Hope of Salvation:
How the *Continuing* Church of God Differs from Protestantism

Polycarp of Smyrna and Martin Luther

Jude's epistle says "to contend earnestly for the faith which was once for all delivered to the saints."

Does the *Continuing* Church of God or Protestantism do this the best?

BOB THIEL, PH.D.

What is a Protestant?

Are all professing Christian churches other than the Roman and Eastern Orthodox Catholics Protestant?

What is a real Christian?

What are many of the doctrines that early Christians held that Protestants do not?

What are important teachings related to the Godhead and salvation that Protestantism does not understand?

Version 1.3. Copyright © 2020 and 2021 by *Nazarene Books*. ISBN 978-1-64106-077-6. Book produced for the *Continuing Church of God and Successor*, a corporation sole. 1036 W. Grand Avenue, Grover Beach, California, 93433 USA.

Covers:
> Martin Luther is considered to be the father of Protestantism. He was not only opposed to Roman Catholic doctrines, but also doctrines held by Church of God adherents in his day.
>
> Polycarp was ordained by one or more of the original apostles and Irenaeus reported "Polycarp related all things in harmony with the Scriptures" (Eusebius. The History of the Church).

Photo credits: Edited Polycarp engraving by Michael Burghers, ca 1685 from Wikipedia and Martin Luther statue from Pixabay.

Back cover has the logo of the *Continuing* Church of God, which was based on a public domain picture.

Scriptural quotes are mostly taken from the New King James Version (Thomas Nelson, Copyright © 1997; used by permission) sometimes abbreviated as NKJV, but normally shown without any abbreviation. Other translations are identified with at least initials such as: AENT-Aramaic English New Testament, AFV-A Faithful Version, ASV-American Standard Version, BLB-Berean Literal Bible, BSB-Berean Study Bible, CSB-Christian Standard Bible, DBT-Darby Bible Translation, DRB-Douay-Rheims Bible, ERV-English Revised Version, ESV-English Standard Version, GNT-Good News Translation, GWT-God's Word Translation, HCSB-Holman Christian Standard Bible, IB-Interlinear Bible, ILB-International Language Bible, ISV-International Standard Version, JB2000-Jubilee Bible 2000, JMNT-James Moffatt New Testament, KJV-King James Version, NAS1977-New American Standard 1977, NASB-New American Standard Bible, NET-NET Bible, NHEB-New Heart English Bible, NIV-New International Version, WEB-Word English Bible, WNT-Weymouth New Testament, YLT-Young's Literal Translation. The use of these brackets { } in this book means that this author inserted something, normally like a scriptural reference, into a quote.

Note: although early texts from post-New Testament writers are not scripture, and some were not preserved as written (hence can contain errors), overall they give clues and other information on what early Christians and other professors of Christ believed.

CONTENTS

1. Protestant vs. Church of God History   P. 7
Start of Protestantism – Martin Luther and Early Reformers – Baptists – Apostolic Succession – Corrupt Claimed Successors – Church of England – Henry VIII – Tertullian's Two Groups – Polycarp – Church of God Succession – Asia Minor, Jerusalem, & Antioch

2. Marcion (the First Protestant) and the Ten Commandments   P.47
First Protestant – False Canon – Doctrine of Antichrist – Most to be Lost? – Denounced by COG Leaders – Lawlessness – Ten Commandments in Effect? – Andy Stanley – Imitate Paul and Jesus – Nailed to the Cross? – Grace – Always Saved? – Who is a Real Christian? – The Christian Life – Character

3. The New Testament, Martin Luther, and the Canon   P.81
Books of the Bible Martin Luther Discounted – Prima Luther – Scriptures Martin Luther Changed – Formation of the Canon – John to Polycarp

4. Passover and Easter Sunday   P.94
Christian Passover – Easter Sunday – Biblical Date – Change of Apostle's Practice – Doctrine of Antichrist – Council of Nicea – Ishtar – Weekly Communion or Annual Memorial? – Bread and Wine – Footwashing – Three Days and Three Nights

5. Views of Jews and the Lost Tribes   P.105
Emperor Constantine – John Chrysostom – Martin Luther's Writings – Lost Tribes – Anglo-Israelism

6. Warfare and Violent Sports   P.119
Early Christian Writings – Constantine's Change – Lutheran Acceptance

7. Baptism, Infants, Sprinkling, and Immersion   P.124
Adult Baptism – Babies – Condemnation from Lutherans – Blessing of Little Children

8. Sola Scriptura or Tradition? — P.128
Sola Scriptura? – Martin Luther King, Jr. – Usefulness of Tradition? – Mystery of Truth? – Rebellious Warning

9. Sabbath vs. Sunday — P.139
Christian Sabbath – Mistranslations – Colossians 2:16-17 – Galatians 4:8-10 – Church Services/Liturgy – Scripture or Greco-Roman Catholic Tradition?

10. Seventh Day Baptists, Adventists, and Messianic Jews — P.169
Seventh Day Baptists – Seventh-day Adventists – Ellen White vs. Herbert W. Armstrong – Messianic Jews

11. The Millennial Kingdom of God — P.196
Early Writings – Lutheran Condemnation – Gospel of the Kingdom – Worldly Politics – Proclaiming the Gospel

12. Saved to Do What? — P.206
The Protestant Message – Why Did God Create Humans? – Beatific Vision – Created for Jesus – Heaven – Humanity's Purpose – Soul Sleep – Annihilation or Eternal Torment?

13. Plan of Salvation — P.233
Offer of Salvation? – Salvation by Chance? Doom of Protestantism – God of Salvation – Real Jesus is Central to the Gospel – Holy Days – Mercy – Three Resurrections – Little Flock – No Partiality – Day of Salvation – Who Will be Totally Lost? – Indescribable Gift

14. Crosses, Trees, Valentine's, and Collars — P.265
Cross not in the Bible – On a Tree – Constantine – An Antichrist Symbol? – Evergreen Trees as Symbols – Valentine's Day – Garb of the Christian Clergy

15. Godhead — P.287
Early Christian Worship – Apostates – Gregory the Wonder Worker – Trinitarian Scriptures? – Ancient of Days – Biblical or Protestant Jesus? – Holy Spirit – Imperial Councils – Deification – Plan of God

16. Tithing   P.333
Words of Jesus – Early Christian Practices – Multiple Tithes? – Change from the Levitical Priesthood

17. Clean and Unclean Meats   P.338
Peter's Vision – Early Christian Practices – Being Holy – Roman Change?

18. Rapture or Fleeing?   P.344
Early Christian Teachings – Pretribulation Rapture? – Place of Safety in the Wilderness? – Gather Together

19. Polycarp or Martin Luther?   P.352
Church of God Leaders – Claimed Protestant Leaders – Comparison of Polycarp and Martin Luther

20. Ecumenism   P.355
Early Protestant Writings – Antichrist – Mystery Babylon – Protestant Ecumenical Supporters – Warnings from Scripture – Signs and Lying Wonders – Ecumenical Position of the Continuing Church of God

21. Summary   P.376
Protestantism's Problem – Chart of Selected Differences – Outward Differences – Hope of SalvationX

Contact Information   P.390
Mailing Address – Websites – Video Channels

1. Protestant vs. Church of God History

How firm is your foundation? Is your faith built upon a rock or sand (Matthew 7:24-27)?

Could Protestantism reflect the original Christian faith?

Or is "the faith once for all delivered" (Jude 3) best represented by a church like the *Continuing* Church of God?

The *Continuing* Church of God (CCOG) explicitly teaches that it is not Protestant.

Many people have wondered about doctrinal and other differences between the CCOG and those known as, or considered to be, Protestants.

In some ways pointing out differences is easy as the CCOG has a published statement of beliefs and other doctrinal literature. There are many clear doctrinal differences.

However, because of the nature of Protestantism, it gets complicated as Protestants have many varying official beliefs.

Part of this is because Protestantism in the 21st century is an amalgam of many groups and denominations.

For the purposes of this book, groups that claim to have developed from the Reformers of the 16th century and/or who claim those Reformers were true and faithful Christians are considered to be Protestant. The title Protestant, therefore, includes most Baptists (who sometimes state they are not Protestant, but hold doctrines like the Protestants) and groups like American Evangelicals (including Pentecostals). But this does not include the Roman and Eastern Orthodox Catholics or genuine Church of God groups.

The *Continuing* Church of God and the Protestant faiths claim to derive their doctrines and teachings from the Bible. But they disagree on many points.

Could the disagreements matter to you? Might they matter to God?

Can you look at doctrines and historical perspectives that may sometimes challenge long-held ideas that you are comfortable with?

Regarding original Christianity, the Book of Acts reported that it was "spoken against everywhere" (Acts 28:22). Sadly, that is often the case still in the 21st century (particularly by critics on the Internet). Can you handle that?

The Apostle Paul wrote to:

> [21] Prove all things; hold fast that which is good. (1 Thessalonians 5:21, KJV)

Can you do that? Can you hold fast to the original doctrines and practices of the Christian church?

Are you willing to be like the Bereans of old, that when they heard teachings that they had not expected, they "received the word with all readiness, and searched the Scriptures daily to find out whether these things were so" (Acts 17:11)?

If so, you should find this book to be a valuable resource to summarize aspects of biblical Christianity.

To help determine which doctrines and practices are more faithful, this book will refer to the Bible as well as historical information which should help make that determination easier for you.

This book is not intended to give detailed documentation on every difference (hence the expression in the title "most Protestants"), but does provide an overview, along with some details and scriptures, about many of the major doctrinal differences between Protestantism and the *Continuing* Church of God.

The Official Start of Protestantism

Let's start with some of the history of Protestantism.

Protestants tend to consider the story of Martin Luther putting his 95 theses on the door of the Wittenberg (Germany) church on October 31, 1517 as the official start of their movement.

His paper called for Rome to fix 95 problems he felt it had. These problems included having priests involved in penance and confession, objections to the usefulness of buying/selling indulgences, the lack of the need for the papal office to be involved in many private matters, and what the Church of Rome actually did with monies it gained from selling indulgences.

Martin Luther was not out, initially, to form a separate church. He hoped that the Church of Rome would make changes to many practices he rightly found to be objectionable. On the surface this seems proper and admirable. However, after politics got involved, his teachings sparked violence and revolt, and ultimately a religion that was separate from the Roman Catholic Church.

Martin Luther was able to quickly gain a large following among many of the German nobles and middle class when he cried:

> Poor Germans that we are—we have been deceived! We were born to be masters, and we have been compelled to bow beneath the yoke of our tyrants, and to become slaves. …. force, power, right, liberty all these have gone over to the popes, who have robbed us of them … It is time the glorious, Teutonic people should cease to be the puppet of the Roman pontiff. (Treatise of 1520 as cited in Bettenson H & Maunder C, eds. Documents of the Christian Church. Oxford University Press, 4th Edition, 2011, p. 209).

So, in an ethnic appeal, Martin Luther reached Germans to support his movement against the Church of Rome.

Technically, the name 'Protestant' came about in 1529, after certain leaders opposed the edict of the Diet (Council) of Speyer. This edict was intended by Charles V (emperor of the so-called 'Holy Roman Empire') to 'restore religious unity.' The opposers were the first individuals known to be called Protestants (Knoll MA. Protestantism: A Very Short

Introduction. Oxford University Press, 2011, p. 19). The Protestants were those who protested against the Church of Rome.

Martin Luther and others like John Calvin and Huldrych Swingli are considered to have been top leaders of the Protestant Reformation in the 16th century. Various churches, like the Anglicans, Lutherans, Episcopalians, Presbyterians, and Methodists came from the reformers or groups that later came out of the earlier reformer groups.

Some Protestants, however, prefer to credit the start of the Reformation to earlier reformers such as Arnold of Brescia, Jan Hus, Tomáš Štítný ze Štítného, John Wycliffe (who, although he translated the Bible, claimed to be a disciple of Augustine), and Girolamo Savonarola.

Non-Catholics who claim to be Christian, who consider any of the above listed in this section to have been their true faithful Christian leaders are considered Protestants for this book.

Baptist Historical Claims

What about Baptists? Does their true history actually start earlier than the Protestant movement?

Various Baptist historians write from the perspective that Baptists existed independently from Roman Catholicism and existed prior to the Protestant Reformation.

Some have a Baptist perpetuity (sometimes called 'successionst') view, which is the claim Baptists have existed since Pentecost in the 2nd chapter of the Book of Acts.

The perpetuity view is often identified with *The Trail of Blood*, a booklet containing five lectures by Dr. James Milton Carrol published in 1931. That booklet claims perpetuity, but an honest reading of it leads to the general conclusion that there are no details to show that Dr. Carroll proved his point on the perpetuity of his faith from the time of Jesus (it mainly points to infant baptism not becoming an issue until after the rise of Emperor Constantine, and persecutions which came to those who disagreed after that). Yet, despite lack of proof, many Baptists still believe it.

The Trail of Blood also contains the following:

> In the first two centuries the individual churches rapidly multiplied and some of the earlier ones, such as Jerusalem, Antioch, Ephesus, Corinth, etc., grew ... serious error to begin creeping in ... the loyal churches declared non-fellowship for those churches which accepted and practiced ... errors ...

While Ephesus and Antioch remained faithful until sometime into the 3rd century (and with the leaders from those areas refuting erroneous changes), Jerusalem and Corinth had apostatized before the end of the 2nd century.

Furthermore, it should be pointed out that in *The Trail of Blood*, the "loyal churches" that Dr. Carroll claims became separate from Rome were NOT actually loyal churches (the truly loyal ones never became part of the Greco-Roman confederacy).

Here is a Baptist claim about early groups that supposedly were "Baptist":

> Novatians were Baptists ... They continued on as Anabaptists ... Hassell lists them right along with the other Baptists of the other ages. "Among the persecuted people of God have been the Novatians, Donatists, Cathari, Paterines, Paulicians, Petrobrusians, Henricans, Arnoldists, Albigenses, Waldenses, Lollards, Mennonites and Baptists, nearly all of whom were occasionally designated Anabaptists or Re-Baptizers by their enemies, because they disregarded infant or unregenerate baptism, and baptized all adults, whether previously baptized or not, who, upon a credible profession of faith, applied to them for membership in their churches -thus insisting upon a spiritual or regenerate church membership, the First and Most Important Mark of the Apostolic Church." (Hissel B. Baptist History Notebook, 3rd ed. Baptist Training Center, 2017, p. 115-116)

While some of those groups held 'Baptist doctrines,' many did not. For example, the Cathari considered the cross to be the "mark of the Beast," yet modern Baptists use crosses as a religious symbol. For another example, the faithful among the Waldenses paid multiple tithes, kept the Sabbath, would not keep Easter, etc.—they were most certainly not modern Baptists.

Here is an assessment from Baptist Pastor Tyler Robbins of certain Baptists claiming the Novatians:

> Were the Novatians Baptists? Many Baptists like to claim the Novatians as their own. ... If the Novatians cannot be claimed as direct descendants, can they be claimed as the distant spiritual kin of modern-day Baptists? Some Baptists would agree.
>
> Much of what has been written of the Novatians by Baptists of any stripe is at best a gloss, and at worst completely incorrect. As an example of the latter, G.H. Orchard, a Landmarkist, wrote (1855):
>
>> One Novatian, a presbyter in the church of Rome, strongly opposed the readmission of apostates, but he was not successful. ... Novatian, with every considerate person, was disgusted with the hasty admission of such apostates to communion, and with the conduct of many pastors, who were more concerned about numbers than purity of communion. (p. 53)
>
> J.M. Carrol, in his infamous treatise *Trail of Blood*, declared that when the errors of compromised local church autonomy, infant baptism and baptismal regeneration crept into true churches, the Novatian Baptists sallied forth for the cause of ecclesiastical purity:
>> Some of the churches vigorously repudiated them. So much so that in A.D. 251, the loyal churches declared non-fellowship for those churches which accepted and practiced these errors. And thus came about the first real official separation among the churches. (2013, Kindle Locations 294-295)

Jack Hoad, a solid historian, likewise missed the boat when he wrote that Novatians were "making a strong protest against the same moral laxity and the weak, almost non-existent disciplinary standards in the churches" (1986, p. 30). Thomas Armitage observed that "[t]he Novatians demanded pure Churches which enforced strict discipline, and so were called Puritans" (178).

All of these brief characterizations are wrong. ...

Dionysius ... claimed that Novatian plied gullible men with liberal amounts of alcohol and "compelled" them to support his rival claim to the Bishopric (6.43.9-10, *NPNF2*, 1:288)! (Robbins T. Were the Novations Early Baptists? Sharper Iron, October 8, 2014)

Novatian himself was baptized by pouring, not immersion, and (3) his baptism was not conducted as a public testimony of his new-found faith—it was done in private, upon a sickbed. ... Novatian's church believed the Holy Spirit was bestowed after baptism and after confirmation by the bishop. Cornelius, Novatian's own successor, criticized him for (1) his irregular baptism, and (2) not having been confirmed. This is not the portrait of a Baptist crusader. (Robbins T. Were the Novatians Early Baptists? Part 2. Sharper Iron, October 17, 2014)

Tyler Robbins is correct that Novatian, who came from the Church of Rome, was not a faithful Christian He is considered the second "antipope" by the Church of Rome, and that church claims Novatian declared himself pope in 251. His faith did not hold to many original Christian teachings. But *The Trail of Blood* points to his 251 declaration to improperly support the Baptist claim of perpetuity.

It should also be pointed out that Dr. Carroll's booklet opposes actual apostolic succession, as it states:

Baptists do not believe in Apostolic Succession.

Since it is true the groups that tend to call themselves Baptists do not have true apostolic succession, obviously they should not claim perpetuity.

Here are some inaccurate perpetuity/successionst assertions by the 19th century Baptist minister G.H. Orchard:

> the Baptists may be considered as the only Christian community which has stood since the times of the Apostles ... all Christian communities during the first three centuries were of the Baptist denomination ... The oriental Baptist Churches, with their successors the Paulicians, continued in their purity until the tenth century when these people visited France ... where they flourished until the crusader army scattered or drown in blood ... offending professors. (Orchard GH. A Concise History of Foreign Baptists. George Wightman Paternoster Row, London, 1838, p. v)

There are many issues with his assertions. The historical reality is that while all faithful Christians believed in baptism by immersion for the repentant, the "oriental ... Churches" (meaning those in Asia Minor) held many doctrines that the modern Baptists oppose (which this book will go into in more detail). Their 'successors' **the Paulicians**, for example, **were binitarian** (Gregory of Nyssa. On the Holy Spirit, Against the Followers of Macedonius. In Nicene and Post-Nicene Fathers, Series Two, Volume 5. Edited by Philip Schaff and Henry Wace. American Edition, 1893), **kept Passover on the 14th day of the first month on the biblical calendar** (Conybeare F.C. The Key of Truth: A Manual of the Paulician Church of Armenia. Clarendon Press, Oxford, 1898, p. clii) as stated in scripture (e.g. Leviticus 23:5)—whereas Baptists call Passover "Easter" and keep in on Sunday, **kept the seventh-day Sabbath while opposing Sunday** (ibid pp. clii, cxciii), **did not keep Christmas** (ibid pp. clii, cxciii), **and the faithful ones called Paulicians were also pacifists** (Fortesque A. Transcribed by Richard L. George. Paulicians. The Catholic Encyclopedia, Volume XI. Copyright © 1911 by Robert Appleton Company). And while we in CCOG would agree that those were original and pure Christian doctrines, Baptists do not hold to them (although Seventh-Day Baptists do often strive to keep the Sabbath).

In his book, Baptist minister G.H. Orchard also claimed "primitive Baptists" essentially began with John the Baptist (ibid, p. 1). Then he later included as "primitive Baptists" Ignatius of Antioch (p. 13), Polycarp of Smyrna (p. 18), Justin Martyr (p. 22), Irenaeus of Lyon (p. 24), Clement of Alexandria (p. 25), and Theophilus of Antioch (p. 26). He also considered writings of John Chrysostom (p. 41) and Augustine of Hippo (p. 44) as "testimonies of the Fathers" and called them "great men" (p.47).

The problem is that not all (if any) of those "primitive Baptist" ministers G.H. Orchard claimed to be Baptists actually held many "Baptist" doctrines. But since relatively few people know much about those early leaders, various Baptists have failed to realize that they held to many doctrines that modern Baptists do not hold.

Consider the following that John the Baptist was prophesied to do:

> [79] To give light to those who sit in darkness and the shadow of death, To guide our feet into the way of peace. (Luke 1:79)

So, John the Baptist was expected to guide God's followers into the way of peace. Now, notice his response to soldiers:

> [14] Likewise the soldiers asked him, saying, "And what shall we do?"
>
> So he said to them, "Do not intimidate anyone or accuse falsely, and be content with your wages" (Luke 3:14).

The word translated as "intimidate" is the Greek word *diaseio* which the KJV translates as "violence." *Strong's Exhaustive Concordance* translates it "to shake thoroughly, to intimidate, to do violence to." It comes from two Greek words *diagnosis* and *seio*; *diagnosis* is translated as examination and *seio* as to rock, agitate, to throw in a tremor. There is no way a soldier cannot 'agitate/intimidate' if they are trying to kill someone.

Thus, John the Baptist's statement here shows that military violence was not for the future followers of God. While early professors of Christ understood that, sadly, most groups who claim Christianity, including modern Baptists, have not understood that. This is one of many ways that modern Baptists do not follow the teachings or practices of John the Baptist.

Furthermore, some leaders that Baptist minister G.H. Orchard referred to in his book were certainly not real Christians. One, Justin Martyr, reported that he lived in no outward way different than the pagans (Dialogue with Trypho. Chapter 10), contrary to the Apostle Paul's teaching in Ephesians 4:17. Two people that G.H. Orchard called "great men," John Chrysostom and Augustine, not only were not real Christians, they both taught infant baptism!

There was no historical perpetuity for what are now the bulk of Baptists. Yet, it is still asserted at times.

Notice the following claims from a 20th century article by Baptist B.M. Cedarholm:

> Historians testify that local churches; which hold the doctrines, beliefs, and practices of today's Bible-believing, separatist Baptists; have had continuous existence since the days of Christ. This cannot be said of any other church, churches, or religious organization. … "as far back as 100 A.D., although without doubt there were Baptist churches then, as all Christians were then Baptists." (Cedarholm BM, editor. Historical Statements Concerning Baptists and their Origins)

While those are merely claims, we in the CCOG believe we can clearly demonstrate it was our doctrines and practices that the 100 A.D. church originally held (see, also, our free book, available online at ccog.org, *Continuing History of the Church of God*). They were NOT those of modern Baptists.

If you were to read that entire article edited by the Baptist B.M. Cedarholm, you would see that it mostly quotes Protestant theologians over the centuries of a Baptist persuasion who agree with part of the initial statement. But they offer no proof. Nor do they provide a real list of beliefs early 'Baptists' held that current Baptists hold. While it is true that all early Christians endorsed baptism, early Christians simply held many doctrines that are in conflict with 21st century Baptists. Modern Baptists who learn of their teachings would not consider their churches the same as those in 100 A.D.

At least partially because King Henry VIII and early Lutherans condemned Anabaptists in the 16th century, Baptists have not always embraced the title Protestant. Yet, modern Baptists agree more with the Protestants than the Anabaptists of old on some of the teachings and practices the Lutherans condemned the Anabaptists for (including the refusal of military service, not being involved in worldly politics, and teaching annihilation of the unrepentant).

It may be because of their differences from the old Anabaptists that the Baptist perpetuity view of history is properly rejected by many modern Baptists.

However, on the Internet in the 21st century, you can still find Baptist ministers who assert their modern religion has true perpetuity without real proof, such as the following (**bolding** in original):

> Calvary Baptist Church believes that the Lord Jesus started the first church – during His earthly ministry. We do not believe that the church started on the Day of Pentecost, but at least three years earlier, and we further believe that Jesus promised His church a continued existence – i.e. perpetuity. … Baptistic churches have existed from the time of Christ to the present day. Those churches have borne many different names in various places. One such name was "Anabaptist (Oldfield KD, pastor. Summary of our Doctrines. http://idahobaptist.com/about/ accessed 01/20/20)
>
> Some of God's People were known as Novatians … In about **the year 250,** … there was **a man in Rome** who was **converted** to Christ while **on his death bed.** Novatian had been a well-known and distinguished **Pagan philosopher**. … **Novatian** was **one** of several **elders in the church at Rome** before the formation of Roman Catholicism. (Oldfield KD, pastor. Some of God's People were known as Novatians. Calvary Independent Baptists Church. Post Falls, Idaho. May 2, 2016.)

It should be pointed out that by 250 A.D., the Church of Rome had already changed on many doctrines and was aligned with regions dominated by apostates, such as Alexandria, Jerusalem, and by that time, Antioch. 2nd century "oriental" Church of God leaders, such as

Polycarp and Polycrates, had chastised Roman bishops for their inappropriate change of the date of Passover. Furthermore, by including the Roman Novatians, Baptists have proven, by their perpetuity declarations, that they do not have original perpetuity.

Now, instead of claiming doctrinal perpetuity from the original New Testament church, the late Baptist minister and civil rights activist, Martin Luther King, Jr., correctly concluded that his church (and other Greco-Roman-Protestant churches) adopted many traditions that they incorporated from Mithraism (King ML. The papers of Martin Luther King, Jr, Volume 4. Clayborne Carson, Ralph Luker, Penny A. Russell editors/compliers. University of California Press, 1992, pp. 222, 224, 307, 309).

Yes, it is a documented fact that modern Baptists adopted beliefs that the early oriental churches and their faithful successors did not hold.

Yet, what are some of the ramifications if the Baptists actually had doctrinal continuity with unknown groups (or portions of known groups) throughout history?

Well, that would be a total of much less than 1% of the world's population during the church age (the time from Acts 2 to present). So since Baptists do not teach God will offer salvation to all, either in this age or the age to come, either the Baptists are teaching that well over 99% of the population will be permanently lost—as they were not their type of Baptist—or if non-Baptists are also to be saved, that perpetuity teaching means it does not matter if one is a Baptist to be saved. It is most likely the latter position (based on various Baptist statements, including those from the late Billy Graham), which makes them like Evangelical Protestants (who also hold to the position that most who ever lived will not be saved).

Practically speaking, modern Baptists tend to hold essentially Protestant doctrinal views, generally in line with Evangelical Protestants. Because of that, they will tend to be grouped in with them in this book. They do NOT have the same hope of salvation that we in the CCOG hold to (for details, see the free online book: *Universal OFFER of Salvation, Apokatastasis: Can God save the lost in an age to come? Hundreds of scriptures reveal God's plan of salvation*).

Apostolic Succession

Within the Protestant world there are two main views of apostolic succession.

One view, which is held by some Baptists and many Evangelicals, is that there is no such thing.

The other view is that Protestantism has direct apostolic succession.

Here is one pro-succession Protestant view of the Church of England published by Angelo Benton (with only selected names shown here for reasons of space), where he claims succession through five regions:

> The succession of the English church from St. Polycarp ... St. James ... is here given. St. Peter ... St. Paul ... St. John ... the English Episcopate has probably twined into one 'cord' more of the separate successions of more than any other communion.

EPHESUS	A.D.
ST. JOHN	96
POLYCARP	107-169

FROM SMYRNA he sends out POTHINUS who survived until A.D. 177

LYONS	A.D.
POTHINUS	177
IRENAEUS	177-202

JERUSALEM	A.D.
ST. JAMES	35
MARCUS I	134
JOHN III	513

Consecrated DAVID of Wales

ROME	A.D.
SS PAUL AND PETER	65
SEXTUS I	119

ANICETUS	157
VICTOR	192
ZEPHRENINUS	201
CALIXTUS	219
VITALIAN	657

Vitalian selected Theodorus ... and sent him to England.

CANTERBURY	A.D.
1. AUGUSTINE	587
2. LAURENTUS	604

Source: Benton, Angelo Ames. The Church Cyclopaedia: A Dictionary of Church Doctrine, History, Organization, and Ritual, and Containing Original Articles on Special Topics, Written Expressly for this Work by Bishops, Presbyters, and Laymen; Designed Especially for the Use of the Laity of the Protestant Episcopal Church in the United States of America. Published by L. R. Hamersly, 1883, pp. 51-52

Notice that people like Anicetus of Rome (whose acceptance of the change to a Sunday Passover was denounced by Polycarp, Victor whose position was denounced by Polycrates of Ephesus, Zephreninus (Zephyrinus) and Calixtus (Callistus) of Rome (both of whom at least one Roman Catholic saint identified as corrupt), the apostate Marcus of Jerusalem, the compromised Irenaeus of Lyon, and the Platonist misogynist Augustine of Hippo are in Angelo Benton's lists. None of them were true Christians and we in the CCOG do not believe there was apostolic succession through them. The Apostle John warned that people who even had apostolic ties, but not apostolic practices, were essentially antichrists (1 John 2:18-19), hence none like that have true apostolic succession.

It should also be noted that although Protestant scholars have long acknowledged that Polycarp "conversed with the Apostles" (e.g. Armitage R. The Primitive Church in Its Episcopacy; with an Essay on Unity, and Counsel for the Present Times. Richard Bentley, 1844, p. 62), and has been considered to be a saint by them (e.g. ibid, p. 116), Polycarp held many positions that nearly all Protestants do not.

Although some Anglicans and Episcopalians have claimed to have apostolic succession through the Apostle John and the bishops of Asia Minor, since those churches do not hold to the doctrines of those leaders, they simply do not have true succession of the original doctrines.

Some writers with ties to the Church of England instead claim succession via Antioch (McClanahan, Russell. The Apostolic Succession of The Most Reverend Russell McClanahan) and Rome (The Episcopal Succession of the Church of England. Copyright Matthew Duckett 1995), but also have problems because they do not hold to several of the original teachings that those in Antioch or Rome once held (and they included people beyond the faithful in their succession lists).

Some Protestants claim that successor leadership for centuries was passed on through Gaul (via Irenaeus of Lyon) from Asia Minor through the Apostle John and the bishops of Asia Minor (Hopkins, Samuel Miles. Manual of Church Polity. Auburn Theological Seminary (N.Y.). Wm. J. Moses' Publ. House, 1878, p. 43-44). Any, however, who claim that faithful apostolic succession passed from Polycarp of Smyrna to Pothinus to Irenaeus of Lyon are in error, as Irenaeus was not a true and faithful Christian.

Consider that Irenaeus supported the Roman Church even though Irenaeus knew that its leadership accepted certain heresies and tolerated heretics that had earlier been condemned by Polycarp. It also may be of interest to note for Protestants to realize that Pope Benedict XVI stated that Irenaeus was the "true founder of Catholic theology" (Pope Benedict XVI. Homily for the Solemnity of Sts. Peter and Paul. June 29, 2005). Many aspects of Irenaeus' theology did not come from the Bible. In reality, Roman 'Catholic theology' ultimately ended up incorporating heresies that apostates such as Simon Magus, Marcion, Valentinus, and many others helped introduce (despite some of Irenaeus' writings against them).

As it turned out, the official "Church of England" itself was not truly formed for reasons that square with the Bible. In 1534, it was really formed because King Henry VIII was denied permission from Pope Clement VII to annul his marriage to Catherine of Aragon, so he could marry Anne Boleyn. Adultery, not theological doctrines, was his motivation. After a time Anne Boleyn miscarried, Henry had her beheaded and then married Jane Seymour. King Henry VIII was not interested in practicing original Christianity.

In the 21st century, even those who do not accept many original Christian doctrines should be able to discount 'apostolic succession' for the Church of England. Not only because of Henry VIII, but because of other beliefs its current bishops hold, particularly in regards to sexual morality that are in clear conflict with the New Testament (cf. Romans 1:18-32).

Tertullian Pointed to Two Groups

By Tertullian of Alexandria's time (circa 195), he concluded that there were basically two possibly apostolic churches, plus the heretics:

> Anyhow the heresies are at best novelties and have no continuity with the teaching of Christ. Perhaps some heretics may claim Apostolic antiquity: we reply: Let them publish the origins of their churches and unroll the catalogue of their bishops till now from the Apostles or from some bishop appointed by the Apostles, as the Smyrnaeans count from Polycarp and John, and the Romans from Clement and Peter; let heretics invent something to match this (Tertullian. *Liber de praescriptione haereticorum*. Circa 200 A.D. as cited in Chapman J. Tertullian. The Catholic Encyclopedia, Volume XIV. Copyright © 1912).

When Tertullian wrote the above, Alexandria and Jerusalem were basically aligned with the Romans, whereas Antioch was still aligned with the Smyrnaeans.

Tertullian must have known (or at least certainly should have known) that the two groups he said had claimed succession had different beliefs. And, of course, that meant only one, at most, could have truly been contending for the original faith (Jude 3; 1 John 2:19).

What became the Roman and Greek Orthodox churches coalesced, and for centuries remained in communion with each other. Ultimately, from the Roman portion, there sprung up the Protestant Reformers.

From the group Tertullian referred to as Smyrnaeans, the Church of God has continued through the entire church age (Matthew 10:23, 16:18; Luke 12:32; Ephesians 2:19-22; Revelation 2 & 3).

The CCOG traces its succession and doctrines back to the New Testament through the apostles and their followers, such as those known as the Smyrnaeans, later through successive eras. There was a written list of successors all the way into the 16th century, but it was lost (see Proceedings of the New York State Historical Association: ... Annual Meeting with Constitution and By-laws and List of Members, Volume 17; Volume 19. The Association, 1919. Original from the University of Michigan Digitized Oct 28, 2005, pp. 190-191). We in the CCOG also have a list from the 1st through 3rd centuries and from the 17th through 21st centuries.

Therefore, although it is neither Eastern Orthodox nor Roman Catholic, the CCOG is not Protestant.

Church of God Succession

When this book uses the term 'Church of God' (or 'COG'), this does not include those groups who also use that name which teach against the Ten Commandments, are non-Sabbatarian, are 'Pentecostal', and/or are trinitarian—most of those groups are Protestant.

Now, like many Protestants, we in the *Continuing* Church of God consider that the Christian church started on the Day of Pentecost mentioned in the second chapter of the Book of Acts.

Like *some* Protestants who believe in 'church eras' (most do not), we in the *Continuing* Church of God consider that we are successors to previous church eras.

In the late 2nd century, Irenaeus wrote:

> ...the **Church in Ephesus**, founded by Paul, and having John remaining among them permanently until the times of Trajan, **is a true witness of the tradition of the apostles** (Irenaeus. Adversus Haereses, Book III, Chapter 3. Excerpted from Ante-

Nicene Fathers, Volume 1. Edited by Alexander Roberts & James Donaldson. American Edition, 1885)

"Rather than distance themselves from their Jewish counterparts, the Jewish Christian community of Ephesus seems to have retained their customs for quite some time, most notable in the link between the dates of Passover" (e.g. Simons J. "Ecclesia enim per universum orbem": Unity in Ephesus as Claimed by Irenaeus. Wheaton College Graduate School, April 2016, p. 37).

Those of us in the *Continuing* Church of God consider ourselves to be the spiritual descendants of the Ephesus era (through 135 A.D.; Revelation 2:1-7), followed by the eras of the Smyrnaeans (c. 135 – 450 A.D.; Revelation 2:8-11), Pergamosians (c. 450-1050; Revelation 2:12-17), Thyatirans, (c. 1050-1600; Revelation 2:18-29), Sardisians (c. 1600-1931; Revelation 3:1-6), and Philadelphians (c. 1931-1986; Revelation 3:7-13). Specifically, we consider ourselves as the most faithful remnant of the Philadelphian church living in the Laodicean church era (c. 1986-present; Revelation 3:14-22).

As far as the church's name goes, here are three 2nd century church name-related references from COG writings:

> Church of God the Father ... the Church which is at Smyrna (Ignatius. Letter to the Smyrnaeans).

> Polycarp, and the presbyters with him, to the Church of God sojourning at Philippi: (Polycarp. Letter to the Philippians)

> The church of God which sojourns at Smyrna to the Church of God which sojourns in Philomelium (Smyrnaeans. Martyrdom of Polycarp).

The predominant biblical name of the true Church in the New Testament is "Church of God." Variants of this expression are clearly stated in singular and plural forms in twelve different places in the New Testament (Acts 20:28; 1 Corinthians 1:2; 10:32; 11:16,22; 15:9; 2 Corinthians 1:1; Galatians 1:13; 1 Thessalonians 2:14; 2 Thessalonians 1:4; 1 Timothy 3:5,15). Throughout Christian history, the true church has normally used a version of the expression 'Church of God' (or

'Churches of Christ,' cf. Romans 16:16) though often with another term, like a geographic region (cf. 1 Corinthians 1:2; 1 Thessalonians 1:1; 2 Thessalonians 1:1) or another word, with it (1 Timothy 3:15). Jesus said that Christians would be kept in His Father's name (John 17:12), which most often is simply "God" in the New Testament, hence 'Church of God.' Since the true Church of God has continued from the time of the original apostles in Acts 2, the name *Continuing* Church of God helps convey that. The Church of God is not just some brand new organization like some claim, but has continued for close to 2,000 years, despite relocations and organizational changes.

Perhaps it should be mentioned that the first time the term 'catholic church' is found in the ancient literature, it was referring to the Church of God in Smyrna (Ignatius. Letter to the Smyrnaeans, 8:2) and that was also where it was next referred to four times (Smyrnaeans. Martyrdom of Polycarp, 1:0, 8:1, 16:2,19:2). So, one could say that the Smyrna church was the original apostolic catholic Church of God, and that the CCOG is the continuation of that church which our doctrines and practices demonstrate (for more information, see the free book, online at ccog.org, titled *Beliefs of the Original Catholic Church*).

It should also be noted that during the Pergamos (c. 450-1050 A.D.) and Thyatira (1050-1600 A.D.) church eras, COG groups considered themselves historical successors to the original apostles:

> The Paulicians claimed to be THE "holy universal and apostolic church" founded by Jesus Christ and his apostles. Of the false churches, they would say: "We do not belong to these, for they have long ago broken connection with the church." (Lesson 50 - I Will Build My Church, Part 2. 58 Lesson: Ambassador College Bible Correspondence Course, 1965)

> The ... Waldenses ... Their own historians assert that the community has remained from apostolic times independent of the church of Rome and they boast they can show a regular apostolic succession of bishops from the earliest period of Christianity, till that of the reformation. (Proceedings of the New York State Historical Association: ... Annual Meeting with Constitution and By-laws and List of Members, Volume 17; Volume 19. The Association, 1919, pp. 190-191)

The term "universal" related to the Paulicians could just as well have been translated as "catholic." Thus, that medieval Church of God continued to use a version of the term 'catholic' for some time and claimed apostolic succession. The Waldenses claimed to not only have an apostolic succession list, they also claimed that they came from the Greek portion of the Church (Martin JH. Historical Sketch of Bethlehem in Pennsylvania With Some Account of the Moravian Church. Philadelphia, 1873, p. 8)—which would have been from Asia Minor. Hence, at least part of their succession list (which has since seemingly been lost, destroyed, or hidden) likely was similar to that which the CCOG points to in the first couple of centuries of the Christian church. In 1749, the validity of a succession list of a group that claimed to have been from the Waldensians was actually accepted by the British Parliament (Atwood CD. Community of the Cross Moravian Piety in Colonial Bethlehem. Penn State Press, 2004, p. 23). So, yes, there are references to a list once that stretched over a millennium of leaders with apostolic succession that were not Greco-Roman Catholics.

Andrew Dugger, a Sardis-era (c. 1600-1931) leader (who lived into the Philadelphian era) taught the true Church of God had apostolic succession:

> **Apostolic Succession** ...
>
> That succession of the apostolic power has come down unbroken ... The Scriptures teach us most emphatically that the apostolic virtue and power was handed down from apostle to apostle by the divine ordinance of laying on of hands and prayer. -- Numbers 8:10, 27:23; Acts 6:6; 13:3; I Timothy 4:14; II Timothy 1:5-6.
>
> That the Sabbath-keeping "Church of God," has a most definite link of connection back through holy men to the days of the apostles is certain. The very same faith, and practice in divine worship, have been definitely handed down to the present (Dugger AN, Dodd CO. A History of True Religion, 3rd ed. (first edition 1936). Jerusalem, 1972 (Church of God, 7th Day). 1990 reprint, p. 308)

Here are two statements from the Philadelphian era (1931-1986):

> God has always, in dealing with humans, worked through ONE MAN at a time — one who believed God! (Armstrong HW. And NOW Christ Sets Church Back On Track Doctrinally. Good News, April 1979)

> The Worldwide Church of God ... is the present generation continuing the Church of God founded A.D.31 by Jesus Christ. ... The Worldwide Church of God today holds to the SAME FAITH, same doctrines, same customs and practices, as the original Church of AD 31, under the original apostles. (Armstrong HW. Worldwide News, July 14, 1980, p. 1)

We in the *Continuing* Church of God believe that apostolic succession continued into the 21st century and that we are "the present generation continuing the Church of God founded {c.} A.D.31 by Jesus Christ."

One of the reasons that the Church of God is not Protestant (nor Roman Catholic) is because the COG began in Jerusalem when God gave His Holy Spirit (Acts 2). The COG did not start as a protest against the Church of Rome, like Protestants did, as the Roman church did not exist until well after Acts 2. The COG also preceded the start of the official formation of Protestantism by about 1,500 years.

For those interested in our 'succession' from the original apostles, this chapter includes lists of succession of leaders from the 1st through as late as the 3rd centuries.

Protestant historian Philip Schaff understood that there were many (at least seventy-two) groups considered to be Cathari (c. 8th--14th centuries), but with claimed ties to the Paulicians and the apostles. He also indicates that some of the doctrines they held we would consider to be Church of God doctrines:

> Agreed as the Cathari were in opposing many customs and doctrines of the established Church, they were divided among themselves and broken up into sects. According to one document seventy-two existed.
>
> There are two Churches they held; one of the wicked and one of the righteous. **They themselves constituted the Church of**

the righteous, outside of which there is no salvation, having received the imposition of hands and done penance according to the teaching of Christ and the Apostles. Its fruits proved that the established Church was not the true Church. The true Church endures persecution, does not prescribe it ... The true church teaches first. The Roman Church baptizes first. ... The Roman Church is the woman of the Apocalypse, a harlot, and the pope anti-Christ. The depositions at their trials indicate that the Cathari made much use of the Scriptures ... The Cathari also renounced priestly vestments, altars, and crosses as idolatrous. They called the cross the mark of the beast, and declared it had no more virtue than a ribbon for binding the hair. It was the instrument of Christ's shame and death, and therefore not to be used. Thorns or a spear would be as appropriate for religious symbols as the cross. They also rejected, as might have been expected, the doctrines of purgatory and indulgences. ... their rejection of judicial oaths and war ... (Schaff, Philip, History of the Christian Church, Chapter X, pp. 474-481)

The Cathari seemed to recognize that there were basically two church groups, and they did not recognize the others are truly Christian. (Note: There were various beliefs among the seventy-two Cathari sects and many were NOT Church of God.) The persecutions from the unfaithful church tended to make the true Christians flee to more mountainous regions as those areas were more remote and thus a safer place to live during that time. Notice also that the Cathari claimed laying on of hands succession.

A laying on of hands succession should be understood to mean, that although there were unfaithful bishops/pastors throughout history, we consider that our members and leaders have an unbroken laying on of hands connection to the original apostles who received God's Holy Spirit in Acts 2:1-4 (and/or the Apostle Paul, cf. Acts 9:17). We also have the "last days" signs of Acts 2:17-18, which we believe shows God's confirmation of our church (cf. Mark 16:20; Hebrews 2:4). Unlike the Church of Rome, we do not claim infallibility for any of our human leaders or any of their writings that are not contained in scripture.

Furthermore, in the 1300s, it was reported about the Albigenses (some of which were COG):

> In the first place, they usually say of themselves that they are good Christians, who do not swear, or lie, or speak evil of others; that they do not kill any man or animal, nor anything having the breath of life, and that they hold the faith of the Lord Jesus Christ and his gospel as the apostles taught. They assert that they occupy the place of the apostles ... (From the Inquisitor's Manual of Bernard Gui [d.1331], early 14th century, translated in J. H. Robinson, Readings in European History, (Boston: Ginn, 1905), pp. 381-383)

It may also be of interest to note, that in a sense, the 'Smyrnaean' leaders that Tertullian referred to could also be considered as the 'succession list' of the "Apostolic see of Ephesus" (Duchesne L, Jenkins C. Early History of the Christian Church: The fifth century Volume 3 of Early History of the Christian Church: From Its Foundation to the End of the Third Century. Longmans, Green, 1924, p. 320). *The Catholic Encyclopedia* teaches that "the See of Ephesus, {was} founded by St. John the Apostle" (Gerland, Ernst. The Byzantine Empire. The Catholic Encyclopedia. Vol. 3. Nihil Obstat. November 1, 1908. Remy Lafort, S.T.D., Censor. Imprimatur. +John Cardinal Farley, Archbishop of New York. New York: Robert Appleton Company, 1908). Protestant historian James Charles Wall wrote of "Polycarp, the successor of St. John in the see of Ephesus" (Wall JC. The first Christians of Britain. Talbot & Co., 1927, p. 34). "See," in this context, is pointing to an area where there was believed to be apostolic succession.

This "See of Ephesus" is mentioned because it was accepted for centuries among the Greco-Romans that there was an apostolic succession in Ephesus/Asia Minor. It could rightly be said that we in the CCOG are the modern descendants and representatives of the original "See of Ephesus."

As far as succession goes, note that according to Protestant minister William Dawson:

> The Keltic Churches of Ireland, of Galloway, and of Iona were at one with the British Church. These claimed, like Southern Gaul and Spain, to have drawn their faith from the Apostolic See of Ephesus. Their liturgies, or such fragments as have come down to us, bear marks of belonging to the Oriental family of liturgies.

(Dawson W. The Keltic Church and English Christianity. Transactions of the Royal Historical Society (New Series), 1884, p. 377)

The CCOG has a 'liturgy' consistent with the original 'Oriental' one at that time. Also, it should be pointed out that those **Celtic churches kept the seventh-Day Sabbath** (Celtic Sabbath-Keeping Study No. 264, from Cherith Chronicle, April-June 1998, pp. 46-47), **observed Passover on the 14th** (McBrien, Richard P. Lives of the Popes: The Pontiffs from St. Peter to Benedict XVI. Harper, San Francisco, 2005 updated ed., p.109), **engaged in footwashing** (Hardinge L. The Celtic Church in Britain. Teach Services, Brushton (NY) 2000, p. 111) and had many practices and beliefs closer to the CCOG than to the Protestant faiths.

Perhaps it should be mentioned that we in the CCOG do not view our 'succession lists' the same way that those in the Roman Catholic or Eastern Orthodox churches view theirs.

We believe that we are the true spiritual descendants of the apostles. We assert that this is not dependent upon a bishop to bishop transfer (or later vote by Cardinals), but a true holding of teachings of the true "little flock" (Luke 12:32) and an unbroken laying on of hands connection back to the original apostles (cf. 1 Timothy 4:14, 5:17-22; 2 Timothy 1:6; Acts 6:3-6).

Early and Late Church of God Succession

We in the *Continuing* Church of God consider that the following, presuming the Greco-Roman historian Eusebius' information was accurate, had apostolic succession in Jerusalem through 134/135 A.D.:

Jerusalem Succession List Per Eusebius

The first, then, was James, the so-called brother of the Lord;
the second, Symeon;
the third, Justus;
the fourth, Zacchæus;
the fifth, Tobias;
the sixth, Benjamin;
the seventh, John;

the eighth, Matthias;
the ninth, Philip;
the tenth, Seneca;
the eleventh, Justus;
the twelfth, Levi;
the thirteenth, Ephres;
the fourteenth, Joseph;
and finally, the fifteenth, Judas.

These are the bishops of Jerusalem that lived between the age of the apostles and the time referred to, all of them belonging to the circumcision. (Eusebius. The History of the Church, Book III, Chapter V, Verses 2,3.& Book IV, Chapter 5, Verses 2-4, pp. 45, 71)

We consider the above Church of God leaders. They held to many COG doctrines that Protestants do not hold to, as Protestant scholars will normally admit. The Christian church originated in Jerusalem of Judea, was based out of Jerusalem for a time, and the twelve apostles reportedly remained there for at least twelve years before venturing out (Eusebius Book V, Chapter 18). The Church of Rome also teaches that the Jerusalem church was the original Christian church (Joyce G. The Church. The Catholic Encyclopedia). According to the Apostle Paul, Gentile Christians should be "imitators of the churches of God which are in Judea in Christ Jesus" (1 Thessalonians 2:14a), but Protestants do not do that.

That being said, we do not consider that a later claimed successor, the 'Latin' Marcus of Jerusalem who compromised with doctrine and came to power 134/135 A.D. (and was allegedly there until 185), as a true successor or part of the Church of God. Nor did Irenaeus of Lyon as he wrote that apostolic fruits in Jerusalem ended immediately before the time Marcus gained power (Irenaeus. Adversus haereses, Book IV, Chapter IV, Verse 1). Even the Roman Catholic monk and historian Jean Briand reported what happened after 134:

135. The direction of the Church in Jerusalem was then entrusted to bishops of pagan origin. (Briand J. The Judeo-Christian Church of Nazareth Franciscan Printing Press, Jerusalem, 1982, p. 13)

Those "bishops of pagan origin" were apostates.

As far as how apostasy could hit Jerusalem, 2nd century writer Hegissipus wrote that the corruption in Jerusalem began a decade or two prior to the rise of Marcus. Hegissipus reported that one called Thebuthis had doctrines of Simon Magus (of Acts 8:9-14) and Marcion of Pontus (discussed in the next chapter), but that the Jewish Christians and their leaders would not then accept them (Eusebius. Church History, Book IV, Chapter 22, verses 1, 4-5).

As it turned out, in order to be 'legally' allowed back into Jerusalem after the Jewish Bar Kochba revolt, history shows Marcus finally implemented some of the false doctrines that Simon (Magus) and Marcion taught. That is why we in the CCOG do not accept Marcus as an apostolic successor (but the Eastern Orthodox do). Anyway, some of the spiritual descendants of the faithful who had to leave Jerusalem were called Nazarenes—consistent with what Christians associated with the Apostle Paul were called (cf. Acts 24:5).

Antioch was originally part of the true Christian church (cf. Acts 11:26-27), and Serapion of Antioch held COG doctrines. We in the CCOG consider that there was apostolic succession in Antioch through his death (died c. 211/212). The following names and dates are from Antiochian Orthodox Christian Archdiocese of North America (http://ww1.antiochian.org/patofant/primates accessed 01/24/20) and may or may not be precisely accurate:

Antiochian Succession List

1 **45-53** The Episcopacy of St. Peter, the Apostle, in Antioch.
2 **53** The Episcopacy of Eudoius in Antioch.
3 **68** The Episcopacy of St. Ignatius (d. 107) in Antioch.
4 **100** The Episcopacy of Heros in Antioch.
5 **127** The Episcopacy of Cornelius in Antioch.
6 **151** The Episcopacy of Heros II in Antioch.
7 **169** The Episcopacy of Theophilus (d. 181/182) in Antioch.
8 **188** The Episcopacy of Maximianus (d. 190/191) in Antioch.
9 **191-212** The Episcopacy of Serapion in Antioch.

Scholars are aware of writings from at least four on that list. Those writings demonstrate that they held Church of God as opposed to Protestant or Eastern Orthodox doctrines on matters such as Passover and the Godhead.

Prior to heretical changes taking hold in Asia Minor, Serapion of Antioch warned of a "lying confederacy" (Serapion. From the epistle to Caricus and Ponticus) of Greco-Roman churches that was forming (and which enveloped Antioch after his death). Also, it should be pointed out that Polycarp in Smyrna had warned earlier of the "vanity of many" (Polycarp. Letter to the Philippians, Chapter VII). Some other leaders who lived in Antioch, NOT on the Orthodox list, such as the binitarian Lucian, who opposed the allegorists (270-312), seemed to be faithful.

Neither Polycarp nor Serapion wanted to be in communion with the growing number of compromisers who would not hold to the original apostolic faith. The "vanity of many" Polycarp warned about led to the "lying confederacy" which Serapion saw develop further that ended up resulting in the Greco-Roman churches, from which Protestantism later sprang.

Note that we do not consider that Asclepiades the Confessor (c. 211/212-220, who is next on Orthodox Church succession lists for Antioch) was a faithful successor to Serapion. Throughout church history, the mystery of iniquity has been present (2 Thessalonians 2:7; 1 John 2:19) and false leaders have appeared.

We in the *Continuing* Church of God consider that the following had laying on of hands apostolic succession in Asia Minor:

Early Asia Minor/Smyrnaean Succession Chart

Apostle Peter died circa 64-68 A.D.
Apostle John died circa 98-102 A.D.
Polycarp died circa 155-158 (oversaw churches from Smyrna of Asia Minor)
Thraseas died circa 160 (oversaw the churches from Eumenia, but died in Smyrna)
Sagaris died circa 166-167 (died in Laodicea of Asia Minor)

Papirius died circa 170 (oversaw churches from Smyrna of Asia Minor)

Melito died circa 170-180 (oversaw churches from Sardis of Asia Minor)

Apollinaris died circa 195 (oversaw churches in Hierapolis)

Polycrates died circa 200 (oversaw churches from Ephesus of Asia Minor)

Apollonius of Ephesus died circa 210 (oversaw churches from Ephesus of Asia Minor)

Camerius of Smyrna through death circa 220 (possibly oversaw churches from Smyrna of Asia Minor)

* Eudaemon of Smyrna through his compromise with the pagans seems to have been a successor that lost the spiritual succession while alive.

Pionius of Smyrna through death circa 250 (was faithful during the time of an unfaithful leader, Eudaemon of Smyrna)

* The actual top mantle of Church leadership from 220 through 254 may have not been in Asia Minor but instead to have been held by the Egyptian Nepos of Arsinoe, then followed by an unnamed Antiochian, and perhaps transferred to Lucian of Antioch from 270 through his martyrdom in 312 (Nepos and Lucian stood against the Greco-Roman allegorists).

Prior to Peter, Timothy was in Ephesus (1 Timothy 1:3) and seemingly had succession from the Apostle Paul, but since the Apostle John moved to Ephesus afterwards, we did not list a non-apostle before him. Furthermore, since Paul wrote ALL in Asia had turned away from him (2 Timothy 1:15), the church had to begin anew in Asia.

Throughout true church history, various ones have fallen away, making the church look to start again elsewhere, and often called by another name—though continuing with an unbroken laying on of hands succession.

We do not consider that the first known leader in certain lists, Pluinos of Ephesus, who rose up after Pionius, was a true Church of God Christian. This is based on a mid to late 2nd century writing from Dionysius, bishop of Alexandria where he said that Asia Minor no longer was divided from Alexandria and Jerusalem (Eusebius. Church History, Book VII, Chapter V, Verse I) as the main leaders became part of the Greco-Roman confederacy—this meant compromise/apostasy took over in much of Asia Minor. And then many of the faithful fled or otherwise became difficult to track.

Many of the leaders in the 'succession list' above in Asia Minor wrote letters or had treatises about them that survive until this day (and parts of several are cited throughout this book).

Roman Catholic scholars have noted that the Greco-Roman Catholic historian Eusebius intentionally did not report later details about those they have considered to be Judeao-Christians (e.g. Briand, p. 66 and Bagatti B. Translated by Eugene Hoade. The Church from the Circumcision. Nihil obstat: Marcus Adinolfi, 13 Maii 1970. Imprimi potest: Herminius Roncari, 14 Junii 1970. Imprimatur: +Albertus Gori, died 26 Junii 1970. Franciscan Printing Press, Jerusalem, 1971, p.11).

Since the 4th century Greco-Roman Eusebius was the official Imperial historian for Emperor Constantine, this is one reason the CCOG early succession lists do not have named Christian leaders past certain points—such as a gap on the names of the faithful after Pionius through the time of Eusebius.

We in the *Continuing* Church of God would call the previously shown list of successors Smyrnaeans, partially because of the time that Polycarp of Smyrna arose in prominence as well as Tertullian's use of the term (plus earlier, Ignatius also wrote that Polycarp was the bishop of the Smyrnaeans in his *Epistle to Polycarp*). However, some of the Greek Orthodox have claimed at least some of these leaders as part of the Patriarch of Ephesus. That is despite the fact that the Greek Orthodox do not hold to many of the teachings these early leaders had.

Whether referred to as Smyrnaeans or the See of Ephesus, the leaders in the list shown above clearly held Church of God doctrines that were later condemned by the Greco-Roman churches (and doctrines often considered as an anathema to Protestant ones).

As far as being faithful to original Christianity and scripture goes, notice the following:

> The lineage of bishops in the region of Asia Minor may be the most important area of all for crystallizing Christian theology by

providing a direct link between the writings of the Scripture and the tradition of the fathers. (Simons J. "Ecclesia enim per universum orbem": Unity in Ephesus as Claimed by Irenaeus. Wheaton College Graduate School, April 2016, p. 57).

And that is why they are often quoted in this book as advocating original Christianity. Further consider that the Asia Minor leaders held beliefs that we in the CCOG still hold that the Greco-Roman-Protestant churches do not. The CCOG truly has spiritual (as well as physical) succession from these leaders, as well as the faithful early leaders in Jerusalem.

In the late 4th century, the Greco-Roman saint Jerome reported that the Christians he did not care for and called Nazarenes, who seemed to have fled into the wilderness (cf. Revelation 12:6), held COG doctrines. But Jerome did not list the leaders' names. The Nazarenes, themselves, claimed to have ties to Jerusalem and seemingly Asia Minor and/or Antioch (Schaff, Philip, History of the Christian Church. Charles Scribner's Sons, 1910).

It is known that various records originally retained by early COG sources were destroyed, lost, and/or supressed (Schaff P. NICENE AND POST-NICENE FATHERS OF THE CHRISTIAN CHURCH. 2nd series, Volume I, Chapter XXVI, Note 1, p. 203). Plus, not everything was written down or retained. What we do know is that in 380 A.D. Emperor Theodosius made various statements (Theodosian Code XVI.1.2.) that seemed to drive the faithful Christians into the wilderness.

We have names of many Sabbath-keeping leaders during the 1260 years in the wilderness (for details, see the free book, online at ccog.org, *Beliefs of the Original Catholic Church*), as well as a more complete list from when that time ended (c. 1640). Starting with leaders in the British Isles in the early 17th century and then leaders in the Americas starting with John Maxson, Jr., here is a tentative list of Sabbath-keeping leaders through the 20th century:

    1617-1619 John Traske
    1620-1652 John Pecke (and possibly others)
    1652-1654 Peter Chamberlen
    1654-1661 James John
    1661-1678 William Saller
    1678-1711 Henry Soursby

1712-1715 John Maulden
1715-1718 John Maxson, Jr.
1718-1737 Joseph Crandall
1737-1748 Joseph Maxson
1748-1778 John Maxson
1779-1796 Unnamed Sabbatarians
1796-1832 Joseph Davis
1823-1850 Peter Davis or 1830-1850 John Cottrell
1850-1871 Asa Bee or Unnamed Sabbatarians
1871-1900 A.C. Long
1900-1905 William C. Long
1905-1921 S. W. Mentzer
1921-1933 Andrew N. Dugger or 1922 - 1933 John S. Stanford
1933-1986 Herbert W. Armstrong

From 1986 through the early 21st century was a time of transition. There were leaders like Aaron Dean, Dibar Apartian, and Roderick Meredith during that transition with the CCOG formally declared in 2012, physically headed up by Bob Thiel (anointed in 2011). For more information, see the free book, online at ccog.org, titled *Continuing History of the Church of God*.

It should perhaps be mentioned that in the CCOG, we also accept that there were saints (Romans 1:7) and apostles beginning with the Apostle Paul) in Rome, but do not trace our succession through 2nd century Roman leaders such as Pius I or Anicetus I.

We further wish to state that we do not believe that the Apostle John was subservient (in God's eyes) to any Roman, Smyrnaean, Antiochian, or other bishop/overseer while John was still alive.

That being said, although the Roman and Eastern Orthodox Catholics consider the leaders in the aforementioned COG succession lists to be saints (as well as do many Protestants), the leaders mentioned held to Church of God doctrines which the Greco-Roman-Protestant churches basically no longer accept (and often have condemned).

Examples include the observance of Passover on the 14th, the binitarian nature of the Godhead, avoidance of biblically unclean meats, and the coming of a literal millennium (though some Protestants and Eastern Orthodox accept millenarianism). However, all of these are still doctrines retained in the *Continuing* Church of God.

Polycarp is a Unique Apostolic Successor

Polycarp grew up in Asia Minor and was converted at a fairly young age (he was baptized at age 18). Here is additional information about him:

> It is significant that after his release John trained Polycarp elder of Smyrna, a city near Ephesus in the province of Asia. ... At neighbouring Smyrna, Polycarp presided over the Church of God for half a century after John's death. Polycarp stood up boldly for the truth while many fell away and began having fellowship with the Catholic bishops of Rome. (Armstrong HW. The Church They Couldn't Destroy. Good News, December 1981)

Here is something from a questionable, but ancient 2nd century document:

> John ... on the seventh day, it being the Lord's day, he said to them: Now it is time for me also to partake of food. ...John went to Ephesus, ... And when he was old and changed, he ordered Polycarp to be bishop over the church. (Acts of the Holy Apostle and Evangelist John the Theologian. Translated by Alexander Walker. From Ante-Nicene Fathers, Vol. 8. Edited by Alexander Roberts, James Donaldson, and A. Cleveland Coxe)

Yes, the original Christian Lord's Day was on Saturday and John and Polycarp kept it.

Notice the following 2nd century report about him from a Greco-Roman saint:

> Polycarp also was not only instructed by apostles, and conversed with many who had seen Christ, but was also, by apostles in Asia, appointed bishop of the Church in Smyrna ... always taught the things which he had learned from the apostles, and which the Church has handed down, and which alone are true. To these things all the Asiatic Churches testify, as do also those men who have succeeded Polycarp down to the present time ... There is also a very powerful Epistle of Polycarp written to the Philippians, from which those who choose to do so, and are anxious about their salvation, can learn the character of his faith, and the preaching of the truth (Irenaeus. Adversus Haereses. Book III, Chapter 3, Verse 4).

Polycarp was clearly appointed by the original apostles and taught the original faith, as did his faithful successors in Asia Minor.

Protestant Charles Merritt Nielsen wrote:

> Polycarp would not tolerate any deviation from the traditions of Christianity as he understood them, and he seemed forever asking his readers to turn back to the faith delivered to us from the beginning. (Nielson CM. *"Polycarp: Model for Seminarians"* Theology Today 30, no. 2 (1973): 178-180 as cited in Polycarp Versus The Progressives. HeidelBlog.net, Copyright © 2020 R. Scott Clark.)

> he was not only unoriginal, he seemed content and determined to be so. For instance, most of his letter is made up of quotations from Christian writings" (Nielson CM. *"Polycarp: Model for Seminarians"* Theology Today 30, no. 2 (1973): 178-180; as cited in Brown JM. Life of Polycarp. Liberty Baptist Theological Seminary, March 1, 2013, p. 6).

Yes, Polycarp stuck to scripture, taught the Bible, and did not act like it should be changed.

Protestant scholar Michael Holmes wrote:

> Conservative and traditional, Polycarp exercised influence far beyond Asia as he sought to protect and maintain the proto-orthodox strand of the early Christian movement. Tradition portrays Polycarp as a prolific writer. (Holmes M. Polycarp of Smyrna, Letter to the Philippians in Foster P. The Writings of the Apostolic Fathers. Bloomsbury Publishing, 2007, p. 109)

Polycarp wrote a lot and quoted scriptures, He did not want to change doctrine—he was truly "orthodox" as far as original Christianity was concerned. Those who accept him, but consider him "proto-orthodox" do so, because they accepted later doctrinal changes that were not part of the original faith.

Although the Church of Rome and Eastern Orthodox consider Polycarp to be a saint (as do Protestant historians), he held doctrines much more consistent with those of the *Continuing* Church of God. Polycarp was not a traditional Greco-Roman leader, but a Church of God leader.

Polycarp held doctrines that the Greco-Romans later declared as anathemas. Nor, despite claims of some, did he attend what would be called a 'Roman Catholic mass,' as the Church of Rome did not have that type of liturgy fully in place until nearly two centuries after Polycarp visited.

Polycarp is unique among any claimed to be a direct successor to any of the apostles:

1. Polycarp is the only possible direct apostolic successor considered by any church I am aware of that there was a letter written to him while he was alive (yes, there were letters written in the New Testament to leaders, but none of them other than to Timothy are in any of the 'accepted' succession lists I have seen).
2. He is the only possible direct apostolic successor considered by any church I am aware of to have written any document that we still possess to this day (there is a letter claimed to have been written by Clement of Rome; however, it does not say that he wrote it, nor is Clement considered to be the direct successor of any apostle--the Roman Catholic Church currently claims that Linus was Peter's direct successor; there are also letters written by Ignatius of Antioch, but the two Antiochian Churches we are aware of claim that Evodius, not Ignatius, was Peter's direct successor).
3. Polycarp is the only possible direct apostolic successor considered by any church I am aware of to have any significant document written about him shortly after his death.
4. Polycarp is the only possible direct successor to the apostles that was clearly called "bishop" while he was alive.
5. Roman Catholic, Orthodox, and Church of God historians all teach that Polycarp was a spiritually faithful Christian leader. Yet, Polycarp refused to accept the authority of the Roman Bishop Anicetus, instead Anicetus acquiesced to Polycarp.
6. Polycarp is also the only possible successor to have a writing perhaps, at least partially, directed to him in the Bible. Some scholars believe that when John wrote to the "angel of the

church in Smyrna" that this actually was addressed to the leader of the church (the Greek term translated as "angel" can mean human representatives, e.g. Luke 7:24) who they feel was Polycarp.
7. The Romans stated about Polycarp: "This is the teacher of Asia, the father of the Christians, and the overthrower of our gods, he who has been teaching many not to sacrifice, or to worship the gods" (*Martyrdom of Polycarp,* 12:2). Even his opponents felt he was important to Christianity.

Polycarp's *Epistle to the Philippians* contains a lot of information about what he believed and taught. There was also the letter written about his martyrdom by the Smyrnaeans which gives some insight into him. Polycarp is discussed in writing by such early writers as Ignatius who write an entire letter to him (circa 108 A.D.).

Furthermore, Irenaeus claimed Polycarp was faithful (circa 170 A.D.) and Polycrates also claimed that Polycarp was faithful (circa 190 A.D.). Tertullian claimed that the true Christian church could be traced through Polycarp (circa 200 A.D.). Eusebius also wrote that Polycarp was faithful to the apostolic traditions (circa 330 A.D.).

Despite Greco-Roman supporters praising Polycarp's faithfulness, they and their Protestant associates often do not hold the doctrinal positions that he and his faithful successors held.

British Isles and Early Beliefs

Perhaps it should be mentioned that there are legends and/or myths that the Apostle Paul and Joseph of Arimathea (Mark 15:43; John 19:38) made it to the British Isles (Wall JC. The first Christians of Britain. Talbot & Co., 1927, pp. 36-40, 168). Note the following claim:

> Christianity was first introduced into Britain by Joseph of Arimathea, AD 36—39; followed by Simon Zelotes, the apostle; then by Aristobulus, the first bishop of the Britons; then by St. Paul. (Morgan RW. St. Paul in Britain; or, the origin of British as opposed to Papal Christianity. J. B. and Jas. Parker, 1861, p. 129)

Though this seems possible, it may only be a later legend or myth. Relatively modern reports seem to be partially based on a writing from 542 by the British historian Gildas:

> We certainly know that Christ, the True Sun, afforded His light, the knowledge of His precepts, to our island in the last year of the reign of Tiberius Caesar. (Cited in Morgan, p. 186)

If accurate, that would have been 36-37 A.D.

Some have claimed that the Episcopal/Anglican Church had apostolic succession from the time of Joseph of Arimathea to present. The late Anglican George F. Jowett wrote:

> The present Mother British Church is the only Christian Church that has maintained an unbroken apostolic succession of Bishops from the beginning, with all the named Episcopal Churches sharing in this distinction. (Jowett G. The Drama of the Lost Disciples. Covenant Publishing, 2009, p. 85)

George Jowett also mentioned that the Druids had crosses and believed in the immortality of the soul prior to Joseph of Arimathea coming to Britain, suggesting that conversion to 'Christianity' was not difficult for them (ibid, pp. 77,86). He claimed that the British King Aviragus was converted by Joseph of Arimathea, and Britain was a warring 'Christian' nation (ibid, pp. 83-85). Yet (as will be explained later in this book), early Christians were not warring, did not believe in the immortality of the soul, and did not use crosses (see also Cross. The Encyclopedia Britannica, 11th ed., 1910, Vol. 7, p. 506).

George Jowett and others need to consider that modern Episcopalians condone aspects of sin that no early Christian did. Consider that Polycarp wrote:

> Knowing, then, that "God is not mocked," we ought to walk worthy of His commandment and glory. In like manner should the deacons be blameless before the face of His righteousness, as being the servants of God and Christ, and not of men. They must not be slanderers, double-tongued, or lovers of money, but temperate in all things, compassionate, industrious, walking

according to the truth of the Lord, who was the servant of all. If we please Him in this present world, we shall receive also the future world, according as He has promised to us that He will raise us again from the dead, and that if we live worthily of Him, "we shall also reign together with Him," provided only we believe. In like manner, let the young men also be blameless in all things, being especially careful to preserve purity, and keeping themselves in, as with a bridle, from every kind of evil. For it is well that they should be cut off from the lusts that are in the world, since "every lust warreth against the spirit;" and "neither fornicators, nor effeminate, nor abusers of themselves with mankind, shall inherit the kingdom of God," nor those who do things inconsistent and unbecoming. (Letter to the Philippians, Chapter 5)

Since many modern Episcopalians, Anglicans, and Methodists, would not agree with Polycarp (or scripture) on several parts of this, it should be obvious that they do not have unbroken apostolic succession.

Regarding Aristobulus (sometimes "Aristibule" in English), he was claimed to be one of "the seventy" that Jesus sent out (Luke 10:1,17) and that he became the first bishop/pastor in Britain (Hippolytus. Where Each Of Them Preached, And Where He Met His End. Translated by J.H. MacMahon. From Ante-Nicene Fathers, Vol. 5. Edited by Alexander Roberts, James Donaldson, and A. Cleveland Coxe. Christian Literature Publishing Co., 1886). It has been claimed he was the brother of the Apostle Barnabas (Acts 14:14) and was mentioned in Romans 16:10 (Holy Apostle Aristobulus of the Seventy, first Bishop of Britain (1st c.). Ancient Faith, a department of Antiochian Orthodox Christian Archdiocese of North America, March 19, 2017).

Presuming that Paul, Joseph, and/or Aristobulus came to Britain, it would be logical to conclude that they would have originally held to Church of God, not Protestant, doctrines. Several historical reports point to that conclusion.

Some of the Celts had footwashing (Hardinge, p. 111), were Arian/Semi-Arian (ibid, pp. 2, 54-55), practiced tithing (ibid, p. 161), avoided unclean meats (ibid, p. 196), forbade sexual intercourse during menstruation consistent with Leviticus 18:19 & Ezekiel 36:17 (ibid, 198), did not observe Easter Sunday, yet kept Passover on the 14th (Bede. The Ecclesiastical History of the English People. Judith McClure and Roger Collins, editor. Oxford University Press, 1999, pp. 71-72). Those are COG, not Protestant positions.

"It has also been asserted, that the Kelts or Culdees were opposed to auricular confession, the worship of saints, and images, purgatory, transubstantiation, the seven sacraments" (Schaff, Philip, *History of the Christian Church*. Oak Harbor, WA: Logos Research Systems, Inc., 1997). On most of those points, Protestants, historically, would be in agreement with the Celts.

When the Roman Catholic Augustine arrived in Britain (c. 597) he was shocked and disappointed to find that people there had early Christian, as opposed to Greco-Roman, practices (Hardinge, p.18). In time, however, many of those in the British Isles changed and mainly adopted Greco-Roman-Protestant practices.

Various reports claim that the Church of God in Britain originally came from places like Asia Minor (Dawson, p. 377), but had other influences that eventually overwhelmed it:

> "The Celtic Church which occupied Ireland, Scotland, and Britain, had the Syriac (Byzantine) scriptures instead of the Latin vulgate of Rome. The Celtic Church, with the Waldenses and the Eastern empire, kept the seventh-day Sabbath" (Celtic Sabbath-Keeping Study No. 264, from *Cherith Chronicle*, April-June 1998, pp. 46-47).

> In its organisation, ... the Celtic Church circumvented the Church of Rome and functioned as a repository for elements of Nazarean tradition transmitted from Egypt, Syria, and Asia Minor. ... In 664, the Synod of Whitby effectively dissolved the Celtic Church, and Ireland was brought into the Roman fold (Baigent M, et. al. The Messianic Legacy: Secret Brotherhoods. The Explosive Alternate History of Christ. Delta, 2004, p. 120).

The "Nazarene" tradition mentioned above would have included various practices Protestants often consider to be Jewish or 'outdated.'

Perhaps it should be pointed out that in the late 1600s, Thomas Bampfield (who had been Speaker of the House of Parliament at one time, under Cromwell) mentioned sabbath continuity in the British Isles:

> Thomas Bampfield ... contended that the seventh day had been kept in England in unbroken succession until the thirteenth century (Ball B. Seventh Day Men: Sabbatarians and Sabbatarianism in England and Wales, 1600-1800, 2nd edition. James Clark & Co., 2009, p. 21).

It should be noted that because of practices of a few of the Lollards in the British Isles, some Sabbath-keeping would have occurred from the thirteenth through seventeenth centuries (Ball, pp. 30-31), so it would have been unbroken for even more centuries than Thomas Bampfield contended. But the official Church of England has never adopted that practice.

The United States government published the following:

> The Church of God (seventh day) was organized in separate church organizations in this country soon after the landing ... here from London, England, in 1620 ... The ... Sabbatarian Christian Church in America was connected with the oldest in London-the Mill Yard Church (RELIGIOUS BODIES: 1936 VOLUME II PART1 DENOMINATIONS A to J STATISTICS, HISTORY, DOCTRINE ORGANIZATION, AND WORK. UNITED STATES DEPARTMENT OF COMMERCE p. 423,424)

Yes, there was a succession connection from the British-Isles to the New World.

Summary

Protestants either claim to have apostolic succession, succession via Rome, perpetual existence, and/ or being a movement that developed within the last five or so centuries.

Baptists, who have looked into perpetuity and the teachings of earlier groups, realize that the modern Baptist church should not claim perpetuity as 1) Novatian was not faithful, 2) the faithful Paulicians

(Cathari, Waldenses, etc.) held Church of God doctrines in conflict with Baptists, and 3) Baptists do not agree with important positions of the 16th century Anabaptists.

The *Continuing* Church of God asserts that it does have succession through the laying on of hands from the original apostles to the ministry to the members today. We further contend that the CCOG holds to the original faith that Jesus' original apostles had (which this book helps document).

When it comes to church history, it should be pointed out that unless one can reasonably determine if early post-New Testament writers were true Christians or not (and the Bible greatly assists with that), church history is basically impossible to properly discern.

In general, the Greco-Roman-Protestant churches consider many early writers saints from nearly all areas, even if those 'saints' contradict scripture or each other.

We in the *Continuing* Church of God assert that by knowing which leaders and regions (like Polycarp of Smyrna) were faithful to biblical and apostolic teachings, we can put together a more accurate picture of church history which shows that the true faith did not die out, and continues to this day.

An understanding of proper true Christian church history exposes many falsehoods and improper traditions that many Protestants and Baptists hold as nearly (or actually) sacred.

Protestants and others interested in learning more about church history should consider reading the free book, available online at ccog.org, *Continuing History of the Church of God*.

2. Marcion (the First Protestant) and the Ten Commandments

For the past couple of centuries, historians have searched in vain for an early religion that resembles modern Protestantism.

Protestants may be surprised to learn that theirs clearly was not the faith of the original Christians.

Now, for sake of simplicity, within Protestantism let's accept that there are two main camps. Let's call them the Martin Luther camp (sometimes referred to as 'mainline' or 'mainstream' Protestant denominations) and the Evangelical camp.

The Evangelical camp (as well as some mainline Protestant denominations) often claims that the Ten Commandments are not fully enjoined upon Christians.

When we look at available records that came out within a century after the last New Testament book was written, we do not see a professing Christian faith that categorically discounted the Ten Commandments, unless you include apostates such as Simon Magus (Acts 8:9-24) and Marcion of Pontus.

Marcion of Pontus

Marcion was an apostate leader who came from a town called Pontus in Asia Minor. He was born around 110 A.D. He came to Rome around 140 A.D. and founded a heretical group around 144 A.D. He strove to push a religion that would be far from biblical Judeo-Christianity.

In the 1800s, Protestant theologian Johann August W. Neander wrote that Marcion had taken certain doctrines from Gnostics (Gnostics have been condemned by nearly all COG, Protestant, and Roman Catholic scholars; and the initial condemnations seem to have started in the New Testament: cf. 1 Timothy 6:20).

Despite his ties to Gnosticism, Dr. Neander wrote that Marcion was a Protestant:

> "Marcion ... a genuine Protestant (if we may transfer to this ancient day this appellation ...)" (Neander JAW. The history of the Christian religion and Church during the three first centuries, tr. By H.J. Rose [from vol.1 of Allgemeine Geschichte der christlichen Religion]. Translated by Henry John Rose. 1841, p. 121).

Lutheran theologian Adolf von Harnack (died 1930) later agreed with Professor Neander's calling Marcion the first Protestant:

> In his first monograph on Marcion, Adolf von Harnack quoted approvingly the opinion of August Neander according to which Marcion was the 'first Protestant.' (Marcion and his impact on church history Volume 150 of Texte und Untersuchungen zur Geschichte der altchristlichen Literatur. Editors: Gerhard May, Katharina Greschat, Martin Meiser. Walter de Gruyter, 2002, p. 131).

> Though celebrated as 'the first Protestant' by Adolf von Harnack for his radical interpretation of the Pauline distinction between Law and gospel, Marcion was the most formidable heretic of the 2nd cent. And the spiritual father of a perennial danger for Christian theology. (Soulen R & R. Handbook of Biblical Criticism. Presbyterian Publishing Corp, 2011, p. 122)

So, Marcion has been considered to be the first 'Protestant' and a most formidable threat to Christian theology.

Baptist-trained Pastor Dr. Carroll R. Bierbower referred to him as the "evangelist Marcion" and has promoted Marcion's theology (Bierbower CR. The Antithesis. http://www.marcionite-scripture.info/CB_The_Antithesis.pdf accessed 02/11/20).

Some have claimed Marcion promoted 'Baptist' doctrines such as "sola fide" and "sola Scriptura" (Emby R. Marcion Heretic or Christian? Possible Progenitor of Three Famous Christian Communities: Baptists, Catholics, Gnostics. Travis Embry, 2001). Yet, it should be pointed out that Marcion did not actually believe in *sola Scriptura* and he did not even accept much of the Bible as truly valid.

Unlike early Christians, Tertullian wrote that "Marcion does not in any wise admit the resurrection of the flesh, and it is only the salvation of the soul which he promises" (Tertullian. Against Marcion, Book V, Chapter 10).

Marcion is said to have gathered scriptures from Jewish tradition, and juxtaposed these against certain of the sayings and teachings of Jesus in a work entitled the *Antithesis*—Marcion opposed the Old Testament.

Some improperly believe Marcion came up with the first canon of the New Testament. His was his own canon of scripture. His canon seems to have his edited version of Luke's gospel and ten edited letters of the Apostle Paul —the list did not include 1 & 2 Timothy and Titus (Bruce FF. The Canon of Scripture. InterVarsity Press, 1988, pp. 137-140).

Marcion called the books of his 'canon' the *Gospel* and the *Apostolikon* (or *Apostle*), which reflected his claim to believe in certain teachings of Jesus and the apostle Paul respectively. Tertullian reported that Marcion "erased" scriptures that did not agree with his teachings (Tertullian. Against Marcion, Books IV and V).

Perhaps the earliest writing that mentions Marcion or his followers was by Justin Martyr (who most Protestants consider to be a saint), writing in the mid-second century:

> And there is Marcion, a man of Pontus, who is even at this day alive, and teaching his disciples to believe in some other god greater than the Creator. And he, by the aid of the devils, has caused many of every nation to speak blasphemies, and to deny that God is the maker of this universe, and to assert that some other being, greater than He, has done greater works. All who take their opinions from these men, are, as we before said, called Christians; just as also those who do not agree with the philosophers in their doctrines, have yet in common with them the name of philosophers given to them. ... Marcion of Pontus, who is even now teaching men to deny that God is the maker of all things in heaven and on earth, and that the Christ predicted by the prophets is His Son, and preaches another god besides the Creator of all, and likewise another son. (Justin. First

Apology, Chapters XXVI, LVIII. Excerpted from Ante-Nicene Fathers, Volume 1. Edited by Alexander Roberts & James Donaldson. American Edition, 1885).

The term 'these men' from Justin refers to Simon Magus, Meander (another apostate), and Marcion. Justin wrote that Marcion denied Jesus was the Son of God. Clearly, Marcion was not a real Christian.

Notice this information about Marcion from Protestant and Harvard scholar Dr. Harold Brown:

> Marcion devised distinctive Christology to solve the problem of the Law and the Gospel. ...
>
> The first great heretic broke drastically with the faith of the early church ... Marcion did not believe in a real incarnation ... Because he was a 'Reformer,' Marcion has enjoyed a certain vogue among later Protestant writers. ...
>
> **Marcion ... expected the majority of mankind to be lost ... he denied the validity of the Old Testament and its Law** ... As the first great heretic, Marcion developed and perfected his heterodox system before orthodoxy had fully defined itself ... Marcion was in a sense a 'fundamentalist,' in that he believed he was correctly interpreting an authoritative written revelation ...
>
> Orthodox Lutheranism sometimes elevates the contrast between Law and Gospel to a degree reminiscent of Marcion (Brown HOJ. Heresies: Heresy and Orthodoxy in the History of the Church. Hendrickson Publishers, Peabody (MA), 1988, pp. 64-66, 455).

In other words, Marcion was essentially the first real anti-law Protestant and he denied Jesus came in the flesh—the denial of which is a doctrine of antichrist (2 John 7)! Notice that Dr. Brown points out Marcion was a "great heretic," that Marcion expected most humans would be permanently lost, and that Marcion's teachings on the Law were similar to those of Orthodox Lutherans.

We could take it a step further and state that in these subjects, Marcion was not different from general Protestantism (except that Protestantism usually talks well of the Law, but generally does not expect people to actually follow it) and that general Protestantism does clearly teach that most of humankind will be lost forever.

Irenaeus of Lyon (whom most Protestant scholars consider to be a saint) wrote that Marcion was a successor of Simon Magus:

> Cerdo was one who took his system from the followers of Simon, ... Marcion of Pontus succeeded him, and developed his doctrine. In so doing, he advanced the most daring blasphemy against Him who is proclaimed as God by the law and the prophets, declaring Him to be the author of evils, to take delight in war, to be infirm of purpose, and even to be contrary to Himself. (Irenaeus. Adversus Haereses, Book 1, Chapter 27:1-2).
>
> And that the Lord did not abrogate the natural [precepts] of the law, by which man is justified, which also those who were justified by faith, and who pleased God, did observe previous to the giving of the law, but that He extended and fulfilled them, is shown from His words. 'For,' He remarks, "it has been said to them of old time, Do not commit adultery. But I say unto you, That every one who hath looked upon a woman to lust after her, hath committed adultery with her already in his heart." And again: "It has been said, Thou shalt not kill. But I say unto you, Every one who is angry with his brother without a cause, shall be in danger of the judgment." And, "It hath been said, Thou shalt not forswear thyself. But I say unto you, Swear not at all; but let your conversation be, Yea, yea, and Nay, nay." And other statements of a like nature. **For all these do not contain or imply an opposition to and an overturning of the [precepts] of the past, as Marcion's followers do strenuously maintain**; but [they exhibit] a fulfilling and an extension of them (Irenaeus. Adversus Haereses, Book IV, Chapter 13:1)

Marcion's 'reforming' had anti-Jewish and anti-law sentiments.

Marcion hated the biblical Sabbath (Tertullian. Against Marcion, Book IV, Chapter 12).

Partially because he made one or more financial contributions, Marcion was tolerated by the Church of Rome for decades (Tertullian. The Prescription against Heretics, Chapter 30), Marcion was denounced by Church of God leaders such as Polycarp of Smyrna, Theophilus of Antioch, and Serapion of Antioch:

> **Polycarp himself replied to Marcion, who met him on one occasion, and said, "Dost thou know me?" "I do know thee, the first-born of Satan."** (Irenaeus. Adversus Haereses. Book III, Chapter 3, Verse 4. Excerpted from Ante-Nicene Fathers, Volume 1. Edited by Alexander Roberts & James Donaldson. American Edition, 1885).
>
> Theophilus ... is celebrated for one treatise, which was ably composed by him against Marcion, (Eusebius of Caesarea, Ecclesiastical History, Syriac version, Book 4 (Extract), Chapter 24. Spicilegium Syriacum, 1855).
>
> Serapion ... Moreover, brethren, we, having discovered to what kind of heresy Marcion adhered, and seen how he contradicted himself, not understanding of what he was speaking, (Serapion of Antioch. Eusebius Church History, VI,12)

Marcion was also denounced by Church of God leader Melito of Sardis in περί σαρκώσεως χριστού (On the Incarnation of Christ), but only fragments of that document remain.

In the early 3rd century, Hippolytus of Rome wrote:

> Marcion, a native of Pontus, ... founded a school full of folly, and attended by men of a sensual mode of life, inasmuch as he himself was one of lustful propensities. (Hippolytus. Refutation of All Heresies (Book VII), Chapter XVII. Translated by J. H. Machmahon. Excerpted from Ante-Nicene Fathers, Volume 5. Edited by Alexander Roberts & James Donaldson. American Edition, 1886)

Notice what the Protestant historian Kenneth Latourette stated about Marcion:

> Marcion insisted that the Church had obscured the Gospel by seeking to combine it with Judaism (Latourette KS. A History of Christianity, Volume 1: to A.D. 1500. HarperCollins, San Francisco, 1975, p. 126).

In other words, the original true Church of God truly did combine faith in Christ with practices that Marcion considered to be too Jewish. And Marcion was denounced by Church of God leaders from Asia Minor and Antioch for rejecting the true faith.

Marcion essentially taught that the Ten Commandments were done away and burdensome (Adversus Heresies, Book IV, Chapter 13:1)—like certain Protestant leaders do this day.

Yet, the Bible teaches:

> [1] Whoever believes that Jesus is the Christ is born of God, and everyone who loves Him who begot also loves him who is begotten of Him. [2] By this we know that we love the children of God, when we love God and keep His commandments. [3] For this is the love of God, that we keep His commandments. And **His commandments are not burdensome**. [4] For whatever is born of God overcomes the world. And this is the victory that has overcome the world — our faith. (1 John 5:1-4)

God's commandments are not burdensome. Consider that the Apostle Paul warned about the mystery of lawlessness:

> [7] For the mystery of lawlessness is already at work; only He who now restrains will do so until He is taken out of the way. (2 Thessalonians 2:7)

While the mystery of lawlessness appears to have started by the time of Simon Magus, Marcion and others promoted it further.

Jesus warned against those who would claim to have done things in His name, yet practiced lawlessness:

> [21] "Not everyone who says to Me, 'Lord, Lord,' shall enter the kingdom of heaven, but he who does the will of My Father in heaven ... [23] And then I will declare to them, 'I never knew you; depart from Me, you who practice lawlessness!' (Matthew 7:21,23)

Marcion promoted practicing lawlessness!

Yet, in order to grasp for historical legitimacy, Protestant scholars have sometimes considered him to be the first Protestant.

Modern Direct Promoters of Lawlessness

Although he did not actually keep the Ten Commandments, Martin Luther wrote:

> The fruits of this sin are afterwards the evil deeds which are forbidden in the Ten Commandments ... we hold that the Law was given by God, first, to restrain sin by threats and the dread of punishment, and by the promise and offer of grace and benefit (Luther M. The Smallclad Papers. 1537).

Protestants originally taught that they were to keep the Ten Commandments.

Yet, in its *Ten Commandments* article, Wikipedia once reported:

> Modern Evangelicalism, under the influence of dispensationalism, commonly denies that the commandments have any abiding validity as a requirement binding upon Christians (Ten Commandments. Wikipedia, viewed 7/30/08).

And sadly, this is a fairly common Protestant view as the following quotes help demonstrate:

The 10 commandments are Abolished

> Today Christians keep the Law of Christ which is superior! 1 Cor 9:21; Gal 6:2 (http://www.bible.ca/7-10-commandments.htm viewed 12/03/19).

The Ten Commandments Were Abolished

Introduction The ten commandments are no longer lawful: they are not binding on the Christian. Christian scripture says the ten commandments were abolished Ephesians 2:15; a bible believing person is no longer bound to follow them; (http://my.opera.com/richardinbellingham/blog/the-ten-commandments-were-abolished viewed 7/30/08).

THE TEN COMMANDMENTS ARE NOT FOR CHRISTIANS
(Richard Bethel. http://www.bethel ministries.com ten_commandments.htm viewed 7/30/08).

The Ten Commandments: Christ Nailed to the Cross (The Ten Commandments: Christ Nailed to the Cross. By William A Worley. Published by the Author?, 1959).

Prof. M.D. Canright, an ordained Baptist preacher says: ... "The Ten Commandments and the whole Jewish law are abolished, and the Sabbath is not binding upon Christians ... we are not under the Ten Commandments, but under Christ" (Religious Delusions: A Psychic Study By J. V. Coombs Published by Kessinger Publishing, 2003, pp. 34-35).

One of the Ten Commandments was not carried over into the Law of Christ...

Not all of the Ten Commandments were carried over into the law of Christ (Jeffrey W. Hamilton, preacher. La Vista Church of Christ. http://www.lavistachurchofchrist.org/LVanswers/2004-11-23.htm viewed 7/30/08).

The Ten Commandments were given to the Jews; and when Christ came and died they were all nailed to the cross (Lindsay Taylor C. The Marked Bible. Pacific Press, 1922, p. 53).

The keeping of the Sabbath as commanded on the tables of stone was nailed to the cross ... The Sabbath of the ten commandments had its mission (Orr CE. The Gospel Day: Or, the Light of Christianity. Gospel Trumpet, 1904, pp. 336-337).

> Andy Stanley, the senior pastor of North Point Community Church in Alpharetta, Georgia … "You are not accountable to the Ten Commandments, we're done with that. God has done something new." (James E. Andy Stanley and the Dismissal of the OT. May 14, 2018. https://thewitnessbcc.com/andy-stanley-and-the-dismissal-of-the-ot/ accessed 08/14/18)

So, various Evangelicals/Protestants have directly taught against the Ten Commandments. They claim to be Christian, but promote lawlessness, which is part of the "mystery of iniquity." Those who are hearers of part of the word of God, but not doers deceive themselves (James 1:22). Often, what they will improperly say is that the Sabbath commandment was not carried over in the New Testament, which is false per Hebrews 4:9-11. Their arguments against the law tend to be intended to justify not keeping the Sabbath commandment.

Jude warned about such people:

4 For certain men have stealthily crept in, those who long ago have been written about, condemning them to this judgment. They are ungodly men, who are perverting the grace of our God, turning it into licentiousness, and are personally denying the only Lord God and our Lord Jesus Christ. (Jude 4, AFV)

Yet, Protestants claim that they accept, but do not deny, Jesus.

The Apostle Paul warned that there would be people who claimed Jesus, but were not Christian:

16 They profess to know God, but in works they deny Him, being abominable, disobedient, and disqualified for every good work. (Titus 1:16)

Worshiping false gods, murder, lying, adultery, coveting, stealing, Sabbath breaking, covetousness, dishonoring parents, and idolatry are wrong—and all of these are part of the Ten Commandments. Furthermore, disobedience often involves not accepting the truth, but accepting fables like the Apostle Paul warned about (2 Timothy 4:3-4). Protestants basically deny Christ in their works, beliefs, and practices.

Speaking of adultery, another area of difference between the CCOG and Protestantism is that Protestantism often accepts non-biblical reasons for divorce and remarriage that CCOG does not—Protestantism should have stuck to the teachings of Jesus (Matthew 5:32) and the Apostle Paul (1 Corinthians 7:10-15) on this.

Consider the following prophecies regarding Jesus:

> [3] A bruised reed He will not break, And smoking flax He will not quench; He will bring forth justice for truth. [4] He will not fail nor be discouraged, Till He has established justice in the earth; And the coastlands shall wait for His law. (Isaiah 42:3-4)

> [4] "Listen to Me, My people; And give ear to Me, O My nation: For law will proceed from Me, And I will make My justice rest As a light of the peoples. [5] My righteousness is near, My salvation has gone forth, And My arms will judge the peoples; The coastlands will wait upon Me, And on My arm they will trust. (Isaiah 51:4-5)

Why would Jesus abolish the Ten Commandments for His Church since scriptures clearly show that there will be truth and justice in His Kingdom as people will keep the law?

Well, obviously He did not abolish those commandments. Sadly, many despise prophecies, even though the New Testament says not to (1 Thessalonians 5:20).

In a podcast, anti-Ten Commandments Protestant minister Andy Stanley said:

> "I'm convinced that we make a better case for Jesus if we leave the Old Testament or the old covenant out of the argument ... you don't need ancient prophs when somebody rises from the dead" (Jonathan Merritt interview of Andy Stanley. Seekers & Speakers, podcast. August 9, 2018).

Well, Andy Stanley's opinion is NOT in line with Jesus (Luke 16:31) nor what the original apostles and Gospel writers did. They all referred to the Old Testament as proof Jesus was the Messiah and taught other truths from the Old Testament. Notice that is what is SUPPOSED to be done:

> [25] ... Jesus Christ, according to the revelation of the mystery kept secret since the world began [26] but now made manifest, and by the prophetic Scriptures ... (Romans 16:25b-26a)

(For more details, also check out the free book, online at ccog.org, *Proof Jesus is the Messiah*.)

Jesus also stated:

> [46] For if you believed Moses, you would believe Me; for he wrote about Me. [47] But if you do not believe his writings, how will you believe My words? (John 5:46-47)

Sadly, many Protestants are like Andy Stanley and do not want to believe what Moses wrote.

Now let's look at some passages from the Old and New Testaments:

> [18] Where there is no revelation, the people cast off restraint; But happy is he who keeps the law. (Proverbs 29:18)

> [14] Always obey the LORD and you will be happy. If you are stubborn, you will be ruined. (Proverbs 28:14, GNT)

> [3] Dear friends, although I have been eager to write to you about our common salvation, I now feel compelled instead to write to encourage you to contend earnestly for the faith that was once for all entrusted to the saints. [4] For certain men have secretly slipped in among you – men who long ago were marked out for the condemnation I am about to describe – ungodly men who have turned the grace of our God into a license for evil and who deny our only Master and Lord, Jesus Christ. (Jude 3-4, NET)

> [1:4] And these things we write to you that your joy may be full. ... [2:3] Now by this we know that we know Him, if we keep His commandments. [4] He who says, "I know Him," and does not keep His commandments, is a liar, and the truth is not in him. [5]

But whoever keeps His word, truly the love of God is perfected in him. By this we know that we are in Him. ⁶ He who says he abides in Him ought himself also to walk just as He walked. (1 John 1:4, 2:3-6)

The Ten Commandments are not a burden, but keeping them helps make one happy (cf. Proverbs 29:18). Anti-Ten Commandments Protestant teachers ignore/rationalize away the commands from the revealed word of God and instead turn grace/favor into license. They deny Jesus by teaching that we do not need to strive to walk as He walked. We are to imitate Jesus, who kept the Ten Commandments (John 15:10), as the Apostle Paul wrote Christians are to do (1 Corinthians 11:1).

The Bible teaches we are to keep God's commandments and statutes for our good (Deuteronomy 10:13). The Bible also teaches that violating the Ten Commandments is evil (e.g. Deuteronomy 4:25, 22:22; 1 Samuel 20:7-33; 1 Corinthians 5:9-12; Colossians 3:5; 2 Timothy 3:13).

A while back, a Protestant scholar named Dr. Kenny Rhodes claimed that "God never gave the Ten Commandments to the Gentiles" and that "not all of the Ten Commandments are reiterated in the New Testament," yet the Bible disagrees (e.g. Exodus 12:49; for more details please see the free book, online at ccog.org titled: *The Ten Commandments: The Decaloque, Christianity, and the Beast*).

Dr. Rhodes also inaccurately claimed that the Ten Commandments did not carry over into the New Testament. For one of his 'proofs,' he correctly said that if we need to keep the Ten Commandments, then we would have to keep the Sabbath command as well. We in the CCOG do, of course, keep the Sabbath commandment. So, that is NOT proof that one does NOT need to keep the commandments.

It is also astounding that various scholars in the past couple of centuries seemingly claim to know how to interpret what the Greek New Testament meant so much better than the early Christians who lived much nearer to the time it was written.

The Apostle Peter told of those who improperly twisted scriptures:

> ^{15} ... Paul, according to the wisdom given to him, has written to you, ^{16} as also in all his epistles, speaking in them of these things, in which are some things hard to understand, which untaught and unstable people twist to their own destruction, as they do also the rest of the Scriptures. (2 Peter 3:15-16)

To this day, many Protestant scholars have twisted the Apostle Paul's writings. Jesus also pointed out that Satan could twist the meaning of scriptures as well (Matthew 4:3-10).

Having been exposed to teachings from the apostles, many early Christians understood *koine* (common) Greek and they understood that they were to strive to keep the Ten Commandments. This is confirmed by writings from 2nd century Gentile Church of God leaders such as Ignatius, Polycarp, Theophilus, and Melito as well as writings from Gentile Greco-Roman leaders such as Clement of Alexandria, Irenaeus of Lyon, and others. Modern scripture twisters should know better.

Consider also that an anonymous 2nd century document that has been called "the oldest complete Christian sermon that has survived" (Holmes MW. The Apostolic Fathers, Greek Texts and English Translations. Baker Books, Grand Rapids (MI), 2004, p. 102) repeatedly teaches that Christians are to keep the commandments (meaning the Ten Commandments) to be God's people (2 Clement 3:4, 4:2-5, 6:7, 8:4, 17:3-7).

Striving to keep the Ten Commandments was part of the original Christian faith. It takes faith to trust God and do that at times, but God says those who actually trust Him are happy for it (Proverbs 16:20).

Yet, notice a Protestant view:

> What does Jesus say about the Ten Commandments? He asks us to look at the Cross of Calvary where he died to set us free. (Ten Commandments and Jesus. Copyright © 2002-2019 AllAboutTruth.org accessed 09/16/19)

No, Jesus did not die to set Christians free from the Ten Commandments. He never asked "to look at the Cross of Calvary" to be freed from obeying God. He died to set us free from the slavery of sin (cf. Romans 6:6), so we could be slaves of righteousness (Romans 6:18).

The Bible teaches that all of God's commandments are righteousness (Psalm 119:172), not something to be set free from. The New Testament teaches that scripture is intended to teach God's people about righteousness (2 Timothy 3:16) so they can be "thoroughly equipped for every good work" (2 Timothy 3:17), so why should any Protestant teach against the commandments it contains?

Notice a statement from a Protestant minister related to a Protestant preacher:

> A preacher once said ..., pointing to the Ten Commandments hanging on the wall ...: "They are an offence to me. Jesus kept them for me. I don't want to have anything to do with them." (Murray W. What Is The True Christian Religion? New Age Press, 1947, p. 24)

Yes, Jesus did keep the commandments, for He said, "I have kept My Father's commandments" (John 15:10). The Bible teaches "All Your commandments are faithful" (Psalm 119:86). Yet, God's Ten Commandments are not an offence to real Christians. Furthermore, Jesus did not say He kept them so others would not need to strive to do so.

Notice that the Apostle Paul wrote:

> [1] Imitate me, just as I also imitate Christ. (1 Corinthians 11:1)

Like Jesus, the Apostle Paul also kept the commandments (cf. Philippians 3:5-6).

While many Protestants like to make statements such as "It's all about Jesus," it is only about *their version* of Jesus, not actually trying to imitate how He lived.

According to Jesus, it's actually 'all about love' (cf. Matthew 22:37-39; John 13:34-35) and while Jesus is certainly part of that (cf. John 3:16-17, 15:9-17), He also taught that the commandments were aspects of that love (Matthew 22:37-40). The Apostle Paul specifically taught that love was the purpose of the commandments (1 Timothy 1:5).

Christians imitate Jesus and the Apostle Paul by striving to keep the Ten Commandments. Many Protestants do not understand that. They also do not understand the statement by Peter and the other apostles that God's Holy Spirit is "given to those who obey Him" (Acts 5:32). Those who say Jesus is Lord, but practice lawlessness, will not be in His Kingdom if they do not truly repent (Matthew 7:21-23). One needs to repent so one's "sins may be blotted out" (Acts 3:19)—many Protestant preachers do not really teach that.

Those who strive to obey the Ten Commandments are those who properly will acquire the fruits of the Spirit:

> [22] But the fruit of the Spirit is love, joy, peace, long-suffering, kindness, goodness, faith, [23] Meekness, self-control; against such things there is no law. [24] But those who are Christ's have crucified the flesh with its passions and lusts. [25] If we live by the Spirit, we should also be walking by the Spirit. (Galatians 5:22-25)

However, some Protestants teach that it is 'Pharisaical' to try to keep the Ten Commandments. Many improperly teach that is why Jesus condemned the Pharisees. Yet, **the Pharisees were condemned for their hypocrisy by Jesus because they did NOT properly keep the Ten Commandments** (cf. Matthew 15:3-9; 23:13-29)—not because they actually did.

The view on the law remains one of the significant differences between many Protestants and the *Continuing* Church of God today.

Let it also be stated that in the Greco-Roman-Protestant world, there are those who profess that the Ten Commandments should be kept, but, like the Pharisees of Jesus' day, they reason around them. This is a "mystery of lawlessness" as well.

The *Continuing* Church of God teaches:

> [105] Your word is a lamp to my feet And a light to my path. ... [115] ... I will keep the commandments of my God! (Psalm 119:105,115)

The true church realizes that God's Ten Commandment law is one of His greatest gifts to humankind. Keeping them reflects love.

The New Testament teaches:

> [5] Now the purpose of the commandment is love ... (1 Timothy 1:5)

Yes, the purpose of the commandments is to show love, make us better, and help others to be better.

> [13] Let us hear the conclusion of the whole matter:
>
> Fear God and keep His commandments, For this is man's all. [14] For God will bring every work into judgment, Including every secret thing, Whether good or evil. (Ecclesiastes 12:13-14)

The Ten Commandments were not some arbitrary rules or burden.

The Ten Commandments were made known to us to help build character in us so that we will be able to be better (cf. Psalm 119:72), love better (cf. James 2:8; Matthew 22:37-40), and make eternity better. We can, in this life, make our own eternity better if we truly trust Him (cf. Proverbs 3:5-8,16:20).

Yet, because of distortions from religious leaders, the Apostle Paul was inspired to write about the "mystery of lawlessness" (2 Thessalonians 2:7). According to Jesus, in these end times, lawlessness will increase and cause the love of many to grow cold (Matthew 24:12). Sadly, this will help lead to the final end time "Mystery Babylon the Great" (Revelation 17:5)—a religious power on the city of seven hills (Revelation 17:9,18).

For more on that and the Ten Commandments, check out the free online booklet: *The Ten Commandments: The Decalogue, Christianity, and the Beast*.

Nailed to the Cross?

Some Protestants teach that the Ten Commandments were "nailed to the cross." Here are a few quotes:

> The Ten Commandments: Christ Nailed to the Cross (Worley W. The Ten Commandments: Christ Nailed to the Cross. 1959).
>
> The Ten Commandments were given to the Jews; and when Christ came and died they were all nailed to the cross (Taylor CL. The marked Bible. 1922, p. 53).
>
> The keeping of the Sabbath as commanded on the tables of stone was nailed to the cross ... The Sabbath of the ten commandments had its mission (Orr C. The Gospel Day: Or, the Light of Christianity. 1904, pp. 336-337).
>
> Colossians 2:14-16 says the 10 commandments are abolished! Colossians 2:14-16 so clearly states the weekly Sabbath was nailed to cross and abolished that Sabbatarians are at a loss to know what to do with it! (Sabbath Keepers Refuted. http://www.bible.ca/7-Col2-14-16.htm accessed 02/08/18)

There is only one scripture that uses the mistranslated "nailed it to the cross" expression (AV/NKJV), it is Colossians 2:13-14, in which Paul states:

> [13] And you, being dead in your trespasses and the uncircumcision of your flesh, He has made alive together with Him, [14] having forgiven you all trespasses, having wiped out the handwriting of requirements that was against us, which was contrary to us. And He has taken it out of the way, having nailed it to the cross.

Were the Ten Commandments the "requirements that was against us, which was contrary to us"?

No, that is not what Paul wrote. He wrote it was the handwriting of requirements that were "nailed to the cross."

Which requirements were wiped out?

It appears that two 'requirements' were wiped out. One would be the requirements of the Levitical priesthood (Hebrews 9:1,6-10).

And why?

> [4] For it is not possible that the blood of bulls and goats could take away sins ... [10] By that will we have been sanctified through the offering of the body of Jesus once for all. (Hebrews 10:4,10)

The other (which is related) would be the ultimate death penalty, as "the wages of sin is death, but the gift of God is eternal life in Christ Jesus our Lord" (Romans 6:23) or other specific ceremonial penalties associated with the Old Testament statutes (such as making a sin offering or washing; cf. Hebrews 9:11-15, 10:17-18).

Please understand that the expression "the handwriting of requirements" (*cheirografon tois dogmasin*) is a Greek legal expression that signifies the penalty which a lawbreaker had to pay. It does not signify the laws that are to be obeyed--only the penalty.

It is only through the acceptance of the sacrifice of Jesus Christ that the penalty was wiped out ("the handwriting of requirements"). But only the penalty, not the law!

It is sort of like if a judge tells someone they do not have to pay a fine for running a traffic signal. That does not mean to go out and ignore traffic signals--it means that the legal penalty for doing so was forgiven.

Even certain Protestant commentators realize this. Notice what *Matthew Henry's Commentary on the Whole Bible* states about Colossians 2:14:

> Whatever was in force against us is taken out of the way. He has obtained for us a legal discharge from the hand-writing of requirements which was against us (v. 14), which may be understood,
>
> 1. Of that obligation to punishment in which consists the guilt of sin. The curse of the law is the hand-writing against us, like the hand-writing on Belshazzar's wall. Cursed is every one who

continues not in every thing. This was a hand-writing which was against us, and contrary to us; for it threatened our eternal ruin. This was removed when he redeemed us from the curse of the law, being made a curse for us, Gal 3:13. (Matthew Henry's Commentary on the Whole Bible: New Modern Edition, 1991)

Some have argued that you still cannot keep the Ten Commandments (for "all have sinned"), even though they are all mentioned as being in effect after Jesus' execution and resurrection.

Does this mean one should not try? No, despite the fact that Christians sin (1 John 1:8), they are to keep His commandments (1 John 2:4).

Furthermore, let's look at another Protestant translation:

> [14] having canceled out the certificate of debt consisting of decrees against us, which was hostile to us; and He has taken it out of the way, having nailed it to the cross (Colossians 2:14, NASB)

It was the handwriting of requirements (often also called the handwriting of ordinances), the certificate of debt, that was wiped away and "nailed to the cross."

Consider:

> [16] This is the covenant that I will make with them after those days, says the LORD: I will put my laws into their hearts, and in their minds I will write them. (Hebrews 10:16).

God's laws should be a way of life written on our hearts.

If Christians were not to keep the Ten Commandments, the Apostle Paul would not, for example, have been inspired to write the following:

> [11] But now I have written to you not to keep company with anyone named a brother, who is sexually immoral, or covetous, or an idolater, or a reviler, or a drunkard, or an extortioner -- not even to eat with such a person. (1 Corinthians 5:11)

⁹ Do you not know that the unrighteous will not inherit the kingdom of God? Do not be deceived. Neither fornicators, nor idolaters, nor adulterers, nor homosexuals, nor sodomites, ¹⁰ nor thieves, nor covetous, nor drunkards, nor revilers, nor extortioners will inherit the kingdom of God. (1 Corinthians 6:9-10)

Christians are to strive to keep the Ten Commandments and not accept someone as a real Christian who does not.

2nd century COG leaders like Polycarp of Smyrna (Letter to the Philippians), Melito of Sardis (A Discourse Which Was in the Presence of Antoninus Caesar), and Theophilus of Antioch (To Autolycus) taught keeping the Ten Commandments.

Saved by Grace for Works

Of course, just striving to keep the Ten Commandments will not save us.

After hearing Peter preach about Jesus, people asked what they should do. Peter responded with:

> ³⁸ ... "Repent, and let every one of you be baptized in the name of Jesus Christ for the remission of sins; and you shall receive the gift of the Holy Spirit. ³⁹ For the promise is to you and to your children, and to all who are afar off, as many as the Lord our God will call." (Acts 2:38-39)

Notice that repentance, baptism, and the acceptance of Jesus are criteria for salvation.

Peter and the other apostles later added clarifying points about following humans and the giving of the Holy Spirit:

> ²⁹ But Peter and the apostles answered and said, "We are obligated to obey God rather than men. ³⁰ The God of our fathers raised up Jesus Whom you killed by hanging Him on a tree. ³¹ Him has God exalted by His right hand to be a Prince and Savior, to give repentance and remission of sins to Israel. ³² And we are His witnesses of these things, as is also the Holy Spirit, which God has given to those who obey Him." (Acts 5:29-32, A Faithful Version)

Therefore, according to the apostles, people desiring to be Christian should not accept orders or traditions of humans that are in conflict with scripture. And notice that God only gives His Spirit to those who obey Him. Without that Spirit, one is NOT a Christian (Romans 8:9-10).

But aren't Christians saved by grace? Yes, as it is written:

> [8] For by grace you have been saved through faith, and that not of yourselves; it is the gift of God, [9] not of works, lest anyone should boast. [10] For we are His workmanship, created in Christ Jesus for good works, which God prepared beforehand that we should walk in them. (Ephesians 2:8-10)

The New Testament Greek word translated "grace" is "*charis.*" *Charis* was a widely used word in the first century; its primary meaning is "that which gives pleasure or delight." 'Grace' means an undeserved free gift of favor, and in context, can also indicate unmerited pardon (forgiveness).

Why is grace essential to salvation?

Because "all have sinned" (Romans 3:23) and "the wages of sin is death" (Romans 6:23). Therefore, all people have earned the death penalty. That penalty has to be paid. Our regret and subsequent good behavior can never pay the penalty for sin, because the penalty is death.

Grace is not deserved, because our sins do not merit it. But undeserved/unmerited does not mean unconditional. One must, for example, repent and accept Jesus, and obey to receive the Holy Spirit (Acts 2:38, 5:32). If we refuse to change our lives — to obey God — God is under no obligation to bestow His grace upon us. God will not allow Christ's sacrifice and His grace to be taken lightly.

Why are all efforts to earn salvation by our own efforts futile?

> [7] Because the carnal mind is enmity against God; for it is not subject to the law of God, nor indeed can be. [8] So then, those who are in the flesh cannot please God. (Romans 8:7-8)

Our best personal efforts are in vain unless God gives humans the help we need. God's grace toward us begins when God begins calling us.

The old Worldwide Church of God published the following:

> Is grace, as many assume, merely unmerited pardon for sin — or is it much more? ...
>
> The Apostle Paul wrote, "God ... called me through His grace" (Galatians 1:15).
>
> The very fact that you can understand the truths of God as revealed in the Bible is because of God's grace. But being called is just the beginning of grace.
>
> The process of conversion requires more than understanding. It requires change, or repentance. We must freely choose to obey God — and unless God shows us what to repent of and the importance of obeying Him, we cannot repent. "The goodness of God leads you to repentance," Paul explained in Romans 2:4.
>
> But being sorry for sinning, and changing, is not enough. So God's grace continues with Jesus Christ's sacrifice: "For all have sinned and fall short of the glory of God, being justified freely by His grace through the redemption that is in Christ Jesus, whom God set forth to be a propitiation [an atoning sacrifice] by His blood, through faith, to demonstrate His righteousness" (Romans 3:23-25).
>
> Jesus Christ paid the penalty of sin, which is death, in our stead. Christ's sacrifice is the supreme expression of divine grace. It is totally unmerited (Romans 5:6-8).
>
> Christ's sacrifice frees us from the penalty of breaking God's law. But it does not do away with the law! Think: Would God now allow the violation of laws that necessitated the death of His own Son? Of course not.
>
> Grace does not nullify God's law. Rather, grace is necessary because God's law is eternally binding. As Paul explained: "Shall we continue in sin [the transgression of God's law —I John 3:4] that grace may abound? Certainly not! How shall we who died to

sin live any longer in it?" (Romans 6:1-2) Continuing in sin would mock Jesus Christ's supreme sacrifice.

Unmerited but not unconditional

Here is where many misunderstand. Grace is unmerited but it is not unconditional. There are two conditions: repentance and faith (Mark 1:5, Acts 2:38). Although we can never earn salvation, God does set certain requirements for receiving His grace.

Let's understand. Once God, by His grace, reveals to us the need to repent and humbly accept Jesus Christ's sacrifice as payment for our sins, we must do our part. We must voluntarily yield ourselves to God, admitting where we have been wrong, and make the necessary changes. Then we must be baptized as an outward expression of our repentance and faith (Romans 6:3-6).

Don't misunderstand — God's grace is free and unmerited, but if we refuse to change our lives — to obey God — He is under no obligation to bestow His grace upon us. God will not allow Christ's sacrifice and His grace to be taken lightly.

The process continues. Peter tells us we must now "grow in grace" (II Peter 3:18, Authorized Version). Grace is unmerited pardon for sin, but it is much more. For if grace were merely the unmerited forgiveness of sin, how could we grow in grace except by sinning more? No, we must, while coming under God's grace, overcome sin.

If you are truly under God's grace, you will be striving diligently to obey God's commandments. Paul said: "For the grace of God that brings salvation has appeared to all men, teaching us that, denying ungodliness and worldly lusts, we should live soberly, righteously, and godly in the present age, looking for the blessed hope and glorious appearing of our great God and Savior Jesus Christ, who gave Himself for us, that He might redeem us from every lawless deed and purify for Himself His own special people, zealous for good works" (Titus 2:11-14). (Peitz DG. Grace: Do You Really Understand It? Good News, January 1985)

Notice the following scriptures:

> ³:¹⁸ And to whom did He swear that they would not enter His rest, but to those who did not obey? ¹⁹ So we see that they could not enter in because of unbelief. ⁴:¹ Therefore, since a promise remains of entering His rest, let us fear lest any of you seem to have come short of it. (Hebrews 3:18-4:1)

> ⁹ ... He became the author of eternal salvation to all who obey Him, (Hebrews 5:9)

The result of unbelief, lack of faith, is disobedience. Entering into God's rest of salvation requires obedience. Not to earn salvation, but obedience is necessary for those who are called and who accept God's great gift to be saved according to the Bible.

The Apostle Paul wrote that there is a mystery to Christ and grace that not all will understand:

> ¹ For this reason I, Paul, the prisoner of Christ Jesus for you Gentiles — ² if indeed you have heard of the dispensation of the grace of God which was given to me for you, ³ how that by revelation He made known to me the mystery (as I have briefly written already, ⁴ by which, when you read, you may understand my knowledge in the mystery of Christ), ⁵ which in other ages was not made known to the sons of men, as it has now been revealed by the Spirit to His holy apostles and prophets: (Ephesians 3:1-5)

The Apostle Peter taught:

> ²⁰ ... Jesus Christ, who was preached to you before, ²¹ whom heaven must receive until the times of restoration of all things, which God has spoken by the mouth of all His holy prophets since the world began. (Acts 3:20-21).

The Protestants teach that relatively few humans will ever experience God's grace as they tend to not understand the apostles or the prophets nor the time of the restoration of all things.

After Jesus returns, He will not be sacrificed again. But since He died for all, He will bring the opportunity for salvation and the opportunity of grace to all:

> [28] ... Christ was offered once to bear the sins of many. To those who eagerly wait for Him He will appear a second time, apart from sin, for salvation. (Hebrews 9:28)

It is the true God, whom those in the true Church of God worship, who is truly the God of grace. The true God, who is love, will grant His grace to almost everyone! God's plan will work:

> [14] The LORD of hosts has sworn, saying, "Surely, as I have thought, so it shall come to pass, And as I have purposed, so it shall stand (Isaiah 14:24).

Does God have a purpose, a plan, that will grant grace to most or few? Does anyone doubt that God has had thoughts about granting His grace to everyone?

A God of love has a purpose to share His grace with more than a minority of humans.

Protestants have limited understanding about God's grace. Furthermore, sadly, they often have turned grace "into a license for immorality" (Jude 4, BSB, NET, NIV).

The Bible teaches that God's word is part of His grace. His law gives direction in how to live in this age (e.g. Deuteronomy 6:24-25), as well as in the millennial Kingdom (cf. Isaiah 2:2-3). The misuse of grace, in an attempt to negate the law, has confused many Protestants. It is because humans violate God's law that they need the type of forgiveness which comes from the grace of God.

Christians are not to live in violation of God's law, but are to eliminate tendencies towards sin:

> [5] Therefore put to death your members which are on the earth: fornication, uncleanness, passion, evil desire, and covetousness, which is idolatry. [6] Because of these things the

wrath of God is coming upon the sons of disobedience, ⁷ in which you yourselves once walked when you lived in them.

⁸ But now you yourselves are to put off all these: anger, wrath, malice, blasphemy, filthy language out of your mouth. ⁹ Do not lie to one another, since you have put off the old man with his deeds, ¹⁰ and have put on the new man who is renewed in knowledge according to the image of Him who created him, (Colossians 3:5-10).

At least six of the Ten Commandments are being referred to above.

Although Christians are NOT saved *by* works, they were created *for* good works. Christians are to walk in the way of good works (Ephesians 2:10). We are to live the way of give, which includes striving to keep the Ten Commandments. Striving to keep them under adversity helps build faith and character.

Martin Luther improperly disapproved of the Book of James. In it, the Bible teaches:

> ¹⁴ What does it profit, my brethren, if someone says he has faith but does not have works? Can faith save him? ¹⁵ If a brother or sister is naked and destitute of daily food, 16 and one of you says to them, "Depart in peace, be warmed and filled," but you do not give them the things which are needed for the body, what does it profit? ¹⁷ Thus also faith by itself, if it does not have works, is dead.
>
> ¹⁸ But someone will say, "You have faith, and I have works." Show me your faith without your works, and I will show you my faith by my works. ¹⁹ You believe that there is one God. You do well. Even the demons believe — and tremble! ²⁰ But do you want to know, O foolish man, that faith without works is dead? ²¹ Was not Abraham our father justified by works when he offered Isaac his son on the altar? ²² Do you see that faith was working together with his works, and by works faith was made perfect? ²³ And the Scripture was fulfilled which says, "Abraham believed God, and it was accounted to him for righteousness."

And he was called the friend of God. ²⁴ **You see then that a man is justified by works, and not by faith only.** (James 2:14-24)

That last statement deeply offended Martin Luther as it disagreed with his opinions. Notice how the English Standard Version renders it:

> ²⁴ You see that a person is justified by works and not by faith alone. (James 2:24, ESV)

Scripture is in direct conflict with some of Martin Luther's cherished opinions.

Hence, in the *Continuing* Church of God, we do not accept Martin Luther's inaccurate doctrine of *sola fide* teaching. We are saved by grace, through faith, for good works.

Once Saved Always Saved? Who is a Real Christian?

Some Protestants teach that if you ever once prayed several seconds for Jesus to be your Saviour that you are saved, no matter what you do or how you live your life.

At least one Protestant 'cartoon' tract tried to illustrate that. One showed a group of men who apparently all died suddenly together (such as from an automobile accident). They were pictured before a judgment seat in heaven. One man was told he was going to heaven, and the rest of the men were told they would be burning in everlasting punishment forever. Since the men all knew each other, they wondered why one man supposedly got to stay in heaven. They pointed out that they did not know he was a Christian, that he did not live differently than them, nor did he ever tell them anything about Jesus.

Well, according to the cartoon tract, once when the man was 9 years of age, he accepted Jesus in response to an emotional appeal. Since this did not happen to them, they were doomed to fry forever. But the man who was allowed to go to heaven obviously failed to repent or meet other biblical requirements for salvation (e.g. Acts 2:38).

This is a cheap, but also false, understanding of grace. It also overlooks various New Testament passages.

For example, the Apostle Paul wrote and warned:

> [11] For the grace of God that brings salvation has appeared to all men, [12] teaching us that, denying ungodliness and worldly lusts, we should live soberly, righteously, and godly in the present age, [13] looking for the blessed hope and glorious appearing of our great God and Savior Jesus Christ, [14] who gave Himself for us, that He might redeem us from every lawless deed and purify for Himself His own special people, zealous for good works. (Titus 2:11-14)
>
> [1] We then, as workers together with Him also plead with you not to receive the grace of God in vain. (2 Corinthians 6:1)

Christians are to live differently once they have repented, accepted Jesus, and been baptized as they are "not to receive the grace of God in vain."

Real Christians have repented, been baptized, and received the Holy Spirit (Acts 2:38).

Here is essentially the biblical definition of who is and who is not a real Christian:

> [9] But you are not in the flesh but in the Spirit, if indeed the Spirit of God dwells in you. Now if anyone does not have the Spirit of Christ, he is not His. (Romans 8:9)

A real Christian has the Spirit of Christ, no one else is a true Christian.

Who receives that Spirit?

Only those who obey are given the Spirit of Christ (Acts 5:32).

Thus, God is the judge of who is, as well as who is not, a real Christian.

The Christian Life

What about how to live a Christian life?

Believe it or not, Martin Luther actually taught:

> Be a sinner, and let your sins be strong, but let your trust in Christ be stronger ... No sin can separate us from Him, even if we were to kill or commit adultery thousands of times each day (Let Your Sins Be Strong: A Letter from Luther to Melanchthon Letter no. 99, 1 August 1521).

We in the CCOG do not believe our sins should be strong. It is not that Jesus cannot forgive all, but notice what the New Testament teaches:

> ^{26} **For if we sin willfully** after we have received the knowledge of the truth, there no longer remains a sacrifice for sins, ^{27} but a certain fearful expectation of judgment, and fiery indignation which will devour the adversaries. ^{28} Anyone who has rejected Moses' law dies without mercy on the testimony of two or three witnesses. ^{29} Of how much worse punishment, do you suppose, will he be thought worthy who has trampled the Son of God underfoot, counted the blood of the covenant by which he was sanctified a common thing, and **insulted the Spirit of grace?** (Hebrews 10:26-29)

Martin Luther's statement was an insult to "the Spirit of grace."

Since Christians are saved by grace, various Protestants simply cannot accept the biblical admonitions about works. Protestants (and many others) do not understand that the Christian life is one of training. In addition to supporting the work of the great commission (Matthew 24:14, 28:19-20), Christians are training to develop character that will impact what they will be doing throughout eternity in the next life. In this sense, many Protestants miss much of the purpose of salvation.

While the Bible teaches that faith without works is dead, it does not teach that people can earn their salvation by their own good works. But what many Protestants do NOT understand is that the Bible teaches that we shall be REWARDED according to our WORKS (Matthew 16:7; Revelation 22:12)! And we will be able to help more people because of that (cf. Luke 19:15-19).

Some Protestants have pointed to the last half of the following scripture from the Apostle Paul to support their views on lawlessness:

> [14] For sin shall not have dominion over you, for you are not under law but under grace. (Romans 6:14)

Since Christians are under grace, does this mean Christians are given license to disobey God's Law?

No, because we do not want sin, which is the "transgression of the law" (1 John 3:4, KJV), to have dominion over us. Jesus said that "whoever commits sin is a slave of sin" (John 8:34).

We can better understand what Paul was teaching by also looking at other verses in Romans 6:

> [1] What shall we say then? Shall we continue in sin that grace may abound? [2] Certainly not! How shall we who died to sin live any longer in it? (Romans 6:1-2)

> [12] Therefore do not let sin reign in your mortal body, that you should obey it in its lusts. [13] And do not present your members as instruments of unrighteousness to sin, but present yourselves to God as being alive from the dead, and your members as instruments of righteousness to God. (Romans 6:12-13)

It should be pointed out that the word of God specifically teaches:

> [172] ... For all Your commandments are righteousness. (Psalm 119:172)

Hence since Christians are to present themselves "as instruments of righteousness" (Romans 6:13), Christians should be striving to obey God's commandments, not let their "sins be strong" as Martin Luther wrote. To learn more about living as a Christian, check out the free book, available online at ccog.org, titled *Christians: Ambassadors for the Kingdom of God, Biblical instructions on living as a Christian*.

Now, to see more about obedience and grace, let's go back to Romans 6:

> [15] What then? Shall we sin because we are not under law but under grace? Certainly not! [16] Do you not know that to whom you present yourselves slaves to obey, you are that one's slaves whom you obey, whether of sin leading to death, or of obedience leading to righteousness? (Romans 6:15-16)

As you can see, Romans 6:15-16, which comes immediately after Romans 6:14, clearly shows that grace is not a license to sin.

Humans are under the law when the law can claim its penalty. Jesus paid the penalty for the sin. Once one becomes a Christian, one is not under the claim/penalty of the law, but under grace.

Character

Character is that capacity of a separate entity, of the individual, to come to its own knowledge of the truth, and to make its own decision, and to will to follow the right instead of the wrong. And the individual created must make that decision. In other words, the individual, human or angelic, has a part in its own creation.

Melito of Sardis also taught that (Melito. A Discourse Which Was in the Presence of Antoninus Caesar; see also the free online book: *The MYSTERY of GOD's PLAN Why Did God Create Anything? Why Did God Make You?*).

By obeying God and accepting His grace, Christians can develop godly character.

A true Christian builds character now through the tests, opportunities, and trials in life (cf. Romans 5:1-4) which will help the Christian be able to personally contribute to the 'better tomorrow'.

Suffering is allowed in this age so that people will be corrected, be trained, build character, and be better from it (see also Romans 5:3-4, 8:17; 2 Thessalonians 1:3-5; James 1:2-4; 2 Peter 1:5-8; Revelation 21:7-8). Trials and problems help build faith, teach humility, teach us lessons, and can help us draw closer to God.

While it can seem overwhelming at times now, God understands and makes it so His people can bear it (1 Corinthians 10:13). Jesus essentially taught to take it one day at a time (Matthew 6:34). And what He has planned in the future is so beyond what physical sufferings will be in this life (Romans 8:18).

By being obedient, having faith, practicing love, and enduring to the end, Christians will not only build character but make their own eternity better.

There are lessons we need to learn in this life in order to build the type of character that will help us make eternity better.

> [1] Therefore, having been justified by faith, we have peace with God through our Lord Jesus Christ, [2] through whom also we have access by faith into this grace in which we stand, and rejoice in hope of the glory of God. [3] And not only that, but we also glory in tribulations, knowing that tribulation produces perseverance; [4] and perseverance, character; and character, hope. (Romans 5:1-4)

> [5] But also for this very reason, giving all diligence, add to your faith virtue, to virtue knowledge, [6] to knowledge self-control, to self-control perseverance, to perseverance godliness, [7] to godliness brotherly kindness, and to brotherly kindness love. [8] For if these things are yours and abound, you will be neither barren nor unfruitful in the knowledge of our Lord Jesus Christ. (2 Peter 1:5-8)

You might not think you benefit from difficulties and trials, but if you are a Christian, you should realize that God's word says that you do. Trials and self-control help build character. Self-control is repeatedly taught in the New Testament (1 Corinthians 7:5,9; 1 Timothy 2:15; 2 Timothy 3:3). But it scares many who are unwilling to truly follow Jesus (cf. Acts 24:24-25).

Notice something that the late Herbert W. Armstrong wrote:

> WHY did the Creator God put MAN on the earth? For God's ultimate supreme purpose of reproducing himself—of recreating himself, as it were, by the supreme objective of

creating the righteous divine character ultimately in millions of unnumbered begotten and born children who shall become God beings, members of the God family. Man was to improve the physical earth as God gave it to him, finishing its creation (which sinning angels had deliberately refused to do) and, in so doing, to RESTORE the GOVERNMENT OF GOD, with God's WAY of life; and further, in this very process FINISHING THE CREATION OF MAN by the development of God's holy, righteous CHARACTER, with man's own assent. Once this perfect and righteous character is instilled in man, and man converted from mortal flesh to immortal spirit, then is to come the INCREDIBLE HUMAN POTENTIAL—man being BORN INTO the divine FAMILY of God, restoring the government of God to the earth, and then participating in the completion of the CREATION over the entire endless expanse of the UNIVERSE! ... God shall have reproduced HIMSELF untold millions of times over! So, on the sixth day of that re-creation week, God (Elohim) said, "Let us make man in our image, after our likeness" (Gen. 1:26). Man was made to have (with his assent) a special relationship with his Maker! He was made in the form and shape of God. He was given a spirit (essence in form) to make the relationship possible (Armstrong HW. *Mystery of the Ages.* Dodd Mead, 1985, pp. 102-103).

Yes, God is reproducing Himself and there are many spiritual lessons from physical aspects of His plan.

The Christian purpose for this life is to build character so you can maximize your potential and increase how much better you can give love in your unique way to make eternity better for everyone in the family of God, including yourself.

Thus, the purpose of building character is to be better and to be able to serve better.

The best way to develop godly character is by obeying God.

And that is for our good (cf. Deuteronomy 6:24).

3. The New Testament, Martin Luther, and the Canon

As far as the books of the New Testament go, understand that the *Continuing* Church of God, Church of Rome, Eastern Orthodox, and the traditional Protestant faiths accept the same 27 books as inspired.

Most Protestant scholars, as well as the CCOG, agree that the New Testament was written in *koine* Greek—the vernacular that was common for Greek speakers in the 1st and 2nd centuries.

Regarding the books of the Old Testament, most of the Protestants and the *Continuing* Church of God point to what are considered now to be 39 books of the Old Testament, whereas the Church of Rome and the Eastern Orthodox point to 46 books (with some 'branches' of the Eastern Orthodox claiming even more).

Most Protestant scholars, as well as the CCOG, agree that the Old Testament was written in Hebrew.

Neither the *Continuing* Church of God, Protestant churches, nor the Roman and Eastern Orthodox Catholic churches, accept the Book of Mormon as divinely inspired.

Martin Luther translated a Bible into German, which was published in 1534, that had the Old Testament, the Apocrypha, and the New Testament, despite the Apocrypha not truly being scripture.

Martin Luther had Problems with New Testament Scripture

Martin Luther, despite claiming *sola Scriptura*, disparaged various books of the New Testament as having questionable value.

Notice some of his writings:

> Up to this point we have had the true and certain chief books of the New Testament. The four which follow have from ancient times had a different reputation. In the first place, the fact that

> Hebrews is not an epistle of St. Paul, or of any other apostle (Luther, M. Prefaces to the Epistle of the Hebrews, 1546).

> St. James' epistle is really an epistle of straw ... for it has nothing of the nature of the gospel about it" (Luther, M. Preface to the New Testament, 1546).

> James ... In the first place it is flatly against St. Paul and all the rest of Scripture in ascribing justification to works ... Besides, he throws things together so chaotically that it seems to me he must have been some good, pious man, who took a few sayings from the disciples of the apostles and thus tossed them off on paper. Or it may perhaps have been written by someone on the basis of his preaching (Luther, M. Preface to the Epistles of St. James and St. Jude, 1546).

> Concerning the epistle of St. Jude, no one can deny that it is an extract or copy of St. Peter's second epistle ... Therefore, although I value this book, it is an epistle that need not be counted among the chief books which are supposed to lay the foundations of faith (Luther, M. Preface to the Epistles of St. James and St. Jude, 1546).

Jesus said, "Scripture cannot be broken" (John 10:35). Therefore, James' epistle is NOT "against St. Paul and all the rest of Scripture", but instead is against Martin Luther's misunderstandings of law and grace.

Contrary to Martin Luther's assertion, it also should be understood that Jude's epistle is not too similar to 2 Peter. Yet, if even it is, should it be discounted?

Maybe Martin Luther discounted it because Jude warns people:

> [3] ... to contend earnestly for the faith which was once for all delivered to the saints (Jude 3).

And this, sadly, is not something that Martin Luther really did (though he did sometimes make some efforts towards that).

Martin Luther had problems with prophetic passages with the gospels. Here is some of what Martin Luther taught about Matthew 24:

> 1. In this chapter there is a description of the end of two kingdoms; of the kingdom of the Jews, and also of the kingdom of the world. But the two Evangelists, Matthew and Mark, unite the two--and do not follow the order as Luke did, for they have nothing more in view than to relate and give the words of Christ, and are not concerned about what was said either before or after. But Luke takes special pains to write clearly and in the true order, and relates this discourse twice; first briefly in the 19th chapter, where he speaks of the destruction of the Jews at Jerusalem; afterwards in the 21st chapter he speaks of both, one following the other.
>
> 2. Notice therefore that Matthew unites the two and at the same time conceives the end, both of the Jewish nation and of the world. He therefore cooks both into one soup. (Luther M. Church Postil. 1525. In Volume V:364-378 of The Sermons of Martin Luther, published by Baker Book House, Grand Rapids, MI, 1983).

We in the CCOG do not believe that Matthew and Mark got the order wrong, but that Martin Luther misunderstood some of what Luke recorded.

Perhaps none of Martin Luther's writings on the Bible were as harsh as what he wrote about its last book, "The Revelation of Jesus Christ" (Revelation 1:1). Specifically, he wrote:

> About this book of the Revelation of John ... I miss more than one thing in this book, and it makes me consider it to be neither apostolic nor prophetic ... **I can in no way detect that the Holy Spirit produced it.** Moreover he seems to me to be going much too far when he commends his own book so highly-indeed, more than any of the other sacred books do, though they are much more important-and threatens that if anyone takes away anything from it, God will take away from him, etc. Again, they are supposed to be blessed who keep what is written in this book; and yet no one knows what that is, to say nothing of

> keeping it. This is just the same as if we did not have the book at all. And there are many far better books available for us to keep ... My spirit cannot accommodate itself to this book. For me this is reason enough not to think highly of it: Christ is neither taught nor known in it" (Luther, M. Preface to the Revelation of St. John, 1522).

Since there is evidence that Martin Luther did not have the Holy Spirit, it should not be a surprise he could not detect that the Holy Spirit helped produce the Book of Revelation.

Martin Luther's comments on Revelation may be part of why he did not accept the millennium and certain other prophetic teachings. The apostate Marcion also rejected the Book of Revelation and the millennium (Tertullian. Against Marcion, Book IV, Chapter 5). Martin Luther's statement that "Christ is neither taught nor known in it" is bizarre as much of the Book of Revelation consists of quotes of Jesus' words, plus He was the one who repeatedly told John to write down in a book what he saw (Revelation 1:9-11,19) as well as various messages (Revelation 2:1,8,12,18; 3:1,7,14) we now read in it.

Martin Luther's discounting of prophecies is dangerous for his followers living in the 21st century. Notice that the Book of Revelation teaches:

> [10] ... Worship God! For **the testimony of Jesus is the spirit of prophecy**. (Revelation 19:10)

Many Protestants do not seem to accept the bolded portion above.

Another reason Martin Luther may not have been able to accommodate this Revelation of Jesus Christ is because he clearly ignored this warning from it:

> [18] For I testify to everyone who hears the words of the prophecy of this book: If anyone adds to these things, God will add to him the plagues that are written in this book; [19] and if anyone takes away from the words of the book of this prophecy, God shall take away his part from the Book of Life, from the holy city, and from the things which are written in this book (Revelation 22:18-19).

Martin Luther took away from that book through his comments about it, and this is the same Martin Luther who, it will be shown, added words to the Bible that were not there. Hence, he and people like him would NOT be in the Book of Life!

Although Martin Luther decried John for penning the Revelation of Jesus Christ, he did like John's Gospel. According to Martin Luther:

> The first three speak of the works of our Lord, rather than His oral teachings; that of St. John is the only sympathetic, the only true Gospel and should undoubtedly be preferred above the others. In like manner the Epistles of St. Peter and St. Paul are superior to the first three Gospels (As cited in: O'Hare PF. The Facts About Luther, 1916–1987 reprint ed., p. 203).

Martin Luther's position on this, and some of his other matters, appear to be blasphemous and in contradiction to 2 Timothy 3:16.

The Bible, in Romans 3:28, states:

> [28] Therefore we conclude that a man is justified by faith apart from the deeds of the law.

Martin Luther, in his German translation of the Bible, specifically added the word *"allein"* (English "alone") to Romans 3:28—a word that is not in the original Greek. Martin Luther wanted people to believe that Romans 3:28 states "a man is justified by faith alone," but the verse does not say that.

Notice what Protestant scholars have admitted:

> ... Martin Luther would once again emphasize ... that we are "justified by faith alone", apart from the works of the Law" (Rom. 3:28), adding the German word allein ("alone") in his translation of the Greek text. There is certainly a trace of Marcion in Luther's move (Brown HOJ. Heresies: Heresy and Orthodoxy in the History of the Church. Hendrickson Publishers, Peabody (MA), 1988, pp. 64-65).

Like Marcion changed scripture, so did Martin Luther. That passage also literally states "works of law," not "the works of the law" as many mistranslate it here and elsewhere in the New Testament (Berry GR. Interlinear Greek-English New Testament. Hinds and Noble, 1897, p. 409).

Furthermore, to justify his change, Martin Luther said:

> You tell me what a great fuss the Papists are making because the word alone is not in the text of Paul ... say right out to him: 'Dr. Martin Luther will have it so', ... I will have it so, and I order it to be so, and my will is reason enough. I know very well that the word 'alone' is not in the Latin or the Greek text (Stoddard J. Rebuilding a Lost Faith. 1922, pp. 101-102; see also Luther M. Amic. Discussion, 1, 127).

This passage strongly suggests that Martin Luther viewed his opinions, and not the actual Bible as the primary authority–a concept which should be *prima Luther* and not *sola Scriptura*. By 'papists' Luther was condemning Roman Catholics.

He also made another change in Romans. Romans 4:15 states:

> ... because the law brings about wrath; for where there is no law there is no transgression.

Yet in his German translation, Martin Luther added the word 'only' before the term 'wrath' to Romans 4:15 (O'Hare, p. 201).

This presumably was to attempt to justify his position to discredit the law.

Matthew 3:2 states:

> "Repent, for the kingdom of heaven is at hand!"

Martin Luther, in his German translation, according to at least one Roman Catholic source, changed the word "repent" to "mend" or "do better" (ibid, p. 201), presumably to justify his position that one does not need to obey God's laws through repentance (others disagree on that point and indicate that the German term chosen can or should be translated as "repent").

But Jesus taught repentance—yet Protestants do not really understand that basic point. To repent means to be willing to change anything and everything you need to change to live God's way. Repentance is more than simply being sorry you sinned (cf. Hebrews 12:16-17).

Jesus' teaching should not be minimized like Martin Luther did!

Acts 19:18, states:

> "And many who had believed came confessing and telling their deeds…"

Yet according to one source, Martin Luther rendered it, "they acknowledged the miracles of the Apostles" (O'Hare, p. 201).

There are several possible reasons why Martin Luther intentionally mistranslated Acts 19:18, but the point here is to show that he reportedly did.

Martin Luther also taught:

> And John 1 says: "The Word was made flesh", when in our judgment it would have been better said, 'The Word was incarnate', or 'made fleshly' (Disputation On the Divinity and Humanity of Christ February 27, 1540 conducted by Dr. Martin Luther, 1483-1546 translated from the Latin text WA 39/2, pp. 92-121 by Christopher B. Brown).

This was apparently done to justify his belief that Jesus was fully God and fully human while on the earth in conflict with Jesus being 'emptied' (Philippians 2:7, literally translated, and as is so translated in the AFV, ASV, BLB, BSB, CSB, DRB, ERV, ESV, HCSB, JB2000, NAS1977, NASB, NET, NHEB, WEB).

Luke 10:28 states:

> "And he said unto him, Thou hast answered right: this do, and thou shalt live" (KJV).

Yet Martin Luther misinterpreted scripture and taught:

> To do means to believe—to keep the law by faith. The passage in Matthew: Do this and thou shalt live, signifies Believe this and thou shalt live. The words Do this, have ironical sense, as if our Lord should say: Thou wilt do it tomorrow, but not today; only make an attempt to keep the Commandments, and the trial will teach thee the ignominy of thy failure (O'Hare, p.205).

It is because of such misinterpretations of what the Bible states that many Protestants have tossed out the necessity to keep the Ten Commandments, even though scholars agree that they were kept by the early Christians. (Note: Although Martin Luther mentioned Matthew's account--which is in Matthew 19:16-21--the quote in question is actually from Luke 10:28.)

Here is something about the apostate Marcion:

> Marcion ... even went so far as to rewrite Matthew 5:17, where Jesus said in the Sermon on the Mount, "Think not that I have come to destroy the Law or the Prophets: I have not come to destroy them but to fulfill them." Marcion turned it around and said that Jesus' actual words were "Think not that I have come to fulfill the Law or the Prophets: I have not come to fulfill them but to destroy them." Further, he took some of Paul's epistles and some sections of the book of Luke and edited them to eliminate any connection with Judaism or the Old Testament. As a result of his actions, church leaders finally branded him a heretic and excommunicated him. (Garr J. Is Christianity Off Base? Vision magazine, Fall 2004)

So, Martin Luther's actions are similar to Marcion. To this day, many Protestant leaders share Marcion's distorted version of Matthew 5:17, despite the fact that even people such as Irenaeus of Lyon (which some

Protestants claim to trace their history through) denounced that view.

Martin Luther also disparaged various books of the Old and New Testaments well:

> "Job spoke not as it stands written in his book, but only had such thoughts. It is merely the argument of a fable. It is probable that Solomon wrote and made this book."...
>
> "Ecclesiastes ought to have been more complete. There is too much incoherent matter in it...Solomon did not, therefore, write this book."...
>
> "The book of Esther I toss into the Elbe. I am such an enemy to the book of Esther that I wish it did not exist, for it Judaizes too much..."
>
> "The history of Jonah is so monstrous that it is absolutely incredible." (as quoted in O'Hare, p. 202).

Furthermore, Martin Luther had little use for the first five books of the Old Testament (sometimes referred to as the Pentateuch):

> Of the Pentateuch he says: "We have no wish either to see or hear Moses" (Ibid, p. 202).

Martin Luther hated the Jews, which may be why he was against Esther, the first five books of the Bible, and other parts of the Hebrew scriptures.

Martin Luther changed and/or diminished the importance of at least 19 books of the Bible (Genesis, Exodus, Leviticus, Numbers, Deuteronomy, Esther, Job, Ecclesiastes, Jonah, Matthew, Mark, Luke, John, Acts, Romans, Hebrews, James, Jude, and Revelation) and, thus, did not truly believe in his *sola Scriptura* rallying cry.

Perhaps it should be mentioned that the "New Agreement" New Testament put out in 2020 by Danish Lutheran supporters did NOT include the word Israel in it, despite it being used in 73 verses of the New Testament (Berkowitz AE. Lutherans Publish New Version of Bible Without the Word 'Israel' in It. Breaking Israel News, April 20, 2020). Apparently, the translators and publishers believe that they can intentionally change the word of God. Do not think it was only Martin Luther who attempted to do such things.

The Canon of the New Testament

The position of the *Continuing* Church of God is that the true Christian church had the canon of the New Testament right after the Apostle John penned the Book of Revelation (as instructed by Jesus) in the very late 1st century A.D. (see also the free online book: *Who Gave the World the Bible? The Canon: Why do we have the books we now do in the Bible?*). It is likely that passages such as Revelation 22:18-19 clarified to John for him to realize that the New Testament canon was complete for the church age.

However, many Protestant scholars do not accept that—they believe that the canonization did not take place for centuries and that many were confused until then about which New Testament books were valid (e.g. Bruce FF. The Canon of Scripture. InterVarsityPress, 1988; Unger M. The New Unger's Bible Dictionary. Moody Press, 2009, p. 204).

While it is true that various leaders whom the Greco-Roman-Protestants improperly considered as real Christians used false 2nd century books for a time (like the wrongly titled *Gospel of Peter* and the *Shepherd of Hermas*), those books were not accepted by actual Church of God leaders.

History demonstrates that false gospels and other false books were produced in the 2nd century. A "certain number of Gospels were written" (false ones) by those who were associated with Marcus of Jerusalem when he apostatized on matters like the Sabbath, unclean meats, and Passover (Pines S. The Jewish Christians of the Early Centuries of Christianity according to a New Source. Proceedings of the Israel Academy of Sciences and Humanities, Volume II, No.13; 1966. Jerusalem, pp. 14-15). Furthermore, both true and false writings appeared in Rome and Alexandria in the second century.

Before going further, it should be noted that some Protestant scholars have realized the truly canonical books were always the word of God and finalized in Asia Minor:

> Although it is out of vogue in some critical circles today, Christians have traditionally believed that the canon is a collection of books that are given by God to his corporate

church. And if the canonical books are what they are by virtue of the divine purpose for which they were given, and not by virtue of their use or acceptance by the community of faith, then, in principle, they can exist as such apart from that community. After all, aren't God's books still God's books—and therefore still authoritative—prior to anyone using them or recognizing them? (Kruger MJ. Question of Canon. InterVarsity Press, 2013, p. 39)

Was not the Apostolic Canon of scripture first formed ... in Asia Minor? Was not Asia Minor ahead of Rome in the formation of the Apostolic, Episcopal, ministry? ...The real thinking upon vital Christianity for centuries was done outside the Roman Church (Excerpt of James Moffatt's review, p.292. In: Bauer W. Orthodoxy and Heresy in Earliest Christianity, 2nd ed. Sigler Press Edition, Mifflitown (PA), 1996).

However, beyond simple assertion, we in the CCOG also point to scripture as well as early documents that back up our claim that the Church of God knew the correct books of the New Testament by the end of the 1st century (which happened as soon as the Book of Revelation was penned).

The New Testament teaches, "All Scripture is given by inspiration of God, and is profitable for doctrine," (2 Timothy 3:16) yet Martin Luther clearly did not think so as he eliminated/changed/downplayed scriptures he felt were not profitable for HIS, as opposed to GOD's, doctrines.

The New Testament also teaches that all scripture is provided so "the man of God may be complete, thoroughly equipped for every good work" (2 Timothy 3:17).

Wouldn't it be logical that the word of God would have been complete by the time that the last of the original apostles died so that their faithful followers could be complete? Obviously, God's plan was not for people to wait many centuries to know what His canon was.

Furthermore, we can prove that through Polycarp. In the early 2nd century, Polycarp made it clear that he and those in Philippi he wrote to, had to have the correct Bible; otherwise, he would not have written:

> For I trust that ye are well versed in the Sacred Scriptures, and that nothing is hid from you; but to me this privilege is not yet granted. It is declared then in these Scriptures, "Be ye angry, and sin not," and, "Let not the sun go down upon your wrath." (Polycarp. Letter to the Philippians, Chapter XII. From *Ante-Nicene Fathers, Volume 1* as edited by Alexander Roberts & James Donaldson. American Edition, 1885).

Note that Polycarp quoted a verse that is in the New Testament, when he used the term Scriptures. They could not have been **well versed in the Sacred Scriptures** if they did not know what they were!

Furthermore, consider that there is a document known as the *Harris Fragments* (ca. 2nd or 3rd century) that also discusses Polycarp. Here are some translated quotes from the *Harris Fragments*, with one grammatical addition in {}:

> There remained [---]ter him a disciple[e ---] name was Polycar[p and] he made him bishop over Smyrna ... He was ... {an} old man, being one hundred and f[our] of age. He continued to walk [i]n the canons which he had learned from his youth from John the a[p]ostle (Weidman, Frederick W. Polycarp and John: The Harris Fragments and Their Challenge to Literary Traditions. University of Notre Dame Press, Notre Dame (IL), 1999, pp. 43-44)

By mentioning the term 'canons', the *Harris Fragments* seems to be suggesting that John passed the knowledge of the proper books of the Bible and proper Christian doctrine to Polycarp-and that would seem to be the case. In his *Letter to Florinus,* Irenaeus states that Polycarp reported that he had often spoken with John (Ecclesiastical History, V. XX.), which would have been how the knowledge of the books would have likely been passed. Furthermore, since it was reported that "Polycarp related all things in harmony with the Scriptures" (Irenaeus as cited in: Eusebius. The History of the Church. Book V, Chapter XX, verses

5-8. Digireads, Stilwel (KS), p. 112), Polycarp would have had to know them.

In the late 2nd century, Polycrates of Ephesus wrote that he (and others in his area) had "gone through every Holy Scripture" (Polycrates. Eusebius. Church History. Book V, Chapter 24) which shows that he claimed to have them all.

In the early 3rd century, COG leader Serapion of Antioch reported that a group in the Alexandria area was not associated with him because they were using the false *Gospel of Peter*. Furthermore, he claimed that the proper New Testament books were 'handed down to us' or 'received' as it has alternatively been translated (Eusebius. The History of the Church, Book VI, Chapter XII, verses 3-4, p. 125-126). This shows that those in his area also knew the books.

Yet, most Protestant scholars accept Roman and Eastern Orthodox traditions and councils as the source of the knowledge of the books of the Bible. This tends to give the Greco-Roman Catholics reasons to claim that THEY gave the world the Bible, as opposed to God and His faithful servants.

The reality is that Church of God leaders knew the books of the New Testament from the beginning. They did NOT need the later councils that many Protestant scholars claim were necessary to determine the canon of the New Testament. They did not dismiss/discount books of the Bible nor change scriptures like Martin Luther did. More on that can be found in the free book, online at ccog.org: *Who Gave the World the Bible? The Canon: Why do we have the books we now do in the Bible?*

The *Continuing* Church of God, furthermore, does not agree with Martin Luther on his discounting biblical books nor his intentional changing of scriptures.

4. Passover and Easter Sunday

The Greco-Romans teach that what was the Christian Passover became known as their Easter Sunday (e.g. Catechism of the Catholic Church. Imprimatur Potest +Joseph Cardinal Ratzinger. Doubleday, NY 1995, p. 332). Most people who observe Easter probably have no idea it was supposed to be a renaming of Passover.

That being said, it is well known that Jews kept Passover on the 14th of the first month of the biblical calendar (cf. Exodus 12:2,6). That is also when Jesus had His last Passover meal (Luke 22:15). The Bible makes it clear that God's people are to "keep the Passover at its appointed time. On the fourteenth day of this month, at twilight, you shall keep it at its appointed time" (Numbers 9:2b-3).

Early Christians, including all the original apostles, observed that time and did NOT believe that God changed the appointed time for Passover or that they should change it. Passover was not observed on a Sunday morning.

However, near 135 A.D., partially because of anti-Semitic pressures from Imperial Rome, many in Rome, Alexandria, and Jerusalem changed to observe a version of Passover on Sunday.

Additionally, some apostates, like Justin Martyr and Tertullian, had a mystical communion rite they wrote that was similar to that of Mithraism. But the practice of those apostates was NOT like the original Christian Passover practices that Jesus initiated, and the faithful in Asia Minor retained.

Although the mid-2nd century Roman Bishop Anicetus wanted Sunday Passover, "Anicetus' acquiescence to Polycarp's views concerning the Pascha ... presumes an accepted representation of some 'apostolic' tradition in the latter. (Hartog P, ed. Polycarp's Epistle to the Philippians and the Martyrdom of Polycarp: Introduction, Text, and Commentary. University Press, 2013, p. 16).

There is also a late 2nd century letter from Polycrates of Ephesus to Roman bishop Victor where he disagrees with Victor's attempt to force a Sunday Passover. Polycrates' letter states that he and others would not accept the opinions of men who changed to a Sunday Passover, but instead would stick to the biblical date of the 14th of Nisan "according to the Gospel" (Eusebius. The History of the Church, Book 5, Chapter XXIV. Digireads.com, 2005, p. 114).

In that letter, Polycrates mentions Church of God leaders who lived in Asia Minor who kept Passover on the 14th, beginning with the Apostles John and Philip, and then later leaders including Polycarp, Thraseas, Sagaris, Papirius, Melito, and he, himself (Ibid). Polycrates specifically stated that the faithful would not listen to threats of men to change their adherence to the biblical date (Ibid).

Now consider that in the New Testament, the Apostle John specifically warned about those who changed, and did not continue in, his practices:

> [18] Little children, it is the last hour; and as you have heard that the Antichrist is coming, even now many antichrists have come, by which we know that it is the last hour. [20] They went out from us, but they were not of us; for if they had been of us, they would have continued with us; but they went out that they might be made manifest, that none of them were of us (1 John 2:18-19).

As it turns out, the first specific departure from the practices of John that we have major historical records of involving John's name is the changing of the date of Passover.

The Apostle John basically taught that there were two groups that professed Christianity: those who followed his teachings who were the faithful ones, and those who did not, who were of the party of the antichrists. God further inspired him to write that he and those truly with him were of God and others were not (1 John 5:19).

So, what may have been the first specific doctrinal departure from the practices of John that we have a clear historical record of?

The changing of the date of Passover (and later, the practices associated with it)!

History records that the Apostles John and Philip continued to keep Passover on the 14th, and not Sunday (e.g. Eusebius. The History of the Church, Book V, Chapter XXIV, Verses 2-7, p. 114; Bede. Edited by Judith McClure and Roger Collins. The Ecclesiastical History of the English People. Oxford University Press, NY, 1999, pp. 155-156).

Would then, the changing of Passover be one of the doctrines of Antichrist that most Protestants have accepted?

While the first time we see a Sunday Passover was in the 2nd century (essentially because of fear of persecution), it turns out that not all of the Greco-Romans accepted that change. In order to have more unity in the Roman Empire, Emperor Constantine convened the Council of Nicea in 325 A.D., at least partially to force unity on the date of Passover. One of its officially agreed to positions was that Passover was to be kept on Sunday, despite the fact that Jesus and the original apostles observed Passover on the evening of the 14th of Nisan. Later in the 4th century, Emperor Theodosius decreed the death penalty on people who kept the Passover on the word of God date of the 14th of Abib (Smith W. A Dictionary of Greek and Roman Biography and Mythology: Oarses-Zygia. J. Murray, 1890 Item notes: v. 3, p. 1064).

In time, the Greco-Roman Passover Sunday observers dropped most Passover practices, and their day is now commonly called Easter. Easter Sunday is NOT the time appointed by God for Passover.

Notice, though, an assertion from a Lutheran source:

> The ancient name for Easter is 'Pascha', from the Greek and Hebrew words for Passover, "for Christ, our paschal lamb, has been sacrificed" (1 Corinthians 5:7). (The church season of Easter. King of Grace Lutheran Church, April 18, 2019)

That is a highly misleading assertion. Early Christians (like Jesus and His disciples) kept Passover which is the Greek word 'Pascha' that is in the New Testament. Christians kept Passover at night as a memorial of Christ's death. Instead of being a memorial of Christ's last Passover, for the Greco-Romans (and then Protestants) it became a claimed resurrection holiday. Pascha is not the ancient name for Easter.

Centuries after many compromisers switched to Sunday, the name of what was supposed to be the observance of Passover was changed in some Teutonic languages (English, German) to Easter.

Easter was the name of a Babylonian sex goddess (often spelled Ishtar, but pronounced about the same as Easter). Ishtar was the "queen of heaven" who was celebrated each Spring by the pagans. Various non-biblical trappings were part of the Ishtar celebration that are similar to many that Protestants use today.

Some have claimed that instead of Ishtar, "Easter" was derived from the pagan-German goddess Eostre/Ostara. She was the "bringer of light" or the "goddess of the dawn," and is sometimes called "the queen of heaven." She was celebrated each Spring. She looks to be a direct tie to Easter sunrise services (since the Bible instead, has Passover right after sunset) as well as rabbits. Her favourite flower was the rose which is also the flower that the Roman Catholics associate with their version of 'Mary' (Philips G. The Virgin Mary Conspiracy: The True Father of Christ and the Tomb of the Virgin. Bear & Company, 2005, pp. 218-219).

1884 portrayal of Eostre/Ostara

Various researchers, such as the late L.L.C. Hamilton, have taught that Ishtar was both the "Ashtoreth" (1 Kings 11:33 NKJV) or "Astarte" (1 Kings 11:33 CEV/GNT/ISV/NET/GWT) condemned in the Old Testament and the Eostre of the Germans (Hamilton LLC. Ishtar and Izdubar, the epic of Babylon; or, The Babylonian goddess of love and the hero and warrior king, restored in mod. verse by L.L.C. Hamilton. 1884, pp. 207-208).

Whether originally from a Babylonian goddess, a later German one or a combination of both, 'Easter' is a term, not for our Saviour, but of a pagan goddess.

The translators of the King James Version mistranslated the Greek word for Passover, which is transliterated as *Pascha,* to *Easter* in Acts 12:4. This intentional mistranslation has resulted in multiple millions not realizing that the Bible did not endorse Easter. Does any thinking person really believe that God wanted the word for Passover changed to the name of a pagan goddess in His word? Though some have claimed that the KJV was carefully checked 14 times to insure no biased translation errors before publication (Daniels DW. New Book. Chick Publications, 2020, p. 7), the fact is that EVERY TRANSLATOR OF THE KJV WHO 'CHECKED' THAT PART OF THE 'TRANSLATION' HAD TO HAVE KNOWN THAT WAS IN ERROR–PARTICULARLY SINCE THAT SAME WORD IS TRANSLATED FROM THE GREEK IN THE KJV 28 OTHER TIMES AS "PASSOVER"! (More translation issues in the KJV are listed in the free online book: *Who Gave the World the Bible? The Canon: Why do we have the books we now do in the Bible?*)

Consider also that Easter's 'hot cross buns' would not have been used by early Christians for many reasons, including the fact that the faithful kept the Days of Unleavened Bread, which comes right after Passover (and hot cross buns are made with leaven). Plus, the Bible warns against making similar cakes to the queen of heaven (Jeremiah 7:18, 44:16-29). Easter bunnies and Easter eggs are certainly not a biblical practice and were not part of early Christian Passover observances. Instead, they were part of the pagan worship of Ishtar/Easter/'Queen of Heaven.' No Christian should take part in worship like that (1 Corinthians 10:20-22, Deuteronomy 12:29-31).

In the CCOG, we observe Passover annually as a memorial on the 14th shortly after sunset, and without the trappings of paganism.

Now, in order to try to justify an Easter Sunday morning observance, some Protestants state that Jesus fulfilled the "wave sheaf offering" of "firstfruits" found in the Old Testament (cf. Leviticus 23:11). While Jesus was the fruitfruits (1 Corinthians 15:20-23) and did fulfil the wave sheaf offering, He did not do that in the morning, instead He did it close to a day after He was resurrected (which is why He did not allow Himself to be touched before ascending as the wave sheaf per John 20:17, but did allow touching after He ascended per John 20:27, Luke 24:39, and Matthew 28:9). Furthermore, the Sunday Jesus fulfilled the wave-sheaf was certainly NOT the Passover—which is what 'Easter' is supposed to be.

Weekly Communion vs. Annual Passover

Most Protestant churches have a ceremony intended to be related to Jesus' last Passover on either a weekly or monthly basis.

They tend to call this the Lord's Supper, communion, breaking of bread, blessed sacrament, and/or the Eucharist. Some Protestants use leavened bread and grape juice. Some use unleavened bread and wine.

Early Christians used unleavened bread and wine in that memorial, which was sometimes referred to as the Eucharist (Ignatius. Letter to the Philadelphians 4:1), but more commonly Passover (e.g. Apollinaris. From the Book Concerning Passover; Melito. Homily on the Passover; Polycrates' Letter to Victor). In ancient times, grape juice would have spoiled from time of harvest in the Fall to Passover in the Spring, hence it is certain that wine was used and NOT grape juice. Protestant practices involving grape juice and/or leavened bread were simply, and absolutely, not part of the original Christian faith.

The bread was broken, per Jesus' example (Luke 22:19), which makes each piece unique. In the CCOG we teach that Jesus' body that was broken and beaten for our sins and that each piece of broken bread points to our individual unique calling (see also the free book, *The MYSTERY of GOD's PLAN: Why Did God Create Anything? Why did God make you?*).

While Passover is biblically an annual event (Exodus 12:6,11,14; cf. Luke 22:7-8; Polycrates' Letter to Victor), Protestants (and various others) point to the following to justify having their commemoration more often:

> [23] For I received from the Lord that which I also delivered to you: that the Lord Jesus on the same night in which He was betrayed took bread; [24] and when He had given thanks, He broke it and said, "Take, eat; this is My body which is broken for you; do this in remembrance of Me." [25] In the same manner He also took the cup after supper, saying, "This cup is the new covenant in My blood. This do, as often as you drink it, in remembrance of Me."
>
> [26] For as often as you eat this bread and drink this cup, you proclaim the Lord's death till He comes. (1 Corinthians 11:23-26)

The Bible calls Passover a memorial (Exodus 12:14) and gives it an annual date (Exodus 12:6,11). And Jesus calls it a remembrance (1 Corinthians 11:24-25)—this is an annual remembrance. Until at least the fifth century, even the Greco-Romans insisted this was an annual event (e.g. Theodoret of Cyrus. Ecclesiastical History, Book I, Chapter IX).

Please understand that the Greek combined term for often, *hosakis ean*, in 1 Corinthians 11:25 and 11:26 does not mean as often as you desire UNLESS the Greek term for 'you desire', *thelo* or *ethelo*, is also present, which it is in Revelation 11:6 (the only other place in the Bible this particular combined term is used). However, since the term for 'you desire' is NOT present in 1 Corinthians 11:25 or 11:26, Paul is NOT telling us Jesus said to observe the Lord's Passover as often as we desire, but that when we are observing it on Passover, it is not just a ceremony, it is showing Christ's death.

Early Christians did not interpret Paul's writing to mean to observe this ordinance more often than annually (cf. Polycrates' Letter to Victor). Early Christians only kept the Passover annually and that observance was after sunset (Calivas AC. The Origins of Pascha and Great Week – Part I. Holy Cross Orthodox Press, 1992).

Protestants who argue against this should also consider that early Christians also performed footwashing during the Passover service as that was part of Jesus' instructions to His followers (John 13:2-17). This is something that Protestants generally do not do. And for Protestants keeping a weekly version of 'Passover', there do not seem to be many (if any) who believe that they have to perform footwashing each week, despite footwashing being an integral part of the Christian Passover.

Taking the unleavened bread and wine, and performing footwashing, annually after sunset, are activities that Jesus taught were to be done during the Christian Passover (Matthew 26:19-28; John 13:1-17). Early Christians observed Passover at night with the biblical symbols (Calivas AC. The Origins of Pascha and Great Week - Part I. Holy Cross Orthodox Press, 1992) and also performed footwashing (Thurston, H. Washing of Feet and Hands. The Catholic Encyclopedia, 1912).

We in the CCOG continue to do so today.

Three Days and Three Nights

How long was Jesus in the grave?

Well, He said three days and three nights (Matthew 12:39-40).

Irenaeus referred to three days and three nights for Jesus to be in the grave:

> [1] ... But the case was, that for three days He dwelt in the place where the dead were, as the prophet says concerning Him: ... And the Lord Himself says, As Jonas remained three days and three nights in the whale's belly, so shall the Son of man be in the heart of the earth. (Against Heresies, Book V, Chapter 31)

Irenaeus is considered to be a major early saint by Roman and Orthodox Catholics, as well as by many Protestants.

But most Protestants do not believe that Jesus was in the grave as long as He stated.

In order to justify a Friday crucifixion and a Sunday morning resurrection, most who do so have relied directly or at least indirectly on the personal opinions of a writer named Augustine of Hippo in the 5th century, who wrote:

> For "He spake this of the temple of His body," as is declared by the most clear and solid testimony of the Gospel; where He said, "For as Jonas was three days and three nights in the whale's belly, so shall the Son of man be three days and three nights in the heart of the earth."
>
> Scripture again witnesses that the space of those three days themselves was not whole and entire, but the first day is counted as a whole from its last part, and the third day is itself also counted as a whole from its first part; but the intervening day, i.e. the second day, was absolutely a whole with its twenty-four hours, twelve of the day and twelve of the night. For He was crucified first by the voices of the Jews in the third hour, when it was the sixth day of the week. Then He hung on the cross itself at the sixth hour, and yielded up His spirit at the ninth hour ... But from the evening of the burial to the dawn of the resurrection are thirty-six hours which is six squared. And this is referred to that ratio of the single to the double wherein there is the greatest consonance of co-adaptation. For twelve added to twenty-four suits the ratio of single added to double and makes thirty-six: namely a whole night with a whole day and a whole night, and this not without the mystery which I have noticed above. For not unfitly do we liken the spirit to the day and the body to the night. For the body of the Lord in His death and resurrection was a figure of our spirit and a type of our body. In this way, then, also that ratio of the single to the double is apparent in the thirty-six hours, when twelve are added to twenty-four (Augustine. On the Trinity (Book IV), Chapters 5 & 6. Translated by Arthur West Haddan, B.D. Revised and annotated by the Professor W.G.T. Shedd, D.D. Excerpted from Nicene and Post-Nicene Fathers, Series One, Volume 3. Edited by Philip Schaff, D.D., LL.D. American Edition, 1887).

Augustine admits that Jesus was to be in the grave for three days, yet decides that he can calculate using a non-accepted form of mathematics to distort the clear meaning of scripture.

Martin Luther, also, basically accepted that wrong math, however, as he wrote:

> How can we say that he rose on the third day, since he lay in the grave only one day and two nights? According to the Jewish calculation it was only a day and a half; how shall we then persist in believing there were three days? To this we reply that he was in the state of death for at least a part of all three days. (Luther M. Of Christ's Resurrection from volume II:238-247 of *The Sermons of Martin Luther*, published by Baker Book House).

It is not that Jewish calculations are off, but that Martin Luther accepted a non-biblical tradition.

Notice also the following from over a century ago:

> **The Church of God believes Christ rose from the dead on the seventh day**. Matt. 28:1 reads, "In the end of the Sabbath as it began to dawn toward the first day of the week came Mary Magdalene and the other Mary to see the sepulchre." The time and object of this visit differs from all the others. The time is the "end" or evening of the Sabbath; the object "to see the sepulchre." This visit was made late on the Sabbath day. It was only beginning to dawn toward the first day of the week, when these women came to visit the sepulchre. The angel on this occasion said to them, "He is risen." Verse 6, As the seventh day always comes twenty-four hours before the first day and the Marys visited the sepulchre late on the ~seventh day and Christ was then risen, he could not have risen on the first day of the week. This testimony of Holy Writ is a clincher and should forever silence the Sunday-resurrection theory. (Dugger AF, Long WC. POINTS OF DIFFERENCE BETWEEN THE CHURCH OF GOD AND THE SEVENTH-DAY ADVENTISTS. THE BIBLE TRACT SERIES, Vol. 5, Num. 5, OCTOBER 15,1899, pp. 7-8)

That being said, some Protestants realize that their traditional understanding of this is off (e.g. Miller M. Bend Time is relative in determining chronology of Holy Week. Weekly News for Oregon. March 16, 2007). The late Jerry Falwell, a Sunday-keeper and chancellor of Liberty University in Lynchburg, Virginia, told *World Net Daily* in 2001, "I personally believe He was crucified on Wednesday ... and rose ... Saturday."

In 1708, Church of God pastor John Mauldin wrote (under the pen name Philotheos) that Jesus was in the grave for three days and three nights and was resurrected on the day we now call Saturday (Philotheos. A Threefold Dialogue, Concerning the Three Chief Points in Controversy amongst Protestants in our Day. London, 1708, pp. 61-64).

In the *Continuing* Church of God we believe Jesus was executed on Wednesday afternoon and rose from the dead Saturday afternoon, which makes three days and three nights.

5. Views of Jews and the Lost Tribes

Jesus was a Jew (John 4:9-10) as were most of His earliest followers.

Here is a report from a Protestant writer about early Christianity:

> It is clear that the Church's attitude towards Jewish Christianity changed significantly over the first four centuries. The attitudes of the first century Apostles were generally tolerant of Jewish Christianity, taking it to be acceptable, if not normative. The second century was a time of transformation in which Jewish Christianity rapidly became the exception rather than the rule, considered a valid, if archaic, expression of Christianity. However, by the time of the third and fourth century, the Church Fathers appear to view any expression of Jewish Christianity, regardless of the theology behind it, as heretical. This change in attitude represented a massive reversal of opinion. It evolved over several centuries, shaped by a variety of complex and interconnected forces. ...
>
> It is clear that at its beginning the Church was a Jewish Christian phenomenon ... the Jewish Christian church of Jerusalem had maintained relatively undisputed authority among Christians in Palestine until 135 C.E. (Howard K. Excommunicating the Faithful: Jewish Christianity in the Early Church, 3rd ed. ASIN: B00HH1K3QQ © 2013 by Kenneth W. Howard, pp. 51-53).

Well, the original faith was one that most Protestants today would identify as Judeo-Christian. It was the 'norm' and was not supposed to be changed (cf. Jude 3). Holding to original Christianity was not heretical. Yet, because of people like Marcion and Roman persecutions, most who professed Christ ended up professing a different faith than the apostles.

Furthermore, antisemitism developed even more than what Marcion pushed for.

The Greco-Roman-Protestant world has a terrible history of antisemitism.

In this chapter, let's start with the pagan Roman emperor Constantine of the fourth century (who is considered as an Eastern Orthodox saint). After his formal declaration in 325 A.D. that Passover should only be observed on Sunday, he stated:

> Let us then have nothing in common with the detestable Jewish crowd; for we have received from our Saviour a different way. (Eusebius' *Life of Constantine*, Book III chapter 18)

The way that Jesus, who was Jewish (Matthew 1:1-3; John 4:9-10), taught differently was about love. Jesus never taught to have "nothing in common with the detestable Jewish crowd."

In 387, the Eastern Orthodox saint and bishop John Chrysostom preached the following in his *Homily Against the Jews* (of which there are at least eight anti-Semitic homilies):

> But do not be surprised that I called the Jews pitiable. They really are pitiable and miserable (I:II:1).

> So the godlessness of the Jews and the pagans is on a par. But the Jews practice a deceit which is more dangerous (I:VI:4).

> Do you see that demons dwell in their souls and that these demons are more dangerous than the ones of old? (I:VI:7).

> Since it is against the Jews that I wish to draw up my battle line, let me extend my instruction further. Let me show that, by fasting now, the Jews dishonor the law and trample underfoot God's commands because they are always doing everything contrary to his decrees. When God wished them to fast, they got fat and flabby (VI:IV:2).

> Indeed, the fasting of the Jews, which is more disgraceful than any drunkenness, is over and gone (VIII:I:5).

John Chrysostom is considered to be a major Roman Catholic saint. He is one of the four 'doctors of the church' who are shown holding up a large black chair that is called the *Cathedra Petri* (Chair of Peter) in St. Peter's Basilica in Vatican City. The late Joseph Tkach of the old

Worldwide Church of God once referred to the *Cathedra Petri* as Satan's throne.

On March 2008, the home page of the Protestant publication *Christianity Today* had a link titled, **"Person of the Week: John Chrysostom"** which went to an article that referred to John Chrysostom as the *"Early church's greatest preacher."* Thus, many Protestants, too, endorsed that anti-Semite.

Furthermore, notice some of what Protestant Reformer Martin Luther wrote about the Jews:

> I had made up my mind to write no more either about the Jews or against them. But since I learned that those miserable and accursed people do not cease to lure to themselves even us, that is, the Christians, I have published this little book, so that I might be found among those who opposed such poisonous activities of the Jews and who warned the Christians to be on their guard against them ... They are so blind and stupid that they see neither the words found in Genesis 17 nor the whole of Scripture, which mightily and explicitly condemns this lie ... They are real liars and bloodhounds who have not only continually perverted and falsified all of Scripture with their mendacious glosses from the beginning until the present day. Their heart's most ardent sighing and yearning and hoping is set on the day on which they can deal with us Gentiles as they did with the Gentiles in Persia at the time of Esther...The worse a Jew is, the more arrogant he is, solely because he is a Jew ... David and other pious Jews were not as conceited as the present-day, incorrigible Jews ... I wanted to present this to us Germans so that we might see what rascals the blind Jews are and how powerfully the truth of God in our midst stands with us and against them (Medieval Sourcebook: Martin Luther (1483-1546): On the Jews and Their Lies, 1543)

Martin Luther's advice about Jews was hateful, not Christian:

> What shall we Christians do with this rejected and condemned people, the Jews? Since they live among us, we dare not tolerate their conduct ... I shall give you my sincere advice:

First to set fire to their synagogues or schools and to bury and cover with dirt whatever will not burn, so that no man will ever again see a stone or cinder of them. This is to be done in honor of our Lord and of Christendom ...

Second, I advise that their houses also be razed and destroyed. For they pursue in them the same aims as in their synagogues. Instead they might be lodged under a roof or in a barn, like the gypsies. This will bring home to them that they are not masters in our country, as they boast, but that they are living in exile and in captivity, as they incessantly wail and lament about us before God.

Third, I advise that all their prayer books and Talmudic writings, in which such idolatry, lies, cursing and blasphemy are taught, be taken from them. ...

Fourth, I advise that their rabbis be forbidden to teach henceforth on pain of loss of life and limb. ...

Fifth, I advise that safe-conduct on the highways be abolished completely for the Jews. For they have no business in the countryside ...

Sixth, I advise that usury be prohibited to them, and that all cash and treasure of silver and gold be taken from them and put aside for safekeeping. ...

Seventh, I commend putting a flail, an ax, a hoe, a spade, a distaff, or a spindle into the hands of young, strong Jews and Jewesses and letting them earn their bread in the sweat of their brow, as was imposed on the children of Adam (Gen 3[:19]}. (Medieval Sourcebook: Martin Luther (1483-1546): On the Jews and Their Lies, 1543)

... burn down Jewish schools and synagogues, and to throw pitch and sulphur into the flames; to destroy their homes; to confiscate their ready money in gold and silver; to take from them their sacred books, even the whole Bible; and if that did not help matters, to hunt them of the country like mad dogs

(Luther's Works, vol. Xx, pp. 2230-2632 as quoted in Stoddard JL. Rebuilding a Lost Faith, 1922, p.99).

Martin Luther was not a true Christian. True Christians were never the persecutors, but have been the persecuted. Peter warned, "there will be false teachers among you" (meaning people who claimed to be real Christians) and that "many will follow their destructive ways, because of whom the way of truth will be blasphemed" (2 Peter 2:1-2). Because many anti-Semites have falsely claimed to be Christian, Jews and others have concluded that Christianity does not have the truth. Sadly, most do not know the true from false churches. For more on the faithful Christian church the free online booklet: *Where is the True Christian Church Today?*

We in the *Continuing* Church of God do not condone antisemitism. We teach that Jesus was a Jew (John 4:9) and most in the nation of Israel are of the same ethnic origin as Jesus. In the 20th century, the late WCG Pastor General met with four prime ministers, four presidents, and numerous leaders in Israel and was honored for his work there. In the 21st century, CCOG's Dr. Thiel has worked with Jewish leaders in and out of Israel to improve relations and to better reach Jews with the gospel of the Kingdom of God. The CCOG also has literature in over 100 languages, including Hebrew and Yiddish.

We strive to reach both Jews and Gentiles about Jesus (see also the free book, online at ccog.org, *Proof Jesus is the Messiah*) and the Father (see also the free book, online at ccog.org, *Is God's Existence Logical?*).

While it does not show antisemitism, notice something Martin Luther reportedly said about a disabled child (who seems to have had symptoms of Prader-Willi Syndrome) as reported in *Table Talks* (essentially a collection of notes from supper guests of Martin Luther):

> Eight years ago, there was one in Dessau whom I, Martinus Luther, saw and grappled with. He was twelve years old, had the use of his eyes and all his senses, so that one might think he was a normal child. But he did nothing but gorge himself as much as four peasants or threshers. He ate, defecated, and drooled and, if anyone tackled him, he screamed. If things didn't go well, he wept. So I said to the Prince of Anhalt: "If I were the Prince, I

should take the child to the Moldau River which flows near Dessau and drown him." But the Prince of Anhalt and the Prince of Saxony, who happened to be present, refused to follow my advice. (T.E.C., Jr. MARTIN LUTHER'S ATTITUDE TOWARD THE MENTALLY RETARDED. Pediatrics, May 1968, VOLUME 41 / ISSUE 5)

Martin Luther also reportedly said that child should be suffocated (Mile M. Martin Luther and Childhood Disability in 16th Century Germany: What did he write? What did he say? Independent Living Institute, 2005). Yet, there are some who have tried to defend his indefensible statements (e.g. Ibid).

When Jesus dealt with a disabled child, He healed him (Mark 9:17-27). He did not advocate for his death like Martin Luther.

Martin Luther had a history of promoting hate and violence.

In modern times, Lutherans and some other Protestants have been involved in supporting anti-Jewish causes and taking steps against Israel (Lapham SS. Ten U.S. Churches Now Sanction Israel—To Some Degree, and with Caveats. Washington Report on Middle East Affairs, March/April 2019, pp. 51-53).

Lost Tribes of Israel

The CCOG teaches that God calls people of all races to salvation in this age and will also do so in the age to come. We do not teach that any race or ethnic group is superior to another and we do teach that, as taught in scriptures such as Romans 10:10-13, race is NOT a salvation matter

Before going further, perhaps it should be mentioned that unlike certain anti-Semitics who deny that the Jews are from the tribe of Judah (Black Israelite groups and some Aryan groups come to mind), we in the CCOG agree that Jews are mainly (though not exclusively, as there has been interbreeding) descended from Judah and are the primary peoples in the tiny nation of Israel.

However, most Protestants take this a step further and think that the people known as Jews are all the modern descendants of Israel—but that is not the historical COG perspective (e.g. Dugger AF, Long WC. POINTS OF DIFFERENCE BETWEEN THE CHURCH OF GOD AND THE SEVENTH-DAY ADVENTISTS. THE BIBLE TRACT SERIES, Vol. 5, Num. 5, OCTOBER 15, 1899, pp. 45-51). Many seem to overlook the fact that God's prophet stated that ten of the tribes of Israel separated from the nation of Judea (which included the descendants of Judah, Benjamin, and Levi—2 Chronicles 11:14) after the death of Solomon (1 Kings 11:31-35).

The Protestant view is in conflict with scripture as the New Testament teaches that there were Israelite tribes scattered abroad (James 1:1), such as part of the Scythians (Colossians 3:11 AFV/DRB).

Israel (whose name originally was Jacob) bestowed the following prophesied blessings on the descendants of the sons of Joseph after he 'adopted' them in Genesis 48:5::

> [13] And Joseph took them both, Ephraim with his right hand toward Israel's left hand, and Manasseh with his left hand toward Israel's right hand, and brought them near him. [14] Then Israel stretched out his right hand and laid it on Ephraim's head, who was the younger, and his left hand on Manasseh's head, guiding his hands knowingly, for Manasseh was the firstborn. [15] And he blessed Joseph, and said:

> "God, before whom my fathers Abraham and Isaac walked, The God who has fed me all my life long to this day, [16] The Angel who has redeemed me from all evil, **Bless the lads; Let my name be named upon them**, And the name of my fathers Abraham and Isaac; And let them grow into a multitude in the midst of the earth."

> [17] Now when Joseph saw that his father laid his right hand on the head of Ephraim, it displeased him; so he took hold of his father's hand to remove it from Ephraim's head to Manasseh's head. [18] And Joseph said to his father, "Not so, my father, for this one is the firstborn; put your right hand on his head."

> [19] But his father refused and said, "I know, my son, I know. He also shall become a people, and he also shall be great; but truly his younger brother shall be greater than he, and his descendants shall become a multitude of nations."
>
> [20] So he blessed them that day, saying, "By you Israel will bless, saying, 'May God make you as Ephraim and as Manasseh!'" And thus he set Ephraim before Manasseh. (Genesis 48:13-20)

The validity of these blessings by Jacob/Israel to Joseph's sons is also confirmed in the New Testament (Hebrews 11:21). If one looks at secular history, it is clear that the Jews did NOT fulfil the prophecies that Israel was inspired to give. Consider also that that name "Israel" was to be prophetically applied to the descendants of Ephraim and Manasseh—this is not otherwise stated for the descendants of Judah (the Jews).

Those of us who believe the Bible realize that these prophecies in Genesis 48 must be fulfilled. And that the Bible points to Ephraim's descendants rising up before Manasseh's.

Looking throughout secular history, we see that the British-descended peoples (Ephraim) became a multitude of nations (Genesis 48:19) and the USA (Manasseh) became a great nation (Genesis 48:19). About ¼ of the land mass of the entire world was once part of the old British Empire.

The British Empire was the largest in history, and the reach of the USA has been great (**bolding** ours):

> In 1913, 412 million people lived under the control of **the British Empire**, 23 percent of the world's population at that time. It **remains the largest empire in human history** and at the peak of its power in 1920, it covered an astonishing 13.71 million square miles - that's close to a quarter of the world's land area. (McCarthy N. The Biggest Empires In Human History. Statista, December 19, 2019).
>
> **The United States is the world's greatest economic power**, measured in terms of gross domestic product (GDP). ... The

> United States is relatively young by world standards, being less than 250 years old; it achieved its current size only in the mid-20th century. … **Probably no other country has a wider range of racial, ethnic, and cultural types than does the United States**. … Annually, the U.S. spends more on its military than the next seven highest-ranking countries in military spending combined. (Harris, JT, et al. United States. Encyclopædia Britannica. Last updated December 22, 2019)

From the 19th century to present, the USA and United Kingdom have dominated the world (though this dominance will be lost by them later in the 21st century). They have received the blessings that God promised them through Jacob.

As far as USA ethnic diversity goes, some of the prophecies related to Manasseh refer to it as 'Samaria' (e.g. Hosea 7:1; Obadiah 1:19; Isaiah 9:8-12,21). By Jesus' time, the Samaritans were only partially, Israelites—even though they have claimed to be from the tribe of Joseph ("Samaritans" in Encyclopaedia Judaica, 1972, Volume 14, col. 727, as cited in Louvish M. Religious life and communities. Keter Books, 1974, p. 61). However, the Bible shows that the Samaritans were highly ethnically mixed (2 Kings 17:24). Protestants tend to mix–some truth with error, so Protestants may be considered to be spiritual Samaritans. Both the physical and spiritual mixtures seems to fit the USA.

There are other scriptures that point to the identities of Ephraim and Manasseh (e.g. Deuteronomy 33:13-17) as well as to the other 'lost tribes' of Israel (such as the 49th chapter of Genesis and 33rd of Deuteronomy). However, most Protestant scholars dismiss them and/or wrongly claim that the USA, for example, is not found in Bible prophecy.

With the understanding that there are mixed ancestries in all nations, notice the list below of Israelitish-descended nations as identified by the old Radio Church of God back in the early 1950s:

1. Reuben – France (dignified but troubled, Genesis 49:3-4).
2. Judah – The nation now called Israel as well as the Jews not in that land but who were from the area near Jerusalem (Ezra 4:12; This tribe is not 'lost'; Genesis: 49:8-12).

3. Simeon – Scattered throughout the tribes (Genesis 49:5-7).
4. Levi – Scattered throughout the tribes (Genesis 49:5-7).
5. Issachar – Finland (sits between Europe and Russia, Genesis 49:14-15).
6. Zebulun – Netherlands (haven by the sea, Genesis 49:13) and a few in South Africa.
7. Gad – Switzerland (will apparently have to temporarily accept European Beast domination, Genesis 49:19).
8. Dan – Denmark, Ireland (on the outskirts–Genesis 49:17; the tribe that named places "Dan", Judges 18:12,29) (those in Northern Ireland mainly are descended from Ephraim).
9. Asher – Belgium, Luxembourg (wealthy, Genesis 49:20).
10. Naphtali – Sweden (attractively described, Genesis 49:21).
11. Benjamin – Norway, Iceland (former Vikings, cf. Genesis 49:27).
12. Ephraim – Britain, Canada, Australia, New Zealand, and probably some in South Africa and Zimbabwe (multitude/company of nations, Genesis 48:19).
13. Manasseh – United States of America (blessed and great nation, Genesis 48:19).

Perhaps it should be pointed out that the author of this book is not predominantly descended from Israel, hence is a Gentile. At the time of this writing, most members of the *Continuing* Church of God are primarily Gentile and not Israelite. Everyone had to descend from people mentioned in the Bible (such as from Adam, Eve, Noah, and Noah's sons), therefore despite claims from naysayers, teaching the biblical truths about God's promises to descendants of biblical figures is not racist.

We in the CCOG do not believe that people in the "lost tribes" are superior to the Gentile-descended peoples, but basically that they received the blessings God inspired Israel/Jacob to give. We also believe that these blessings are the cause of the physical wealth of these peoples, but that those same people are in the process of losing those blessings because of rebellion against the laws of God.

Notice another prophesy about Joseph's descendants:

> [22] "Joseph is a fruitful bough, A fruitful bough by a well; His branches run over the wall. [23] The archers have bitterly grieved

him, Shot at him and hated him. ²⁴ But his bow remained in strength, And the arms of his hands were made strong By the hands of the Mighty God of Jacob (From there is the Shepherd, the Stone of Israel), (Genesis 49:22-24)

The statement "His branches run over the wall" is a prophecy about a colonizing people. Clearly the old British Commonwealth was that. Furthermore, consider that the USA has had military 'branches' all around the world that many resent and even hate the USA for. God's word said Joseph's descendants would be "made strong." The USA and UK truly have fulfilled prophecies promised to the descendants of Joseph.

Consider that if the British-American descendants of Joseph did not fulfil these prophecies, then who did?

Protestants generally ignore this or claim that they were somehow fulfilled before Jesus' birth, but without proof.

Oddly, Protestant critic Walter Martin claimed that the Book of Amos disproved "Anglo-Israelism." Notice what he wrote:

> The *coup de grace* to Anglo-Israelism's fragmented exegesis is given by the prophet Amos of Judah ... (Amos, dwelling in Bethel, prophesied against Israel's restoration as a separate kingdom [Amos 9:8-12]). We learn from this prophecy that as a kingdom, the ten-tribes were to suffer destruction, and their restoration would never be realized. How then is it possible for them to be 'lost' and reappear three millenniums later as the British Kingdom when that Kingdom was never to be restored? (Martin W. Martin W. The Kingdom of the Cults. Baker Books, 2003, p. 518)

Let's look at what the book of Amos actually teaches:

> ⁸ "Behold, the eyes of the Lord God are on the sinful kingdom, And I will destroy it from the face of the earth; Yet I will not utterly destroy the house of Jacob,"
>
> Says the Lord.

> [9] "For surely I will command, And will sift the house of Israel among all nations, As grain is sifted in a sieve; Yet not the smallest grain shall fall to the ground. [10] All the sinners of My people shall die by the sword, Who say, 'The calamity shall not overtake nor confront us.' (Amos 9:8-10)

Amos 9:8-10 teaches that God would make it so the ancient kingdom of Israel would no longer be able to exist (it still does not), that Jacob though would still remain (his descendants still do), that those people would be sifted through the nations (which they have been), and that the sinners among them will be punished (which will happen; with verses 11-12 telling something that will happen later). Since those of us in the CCOG believe all that, we would tend to state that Amos 9:8-12 supports, and does not disprove, British-Israelism. British-Israelism, as understood in the CCOG, does not mean all ten tribes became the British Empire, but mainly one (Ephraim) did, along with another (Manasseh) that became the USA.

Perhaps it should also be noted that Jeremiah 51:5-6, especially when compared to Revelation 18:2-8 and Ezekiel 37:15-26, shows that into the present century that God still considers that Israel is separate from Judah. Therefore, despite comments from critics, the Bible does teach many aspects of "British-Israelism."

But most Protestants typically cannot see the USA in prophecy. Notice a statement from the evangelical Protestant Greg Laurie:

> When I look at Bible prophecy, one thing that is of great interest to me, and of great concern, is the absence of the United States. (Laurie G. Where is the United States in the End-Times Scenario? July 13th, 2013.

But is the USA truly absent from prophecy? Consider the following:

> [39] Thus he shall act against the strongest fortresses with a foreign god, which he shall acknowledge, and advance its glory; and he shall cause them to rule over many, and divide the land for gain. (Daniel 11:39)

Who currently has the strongest military in the world? Who has the "strongest fortresses"?

The "strongest fortresses" in the world belong to the USA, and to a lesser degree (and mainly because of alliances with the USA), its Anglo-allies. It should be pointed out that the nation commonly called Israel does not have the strongest fortresses. This passage is referring to the USA, not the Israel in Palestine, being taken over by the European King of the North (the "he" of Daniel 11:39).

Furthermore, dividing the Anglo-lands would bring much more gain, than the land of Judea.

Predictions and Prophecies

It is because of our understanding of biblical prophecies that for at least 50 years (e.g. McNair R. A Strong United Europe. Tomorrow's World, February 1970, p. 17), Church of God writers predicted that the United Kingdom would NOT remain part of a united Europe. And that departure officially took place on January 31, 2020.

Furthermore, in c. 1992, the author of this book told a British man that one day the UK would separate from Europe. The British man stated that could not possibly happen. And he gave his reasons—but they were not biblical ones—so this author told him he was in error. And the fact of 'Brexit' has proved that as it is consistent with our understanding of biblical prophecies and the identity of the British and American peoples.

Additionally, it should be noted that we teach the Great Tribulation will affect the Anglo-American peoples before others (cf. Jeremiah 30:7) and that the tribes of Israel will also suffer greatly for refusing to repent (Ezekiel 5:1-5).

We in the CCOG do NOT believe that the physical promises given in Genesis are related to salvation as there is no racial difference for God.

However, since God did promise physical blessings to the descendants of Abraham, Isaac, and Jacob, those who believe the Bible realize that some peoples had to be the recipients of those blessings. We believe that God kept His promises and provided those blessings in the 19th-21st

centuries. THOSE WHO CLAIM ALL VERSIONS OF ANGLO-ISRAELISM are unsound have never succeeded in explaining how any, other than the old British Empire and the USA, could have fulfilled God's prophetic promises. And since God's word can be counted on, it is biblically sound to accept that there is truth associated with British-Israelism.

Additionally, we teach that unless there is massive repentance, the physical blessings will be taken away from the descendants of Israel, including the USA and its British-descended allies, in the 21st century (cf. Daniel 8:24-25; 11:39; Isaiah 10:5-11; 17:3).

Most Protestants neither understand nor teach these concepts, despite claiming to believe the Bible.

6. Warfare and Violent Sports

Many may be surprised to learn that early Christians would not participate in carnal warfare nor watch violent sporting events.

Polycarp of Smyrna wrote:

> But He who raised Him up from the dead will raise up us also, if we do His will, and walk in His commandments, and love what He loved, keeping ourselves from all unrighteousness, covetousness, love of money, evil speaking, falsewitness; "not rendering evil for evil, or railing for railing," or blow for blow, or cursing for cursing (Polycarp. Letter to the Philippians, Chapter II. From Ante-Nicene Fathers, Volume 1as edited by Alexander Roberts & James Donaldson. American Edition, 1885).

It would be impossible to love what Jesus loved and to kill people. The admonition to not retaliate blow for blow should be seen as a stance that supports the concept that the second century church was against military service.

Theophilus of Antioch, around 180 A.D., wrote:

> Consider, therefore, whether those who teach such things can possibly live indifferently, and be commingled in unlawful intercourse, or, most impious of all, eat human flesh, especially when we are forbidden so much as to witness shows of gladiators, lest we become partakers and abettors of murders. But neither may we see the other spectacles, lest our eyes and ears be defiled, participating in the utterances there sung. (Theophilus of Antioch. To Autolycus, Book III, Chapter XV)

True Christians did not believe that they were to fight or even watch the violent sports that were popular in the second century.

This was based on several passages from the New Testament.

Paul wrote:

> [19] **Now the works of the flesh are evident**, which are: adultery, fornication, uncleanness, lewdness, [20] idolatry, sorcery, **hatred, contentions, jealousies, outbursts of wrath, selfish ambitions**, dissensions, heresies, [21] envy, **murders**, drunkenness, revelries, and the like; of which I tell you beforehand, just as I also told you in time past, that **those who practice such things will not inherit the kingdom of God** (Galatians 5:19-21).

Those who practice (as opposed to formerly practiced) military behaviors in this life WILL NOT BE IN THE KINGDOM OF GOD!

Notice that the New Testament admonishes Christians to:

> [14] Pursue peace with all people, and holiness, without which no one will see the Lord (Hebrews 12:14).

You cannot observe the above if you are engaging in carnal warfare.

Paul also wrote:

> [15] But God has called us to peace (1 Corinthians 7:15).

> [11] Finally, brethren, farewell. Become complete. Be of good comfort, be of one mind, live in peace; and the God of love and peace will be with you (2 Corinthians 13:11).

> [18] If it is possible, as much as depends on you, live peaceably with all men. [19] Beloved, do not avenge yourselves, but rather give place to wrath; for it is written, "Vengeance is Mine, I will repay," says the Lord. [20] Therefore "If your enemy is hungry, feed him; If he is thirsty, give him a drink; For in so doing you will heap coals of fire on his head." [21] Do not be overcome by evil, but overcome evil with good. (Romans 12:18-21)

Vengeance is God's. Christians are to live peaceably.

While it is true that the resurrected saints will help Christ crush His enemies (Jude 14-15), the saints are changed and not physical humans at that time (cf. 1 Corinthians 15:51-52; 1 Thessalonians 4:16-17).

Peter wrote about Christian behavior in this life:

> [10] For "He who would love life And see good days, Let him refrain his tongue from evil, And his lips from speaking deceit. [11] Let him turn away from evil and do good; Let him seek peace and pursue it …" (1 Peter 3:10-11).

John the Baptist addressed the military this way:

> [14] Likewise the soldiers asked him, saying, "And what shall we do?" So he said to them, "Do not intimidate anyone or accuse falsely, and be content with your wages" (Luke 3:14).

The word translated as 'intimidate' is the Greek word transliterated as *diaseio* which the KJV translates as 'violence'. *Strong's* translates it "to shake thoroughly, to intimidate, to do violence to". It comes from two Greek words *diagnosis* and *seio*; *diagnosis* is translated as examination and *seio* as to rock, agitate, to throw in a tremor. There is no way a soldier cannot agitate/intimidate if they are trying to kill someone.

Jesus had some comments that should be mentioned here:

> [21] "You have heard that it was said to the ancients, 'Thou shalt not commit murder', and whoever commits murder will be answerable to the magistrate. [22] But I say to you that every one who becomes angry with his brother shall be answerable to the magistrate; that whoever says to his brother 'Raca,' shall be answerable to the Sanhedrin; and that whoever says, 'You fool!' shall be liable to the Gehenna of Fire. (Matthew 5:21-22, Weymouth New Testament)

> [18] … Jesus said, "'You shall not murder…" (Matthew 19:18, NKJV)

As Jesus' comments in Matthew 5:21-22 demonstrate, He expanded the restrictions against murder. Those expansions generally do not condone carnal warfare nor encourage violence in sports. Many get inappropriately angry who are fans of violent sports.

The Apostle John was inspired to record:

> ⁹ If anyone has an ear, let him hear. ¹⁰ He who leads into captivity shall go into captivity; he who kills with the sword must be killed with the sword. Here is the patience and the faith of the saints (Revelation 13:9-10).

Notice that even until the end, **saints are to be patient and NOT be among those who kill with the sword**.

Is it any wonder that Martin Luther discounted the literal understanding of the Book of Revelation? Otherwise he and his followers would have to change their positions on warfare

Even most of the Greco-Romans tended to be pacifists and did not watch violent sports (cf. Hippolytus. The Apostolic Tradition of Hippolytus of Rome) until during the rise of Emperor Constantine.

Constantine followed the pagan religion of Mithraism. "Mithraism was first and foremost a military cult" (Aiken CF. Mithraism. The Catholic University bulletin, Volume 19, 1913. p. 255).

The pagan Emperor Constantine had his soldiers paint crosses on their shields to fight in 312. Shortly thereafter, he pushed his "Constantinian Christianity" on the Greco-Romans and they changed to embrace military participation for their members—which they still embrace to this day (as have most Protestants).

After Pope Urban II called on the Greco-Romans in 1095 to take Jerusalem back from the Muslims, the soldiers were called crusaders (meaning cross-bearers) because they, like Constantine's soldiers, had crosses painted on their shields.

Martin Luther, himself, was a type of lying warmonger:

> I, Martin Luther, slew all the peasants in the rebellion, for I said that they should be slain; all their blood is upon my head. But I cast it on the Lord God, who commanded me to speak this way (Werke, Erl. Edition, lix, p. 284 'Table Talk' as quoted in Stoddard JL. Rebuilding a Lost Faith, 1922, p.96).

> Pure devilry is urging on the peasants ... Therefore let all who are able, mow them down, slaughter and stab them, openly or in secret, and remember that there is nothing more poisonous, noxious and utterly devilish than a rebel. You must kill him as you would a mad dog ...
>
> The authorities must resolve to chastise and slay as long as they can raise a finger ... The present time is so strange that a prince can gain Heaven easier by spilling blood than by praying (Luther M. Against the Murderous and Rapacious Hordes of the Peasants, May 4, 1525-Erl, 24, 287, ff. As cited in O'Hare PF. The Facts About Luther, p. 232).

It was reported that 100,000 perished at that time. God did NOT command Martin Luther to speak that way—that is Satan's way. Many Protestants do not act like they believe Satan is the "god of this world," but he currently is (2 Corinthians 4:4, KJV).

The followers of Martin Luther also condemned those who were not willing to be warriors. And they officially declared "it is right for Christians ... to engage in just wars, to serve as soldiers". (Melanchthon P. The Augsburg Confession, Article XVI).

We in the *Continuing* Church of God hold to the original Christian teaching on this. Therefore, we do not participate as soldiers in carnal warfare nor do we endorse watching intentionally violent sporting events.

7. Baptism, Infants, Sprinkling, and Immersion

Should infants be baptized?

The Bible never shows that infants were baptized.

In the 20th century Franciscan Catholic Jean Briand reported:

> **Authors of old only described adult baptisms**. (Briand, p. 54)

Polycarp died at age 104 (Weidman, Frederick W. Polycarp and John: The Harris Fragments and Their Challenge to Literary Traditions. University of Notre Dame Press, Notre Dame (IL), 1999, pp. 43,44) and said he had been a Christian for 86 years (Martyrdom of Polycarp). Therefore, he would have been baptized at age 18 (104-86=18).

After reviewing documents and other evidence, Roman Catholic scholar and priest Bagatti correctly concluded that Judeo-Christians did not baptize infants, "following the example of the Lord" (Bagatti, From the Church of the Circumcision, p. 239).

But the Greco-Romans changed from the original teaching.

Martin Luther accepted that change and later taught:

> "Why are babies to be baptized?
>
> 29. Babies are to baptized because they are included in the words 'all nations' (Luther's Small Catechism with Explanation. Concordia Publishing House, St. Louis, 1986, p.202).

As a Roman Catholic, Martin Luther, himself, would have been baptized as an infant by a priest. Faithful Christians would not consider that to have met the biblical criteria.

The followers of Martin Luther made the following official condemnation of those whose views were more faithful:

> They condemn the Anabaptists, who reject the baptism of children ... (Melanchthon P. The Augsburg Confession of 1530, Article IX).

Other Protestant Reformers, like Ulriucus Zuinglius and John Calvin supported infant baptism and also condemned those who disagreed:

> Zuinglius, who, when questioned regarding the fate of certain Anabaptists, replied, "Drown the Dippers" (Davis, Tamar. A General History of the Sabbatarian Churches. 1851; Reprinted 1995 by Commonwealth Publishing, Salt Lake City, p. 106).

> John Calvin wrote, "We see that the practice which we have of baptizing little children is impugned and assailed by some malignant spirits, as if it had not been appointed by God, but newly invented by men, or at least some years after the days of the Apostles" (Calvin J. Works, Volume 51. Calvin Translation Society, 1846, p. 351)

Notice that John Calvin claimed something contrary to Peter's baptismal instructions (cf. Acts 2:38) was supposedly ordained by God—he could not admit it was a false tradition that was not based on the scriptures. People who felt that infant baptism was invalid were called Anabaptists (re-baptizers).

The Bible shows that those who received John the Baptist's baptism had to be 're-baptized' to be Christian (Acts 19:3-5). The Bible also shows that those baptized needed to repent and accept Jesus (Acts 2:38) and obey Him to receive the Holy Spirit (Acts 5:31-32)—which is something that Infants cannot do.

Part of the non-biblical rationale for infant baptism is that people like John Calvin otherwise condemned infants to eternal torment.

John Calvin taught the following about babies:

> And so INFANTS THEMSELVES, as they bring their DAMNATION with them from their mothers' womb, are bound, not by the sin of another, but by their own. For they have not produced the fruits of iniquity, they have the seed of it inclosed within them;

nay their whole nature is, as it were, a seed of sin; so that it cannot but be odious and abominable to God. (Calvin J. Institut. Lib. II. c. ii, as cited in Palfrey EJ, et al. The Christian Examiner and Theological Review, Volume 4. 1827, p. 432)

This seems to be the basis of John Calvin condemning babies who die to everlasting torment with no chance of reprieve. This is not something a loving God, who made people upright (Ecclesiastes 7:29), would do.

Sadly, Protestants like John Calvin and Martin Luther did not understand God's plan of salvation (some details of which are in the free book, online at ccog.org, titled *Universal OFFER of Salvation, Apokatastasis: Can God save the lost in an age to come? Hundreds of scriptures reveal God's plan of salvation*).

John Calvin's statements were condemned in 1708 by Church of God pastor John Mauldin who also wrote that God was not condemning babies to eternal torment (Philotheos. A Threefold Dialogue, Concerning the Three Chief Points in Controversy amongst Protestants in our Day. London, 1708, pp. 30-32).

Jesus did not condemn infants and little children like John Calvin did. Instead He taught:

> [3] ... Assuredly, I say to you, unless you are converted and become as little children, you will by no means enter the kingdom of heaven. (Matthew 18:3)

Little children can be blest, and Jesus did that to them (Mark 10:16).

And if one or both of their parents are truly Christians, the Bible teaches that their children are holy (1 Corinthians 7:14). However, even if not, all children can be blest as Jesus did not distinguish based upon parenthood (Mark 10:13-14).

Getting back to baptism, since the Bible teaches that requires repentance (cf. Acts 2:38), and life shows us that infants cannot do that, we do not violate scripture by baptizing infants.

Because some churches baptize infants, as well as for general convenience, sprinkling is used by some Protestants. But even the Church of Rome admits that immersion was the original practice:

> The word *Baptism* is derived from the Greek word, *bapto*, or *baptizo*, to wash or to immerse. It signifies, therefore, that washing is of the essential idea of the sacrament ... The most ancient form usually employed was unquestionably immersion. This is not only evident from the writings of the Fathers and the early rituals of both the Latin and Oriental Churches, but it can also be gathered from the Epistles of St. Paul, who speaks of baptism as a bath (Ephesians 5:26; Romans 6:4; Titus 3:5). In the Latin Church, immersion seems to have prevailed until the twelfth century. After that time it is found in some places even as late as the sixteenth century. Infusion and aspersion, however, were growing common in the thirteenth century and gradually prevailed in the Western Church. The Oriental Churches have retained immersion (Fanning, William H.W. Transcribed by Charles Sweeney, S.J. Baptism. The Catholic Encyclopedia, Volume II. Published 1907. New York: Robert Appleton Company. Nihil Obstat, 1907. Remy Lafort, S.T.D., Censor. Imprimatur. +John M. Farley, Archbishop of New York).

We in the *Continuing* Church of God continue with the original practice of baptizing converted adults via immersion.

Jesus blessed little children (Matthew 19:13-15; Mark 10:14-16; Luke 18:15-17). It looks as though a misunderstanding of that practice was at least part of the unbiblical basis of infant baptism (cf. Fanning W. "Baptism." The Catholic Encyclopedia. Vol. 2. New York: Robert Appleton Company, 1907).

Following Jesus' example, we in the CCOG have a ceremony in which we bless little children, but we do not baptize them.

8. Sola Scriptura or Tradition?

We in the *Continuing* Church of God agree with the professed view of Protestants that *sola Scriptura* is the best source for doctrine (2 Timothy 3:16-17).

Yet, is Protestantism really only based on scripture or is it actually a combination of a lot of tradition and some scriptures?

Despite claiming *sola Scriptura* (Latin for 'Scripture alone'), Protestants accept many doctrines based more on tradition than the Bible.

Notice that even *The Catholic Encyclopedia* admits that infant baptism, Sunday worship, and other practices are simply based upon tradition:

> **Divine traditions not contained in Holy Scripture ...**
>
> The designation of unwritten Divine traditions was not always given all the clearness desirable especially in early times; however Catholic controversialists soon proved to the Protestants that to be logical and consistent they must admit unwritten traditions as revealed. Otherwise by what right did they rest on Sunday and not on Saturday? How could they regard infant baptism as valid, or baptism by infusion? How could they permit the taking of an oath, since Christ had commanded that we swear not at all? The Quakers were more logical in refusing all oaths, the Anabaptists in re-baptizing adults, the Sabbatarians in resting on Saturday. But none were so consistent as not to be open to criticism on some point. (Bainvel J. Transcribed by Tomas Hancil. *Tradition and Living Magisterium*. The Catholic Encyclopedia, Volume XV. Published 1912. New York: Robert Appleton Company. Nihil Obstat, October 1, 1912. Remy Lafort, S.T.D., Censor. Imprimatur. +John Cardinal Farley, Archbishop of New York).

It is true that most of the traditions mentioned above are clearly not practices of early Christians, and yet they are practices that most in the Roman Catholic, Orthodox, and Protestant churches accept. Since those traditions do contradict the biblical accounts (and even *The Catholic*

Encyclopedia essentially admitted that on most of them), those practices should be rejected and should not be part of the traditions of either of those groups.

We in the CCOG do rest on Saturday, do not regard infant baptism as valid, and do not swear oaths. Thus, we are consistent in rejecting all those anti-biblical traditions. Protestant acceptance of non-biblical traditions is one reason that many Roman Catholics considered them hypocritical regarding *sola Scriptura*.

Also, we do not observe pagan holidays nor have we adopted many of the other non-biblical trappings that Protestant faiths hold to.

As far as swearing goes, Martin Luther endorsed it (Luther M. The Large Catechism. Translated by F. Bente and W.H.T. Dau. Triglot Concordia: The Symbolical Books of the Ev. Lutheran Church, St. Louis: Concordia Publishing House, 1921). Interestingly in 1618, a Roman Catholic priests noted that those who held to COG doctrines believed "nothing not expresly mentioned in Scriptures, or thence necessarily deduced" were more scriptural than Protestants he had dealt with (Falconer J. A briefe refutation of Iohn Traskes iudaical and nouel fancyes Stiling himselfe Minister of Gods Word, imprisoned for the lawes eternall perfection, or God's lawes perfect eternity. English College Press, 1618, p. 32).

Many of the 'traditional' beliefs that Protestants hold can be traced back to the time of Emperor Constantine. He was able to get many aspects of the militaristic religion of Mithraism accepted by the Greco-Romans. The late Baptist minister and civil rights activist, Martin Luther King, Jr. also concluded this was so in some of his early theological research from 1949 and 1950:

> When Mithraism is compared to Christianity, there are surprisingly many points of similarity. Of all the mystery cults, Mithraism was the greatest competitor of Christianity ...
>
> That Christians did copy and borrow from Mithraism cannot be denied ...
>
> Mithraism ... was suppressed by the Christians sometime in the latter part of the fourth century A.D.: but its collapse seems to

have been due to the fact that by that time many of its doctrines had been adopted by the church, so that it was practically absorbed by its rival.

… the Church made a sacred day out of Sunday partially because … of the resurrection. But when we observe a little further we find that as a solar festival, Sunday was the sacred day of Mithra: it is also interesting to notice that since Mithra was addressed as Lord, Sunday must have been 'the Lord's Day' long before Christian use. It is also to be noticed that our Christmas, December 25th, was the birthday of Mithra, and was only taken over in the Fourth Century as the date, actually unknown, of the birth of Jesus.

To make the picture a little more clear, we may list a few of the similarities between these two religions: (1) Both regard Sunday as a Holy Day. (2) December 25 came to be considered as the anniversary of the birth of Mithra and Christ also. (3) Baptism and a ritual meal were important parts of both groups …

In summary we may say that the belief in immortality, a mediator between god and man, the observance of certain sacramental rites … were common to Mithraism and Christianity. (King ML. The papers of Martin Luther King, Jr, Volume 4. Clayborne Carson, Ralph Luker, Penny A. Russell editors/compliers. University of California Press, 1992, pp. 222, 224, 307, 309.)

Notice that Dr. King clearly understood that the Sunday churches dropped the Sabbath, that "the Lord's Day" essentially first meant the day of Mithra, and that the worlds' churches did adopt many practices from Mithraism. Much of what now is called 'Christianity' is a compromise with the religion of Mithraism.

While Protestants tend to blast Roman Catholics for relying on traditions of men above the Bible, the simple truth is that Protestant scholars not only realize that Protestants do this, they actually teach that relying on human traditions is more important than the Bible.

Look at these admissions from the Protestant scholar and theologian H. Brown:

> **It is impossible to document what we now call orthodoxy in the first two centuries of Christianity.** ... but we can document orthodoxy for all the centuries since then—in other words for close to seventeen centuries of the church's existence. Brown HOJ. Heresies: Heresy and Orthodoxy in the History of the Church. Hendrickson Publishers, Peabody (MA), 1988, pp. 5)

Early Greco-Roman-Protestant "orthodoxy" cannot be documented, because much of it is not part of the original Christian faith. A lot of the 'documentation' began in the 300s A.D. and much can be traced to Mithraism and the influence of Emperor Constantine.

Dr. Brown also wrote:

> Although classical theology is certainly not without its problems, historically it is almost always the case that **the appeal to the Bible alone ... leads to the reemergence of ancient heresies** ... The Reformation began with the slogan "To the sources!" and sought to deal a fatal blow to the place of church tradition in shaping life and faith ... Despite their efforts not to be influenced by the authority of tradition, each of the major Reformation churches found itself borrowing from the past and building up a traditionalism of its own ... **when the Anabaptists and other radicals discovered Scripture to be teaching things the Lutherans found detestable, Lutherans learned the usefulness of tradition** ... (ibid, pp. 335,350-351).

So, Protestant scholars actually claim that relying on the Bible alone leads to the emergence of early Christian views that they consider to be heretical. "Tradition" is NOT useful against scripture! How can appealing to the Bible be heresy?

The historical reality is that when early Protestants did not like biblical teachings, they latched onto traditions of men. Jesus condemned supposedly 'Bible believing' people for doing that:

> [9] ... "All too well you reject the commandment of God, that you may keep your tradition. ... [13] making the word of God of no effect through your tradition which you have handed down. And many such things you do." (Mark 7:9-13)

Do you follow the Jesus of the Bible or do you prefer traditions accepted by Protestants and others?

Around 1918, a COG Sabbatarian named G.G. Rupert wrote:

> We say that the Greek, the Roman, and the Protestant organizations are all the daughters of modern Babylon, the Baal woman, who is the representative of the work of Satan in every age. (Rupert GG. The Seven Churches. Union Publishing Company, c. 1918, pp. 5,10, 22)

The position of the mid 20th century Worldwide Church of God was that since Protestants and others compromised and accepted many non-biblical doctrines and practices of the Church of Rome, that they were the among harlot daughters of Babylon (Revelation 17:4-5) and daughters of Jezebel (Revelation 2:22-23) and would be destroyed after the start of the Great Tribulation consistent with Revelation 2:23 (LESSON 51, AMBASSADOR COLLEGE BIBLE CORRESPONDENCE COURSE "And the woman fled into the wilderness, where she hath a place ..." Rev. 12:6. Ambassador College, 1968).

Mystery of Truth

The *Cambridge Dictionary* defines "the truth" as follows:

> **the truth** the real facts about a situation, event, or person:

The truth is something that is genuinely accurate. Yet philosophers, common people, and leaders have long wondered about the truth.

Notice how the *Cambridge Dictionary* defines "formal" truth:

> a fact or principle that is thought to be true by most people:

But the above is most certainly not always true. And many have long realized that.

When speaking with Jesus, the Roman Prefect Pontius Pilate asked about it:

> [37] Pilate therefore said to Him, "Are You a king then?"
>
> Jesus answered, "You say rightly that I am a king. For this cause I was born, and for this cause I have come into the world, that I should bear witness to the truth. Everyone who is of the truth hears My voice."
>
> [38] Pilate said to Him, "What is truth?" And when he had said this, he went out again to the Jews, and said to them, "I find no fault in Him at all." (John 18:37-38)

While Jesus did not answer Pilate's last question, as it appears that Pilate went out not expecting an answer, Jesus did say what the truth was. Jesus said that saying a statement that was accurate was right, consistent with the truth.

Elsewhere, Jesus did state what the truth was:

> [17] Sanctify them by Your truth. Your word is truth. (John 17:17)

The Bible teaches that God cannot lie (Hebrews 6:18, Titus 1:2).

So, whatever God says is the truth. A lie is something that is opposed to the truth.

Some believe that they should "let their conscience be their guide," but without God's Spirit the carnal mind cannot discern as it should (1 Corinthians 2:14) as the heart can be deceitful and desperately wicked (Jeremiah 17:9).

Jesus said Christians are to live "by every word that proceeds from the mouth of God" (Matthew 4:4), not human tradition.

The Apostle Paul wrote:

> [13] For this reason we also thank God without ceasing, because when you received the word of God which you heard from us, you welcomed it not as the word of men, but as it is in truth, the word of God, which also effectively works in you who believe. [14.] For you, brethren, became imitators of the churches of God which are in Judea in Christ Jesus. (1 Thessalonians 2:13-14a).

> [7] ... the word of truth, (2 Corinthians 6:7)

> [13] In Him you also trusted, after you heard the word of truth, the gospel of your salvation; (Ephesians 1:13)

> [5] the hope which is laid up for you in heaven, of which you heard before in the word of the truth of the gospel, (Colossians 1:5)

The truth is a mystery to most, because most do not fully trust the true word of God (cf. Colossian 1:5,-6,25-27; 1 Thessalonians 2:13). Most trust in other humans, who themselves have been deceived by Satan (Revelation 12:9).

Trusting more in other humans than God's word leads to vain worship and leads people away from the truth (Matthew 15:8-9, 2 Timothy 3:13).

Yet, the truth can be known.

The Apostle John wrote:

> [31] Then Jesus said to those Jews who believed Him, "If you abide in My word, you are My disciples indeed. [32] And you shall know the truth, and the truth shall make you free." (John 8:31-32)

> [46] And if I tell the truth, why do you not believe Me? [47] He who is of God hears God's words; therefore you do not hear, because you are not of God. (John 8:46-47)

> [37] ...I have come into the world, that I should bear witness to the truth. Everyone who is of the truth hears My voice (John 18:37).

> [6] If we say that we have fellowship with Him, and walk in darkness, we lie and do not practice the truth. [7] But if we walk in the light as He is in the light, we have fellowship with one another, and the blood of Jesus Christ His Son cleanses us from all sin. (1 John 1:6-7)
>
> [4] He who says, "I know Him," and does not keep His commandments, is a liar, and the truth is not in him. [5] But whoever keeps His word, truly the love of God is perfected in him. By this we know that we are in Him. [6] He who says he abides in Him ought himself also to walk just as He walked. (1 John 2:4-6)
>
> [18] My little children, let us not love in word or in tongue, but in deed and in truth. [19] And by this we know that we are of the truth, and shall assure our hearts before Him. (1 John 3:18-19)
>
> [3] For I rejoiced greatly when brethren came and testified of the truth that is in you, just as you walk in the truth. [4] I have no greater joy than to hear that my children walk in truth. (3 John 3-4)

Despite what the Bible says, the connection between the truth being the word of God and understood by those who obey God is a mystery to many. Biblically, Protestantism does not have enough of the truth.

Tradition does NOT trump scripture. But, in various ways, it has within Protestantism.

John's Gospel tells of those who "loved the praise of men more than the praise of God" (John 12:43). Sadly, many prefer human opinion over the word of God.

John also penned the following:

> [3] ... Just and true are Your ways, O King of the saints! (Revelation 15:3)

Walking in God's ways helps us better understand the truth as we live by the truth.

Do These Warnings Include Protestants?

There are warnings in scripture that seem to include Protestantism.

Consider the following:

> [1] "Woe to the rebellious children," says the LORD, "Who take counsel, but not of Me, And who devise plans, but not of My Spirit, That they may add sin to sin; ... [8] Now go, write it before them on a tablet, And note it on a scroll, That it may be for time to come, Forever and ever: [9] That this is a rebellious people, Lying children, Children who will not hear the law of the LORD ... [12] you despise this word (Isaiah 30:1,8-9,12)

Because of the acceptance of traditions, some of which came from councils of men, most Protestants will not hear, at least parts of, the law of the Lord and His word.

A major problem Jesus encountered in His day was religious leaders who thought they knew the scriptures, but based much of their understanding on 'exceptions' and traditions of men.

Notice Jesus' words to the Pharisees:

> [3] ... "Why do you also transgress the commandment of God because of your tradition? [6] ... you have made the commandment of God of no effect by your tradition. [7] Hypocrites! Well did Isaiah prophesy about you, saying:
>
> [8] "These people draw near to Me with their mouth, And honor Me with their lips, But their heart is far from Me. [9] And in vain they worship Me, Teaching as doctrines the commandments of men.'" (Matthew 15:3b,6b-9)

The Pharisees used tradition to not obey what the Bible taught.

Protestantism does that. True Christians worship God through obeying Him.

Notice more of Jesus' words to people who claimed to believe the word of God:

> ^{39} You search the Scriptures, for in them you think you have eternal life; and these are they which testify of Me. ^{40} But you are not willing to come to Me that you may have life. (John 5:39-40)

Even today, many do not want to accept the real Jesus as Messiah.

The Pharisees were enslaved by their fear of men and their longstanding devotion to traditions that they falsely thought were biblical. They wouldn't change, even though Jesus told them the truth (John 8:45-46), because they were 'not of God' and therefore could not 'hear' His words (John 8:43,47).

> ^{7} ... Today, if you will hear His voice, Do not harden your hearts. (Hebrews 4:7)

Do not be like the Pharisees! They had their own ways of discounting scriptures and dismissing proper doctrines.

Notice something Jesus warned to those who claim to be His disciples:

> ^{46} "But why do you call Me 'Lord, Lord,' and not do the things which I say? ^{47} Whoever comes to Me, and hears My sayings and does them, I will show you whom he is like: ^{48} He is like a man building a house, who dug deep and laid the foundation on the rock. And when the flood arose, the stream beat vehemently against that house, and could not shake it, for it was founded on the rock. ^{49} But he who heard and did nothing is like a man who built a house on the earth without a foundation, against which the stream beat vehemently; and immediately it fell. And the ruin of that house was great." (Luke 6:46-49)

All who call Jesus 'Lord' should do what He says in His word. Using non-biblical traditions as a foundational part of Protestant belief (such as holding to the trinitarian doctrine) will ultimately result in ruin (cf. Revelation 18:2-3).

Further, notice the following:

> [45] But because I tell the truth, you do not believe Me. [46] Which of you convicts Me of sin? And if I tell the truth, why do you not believe Me? [47] He who is of God hears God's words; therefore you do not hear, because you are not of God. (John 8:45-47)

> [20] Seeing many things, but you do not observe; Opening the ears, but he does not hear (Isaiah 42:20)

Because Protestants often read the Bible, they have seen many things-- many of which they should, but do not, observe.

And they are subject to being punished for that:

> [12] Therefore I will number you for the sword, And you shall all bow down to the slaughter; Because, when I called, you did not answer; When I spoke, you did not hear, But did evil before My eyes, And chose that in which I do not delight. (Isaiah 65:12)

Most Protestants have accepted many traditions over what the Bible teaches. Most Protestants are dismissive of many Church of God doctrines, because they do not fit within the traditions their leaders have adopted.

Protestantism does not really accept *sola Scriptura* as it accepts many positions and doctrines that are in conflict with scripture.

9. Sabbath vs. Sunday

With some exceptions (see chapter 10), most Protestants do not even try to keep the seventh-day Sabbath. Many Protestants have even argued that the New Testament does not enjoin the seventh-day Sabbath, but that is an erroneous belief.

Consider that Jesus taught:

> [4] "It is written, 'Man shall not live by bread alone, but by every word that proceeds from the mouth of God.'" (Matthew 4:4)

Jesus was specifically referring to the Hebrew scriptures, commonly referred to as the Old Testament.

We know that the Old Testament enjoined the seventh-day Sabbath (e.g. Exodus 20:8-11) on at least the children of Israel (and those who dwelt among them, cf. Exodus 12:49).

But does the portion of scripture known as the New Testament enjoin keeping the Sabbath for Christians?

Yes.

Our Lord Jesus kept the Sabbath (e.g. Mark 6:2). Jesus taught that He was the "Lord of the Sabbath" (Mark 2:28).

The Apostle Paul kept the Sabbath (Acts 13:14,42-44, 17:1-4, 18:4; Philippians 3:5-6).

Notice what the New Testament Book of Hebrews (traditionally considered to have been written/dictated by the Apostle Paul) teaches using three Protestant translations:

> [3] Now we who have believed enter that rest, just as God has said, "So I declared on oath in my anger, 'They shall never enter my rest.'" And yet his work has been finished since the creation of the world. [4] For somewhere he has spoken about the seventh day in these words: "And on the seventh day God rested from

all his work." ⁵ And again in the passage above he says, "They shall never enter my rest." ⁶ It still remains that some will enter that rest, and those who formerly had the gospel preached to them did not go in, because of their disobedience...⁹ There remains, then, a Sabbath-rest for the people of God; ¹⁰ for anyone who enters God's rest also rests from his own work, just as God did from his. ¹¹ Let us, therefore, make every effort to enter that rest, so that no one will fall by following their example of disobedience (Hebrews 4:3-6,9-11, NIV).

³ For we who have believed enter that rest, just as He has said, "AS I SWORE IN MY WRATH, THEY SHALL NOT ENTER MY REST," although His works were finished from the foundation of the world. ⁴ For He has said somewhere concerning the seventh day: "AND GOD RESTED ON THE SEVENTH DAY FROM ALL HIS WORKS"; ⁵ and again in this passage, "THEY SHALL NOT ENTER MY REST." ⁶ Therefore, since it remains for some to enter it, and those who formerly had good news preached to them failed to enter because of disobedience,.. ⁹ So there remains a Sabbath rest for the people of God. ¹⁰ For the one who has entered His rest has himself also rested from his works, as God did from His. ¹¹ Therefore let us be diligent to enter that rest, so that no one will fall, through following the same example of disobedience. (Hebrews 4:3-6,9-11, NASB)

³ for we do enter into the rest — we who did believe, as He said, 'So I sware in My anger, If they shall enter into My rest — ;' and yet the works were done from the foundation of the world, ⁴ for He spake in a certain place concerning the seventh [day] thus: 'And God did rest in the seventh day from all His works;' ⁵ and in this [place] again, 'If they shall enter into My rest — ;' ⁶ since then, it remaineth for certain to enter into it, and those who did first hear good news entered not in because of unbelief ⋯ ⁹ there doth remain, then, a sabbatic rest to the people of God, ¹⁰ for he who did enter into his rest, he also rested from his works, as God from His own. ¹¹ May we be diligent, then, to enter into that rest, that no one in the same example of the unbelief may fall, (Hebrews 4:3-6,9-11, Young's Literal Translation)

Thus, this clearly shows that the command to keep the seventh day Sabbath is in the New Testament. The New Testament also shows that only those who will not observe it because of their disobedience argue otherwise. Early Christians realized that the Sabbath was in place for God's people.

In the late 2nd/early 3rd century, despite his flaws, even Origen of Alexandria understood some of this as he wrote:

> But what is the feast of the Sabbath except that which the apostle speaks, "There remaineth therefore a Sabbatism," that is, the observance of the Sabbath, by the people of God ... let us see how the Sabbath ought to be observed by a Christian. On the Sabbath-day all worldly labors ought to be abstained from ... give yourselves up to spiritual exercises, repairing to church, attending to sacred reading and instruction ... this is the observance of the Christian Sabbath (Translated from Origen's Opera 2, Paris, 1733 as cited in Andrews J.N. in History of the Sabbath, 3rd edition, 1887, pp. 324-325).

Sadly, most Protestants, through a state of disobedience and unbelief in the word of God, do not strive to keep the Sabbath God established for His people.

Although over 20 Protestant translations make it clear that Hebrews 4:9 is pointing to the weekly seventh-day Sabbath (ASV, BLB, BSB, CSB, DBT, ERV, ESV, GNT, HCSB, IB, ILB, ISV, JMNT, JB2000, NASB, NETB, NHEB, NIV, RSV, WEB, WNT, YLT), one reason that many do not understand this is that several Protestant translators have intentionally mistranslated the Greek term *sabbatismos* (ςαββατισμός) which is specifically found in Hebrews 4:9 (Green JP. The Interlinear Bible, 2nd edition. Hendrickson Publishers, 1986, p. 930).

For example, the widely used Protestant KJV and NKJV mistranslate that word as "rest."

Yet, there is a different Greek term, *katapausin*, translated as "rest" in the New Testament.

In Hebrews 4:9, the term *sabbatismos* is used. *Sabbatismos* clearly refers to a sabbath-rest and forthright scholars will all admit that.

At least partially because of the mistranslations/improper teachings ("stammering lips," cf. Isaiah 28:11-12), most Protestants today do not seem to realize that the seventh-day Sabbath was specifically enjoined for Christians in the New Testament.

Decades ago, a Protestant mentioned to this book's author that the reason he did not keep the seventh-day Sabbath was because it was not taught for Christians in the New Testament. So, he was handed an RSV Bible and told to read Hebrews 4. After doing so, the man said because he felt his grandmother, who did not keep the Sabbath, was a 'good Christian,' he felt that he did not need to obey the New Testament. He failed to truly rely on the Bible, but instead relied on false tradition (cf. Mark 7:6-8). Sadly, most who profess Christianity do not keep the seventh-day Sabbath and rely mainly on improper traditions, whether they realize it or not.

The Apostle Paul commended the Gentiles in Thessalonica because they "became imitators of the churches of God which are in Judea in Christ Jesus" (1 Thessalonians 2:14)—and the Churches of God in Judea kept the seventh-day Sabbath. Gentiles clearly understood that they were to keep the Sabbath. As late as the 5th century, the historian Socrates Scholasticus noted:

> For although almost all churches throughout the world celebrate the sacred mysteries on the sabbath of every week, yet the Christians of Alexandria and at Rome, on account of some ancient tradition, have ceased to do this. (Socrates Scholasticus. Ecclesiastical History, Book V, Chapter XXII. Excerpted from Nicene and Post-Nicene Fathers, Second Series, Volume 2. Edited by Philip Schaff and Henry Wace. American Edition, 1890.

So, professing Christians, except the main groups in Rome and Alexandria (Egypt), kept the Sabbath—and those two cities did not change from the Sabbath based on scripture. And, it should be noted that elsewhere in Italy (outside of Rome), Gentiles were still keeping the Sabbath.

Protestant historian K.S. Latourette wrote:

> for centuries even many Gentile Christians also observed the seventh day, or Sabbath (Latourette K.S. A History of Christianity, Volume 1, Beginnings to 1500. Harper Collins, San Francisco, 1975, p.198).

This included non-Jews in the British Isles, Africa, Asia Minor (including Polycarp), and Spain.

On the Protestant *Kerry Shook* telecast, Chris Shook (Kerry's wife) read the fourth commandment including the part that said that God made the *seventh-day* holy.

She also cited the following as an admonition to keep the Sabbath commandment:

> [1] So here's what I want you to do, God helping you: Take your everyday, ordinary life—your sleeping, eating, going-to-work, and walking-around life—and place it before God as an offering. [2] Embracing what God does for you is the best thing you can do for him. Don't become so well-adjusted to your culture that you fit into it without even thinking. Instead, fix your attention on God. You'll be changed from the inside out. Readily recognize what he wants from you, and quickly respond to it. Unlike the culture around you, always dragging you down to its level of immaturity, God brings the best out of you, develops well-formed maturity in you. (Romans 12:1-2, The Message)

Truly, people should change to keep the Sabbath and not let their culture or aspects of their routine keep them from turning to God.

Chris Shook also cited the following scripture:

> [10] Be still, and know that I am God! (Psalm 46:10a, NLT)

She said that in order to know God, you needed to keep the Sabbath command. She complained that people often make excuses instead of resting one of seven days. And although she and her husband rest on Monday (yes, that is not a typo), her basic scriptural points (which her husband endorsed) were valid—though she and her husband should go all the way and properly keep the Sabbath when God says to.

It takes faith in God to keep the Sabbath commandment in a society that does not support it. But those of us who truly trust God know He is faithful and "all things work together for good to those who love God" (Romans 8:28). Those who love Jesus keep the commandments (John 14:15), including the Sabbath one—Jesus said He was "Lord of the Sabbath" in Matthew 12:8, Mark 2:28, and Luke 6:5. God would not have had that recorded so often if He did not want Christians to **keep the seventh-day Sabbath**. God gave the Sabbath as a physical and spiritual blessing for humanity.

Sadly, many rationalize their lack of true belief and real faith in God with false arguments against keeping the Sabbath.

Although the Sabbath is a time of refreshing rest, many ignore that and consider it a burden. Notice the following prophecy that seems to apply to those who do not keep the Sabbath:

> [11] For with stammering lips and another tongue He will speak to this people, [12] To whom He said, "This is the rest with which You may cause the weary to rest," And, "This is the refreshing"; Yet they would not hear. (Isaiah 28:11-12)

That "refreshing rest" is what is commanded for the Sabbath (Exodus 20:11). Will you hear?

There was a popular song titled *Turn Me Loose* that hit the charts in 1980. Notice the following line from it:

> I gotta do it my way or no way at all

Many people are like that. Hopefully, that is not YOUR attitude. If you believe in the authority of the God of the Bible, you instead would say that you need to worship GOD'S WAY as "those who worship Him must worship in spirit and truth" (John 4:24).

The seventh-day Sabbath remains for the true people of God. The biblical Sabbath is kept from sunset on the day commonly called Friday through sunset on the day commonly called Saturday.

Now, notice the following:

> [13] "If you turn away your foot from the Sabbath,
> From doing your pleasure on My holy day,
> And call the Sabbath a delight,
> The holy day of the Lord honorable,
> And shall honor Him, not doing your own ways,
> Nor finding your own pleasure,
> Nor speaking your own words,
> [14] Then you shall delight yourself in the Lord;
> And I will cause you to ride on the high hills of the earth,
> And feed you with the heritage of Jacob your father.
> The mouth of the Lord has spoken." (Isaiah 58:13-14)

Notice that God calls the Sabbath *His* holy day, "the holy day of the Lord." The Bible teaches that the Sabbath is to be called a delight. Yet, many Protestants call it an *unnecessary burden*.

Christians are spiritually Israelites (cf. Romans 2:28-29; Revelation 3:7-9) and heirs to the promises (Galatians 3:9). So, notice that the promises to Israel (Jacob) can be ours if we properly keep God's Sabbath, His Holy Day.

Notice a report about John Calvin published in 1650:

> Mr. Calvin [in his Institutions, lib. 3: chap, 8. sect, 33.] saith, The old Fathers, not without choice of their owne, put in place of the Sabbath, the day we call Sunday, etc. And a little after exhorte thus, to follow the order, by the Church appointed; etc. (Ockford J. The Fourth Commandment Deformed by Popery Reformed and Restored to Its Primitive Purity. London, Printed by G. Dawson, 1650)

In other words, John Calvin admitted and accepted that Greco-Roman leaders, not Jesus or the Bible, choose to switch to Sunday. Later his followers and others attempted to absurdly claim that Sunday is the "eighth day" prophesied to be kept in Ezekiel 43:27 and that justified changing to Sunday (Erskine E, Fisher J. The Westminster Assembly's Shorter Catechism Explained. William S. Young publisher, 1840, p. 81).

Consider that God inspired the prophet Ezekiel to write:

> [26] Her priests have violated My law and profaned My holy things; they have not distinguished between the holy and unholy, nor have they made known the difference between the unclean and the clean; and they have hidden their eyes from My Sabbaths, so that I am profaned among them. (Ezekiel 22:26)

So, yes, religious leaders like many Protestant ministers do not distinguish between the clean and unclean and have hidden their eyes to the truth about the Sabbaths (which includes God's Holy Days, the annual Sabbaths). They are helping to fulfil Ezekiel's prophecy, and not the one in in Ezekiel 43:27.

While it also has millennial ramifications, in this current age, the Bible teaches that the Sabbath is to be a blessing:

> [1] Thus says the Lord:
> "Keep justice, and do righteousness,
> For My salvation is about to come,
> And My righteousness to be revealed.
> [2] Blessed is the man who does this,
> And the son of man who lays hold on it;
> Who keeps from defiling the Sabbath,
> And keeps his hand from doing any evil." (Isaiah 56:1-2)

The Bible teaches that ALL of God's "commandments are righteousness" (Psalm 119:172), and that obviously includes the Sabbath as Isaiah 56:1-2 points out.

The righteous keep the Sabbath.

But people like the apostate Marcion of Pontus did not. In his book *Against Marcion*, Tertullian wrote:

> **Marcion ... displayed a hatred** against the Jews' most solemn day, He was only professedly following the Creator, as being His Christ, in this very hatred **of the Sabbath** (Tertullian. Against Marcion, Book IV, Chapter 12).

Christianity was originally considered by Roman Imperial authorities to be a sect of the Jews. Antisemitism and fear of reprisal by Imperial authorities for looking like the Jews (especially because of their Bar Kochba revolt from 132-135 A.D.) led to various ones adopting Sunday (as well as adopting 'Easter Sunday').

Fourth Commandment Before Sinai, from Jesus, and After Jesus' Death

Some Protestant leaders have incorrectly claimed that the Sabbath commandment was not in place before the Ten Commandments were engraved in stone on Mount Sinai and/or that it was nullified by Jesus' teachings, death, and/or resurrection.

The Bible shows the fourth commandment was in place before Mt. Sinai:

> "And on the seventh day God ended His work which He had done, and He rested on the seventh day from all His work which He had done. Then God blessed the seventh day and sanctified it, because in it He rested from all His work which God had created and made" (Genesis 2:2-3).
>
> "Is there not a time of hard service for man on the earth" (Job 7:1).
>
> "the triumphing of the wicked is short...Because he knows no quietness in his heart" (Job 20:5,20).
>
> "Tomorrow is a Sabbath rest, a holy Sabbath to the LORD ... How long do you refuse to keep My commandments and My laws? See! For the Lord has given you the Sabbath ... So the people rested on the seventh day" (Exodus 16:23, 28-30; this was *before* the "giving" of the Ten Commandments in Exodus 20).
>
> "The Sabbath was made for man" (Mark 2:27).

Jesus taught and expanded the fourth commandment:

> "What man is there among you who has one sheep, and it falls into a pit on the Sabbath, will not lay hold of it and lift it out? Of how much more value then is a man than a sheep? Therefore, it is lawful to do good on the Sabbath" (Matthew 12:11-12).
>
> "And pray that your flight may not be in winter or on the Sabbath" (Matthew 24:20); there would be no reason to pray this if the Sabbath was not going to be in existence.
>
> "And He said to them, 'The Sabbath was made for man, and not man for the Sabbath. Therefore the Son of Man is also Lord of the Sabbath'" (Mark 2:27); this verse tells all who will see which day is the Lord's Day.
>
> "And when the Sabbath had come, He began to teach in the synagogue" (Mark 6:2).
>
> "And as His custom was, He went into the synagogue on the Sabbath day, and stood up to read" (Luke 4:16).
>
> "Then He went down to Capernaum, a city of Galilee, and was teaching them on the Sabbaths" (Luke 4:31).
>
> "The Son of Man is also Lord of the Sabbath … Is it lawful on the Sabbath to do good or to do evil, to save life or to destroy?" (Luke 6:5,9).
>
> "But the ruler of the synagogue answered with indignation, because Jesus had healed on the Sabbath …The Lord then answered him and said, 'Hypocrite … So ought not this woman … be loosed from this bond on the Sabbath?'" (Luke 13:14-16).
>
> "'Is it lawful to heal on the Sabbath?'… And they could not answer Him regarding these things" (Luke 14:3,6).
>
> "are you angry with Me because I made a man completely well on the Sabbath?" (John 7:23).

Jesus did not 'do away with the Sabbath'. Jesus eliminated extra 'traditions' that the Pharisees added to the Sabbath commandment. He emphasized that the Sabbath was for doing good.

Jesus never taught that the Sabbath was supposed to be on Sunday. The commandment was in place after He was killed (Luke 23:56).

After Jesus was resurrected, the New Testament continued to teach the fourth commandment:

> "Then Paul, as his custom was, went in to them and for three Sabbaths reasoned with them from the Scriptures…And he reasoned in the synagogue every Sabbath, and persuaded both Jews and Greeks" (Acts 17:2;18:4 see also Acts 13:14,27,42,44).

> "let him labor, working with his hands what is good, that he may have something to give to him who has need" (Ephesians 4:28) and "For even when we were with you, we commanded you this: 'If anyone will not work, neither shall he eat'" (2 Thessalonians 3:10); (recall that the requirement to work is also part of the Sabbath command, thus even that portion of the commandment is repeated in the New Testament.)

> "And to whom did He swear they would not enter His rest, but to those who did not obey?" (Hebrews 3:18). "For He has spoken in a certain place of the seventh day in this way: 'And God rested on the seventh day from all His works'" (Hebrews 4:4). "There remains therefore a rest (literally *sabbatismos*, 'Sabbath rest') for the people of God. For he who has entered His rest has himself also ceased from his works as God did from His" (Hebrews 4:9-10).

> "That day was the Preparation and the Sabbath drew near … And they rested on the Sabbath in accordance with the commandment" (Luke 23:54,56).

> "But when they departed from Perga, they came to Antioch in Pisidia, and went into the synagogue on the Sabbath day and sat down" (Acts 13:14)

The early Christians seemed to be following this admonition from John, "He who says he abides in Him ought also to walk just as He walked" (I John 2:6), since Jesus always went to the synagogues on the Sabbath (Luke 4:16).

The Bible clearly teaches that God blessed the seventh day, not that humans could pick any other day they choose out of the seven in a week.

Many deceive themselves into thinking that one day is the same as another. While that is often true for optional fasting days (Romans 14:5-6), consider the following in light of the Sabbath command:

> ² A wise man's heart is at his right hand, But a fool's heart at his left. (Ecclesiastes 10:2)

Consider that since humans need both halves of their heart, one side or the other would not seem better (both parts are needed) than the other. But God says there is a difference. He also specified the seventh-day as a day of rest. God did not say to pick any one day out of seven.

The 7th day is specifically referred to in Hebrews 4, which also warns "make every effort to enter THAT REST, so that no one will perish by following their example of disobedience" (Hebrews 4:11, NIV). According to the Protestant *Jamieson, Faucett, & Brown Bible Commentary*, the Greek term translated as 'make every effort' (σπουδάσωμεν), also means "strive diligently." The Greek term translated as "that" (ἐκείνος) is in the original biblical text (and can be considered as an intensifier), as is the definite article (τῆς) "the" (which the NIV translators left out). Therefore, the Greek points to Hebrews 4 specifically referring to THE 7th day, not A one in seven day, rest—and that Jesus' true followers will make all efforts to keep it.

Therefore, those who will obey the God of the Bible will not change God's day of rest based on their own authority or on false tradition (cf. Deuteronomy 12:8; Proverbs 12:15, 16:25). Only God, not man, can make a day holy. And He commands people to "keep" (not make) it holy by observing it (Deuteronomy 5:12).

Consider the following:

[16] Do you not know that to whom you present yourselves slaves to obey, you are that one's slaves whom you obey, whether of sin leading to death, or of obedience leading to righteousness? (Romans 6:16)

[15] And if it seems evil to you to serve the Lord, choose for yourselves this day whom you will serve, whether the gods which your fathers served that were on the other side of the River, or the gods of the Amorites, in whose land you dwell. But as for me and my house, we will serve the Lord. (Joshua 24:15)

Christians are to keep the Sabbath, not the day used by pagan sun worshippers (cf. 1 Corinthians 10:19-22). No one in the New Testament is shown teaching that Sunday was the replacement for Saturday.

Those willing to "live by … every word that proceeds from the mouth of God" (Matthew 4:4) keep the seventh-day Sabbath (more on the Sabbath can be found at https://cg7.org).

Early Church Leaders Kept the Seventh-Day Sabbath

Early faithful Christian leaders kept the Sabbath. Notice what the 4th century Greco-Roman historian Eusebius wrote:

> James, the first that had obtained the episcopal seat in Jerusalem after the ascension of our Saviour … until the siege of the Jews, which took place under Adrian, there were fifteen bishops in succession there, all of whom are said to have been of Hebrew descent, and to have received the knowledge of Christ in purity, … For their whole church consisted then of believing Hebrews who continued from the days of the apostles until the siege which took place at this time … the bishops of Jerusalem that lived between the age of the apostles and the time referred to, all of them belonging to the circumcision. (Eusebius. The History of the Church, Book III, Chapter V, Verses 2,3, & Book IV, Chapter 5, Verses 2-4, pp. 45, 71)

The 1st and early 2nd century Christian leaders in Jerusalem were all Jews who kept the seventh-day Sabbath. Since these early bishops/overseers "received the knowledge of Christ in purity," their teachings should have been continued. Instead, Protestant leaders tend to slyly teach that God wanted Gentiles, so He no longer wanted Sabbath observance.

Those Jerusalem bishops/pastors were keeping the Sabbath until the last one died (c. 134-135 A.D.) and Emperor Hadrian took over Jerusalem. These Jewish Christian leaders obviously did not believe that the Sabbath was done away or "nailed to the cross."

Because of the Jewish revolt, Emperor Hadrian outlawed many practices considered to be Jewish, including the Sabbath (as well as Passover on the 14th). The 20th century historian Salo W. Barron wrote:

> Hadrian . . . According to rabbinic sources, he prohibited public gatherings for instruction in Jewish law, forbade the proper observance of the Sabbath and holidays and outlawed many important rituals (Barron SW. Social and Religious History of the Jews, Volume 2: Christian Era: the First Five Centuries. Columbia University Press, 1952, p. 107).

In the early 2nd century, the Christians in Judea were forced to make a decision. They either could continue to keep the Sabbath and the rest of God's law and flee, or they could compromise and support a religious leader (Marcus) who would not keep the Sabbath, etc. Sadly, many who claimed Christ made the wrong choice.

However, it was not just people in Judea who kept the Sabbath in the 2nd century.

Christians in Asia Minor, like Polycarp, kept the Sabbath (Hartog P, ed. Polycarp's Epistle to the Philippians and the Martyrdom of Polycarp: Introduction, Text, and Commentary. University Press, 2013, pp. 6, 197; The Martyrdom of Polycarp. In: Holmes M. The Apostolic Fathers--Greek Text and English Translations, 3rd printing 2004, pp 222-249; Sozomen. THE ECCLESIASTICAL HISTORY OF SOZOMEN. Comprising a History of the Church, from a.d. 323 to a.d. 425. Book VII, Chapter XIX. T&T CLARK, EDINBURGH, circa 1846).

The Gentile Theophilus of Antioch taught the following about the Sabbath:

> And on the sixth day God finished His works which He made, and rested on the seventh day from all His works which He made. And God blessed the seventh day, and sanctified it; because in it He rested from all His works which God began to create ... Moreover, [they spoke] concerning the seventh day, which all men acknowledge; but the most know not that what among the Hebrews is called the 'Sabbath,' is translated into Greek the 'Seventh' (ebdomas), a name which is adopted by every nation, although they know not the reason of the appellation. (Theophilus of Antioch. To Autolycus, Book 2, Chapters XI, XII).

Theophilus observed the seventh-day Sabbath.

Although they have their own biases, even the Protestant writers Jeremy Taylor, Philip Schaff, and Johann Gieseler correctly understood that early Christians kept the seventh-day Sabbath:

> The primitive Christians did keep the Sabbath of the Jews . . . therefore the Christians, for a long time together, did keep their conventions upon the Sabbath, in which some portions of the law were read: and this continued till the time of the Laodicean council." *The Whole Works of Jeremy Taylor*, Vol. IX, p. 416 (R. Heber's Edition, Vol. XII, p. 416)

> The Jewish Christians, at least in Palestine, conformed as closely as possible to the venerable forms of the cultus of their fathers, which in truth were divinely ordained, and were an expressive type of the Christian worship. So far as we know, they scrupulously observed the Sabbath, the annual Jewish feasts, the hours of daily prayer, and the whole Mosaic ritual (Schaff, Philip, History of the Christian Church, Chapter 9. Oak Harbor, WA: Logos Research Systems, Inc. 1997).

> While the Jewish Christians of Palestine retained the entire Mosaic law, and consequently the Jewish festivals, **the Gentile Christians observed also the Sabbath and the passover** (1 Cor. v. 6-8), with reference to the last scenes of Jesus' life, but without Jewish superstition (Gal. iv. 10 ; Col. ii. 16) (Gieseler,

Johann Karl Ludwig. A text-book of church history, Volume I, Chapter II. New York: Harper & brothers. Date 1857-80)

In other words, it is known that the true early Christians did keep the Sabbath and God's biblical Holy Days. We in the *Continuing* Church of God continue to do so to this day. As far as Gentiles go, they were prophesied to keep the Sabbath (Isaiah 56:1-7).

Let it also be pointed out, mistranslations aside, early writings show that Ignatius of Antioch also kept the Sabbath (see https://www.cogwriter.com/ignatius.htm), as did other Church of God leaders like Polycarp of Smyrna and Theophilus of Antioch.

The faithful, according to Arabic sources in the second through basically fifth centuries A.D. concluded:

> Christ also observed the Jewish day of fast and not the fifty days fast ... Neither did he establish Sunday as a day of rest, or abolish for even an hour the observance of Saturday. (Pines S. The Jewish Christians of the Early Centuries of Christianity according to a New Source. Proceedings of the Israel Academy of Sciences and Humanities, Volume II, No.13; 1966. Jerusalem, pp. 7).

People in the British Isles, including Ireland, may be shocked to learn this, but the Sabbath was kept in the isles by many until an English woman married Malcom III king of the Scots, and later forced Sunday upon her husband's subjects. Protestant theologian James Moffat reported:

> It seems to have been customary in the Celtic churches of early times, in Ireland as well as Scotland, to keep Saturday, the Jewish Sabbath, as a day of rest from labor, and Sunday, commemorative of the Lord's resurrection, as one of rejoicing, with exercises of public worship. In that case they obeyed the fourth commandment literally upon the seventh day of the week ...
>
> **The queen insisted upon the single and strict observance of the Lord's Day.** People and clergy alike submitted, but without entirely giving up their reverence for Saturday, which

subsequently sank into a half-holy day preparatory for Sunday (Moffat, James Clement. The Church in Scotland: A History of Its Antecedents, it Conflicts, and Its Advocates, from the Earliest Recorded Times to the First Assembly of the Reformed Church. Published by Presbyterian Board of Education, 1882, p. 140).

The queen mentioned above was Margaret who died in 1093. Margaret (who was technically 'the Queen consort of Malcolm III') was canonized a Roman Catholic saint in the year 1250 by Pope Innocent IV.

Here is an old report from old English (where the letter 'f' was often used instead of the letter 's,' so it is changed below) from a Baptist historian in the 18th century:

> Some of the inhabitants of the Pyrenees, and of the adjacent states, and not those of the vallies of Piedmont, were the true original Waldenses, for to them and to them only do the descriptions in the books of the inquisitors agree. True it is, at the reformation a people appeared in the vallies of Piedmont, who gave good proof of their antiquity, and produced some writings, which indicated their connection with the Catalonians; as will be observed in its due place: but there is one demonstrative proof mentioned by Leger, that they were not the ancient Waldenses of ecclesiastical history. The Piedmontese were trinitarians, uniform in religious: But the old Waldenses had no notion of uniformity, and many of them were Manicheans and Arians. The Piedmontese did not understand liberty: the Pyreneans did. The Piedmontese were a handful: the Pyreneans were thousands and tens of thousands. The Piedmontese were a tame dejected people: the Pyreneans high spirited and ardent for universal freedom, as their ancestors had been. Here lay the snare; the reformers, as fond of the doctrine of succession as the catholicks, laboured with all their might to find out a succession of christians of the same faith and order as themselves. Such a people they found in the vallies of Savoy, and by dextrously applying to them whatever had been said of the inhabitants of other vallies they surmounted all obstacles except one. The catholicks objected that the old Waldenses held all forts of errours, and were as different from the reformers as from the church of Rome. The resformers

> extricated themselves from this difficulty by replying: that inquisitors, monks and historians were flanderers; and that all the Waldenses believed as they and the Piedmontese believed. The worst of this reply is, it is not true. ...
>
> Some of these christians were called Sabbati, Sabbatati, and Insabbatati, and more frequently Inzabbatati. Led astray by found without attending to facts, one says, they were so named from the hebrew word sabbath, because they kept the saturday for the Lord's day. Another says, they were so called because they rejected all the festivals, or sabbaths, in the low latin sense of the word, which the catholick church religiously observed. (Robinson R. Ecclesiastical Researches. Francis Hodson, publisher. 1792. Original from University of Chicago, Digitized Nov 19, 2015, pp. 299-300, pp. 303-304)

So, a Baptist historian realized that there were multiple types of Waldenses, those with true apostolic succession were not like the Protestants, most were not trinitarian, and many kept the seventh-day Sabbath. He also recognized that Protestants could not trace themselves through the original Waldensians. And today, Protestants still cannot trace their movement back to early faithful Christians.

Some have been critical of the position that some of the Waldenses kept the Sabbath. However, notice the following about a Roman Catholic Priest name Gretzer:

> Gretzer, a Jesuit, had examined the subject fully, and who had every opportunity of knowing, admits the great antiquity of the heretics, and moreover, expresses his firm belief that the Toulousians, Albigenses, Pasaginians, Arnoldists, Josephists, and the other heretical factions, who, at that time, were engaging the attention of the popes, were no other than Waldenses. This opinion he collaborates by showing wherein they resembled each other. Among other points he mentions is the following:
>
>> "Moreover, all these heretics despise the feasts and fasts of the church, such as Candlemas, Easter, and the Dominical day; in short, all approved ecclesiastical

> customs for which they did not find a warrant in scripture. They say, also, that God enjoined rest and holy meditation upon the seventh day, and that they cannot feel justified in the observance of any other" (Quoted from Davis, Tamar. A General History of the Sabbatarian Churches. 1851; Reprinted 1995 by Commonwealth Publishing, Salt Lake City, p. 65).

So, those Waldensians kept the Sabbath, but not Sunday or Easter.

Here is a report from the Lutheran historian Johann Moshein concerning a group in the 12th century and two of their tenets:

> the denomination of the Pasaginians ... The first was a notion, that the observance of the law of Moses, in everything except the offering of sacrifices, was obligatory upon Christians; in consequence of which they circumcised their followers, abstained from those meats, the use of which was prohibited under the Mosaic economy, and celebrated the Jewish sabbath. The second tenet that distinguished this sect was advanced in opposition to the doctrine of three persons in the divine nature. (Mosheim JL, Coote C, Gleig G. An Ecclesiastical History, Ancient and Modern: In which the Rise, Progress, and Variations of Church Power, are Considered in Their Connexion with the State of Learning and Philosophy, and the Political History of Europe During that Period, Volume 1. Translated by Archibald Maclaine. Plaskitt & Cugle, p. 333)

Again, we see Gentiles who kept the Sabbath, abstained from unclean meats, and were opposed to the trinitarian view. While not all the views that Mosheim had about the Pasaginians were Church of God views, apparently some called by that name were Church of God Christians. It should also be noted that Mosheim believed that there were two types of Waldnesians. One considered that the Church of Rome was a real Christian church, whereas the other considered the Church of Rome to be the harlot of Revelation 17 (Moshiem, p. 333).

Notice that in 1719 England, John Ozell, a non-Sabbath-keeping Protestant, wrote the following about some of the Sabbath keepers in that land:

> People, who ... go by the name Sabbatarian make Profession of expecting a Reign of a Thousand Years ... These Sabbatarians are so call'd, because they will not remove the Day of Rest from Saturday to Sunday ... They administer Baptism only to adult People ... The major part of them will not eat Pork, nor blood ... their outward conduct is pious and Christian-like (Ozell JM. Mission Observations in His Travels over England. 1719. As cited in Ball, p. 9).

Those John Ozell wrote about sounded like Church of God Christians.

Colossians 2:16-17 and Galatians 4:8-10

Many Protestants have been misled by what seems to be an intentional mistranslation of one of Paul's writings, Colossians 2:16-17, to do away with the Sabbath. Yet, when properly translated it endorses, and does not condemn nor do away with Sabbath observances.

Let's examine one slight mistranslation of it:

> [16] Let no man therefore judge you in meat, or in drink, or in respect of an holyday, or of the new moon, or of the sabbath days: [17] Which are a shadow of things to come; but the body *is* of Christ (Colossians 2:16-17, KJV).

The above translation is close to accurate, however, it added the word "is" (which is why the KJV translators put *is* in *italics*) which is not in the original Greek.

A truly literal translation would leave it out as it is not in there. Notice the *Strong's Concordance* numbers and related words for verse 17:

> 3739. 2076 4639... 3588... 3195....3588 1161 4983 9999 3588 5547
>
> Which are a shadow of things to come; the.... but.... body .... of... Christ.

It should be noted that 9999 means that there was no word in the biblical text—the word "is" is not in this scripture.

Because the same three *Strong's* words (#4983, 3588, & 5547) are used four other times in the New Testament and in those times the KJV translates them as 'body of Christ' (Romans 7:4; 1 Corinthians 10:16; 1 Corinthians 12:27; Ephesians 4:12)—as does the NKJV—so should have the KJV.

Therefore, if those translators were simply consistent with themselves, they would have translated Colossians 2:16-17 to state (and included parentheses or commas):

> [16] Therefore let no man judge YOU in eating and drinking or in respect of a festival or of an observance of the new moon or of a sabbath [17] (for those things are a shadow of the things to come), but the body of Christ.

Or in other words, do not let those outside the "body of Christ" (the true church, Colossians 1:18) judge you regarding Holy Days, but only the true church itself. Colossians 2:16-17 is not saying that the Sabbath and Holy Days are done away.

Even the 4th century Orthodox bishop Ambrose of Milan recognized that Colossians 2:17 was referring to the 'body of Christ' as he wrote the following commenting on that verse:

> Shall we esteem festival days by eating and drinking? But let no man judge us in respect of eating ... Let us, then, seek the body of Christ ... where the body of Christ is, there is the truth. (Ambrose of Milan. Book II. On the Belief in the Resurrection, section 108)

It is sad that modern translators of the Greek have often ignored what the expression really meant.

It is poor exegesis (biblical interpretation) to rely on a mistranslation to claim that the Sabbath and Holy Days are done away with.

Another common objection from Protestants to keeping the Sabbath and Holy Days is to misunderstand the context of Galatians 4:8-10.

Some Protestants tend to use this to say that no biblical dates are to be observed. But, let's look at what those scriptures actually teach:

> ⁸ But then, indeed, when you did not know God, you served those which by nature are not gods. ⁹ But now after you have known God, or rather are known by God, how is it that you turn again to the weak and beggarly elements, to which you desire again to be in bondage? ¹⁰ You observe days and months and seasons and years. (Galatians 4:8-10)

There are several problems with the anti-Holy Day argument here.

One is that the Galatians were Gentiles (although there were apparently some Jews addressed in later verses) and were NOT keeping the biblical Holy Days prior to conversion.

Plus, there is no way that the Bible would call biblical requirements as "beggarly elements." Paul was clearly warning against pagan observances as the Galatians had "served those which by nature were not gods."

Another is that Roman Catholics/Protestants/Eastern Orthodox should consider that they often do observe various non-biblical days and years (e.g. Sunday, Easter, Christmas, New Year's, Valentine's, Halloween), so they should not observe anything if they feel that no religious days are to be observed.

Galatians 4:8-10 is not doing away with the Sabbath or biblical Holy Days, but instead is a warning against clinging to non-biblical observances.

Protestants should consider that the true church was supposed to continue (Matthew 16:18; Jude 3) and that early Christians understood *koine* Greek better than modern Protestant scholars do.

Early Christians did keep the seventh-day Sabbath as well as the biblical Holy Days.

God made the Sabbath day holy when He rested on it (Genesis 2:1-2), faithful Christians kept it from the time of Jesus, and Christians who actually believe the Bible still keep it (Hebrews 4:9).

Church Services

What about the liturgy, if you will, of church services?

Here is a definition of *liturgy* from the *Cambridge Dictionary*:

> (a particular set of) the words, music, and actions used in ceremonies in some religions, especially Christianity

As far as the original liturgy of the Christian church goes, understand that Saturday was considered as the Christian day of rest (no carnal employment) and that is when faithful early Christians attended church services.

Most Protestant denominations hold regular church services on Sunday.

Early Church services were led by men. Men were the only ones that gave the sermon-type messages during church services, consistent with the practices and writings of the Apostle Paul (Acts 13:13-24, 17:1-3; 1 Timothy 2:12). This differs from the Gnostics, which have been condemned as heretical by pretty much all Protestant scholars, as they allowed women to preach and function as ministers.

Consistent with scripture (Romans 16:1, ISV), the CCOG has deaconesses who assist in various functions. Yet, unlike some Protestants, we do not have female ministers, preachers, or pastors/bishops as only males are authorized for those roles in the Bible (cf. 1 Timothy 3:1-2; Titus 1:5-6). Females are specifically prohibited from being preachers in church services in the New Testament (1 Corinthians 14:34-35; 1 Timothy 2:11-12).

We do, however, also accept that God can give dreams to women (cf. Numbers 12:6; Acts 2:17-18) as well as to have them sometimes in a prophetic role (cf. Judges 4:4-16, Luke 2:36). Christian women also have other roles, as well as serve God in many ways, including prayer and fasting (cf. Luke 2:37), financially (cf. Luke 8:3) and otherwise supporting the work (Romans 16:3), teaching younger women (Titus 2:3-5), letting their lights shine (Matthew 4:14-16), studying the word of God (cf. Acts 17:10-13), being able to answer doctrinal questions (1 Peter 3:15-16), teaching (Acts 18:24-26; 2 Timothy 3:14-15; cf. Deuteronomy 6:6-7), growing in grace and knowledge (2 Peter 3:18), etc.

As far as early church services, themselves, they were informational (1 Thessalonians 5:27; 1 Timothy 4:13) as opposed to sacramental or entertainment focused.

The Apostle Paul wrote the following:

> [13] Till I come, give attention to reading, to exhortation, to doctrine. (1 Timothy 4:13)
>
> [27] I charge you by the Lord that this epistle be read to all the holy brethren. (1 Thessalonians 5:27)
>
> [16] Now when this epistle is read among you, see that it is read also in the church of the Laodiceans, and that you likewise read the epistle from Laodicea. (Colossians 4:16)

This is basically showing that having scriptures read and explained was to be a major part of church services.

The Apostle Paul also wrote:

> [13] Hold fast the pattern of sound words which you have heard from me, in faith and love which are in Christ Jesus. (2 Timothy 1:13)

That would seem to be including the idea to hold fast to the basic pattern of church services.

Protestant writer Mike Gendron warned against the following:

> Have you noticed how many church attenders are choosing to follow their favorite Christian celebrities rather than the Word of God? Too often these celebrity pastors tell them what they want to hear, instead of what is true. The apostle Paul described it this way: "For the time will come when they will not endure sound doctrine; but wanting to have their ears tickled, they will accumulate for themselves teachers in accordance to their own

desires" (2 Tim. 4:3). ... We must warn those who follow such popular celebrities. The apostle Paul said, "Now I urge you, brethren, keep your eye on those who cause dissensions and hindrances contrary to the teaching which you learned, and turn away from them. For such men are slaves, not of our Lord Christ but of their own appetites; and by their smooth and flattering speech they deceive the hearts of the unsuspecting" (Rom. 16:17-18). (Gendron M. Proclaiming the Gospel newsletter, January 1, 2020)

Yes, people are often more interested in smooth talking entertainment and hearing what they want to hear, instead of what they should hear. For many, church is often a social club that they attend because of emotion. Certain Protestant churches, such as Hillsong for example, place their focus on entertainment as well as push ecumenism.

Hopefully, you realize that scriptures and facts are more important than ministers who appear good (2 Corinthians 11:12-15) or follow the partying will of the Gentiles (cf. 1 Peter 4:3-5). Jesus said to not let social pressures, including family ones (Matthew 10:34-39), prevent you from properly following Him.

Modern Protestant church services are normally not done like early church services were, though sometimes there are some similarities.

While there was a certain leeway in ancient practices, some modern Protestant services are primarily-music focused, without much in the way of expounding scriptures. Others are more focused on ritual, that early Christians did not focus on. Furthermore, early churches were not like many modern Pentecostal services where one or more is trying to call down the Holy Spirit to be filled with it.

The 'liturgy' of early church services tended to consist of one or more prayers (cf. Ephesians 5:20), the singing of hymns (1 Corinthians 14:26; Colossians 3:16), and apparently one or more short scripture readings (or other messages) and a longer sermon (Ehrman B. From Jesus to Constantine: A History of Early Christianity, Part 2. The Teaching Company, Chantilly (VA), 2004, p. 35; Troutman TA. Christian Worship in the First Century. June 17, 2010. © 2017 Called to Communion). They focused on a biblically-sound message. This is consistent with the present practice of the CCOG, but not many Protestant services.

CCOG services normally begin with singing of hymns, followed by an opening prayer, followed by a short message (called a sermonette), followed by the singing of one hymn, often followed by announcements, then followed by a longer sermon, followed by the singing of one hymn, and concluded with prayer. The practice of expounding of scripture is consistent with information related to Polycarp (Life of Polycarp, Chapter 24. (1889) from J. B. Lightfoot, The Apostolic Fathers, vol. 3.2, pp. 488-506) and that, plus dual messages, with services involving Melito (Melito. Homily on the Passover).

Early Christians mainly sung biblical psalms (1 Corinthians 14:26; Colossians 3:16; Ephesians 5:19), translated into the language of the attendees (Latourette K.S. A History of Christianity, Volume 1: Beginnings to 1500. Harper Collins, San Francisco, 1975, pp. 206-207).

This is somewhat similar to *The Bible Hymnal* used by the CCOG which is predominantly (over 80%) translated biblical Psalms set to music. There are also some other spiritual songs, which often are other biblical passages. Protestant music tends to be less directly scriptural, and much of the Protestant message is not what early Christians taught as this book is helping to point out.

Why Do Protestants Keep Sunday?

Since the Bible enjoins the seventh-day Sabbath for services, where did most Protestants get Sunday?

Despite Martin Luther's rallying cry of *sola Scriptura*, they did not get it from the Bible itself. They accepted traditions/pronouncements of the Church of Rome.

Notice that the Lutherans, in 1530, admitted that the Greco-Roman bishops changed the Sabbath command:

> 30] It is also debated whether bishops or pastors have the right to introduce ceremonies in the church and to make laws about eating meat, celebrating holy days, about the various levels or

types of ministry, and so on. 31] Those who say that bishops have this right, refer to this passage, "I have much more to say to you, more than you can now bear. But ... the Spirit of truth ... will guide you into all truth" (John 16:12,13).

32] They also refer to the example of the apostles, who commanded Christians not to eat blood and animals that had been strangled (Acts 15:29). 33] They say that the Sabbath Day was changed into the Lord's Day, although this seems to be contrary to the Ten Commandments. There is no example they make so much of as this changing of the Sabbath Day. The power of the church is very great, they say, since it has done away with one of the Ten Commandments! (The Augsburg Confession of 1530. Article 28, subsections 30-33)

Despite the above, the Lutherans accepted 'the Lord's Day' instead of the Sabbath. Therefore, they are guilty of doing away with the same commandment that they complained the Greco-Roman bishops did! And the bulk of Protestantism has gone along with this.

Notice also the following Protestant admissions:

Dr. Edward T. Hiscox, author of "The BAPTIST MANUAL," ... went on to say: "Earnestly desiring information on this subject, which I have studied for many years, I ask, Where can the record of such a transaction (from seventh day to the first day) be found? NOT IN THE NEW TESTAMENT, ABSOLUTELY NOT. THERE IS NO SCRIPTURAL EVIDENCE OF THE CHANGE OF THE SABBATH INSTITUTION FROM THE SEVENTH TO THE FIRST DAY OF THE WEEK."

What an admission!

Now a quotation from the LUTHERAN CHURCH. "THE OBSERVANCE of the Lord's day (meaning Sunday) IS FOUNDED NOT ON ANY COMMAND OF GOD, but on the authority of the church," states the "Augsburg Confession," part 2, chapter 1, sec. 10. Also we discover the following statement in Article 28 of the "Augsburg Confession": "They [Catholics] allege the Sabbath changed into Sunday, the Lord's day, contrary to the Decalogue, as it appears; NEITHER IS THERE ANY EXAMPLE MORE BOASTED OF THAN THE CHANGING OF THE SABBATH DAY. GREAT, SAY

THEY, IS THE POWER AND THE AUTHORITY OF THE [Catholic] CHURCH SINCE IT DISPENSED WITH ONE OF THE TEN COMMANDMENTS."

Next, let us hear from a PRESBYTERIAN source, "The Christian at Work," April 19, 1883, and January, 1884. "SOME HAVE TRIED TO BUILD THE OBSERVANCE OF SUNDAY UPON APOSTOLIC COMMAND, WHERE AS THE APOSTLES GAVE NO COMMAND ON THE MATTER AT ALL... The truth is, as soon as we appeal to the LITERAL WRITING OF THE BIBLE, THE SABBATARIANS [Sabbath keepers] HAVE THE BEST OF THE ARGUMENT. (McNair R. The TRUTH About Sunday Observance. Good News, February 1961)

The Archbishop of Reggio (Gaspar [Ricciulli] de Fosso) said the following at the last opening session of Trent, (17th Session) reconvened under Pope Pius IV) on the 18th of January, 1562:

> The Protestants claim to stand upon the written word only. They profess to hold the Scripture alone as the standard of faith. They justify their revolt by the plea that the Church has apostatized from the written word and follows tradition. Now the Protestants claim, that they stand upon the written word only, is not true. Their profession of holding the Scripture alone as the standard of faith, is false. PROOF: The written word explicitly enjoins the observance of the seventh day as the Sabbath. They do not observe the seventh day, but reject it. If they do truly hold the scripture alone as their standard, they would be observing the seventh day as is enjoined in the Scripture throughout. Yet they not only reject the observance of the Sabbath enjoined in the written word, but they have adopted and do practice the observance of Sunday, for which they have only the tradition of the Church. Consequently the claim of 'Scripture alone as the standard', *fails;* and the doctrine of 'Scripture *and tradition'* as essential, is fully established, the Protestants themselves being judges. (as cited in Fifield GE. The Sabbath, the Fathers, and the Reformation. Signs of the Times, Vol. 25, No. 47, Nov. 22, 1899, pgs. 6-7)

The adoption of Sunday was proof to the Church of Rome that the Protestant Reformers really did not believe in *sola Scriptura*.

Let it be understood that although many Protestants claim that the New Testament did away with the Sabbath and/or replaced it with Sunday, this is simply not true. Interestingly, a Roman Catholic publication called *The Catholic Mirror* went through pretty much all the usual Protestant scriptural arguments against Saturday in the late 19th century and correctly concluded that the New Testament was not the reason Protestants do not keep the seventh-day Sabbath.

Furthermore, Martin Luther himself seemed to believe that the Sabbath command had to do with learning about God's word, as opposed to rest, as he wrote about it:

> What does this mean? We should fear and love God so that we do not despise preaching and His Word, but hold it sacred and gladly hear and learn it (Luther's Small Catechism with Explanation. Concordia Publishing House, St. Louis, 1986, p. 10).

> "We sin against the Third Commandment when we despise preaching and the Word of God ... What does God require of us in the Third Commandment? A. We should hold preaching and the Word of God sacred" (Ibid, p. 68).

The Lutheran Confessions admit:

> As we study Luther's expositions of the Decalog, or the Ten Commandments, we find that he does not quote the Third Commandment in its Old Testament form: "Remember the Sabbath Day to keep it holy", but rather in the spirit of the New Testament: 'Thou shalt sanctify the holy day' (Mueller, John Theodore. The Lutheran Confessions. Circa 1953, p.10).

In another place, Martin Luther wrote:

> Now follows the Third Commandment: "Thou shalt hallow the day of rest". (Luther, M. A treatise on Good Works together with the Letter of Dedication, published 1520. In Works of Martin Luther. Adolph Spaeth, L.D. Reed, Henry Eyster Jacobs, et Al., Trans. & Eds. Philadelphia: A. J. Holman Company, 1915, Vol. 1, pp. 173-285).

It should be noted that Lutherans (and Roman Catholics) consider the Sabbath to be the Third, not Fourth, Commandment. The order that Martin Luther chose to accept was an order changed by Augustine and is not the order from the Bible or that as understood by the early Church (please see the free book, online at ccog.org, titled *The Ten Commandments: The Decalogue, Christianity, and the Beast*).

Sadly, Martin Luther often accepted Roman Catholic changes instead of believing what the Bible actually taught. In addition, he also came up with other teachings that neither the Bible nor the Roman Church supported.

Few realize that Martin Luther's other compromise with the Sabbath—like deciding it was Sunday—was a significant factor for many in the Church of Rome to denounce his movement. This proved to them that Martin Luther DID NOT BELIEVE IN SOLA SCRIPTURA.

Because of not having the proper reverence for the Bible, doctrinal and other errors have been part of the Protestant message. And that is more than what day of the week people rest on.

10. Seventh Day Baptists, Adventists, and Messianic Jews

Now, not all Protestants keep Sunday. There are several Protestant groups that believe they are to keep the seventh-day Sabbath, such as the Seventh-Day Baptists, Seventh-day Adventists, and Messianic Jews.

These groups tend to consider themselves to be Protestant and share various Protestant viewpoints on salvation, the Godhead, and numerous other points.

The largest such group is the Seventh-day Adventists. The oldest of such groups, however, seems to be the Seventh-Day Baptists.

Seventh-Day Baptists

The Seventh Day Baptists (SDBs) go to church on Saturday. But basically they hold Protestant doctrines, and primarily consider themselves as Baptists.

Although they claim a long history, in their claims they include early Sabbath keepers who do not hold their present doctrines like 4th century Semi-Arians in Armenia and 6th century Holy Day keepers in the British Isles (Davis T. A General History of the Sabbatarian Churches. 1851; Reprinted 1995 by Commonwealth Publishing, Salt Lake City, pp. 20, 108). In this respect, they are like the Greco-Roman Catholics who claim as their own, their predecessors as well as COG leaders who opposed their beliefs.

The SDBs are actually trinitarian (Stillman W. Miscellaneous Compositions in Poetry and Prose. F.H. Bacon, New-London 1852; pp. 3-4) and do not keep the biblical Holy Days. They also include in their claimed history earlier groups who accepted "church eras" (Davis, p. 31), the Anabaptists who taught apocatastasis (Batiffel, Pierre. Transcribed by Elizabeth T. Knuth. Apocatastasis. The Catholic Encyclopedia, Volume I. Published 1907), kept Passover and the Days of Unleavened Bread (Falconer, pp. 57-58. As cited in Ball, B. Seventh Day Men: Sabbatarians and Sabbatarianism in England and Wales, 1600-1800, 2nd edition. James Clark & Co., 2009, pp. 49-51), did not eat pork

(Ozell J. M. Mission Observations in His Travels over England. 1719. As cited in Ball, p. 9)—yet Seventh Day Baptists do eat pork, as well as many who called themselves "Church of God" and not Seventh Day Baptists (Duggar, pp. 275-277).

The late COG historian Richard Nickels made several points about the SDBs and history:

> Seventh Day Baptists cannot validly claim exclusive "ownership" of the history of Sabbatarians. **SDB's today do not agree doctrinally with their Sabbatarian ancestors!** Actually, today's faithful Church of God brethren are doctrinally *closer* to early English and American Sabbath-keepers than are today's liberal SDB's. Early American Sabbatarians rejected Trinity and immortal soul teaching, eschewed Christmas and Easter, promoted their faith much more than SDB's do today, and traced their spiritual ancestry directly to English Lollards, Waldensians, and the first century Church … The oldest existing Seventh Day Baptist Church, the Mill Yard Church in London, England, began during the mid 1600's. The Mill Yard Church has apparently *always* kept the "Lord's Supper" on the fourteenth day of the first Hebrew month, but almost no American SDB churches have followed this practice. Today, SDB's accept Christmas, the Trinity, and immortal soul teaching. (Nickels R. Six Papers on the History of the Church of God. Sharing & Giving, Neck City (MO), 1993, p. 83).

In the area of England in the 1600s, there were two basic groups of baptism by immersion Sabbath keepers, which some have identified as General and Particular (Ball, pp. 102-103; Brackney WH. The Baptists. ABC-CLIO, 1994, pp. 6-7). Those called General believed Jesus died for all, the doctrine of the laying on of hands, avoiding pork, keeping Passover on the 14th, footwashing, millenarianism, anointing the sick, "Jewish ceremonies" (possibly a reference to biblical Holy Days or Passover), and a soon coming kingdom of God (Ball, p. 9-10,15,49,59,102; see also Brackney, p. 7). The group called Particular Baptists were Calvinists (Brackney, p. 6) who believed Jesus only died for the elect (Ball, p. 102)—this group, in time, became more ecumenically Protestant and more like first day Baptists. Note the faithful used the term "Church of God" then (Philotheos, pp. 26-27), not "Baptist."

By the late 1700s, those now called Seventh Day Baptists adopted even more Protestant positions and also started calling themselves Sabbatarian Baptists. They began to use the title Reverend for their ministers (Randolph CF. A History of the Seventh Day Baptists in West Virginia, 1905. Reprint 2005. Heritage Books, Westminster (MD), p. 28), insist on the immortality of the soul (Dugger AN, Dodd CO. A History of True Religion, 3rd ed. Jerusalem, 1972. Church of God, 7th Day. 1990 reprint, p. 277; Randolf, p. 87), put steeples on their church buildings (Randolf pages 74a, 100a, 160a, 208a, 214a, 238a, and 242a shows pictures of church buildings without steeples, but shows steeples on pages 104a, 106a, 246a, and 344a), and became separate from Church of God brethren that they claim to have been their ancestors (Stillman, pp. 3-4; Randolf, p. 87).

In 1811, a SDB writer declared that the idea "that the Father, Son, and Holy Ghost, are three absolute distinct persons, coequal, coessential, and coeternal Gods" ... flew "in the face of scripture" and was "repugnant to right reason." (Clarke H. A History of the Sabbatarians Or Seventh Day Baptists, in America; Containing Their Rise and Progress to the Year 1811, with Their Leaders' Names, and Their Distinguishing Tenets, etc. Utica, 181, pp. 61-62). But in 1833, the SDBs made a trinitarian declaration in a document titled *Expose of Sentiments*. By the early 1800s, many SDBs considered Protestants to be true Christian brothers (Randolph, pp. 138-140).

Though the SDBs and Seventh-day Adventists claimed to represent nearly all of the Sabbath keepers in the U.S.A. in the 19th century, that was not the case. Notice something written by H.E. Carver (who was then a leader in Church of God, Adventist) to the SDBs that was published in the February 8, 1872, Seventh Day Baptist *Sabbath Recorder*:

> There are hundreds, perhaps thousands, of Sabbath-keepers scattered over the land, from the Atlantic coast to the shores of the Pacific, who do not belong either to your church organization, or that of the Seventh-day Adventists. (As cited in Briggs, Lawson. What Became of the Church Jesus Built? Thesis

for Ambassador College, April 1972, pp. 265,267)

Although some leaders had some contact with the groups called the Seventh Day Baptists and the Seventh-day Adventists (SDAs), those organizations were never COG.

What about the modern SDBs?

Currently, SDBs are clearly Protestants, with their main difference that they normally go to church on Saturday.

The SDBs use crosses as their current logo below shows:

SEVENTH DAY BAPTIST

Here is a 21st century report about the SDBs:

> Are Christians wrong to worship on Sunday when the biblical Sabbath is Saturday? Rob Appel, executive director of the Seventh Day Baptist General Conference answers with a question of his own: "What day did Christ go to church? Saturday. OK, let's be Christ like."
>
> ... Saturday worship is not a definitive marker over which the church is willing to fight.
>
> "It's not a big thing," said Appel ... "We are Baptist," Appel said. "We just have a different day of worship" ...
>
> Early members were persecuted because of their Sabbath worship, which prompted "a tendency to keep to ourselves."
>
> "That mentality permeated from generation to generation," he said. "We don't feel that anymore ..."...
>
> Seventh Day Baptists leave women's ordination up to the local church. The Conference has issued no statement on ordination, although it has accredited some female pastors ...

The Sabbath theology takes second place, or third ...

"We're Baptists first," Kersten said. "When I send kids off to college, I encourage them to keep the Sabbath and find a good Sunday Baptist Church." He said there are "so many theological problems" in other Sabbatarian groups that "Baptist" is more important than Saturday worship. (Jameson N. 'Baptist' comes first for Seventh Day Baptists. Associated Baptist Press, June 29, 2011. This article was commissioned by the North American Baptist Fellowship)

There is no historical evidence that early SDBs ordained any women, and there is evidence that they would take stronger stands on the Sabbath than they now do.

The "theological problems" that the SDBs have with groups like the *Continuing* Church of God seem to include the fact that we have retained historical Christian beliefs on matters such as the Godhead as well as other doctrines they do not hold.

Seventh-day Adventists

Although they go to church on Saturday and do not eat biblically unclean meats, the Seventh-day Adventists are not close to the *Continuing* Church of God in many ways.

The biggest differences include the fact that the SDAs do NOT properly understand the plan of God and have been greatly influenced by a false prophetess named Ellen G. White. Here is a summary of 28 differences:

Seventh-day Adventist logo

1. The SDAs accept Ellen White as God's prophetess. CCOG does not. We see her as false on many points. Hence, CCOG sees no need to heed her pronouncements from a biblical perspective as some are in conflict with scripture and reality.
2. Like the Jehovah's Witnesses, Ellen White taught that the angel Michael became Jesus, "Christ is called the Word of God. John

1:1-3. He is so called because God gave His revelations to man in all ages through Christ. It was His Spirit that inspired the prophets. 1 Peter 1:10, 11. He was revealed to them as the Angel of Jehovah, the Captain of the Lord's host, Michael the Archangel." (White EG. The Great Controversy Between Christ and Satan as Illustrated in the Lives of Patriarchs and Prophets. 1890, page 760). CCOG strongly disagrees and considers this a doctrine of Antichrist (cf. 1 John 4:3).
3. Ellen White falsely taught that the Day of Atonement was October 22 in 1844, whereas in 1844, the Day of Atonement began at sunset September 22 and ran through sunset September 23rd.
4. SDAs believe 1844 has a significance that CCOG says the Bible does not support.
5. The SDAs were originally binitarian (Semi-Arian), but they changed to accept the Greco-Roman trinity. CCOG does not accept that trinitarian change.
6. The SDAs teach a Sunday morning resurrection, whereas the CCOG teaches Jesus was resurrected on a Saturday afternoon.
7. The SDAs originally opposed, then accepted, pagan holidays like Christmas (and now often also uses Christmas trees) and Easter (What Christ's resurrection means to you. Aventist.org July 3, 2013). CCOG does not (see the free online book: *Should You Keep God's Holy Days or Demonic Holidays?*).
8. Though perhaps not officially, most SDAs seem to accept that it is fine to observe such Roman Catholic holidays such as St. Patrick's Day, Valentine's Day, and Halloween. The CCOG does not.
9. The SDAs consider themselves Protestant and the Protestants as Christians. CCOG does not accept insufficiently repented Protestants as true Christians.
10. SDAs do not keep God's Holy Days. CCOG does (see the free online book: *Should You Keep God's Holy Days or Demonic Holidays?*).
11. CCOG keeps Passover annually in accordance with the scriptures, whereas the SDAs keep some version of it quarterly, which is not biblical.
12. SDAs do not fully understand God's plan of salvation. CCOG understands that God will offer salvation to all that ever lived (see the free online book: *Universal OFFER of Salvation,*

Apokatastasis: Can God save the lost in an age to come? Hundreds of scriptures reveal God's plan of salvation).
13. Ellen White and other SDAs put forth the view that the United States of America is the two-horned beast of Revelation 13:11. We in the CCOG teach Revelation 13:11 is a reference to the "false prophet" (Revelation 16:13,19:20) and final "Antichrist" (1 John 4:1-3).
14. SDAs believe swearing oaths is fine (White EG. Thoughts from the Mount of Blessing), the CCOG does not.
15. SDAs do not clearly teach that 666 is the European Beast of the Sea, but CCOG does.
16. SDAs do not believe that saints will be on the Earth during the millennium, CCOG does (cf. Revelation 5:10; 20:4-6).
17. SDAs use crosses as part of the symbols for their religion, whereas CCOG does not.
18. The CCOG teaches an "age to come" (Matthew 12:32; Mark 10:30; Luke 18:30; Hebrews 6:5), whereas because of a vision from Ellen White, the SDAs do not teach that.
19. SDAs call the truth that Jesus was killed on a Wednesday "unscriptural" (Standish RR, Standish C. The General Conference Confronts Apostasy. Hartland Publications, 2006, p. 84), whereas the CCOG accepts that Jesus died then.
20. CCOG teaches the good news of the Kingdom of God and we do not believe the SDA church understands the full gospel or that it teaches it (see also the free online book: *The Gospel of the Kingdom of God*).
21. CCOG's priorities are essentially Matthew 24:14 and 28:19-20, while the SDAs do not consider those the same way as CCOG.
22. CCOG traces its history from Acts 2 to present—and were never Millerites. The SDA church traces itself from the Protestant and Millerite Advent movements (see also the free online book: *Continuing History of the Church of God*).
23. SDAs improperly teach that the Church of God came out of their church. The CCOG teaches that the early SDAs has some exposure to COG doctrines, but ended up rejecting many to follow Ellen White. The COG preceded the formation of the SDA movement by over 18 centuries (see also the free online book: *Continuing History of the Church of God*).
24. The SDAs remnant teaching about itself is mistaken as the 'remnant' taught about in Revelation 12:17 are non-

Philadelphian Christians who are not protected in a place in the wilderness during the Great Tribulation and Day of the Lord.

25. SDAs don't teach that God is calling some now, with all others to be called later, but CCOG does (see also, the free online book: *Is God Calling You?*).
26. The CCOG teaches more fully the meaning of life than the SDAs (see also the free online book: *The MYSTERY of GOD's PLAN Why Did God Create Anything? Why Did God Make You?*).
27. CCOG seems to more clearly teach deification than the SDAs (see also the free online book: *Universal OFFER of Salvation, Apokatastasis: Can God save the lost in an age to come? Hundreds of scriptures reveal God's plan of salvation*).
28. The CCOG teaches more fully how to live as a Christian than the SDAs (see also the free online book: *Christians: Ambassadors for the Kingdom of God, Biblical instructions on living as a Christian*).

Notice the following by SDA scholar Gerhard Pfandl:

> A number of Adventist authors today who are opposed to the doctrine of the Trinity are trying to resurrect the views of our early pioneers on these issues. They are urging the church to forsake the "Roman doctrine" of the Trinity and to accept again the semi-Arian position of our pioneers ... **J. N. Loughborough**, in response to the question "**What serious objection is there to the doctrine of the Trinity?**" wrote, "There are many objections which we might urge, but on account of our limited space we shall reduce them to the three following: 1. It is contrary to common sense. 2. **It is contrary to scripture**. 3. **Its origin is Pagan** and fabulous." (Pfandl G. The Doctrine of the Trinity Among Seventh-day Adventists. Journal of the Adventist Theological Society, 17/1, Spring 2006: 160–179)

Thus, a founder of the SDAs claimed that the trinity was pagan, but that group has now adopted it.

Notice what James White (the husband of Ellen White) wrote:

> The Father is the greatest ... The Son is next in authority ... The inexplicable Trinity that makes the godhead three in one and

> one in three, is bad enough ... (Quoted in Wiebe E. Who Is the Adventist Jesus? Published by Xulon Press, 2005, p. 167).
>
> ... the Trinity does away with the personality of God ... (ibid, p. 88).
>
> The greatest fault we can find in the Reformers is, the Reformers stopped reforming. Had they gone on, and onward, till they had left the last vestige of the Papacy behind such as the natural immortality, sprinkling, *the trinity*, and Sundaykeeping, the church would now be free her unscriptural errors (Ibid, p. 89).

Yes, the Protestant Reformers should have reformed more, and much more than what James White listed. It is interesting that he considered the trinity to be in the same category as Sunday-keeping. Do SDAs realize this?

Another non-biblical change that the SDAs seem to be moving towards in more recent times is the ordination of women as ministers. There are other non-biblical doctrines that have been adopted or are under at least some considerations.

Ellen White, herself, had been a Methodist. And while she seemed to renounce some of their doctrines, she ended up accepting many of them.

She ended up believing in the Millerite movement:

> In the 1830s, a farmer, military veteran and devout Baptist named William Miller continued the fervor of the spiritual "awakening" ... He eventually concluded Christ's Second Coming would be ... October 22, 1844.
>
> Obviously, however, the literal Second Coming of Christ did not happen by October 22, 1844. (Official Seventh-day Adventist Church website. https://www.adventist.org/church/what-do-seventh-day-adventists-believe/history-of-seventh-day-adventists/ accessed 12/30/19)

Instead of accepting that this movement was a failure, Ellen White claimed to have a vision where she said that God had a special meaning for that date and that it was the biblical Day of Atonement (which it was not). We in the CCOG reject the Millerite movement, and despite statements from uninformed critics, we do not trace our history through it as those truly in the COG were not caught up in it.

Now, in addition to tracing themselves through the Millerite movement, the SDAs trace their history through Protestants and hold many Protestant doctrines:

> We consider our movement to be the result of the Protestant conviction Sola Scriptura … (Official Seventh-day Adventist Church website. https://www.adventist.org/en/beliefs/ accessed 12/29/19)

> Before becoming Seventh-day Adventists, the founders of the denomination were sitting in the pews of other protestant churches in the early-to-mid 1800s. … Several separate groups of these devout Christians were dispersed … and what began as the "Advent Movement" is now a worldwide Christian protestant denomination (Official Seventh-day Adventist Church website. https://www.adventist.org/church/what-do-seventh-day-adventists-believe/history-of-seventh-day-adventists/ accessed 12/29/19)

> G. Alexander Bryant, the executive secretary for Seventh-day Adventists of North America … The current Seventh-day Adventist Church considers itself to be Protestant. "If you know our faith, you can't say we don't have the same beliefs as other Protestants," Bryant says. (Taylor J. All Your Questions About Seventh-Day Adventism And Ben Carson Answered. NPR, October 27, 2015)

Regarding history, perhaps this would be a good place to include a quote from Jacob Brinkerhoff who was editor of the *Bible Advocate*, a Church of God publication, in its November 23, 1909 issue:

> Some people have a mistaken idea of the members of the Church of God, or most of them, having previously being connected to the Seventh-day Adventists, when the fact is that **not many of them ever were**. (As cited in Briggs, Lawson. What Became of the Church Jesus Built? Thesis for Ambassador College, April 1972, p. 273)

COG evangelist Dean Blackwell wrote:

> Adventists ... the true church ... they never were as we found from their own writings now in searching. They never were. Just like the Seventh Day Baptists never were the true church. (Blackwell D. A HANDBOOK OF CHURCH HISTORY. A Thesis Presented to the Faculty of the Ambassador College Graduate School of Theology, April 1973, p. 210)

The COG was not an offshoot of the SDAs as the SDAs tend to teach. We trace our history and doctrines from Acts 2 to present, whereas the SDAs tend to trace most of theirs from the 1800s, and before then, the Protestant Reformation.

But beyond Protestant and historical errors, there are many issues because of Ellen White.

Ellen White Issues

Although SDA members seem to be sincere individuals, to a great degree the SDA movement is based upon a non-biblical message from its "prophetess," Ellen White.

Which message?

The non-biblical message is the inaccurate sanctuary interpretation of 1844 by Ellen White that she taught essentially explained "a complete system of truth." Notice what she wrote:

> THE SUBJECT OF THE sanctuary was the key which unlocked the mystery of the disappointment of 1844. It opened to view a complete system of truth, connected and harmonious, showing that God's hand directed the great advent movement, and

revealing present duty as it brought to light the position and work of His people (White E.G. Will America Survive? 1888; Reprint, 1988 by Inspiration Books East, Jemison (AL), p. 405).

Now while Ellen White was correct that prophecy is important, the message of the Bible is that the Advent movement is NOT correct because of her sanctuary interpretation. It is the Bible, and not Ellen White's interpretations, that unlock the mysteries of God and which is the complete system of truth. Ellen White's sanctuary explanation was an attempt to say that a false prophecy about Jesus' return was not false. Jesus did not return in 1844 and the 'explanation' was not true, but looks to be a message from the devil.

Ellen G. White pushed the wrong date for the Day of Atonement:

> "The tenth day of the seventh month, the great Day of Atonement, *the time of the cleansing of the sanctuary,* which in the year 1844 fell upon the 22d of October, was regarded as the time of the Lord's coming. This was in harmony with the proofs already presented that the 2300 days would terminate in the autumn ... The computation of the prophetic periods, on which that message was based, *the* close of the 2300 days in the autumn of 1844, stand without impeachment. (White EG. The Great Controversy Between Christ and Satan During the Christian Dispensation. 1888, pp. 400, 457)

Her timing of this event and claiming it was related to the Day of Atonement was an error, as the Day of Atonement was not the day she claimed in 1844. But this was her first big "prophetic" insight—and truly was biblically in error.

Some have improperly claimed that October 22, 1844, was the Day of Atonement according to the Karite Calendar. The actual date of the Day of Atonement was Monday, September 23, 1844. As it turned out, the Day of Atonement in 1844 was on the same date on both the Rabbinical Perpetual Calendar and the Karite Calendar.

> Edward S. Ballenger (1864-1955), a former Adventist and for a time pastor of the Seventh-day Baptist Church in Los Angeles,

came to understand this fact through a response from the Karaite Rabbi Youseff Ibrahim Marzork.

The defenders of the creed declare that while the orthodox Jews may have celebrated the Day of Atonement on Sept. 23, the Karaite Jews observed it on Oct 22. We have made careful investigation, and we find that this is a false claim. The leading Karaite rabbi of Cairo, Egypt, Youseff Ibrahim Marzork, in reply to an inquiry as to the day on which they celebrated the atonement in 1844, wrote: As to the dates of the Passover and Yom Kippur they are the following: "According to the Karaite Jews in the year 1843 the Yom Kippur is on Wednesday the 4th October, and just the same date according to the Rabinnical." "In the year 1844 it is on Monday 23rd September for the Karaite and Rabinnical." (Ballenger ES. *The Gathering Call*, May-June 1941, pp. 14-15, 1941, pp. 14-15).

Ellen White's explanation must be considered false, as October 22nd was not the Day of Atonement in 1844.

If you are an Adventist, should your "system of truth" be the Bible or traditions outside of it? Please pray about that.

Furthermore, Ellen White initially claimed that the sanctuary doors were closed:

> Mr. Russell stated that the outer door of the Sanctuary was closed in 1844. Brother Cranmer asked him the nature of his proof, and he drew from his pocket Ellen G. White's book of visions and said there was his proof.
>
> Brother Cranmer answered, "Perhaps Mrs. White's visions are proof to you, but they are not to me".
>
> Some of the church got very much excited over the course Brother Cranmer proposed to pursue in regard to the "shut-door" question, and Mr. George Leighton went to Battle Creek to confer with Elder White on the subject. ...
>
> Mr. Leighton said in our presence that the visions were inspired,

> that they were better than the Bible because they were warm and fresh from the throne of God, and that anyone who did not accept them as inspiration absolutely would be {condemned by God} ... These statements we solemnly aver to be true (Perkins Joseph, Perkins Louise. Cited in Branch, p. 12).

However, the SDAs ultimately abandoned the shut-door doctrine themselves:

> Joseph Bates and James White ... both accepted the shut-door theory, and Ellen G. White experienced a vision in December 1844 that appeared to support this understanding. In 1849, however she had another vision that portrayed Jesus as shutting the door to the Holy Place of the heavenly sanctuary and opening the door to the most Holy Place ... Soon some Sabbatarian Adventists where speaking of both a shut door, referring to those that had rejected the gospel message, and an open door that was available to certain individuals despite the fact that they had not believed that Christ was coming in 1844 .

> Joseph Bates and James White concluded that their shut door views were wrong and by 1854 had largely abandoned shut door/open door language. (Land G. Historical Dictionary Of Seventh-Day Adventists: Historical Dictionaries of Religions Philosophies, and Movements, No. 56. Published by Scarecrow Press, 2005, p. 273).

There were many problems with Ellen White's visions which demonstrate that they were not from God.

The following is from a book titled "More than a Prophet" by SDA scholar Graeme Bradford. Note: This scholar is supportive of Ellen G. White and the Seventh Day Adventist Church. The point of showing this information is to point out the fact that SDA leaders have long known about problems with Mrs. White's life and writings. Anyway, here is some of what SDA scholars acknowledge about Mrs. White:

> They still believed in Ellen White, even though they were also aware of weaknesses in her life. And they could have listed them as well:

1. She did have some problems in her marriage. There were times when she and her husband worked apart.
2. She had problems with her children. She tended to favour Willie as the "good boy." James Edson, the only other of her four sons who survived to adulthood, turned away from the faith, but she won him back and he became a missionary to former slaves in the south of the United States.
3. She often became despondent over the criticism she faced. She could even doubt her own experience in Christ.
4. She could be forgetful.
5. She may not have always been as open about her use of other sources as she could have been.
6. She struggled to give up eating flesh foods and live up to the health counsel she had given to others. ...

It can be unsettling for some to come to grips with the fact that there are historical inaccuracies in her writings ... In other words, she is not a historian. Rather, she is giving a meaning to history. She is interpreting history for Christians. Today these historical inaccuracies are acknowledged by the White Estate; but this should not a problem for those who have a correct view of her work. ...

This point is made even stronger when we read a letter written to W. W. Prescott from her secretary Clarence E Crisler. In this letter he appeals to Prescott to come to give some help in the work of Ezra (which must have been for writing the book Prophets and Kings). In this letter he makes a list of the problem areas they need help and then says at the end, "I am sure that Sister White would be specially pleased and cheered, if she could know that you were coming soon to help us over hard places." ...

Even in her day, not everyone had this idea clearly in mind and they gave her writings an authority beyond what was appropriate. This could account for the protest that Prescott made to Willie in the year that Ellen White died. "It seems to me that a large responsibility rests upon those of us who know that there are serious errors in our authorized books and yet make no special effort to correct them. The people and our average ministers trust us to furnish them with reliable statements, and they use them as sufficient authority in their sermons, but we let them go on year after year asserting things we know to be untrue. . . .

"The way your mother's writings have been handled and the false impression concerning them which is still fostered among the people have brought great perplexity and trial to me. It seems to me that what amounts to deception, though probably not intentional, has been practiced in making some of her books, and that no serious effort has been made to disabuse the minds of the people of what was known to be their wrong view concerning her writings. But it is no use to go into these matters. I have talked to you for years about them, but it brings no change. I think however that we are drifting toward a crisis which will come sooner or later and perhaps sooner. A very strong reaction has already set in."

Adventists Should be Better Informed About Ellen White's Writings

Prescott's letter is indeed a serious one. It seems Willie White and Prescott held to the same ideas regarding how Ellen White's work was produced, their difference lay in the fact that Prescott felt Adventists should be better informed. What he says is hinted at in the conversation of the 1919 Bible Conference after-meeting. It seems many Adventists held to a view of verbal inspiration regarding her writings. J. N. Anderson asks the question, "Is it well to let our people in general to go on holding to the verbal inspiration of the Testimonies? When we do that, aren't we preparing for a crisis that will be very serious some day?"

Some say that when she states "I saw," her words have special authority. However, we know there were times when she used these words and then quoted from the works of others. It could be that the words "I saw" or "I was shown" mean "she saw" or "was shown" through the study of books. There are even times when she uses the words of authors when describing words she had heard spoken in vision. Ron Graybill, an Associate Secretary of the White Estate, made the following comments in a series of General Conference Worships in 1981.

"Did Mrs White ever borrow when she was reporting a vision? Did she ever say 'I was shown' and then proceed to borrow? The answer to that is 'yes,' although examples of it are not very plentiful. They are quite rare. I know of only three clear and unequivocal examples."

(Bradford, Graeme. Excerpt from *More than a Prophet*. ENDTIME ISSUES NEWSLETTER No. 151, July 11, 2006).

In other words, some of her inaccuracies and blatant hypocrisy have long been apparent to many Adventist leaders. Also, the fact that all know that she CHANGED the view of the Godhead is clear proof that the SDAs do not hold "the faith once for all delivered to the saints" (Jude 3).

The Ellen White Adventists did not officially adopt the name Seventh-day Adventists until October 1, 1860.

Ellen White made the following comments as part of her "Testimony for the Church," No. 6:

> "No name which we can take will be appropriate but that which accords with our profession, and expresses our faith, and marks us as a peculiar people...
>
> "The name Seventh-day Adventist carries the true features of our faith in front, and will convict the inquiring mind. Like an arrow from the Lord's quiver, it will wound the transgressors of God's law, and will lead to repentance toward God and faith in our Lord Jesus Christ.
>
> "I was shown that almost every fanatic who has arisen, who wishes to hide his sentiments that he may lead away others, claims to belong to the Church of God. Such a name would at once excite suspicion; for it is employed to conceal the most absurd errors."
>
> (As cited in Loughborough JN. Rise and progress of the Seventh-

day Adventists: with tokens of God's hand in the movement and a brief sketch of the Advent cause from 1831 to 1844. General Conference Association of the Seventh-day Adventists, 1892, p. 227)

So, according to Ellen White's sixth "Testimony," nearly all who opposed her claimed to be part of the Church of God. And despite "Church of God" being a biblical term (Acts 20:28; 1 Corinthians 1:2; 10:32; 11:16,22; 15:9; 2 Corinthians 1:1; Galatians 1:13; 1 Thessalonians 2:14; 2 Thessalonians 1:4; 1 Timothy 3:5,15) that faithful Sabbatarian Christians used throughout history, Ellen White considered those who held to the biblical name in this case to be fanatics.

Regarding her testimonies, Richard Nickels reported the falseness of at least one of Ellen G. White's "visions":

1856 Vision Proven False

Ellen G. White wrote in her Testimonies for the Church that "At the General Conference at Battle Creek, May 27, 1856, I was shown in vision some things which concern the church generally; . . . I was shown the company present at the Conference. Said the angel, 'Some food for worms, some subjects of the seven last plagues, some will be alive and remain upon the earth to be translated at the coming of Jesus'." (Nickels R. History of the Seventh Day Church of God, Volume I. Chapter IV)

The seven last plagues still have not begun, Jesus has still not returned, and all that attended that Conference are dead. Ellen White's vision was false.

Also notice this warning from Ellen White:

It is not really wise to have children now. Time is short, the perils of the last days are upon us, and the little children will largely be swept off before this. –Letter 48, 1876 (White E. Last Day Events: Facing Earth's Final Crisis. As printed by Pacific Press Publishing, 2002, p. 36)

As far as I have been able to see, the Adventist children were not "swept off" then as it was not time for "the perils of the last days" that Ellen White discussed in 1876.

Here is another prediction from Ellen White:

> Testimonies Volume 1 ... "January 4, 1862, I was shown some things in regard to our nation ... it is all a bitter denunciation of Lincoln's administration and management of the war. Every move had been wrong and only defeat was prophesied..." (Cornelius J. The Commandments of Men. Xulon Press, 2008, p. 286)

But Lincoln's side did win that war (granted at a major cost). Thus saying she "was shown" that Lincoln's side would be defeated is proof that she was not shown by God. The SDA church still claims that Ellen White was "a true prophet" (https://www.adventist.org/articles/the-gift-of-prophecy/ accessed 12/29/19).

While Ellen G. White may have correctly stated some events before they occurred, the falseness of many of her "predictions" indicates that she was not truly God's prophetess.

Notice what the Bible teaches:

> [21] And if you say in your heart, 'How shall we know the word which the Lord has not spoken?' — [22] when a prophet speaks in the name of the Lord, if the thing does not happen or come to pass, that is the thing which the Lord has not spoken; the prophet has spoken it presumptuously; you shall not be afraid of him. (Deuteronomy 18:21-22)

Yet, Ellen White claimed:

> In these letters which I write, in the testimonies I bear, I am presenting to you that which the Lord has presented to me. I do not write one article in the paper expressing merely my own views. They are what God has opened to me in vision—the precious rays of light shining from the throne (White EGH. Testimonies for the church, Issue 31. Pacific Press, 1882, p. 63).

Notice she claimed the testimonies came from God. God does NOT give His prophetic messengers false prophecies.

Furthermore, how she sometimes got her visions is an issue. Notice this account of one of her visions by supporter J.N. Loughborough:

> While she was in the vision, Elder White and myself were sitting by one side of the bed, and Elder Andrews on the other side. Her hands were alternately clasped over her breast or moved with her arms in her usual graceful manner toward the different scenes she was viewing. The upper portion of her body was raised from the bed so that there was a space of some eight or nine inches between her shoulders and the pillow. In other words, the body from the hips upward was flexed at an angle of about thirty degrees. And in that position she remained during the continuance of the vision, which was thirty minutes. No one could naturally assume that posture, unsupported by hands and arms, much less hold himself there for that length of time. Here again was proof that some power over which she had no control was connected with the vision (Loughborough JN. Rise and progress of the Seventh-day Adventists: with tokens of God's hand in the movement and a brief sketch of the Advent cause from 1831 to 1844. General Conference Association of the Seventh-day Adventists, 1892, p. 219).

Here is one analysis of this by the late R. Nickels (**bolding** in source):

> The Bible, however, shows that God's true prophets are never possessed with such a spirit. "The spirits of the prophets are subject to the control of the prophets" (**I Corinthians 14:32**, NIV). **Verse 14** of **Romans 8** shows that God's Spirit leads and does not take over and control us apart from our own will. From her childhood, when she was struck in the head by a rock and was in a coma for days, until later in life, Mrs. White suffered nervous and physical disorders (Nickels R. What Seventh-Day Adventists Should Know About Other Sabbath-keepers, p. 15).

It should be noted that the same cautions hold true for various "Catholic," Pentecostal, and other mystics. The way many of them claimed to receive their "prophecies" was not biblical. Roman Catholic "prophets" have also gotten some events correct, but as they have gotten others wrong and contradict the Bible, just because a prophet sometimes is correct, does NOT make him or her God's messenger. And since according to Ellen White her "testimonies" were always from God, since they were not always correct, she truly did not represent the true God.

Here is information on another vision:

> ... in 1851, Ellen White, through a vision, helped a church member who was confused with the "age to come" error. (Douglass HE. Messenger of the Lord. Pacific Press Publishing Association, 1998, p. 436)

Yet, an "age to come" is biblical (Matthew 12:32; Mark 10:30; Luke 18:30; Hebrews 6:5). We in the CCOG specifically still teach it (see the free online book: *Universal OFFER of Salvation, Apokatastasis: Can God save the lost in an age to come? Hundreds of scriptures reveal God's plan of salvation*).

Originally Ellen White had positions on the Holy Spirit that were quite close to those held by the CCOG. Notice what Ellen White's statements about the Holy Spirit suggest (note someone from an SDA background provided us the following statements including the source cited):

> The Spirit is freely given us of God if we will appreciate and accept it. And what is it? The representative of Jesus Christ. It is to be our constant helper. It is through the Spirit that Christ fulfills the promise, "I will never leave thee nor forsake thee." "Verily, verily, I say unto you, He that believeth on me hath everlasting life". (The bell is sounding for morning worship, I must stop here) (1888 Materials, pp. 1538, 1539, Letter to S. N. Haskell, May 30, 1896).
>
> The church members need to know from experience what the
>
> Holy Spirit will do for them. It will bless the receiver, and make him a blessing. It is sad that every soul is not praying for the vital breath of the Spirit, for we are ready to die if it breath not on us.
>
> We are to pray for the impartation of the Spirit as the remedy for

sin-sick souls. The church needs to be converted, and why should we not prostrate ourselves at the throne of grace, as representatives of the church, and from a broken heart and contrite spirit make earnest supplication that the Holy Spirit shall be poured out upon us from on high? Let us pray that when it shall be graciously bestowed, our cold hearts may be revived, and we may have discernment to understand that it is from God, and receive it with joy. Some have treated the Spirit as an unwelcome guest, refusing to receive the rich gift, refusing to acknowledge it, turning from it, and condemning it as fanaticism. When the Holy Spirit works the human agent, it does not ask us in what way it shall operate. Often it moves in unexpected ways. Christ did not come as the Jews expected. He did not come in a manner to glorify them as a nation. His forerunner came to prepare the way for him by calling upon the people to repent of their sins and be converted, and be baptized. Christ's message was, "The kingdom of heaven is at hand; repent ye and believe the gospel." The Jews refused to receive Christ, because he did not come in accordance with their expectations (Ibid., p. 1540).

And Jesus said He would give us the Comforter. What is the Comforter? It is the Holy Spirit of God. What is the Holy Spirit? It is the representative of Jesus Christ, it is our Advocate that stands by our side and places our petitions before the Father all fragrant with His merits (Reflecting Christ, p. 285).

It is the Spirit of Truth ... It is the Spirit that makes effectual what has been wrought by the world's Redeemer ... The Holy Spirit is the breath of the spiritual life of the soul ... It imbues the receiver with the attributes of Christ. (White EH. The Desire of the Ages. Originally published in 1898. Nabu Press, 2012 paperback edition, pp. 419,501)

The Lord would have every one of His children rich in faith, and this faith is the fruit of the working of the Holy Spirit upon the mind. It dwells with each soul who will receive it, speaking to the impenitent in words of warning, and pointing them to Jesus, the Lamb of God, that taketh away the sin of the world. It causes light to shine into the minds of those who are seeking to co-operate with God, giving them efficiency and wisdom to do His work

(White EG. The Outpouring of the Spirit, No, 2. September 27, 1899. In Signs of the Times Articles - Book III of II, Lulu Press).

Like the CCOG, Mrs. White then realized that the Holy Spirit was not a person. They both have referred to the Holy Spirit as "it."

Regarding crosses, Ellen White wrote:

> Papists place crosses upon their churches, upon their altars, and upon their garments. Everywhere is seen the insignia of the cross. Everywhere it is outwardly honored and exalted. But the teachings of Christ are buried beneath a mass of senseless traditions, false interpretations, and rigorous exactions. ... The worship of images and relics, the invocation of saints, and the exaltation of the pope, are devices of Satan to attract the minds of the people from God and from His Son. (White EG. The Great Controversy Between Christ and Satan. Guttenberg Project edition, p. 590)

How was that interpreted?

Historically our Adventist church viewed the cross as a pagan symbol (Bacchiocchi S. Is the Cross a Pagan Symbol? Endtime Issues Newsletter, 124, 2005, p. 17)

But that changed. Since no later than 1997, a cross containing logo has been in use by the official SDA church. Some have indicated part of the reason was to make the SDAs more acceptable to other Protestants and Rome (cf. Nyazika P. The Final Call. Lulu.com, pp. 131, 176).

Ellen White vs. Herbert W. Armstrong

An important difference between the CCOG and SDA church is how they view some of their deceased major leaders, such as Herbert W. Armstrong and Ellen White.

Ellen White's writings are referred to by many SDA writers as "Inspiration" (Plain View, a magazine by Seventh-day Adventists. Jan-Mar 2005). The faithful of us in CCOG do NOT refer to Herbert Armstrong's writings as "inspiration." He had various issues and many times made statements about dates related to biblical prophecies that were wrong.

Although there are some in the SDA movement who do not do so, the major position among SDAs seems to be that Ellen White was God's prophetess. Herbert W. Armstrong was NOT a prophet.

While, we in the *Continuing* Church of God do acknowledge that some fringe individuals/groups do have an improperly excessive view of Herbert Armstrong, that view is simply that: a fringe view not held by most in the various Church of God groups, and certainly is not held by the CCOG.

Notice what Herbert W. Armstrong wrote about himself:

> Emphatically I am NOT a prophet, in the sense of one to whom God speaks directly, revealing personally a future event to happen or new truth, or new or special instruction from God-- separate from, and apart from what is contained in the Bible. And I never have claimed to be (Armstrong Herbert W. Tomorrow's World, June 1972).

Additionally, Herbert Armstrong taught:

> *Don't* believe *me* – BELIEVE YOUR BIBLE – BELIEVE *GOD!* I always say ... check up! Listen without prejudice, with open mind, then *check up*--go to your BIBLE, and BELIEVE what you read *there*. (Armstrong HW. Personal from the Editor. Plain Truth. September 1963.)

That is great advice. We in CCOG do not accept anyone's writings, including those of Herbert W. Armstrong, if they are in conflict with the truth.

As far as history goes, the plain truth is that the Church of God people had a lot of biblical doctrines in the 1800s. The Whites came in contact with some of them (and others) and accepted many of their COG doctrines, and hence did teach many biblical truths. This made them look like COG to some, when they really were not (cf. 2 Corinthians 11:13-14; Revelation 3:9).

Because of their excessive fixation on Ellen White's prophetic interpretations, combined with the fact that she (and ultimately nearly all other SDAs) began to lose many biblical doctrines showed the truly faithful that the SDAs were simply not part of the true Church of God (though some who believe that they are in that movement possibly may be). This was the conclusion of the COG groups who had an affiliation with the Whites: once they understood that the Whites did not hold to the original faith, they stayed separate from them (2 Corinthians 6:17). In time, the SDAs lost more of their doctrines that the COGs have.

The SDAs now consider themselves to be Protestant, which no one in the CCOG would wish to be. Just keeping the Sabbath does not make one a true Christian.

But as scripture shows, true Christians do keep the Sabbath, like Jesus (Luke 4:16; John 15:10) and the Apostle Paul did (Acts 17:1-4, 28:17). Christians are to imitate them (1 John 2:6; 1 Corinthians 11:1).

Messianic Jews

Although they keep the Sabbath and Holy Days, plus do not eat biblically unclean animals, Messianic Jews are NOT in the Church of God.

Here is some of what one Messianic group says about their history:

> Messianic Judaism continued into the seventh century AD. First, non-Messianic rabbis pressured Messianic Jews to relinquish their faith in Yeshua as the Messiah. In addition, the dominant Gentile expression of Christianity pressured Messianic Jews to abandon their Jewishness ... Messianic Judaism as a distinct movement faded in the seventh century ... Beginning in the early 1800s increasing numbers of Jewish people began believing in Yeshua. The modern Messianic Jewish movement came to fruition in the 1960s and 1970s. (What is Messianic Judaism? Congregation Shema Yisrael. viewed 09/07/14)

So, the movement is not believed to have been continuous.

Furthermore, the Messianic Jews tend to push 613 requirements:

So what relationship does the Gentile Christian have to the 613 laws of the Torah? The book of Acts records that Messiah's Emissaries (the Apostles) and the Elders of Messiah's Holy Community met to decide this very issue. In the Messianic Jewish community we commonly refer to this meeting, recorded in Acts 15, as "the First Jerusalem Council". (What is Messianic Judaism. Congregation Shema Yisrael. http://shema.com/messianic-judaism/what-is-it/ viewed 12/30/19)

Let it be stated that scripture does not teach that the apostles met to discuss the "613 laws of the Torah" in Acts 15. There is no such thing biblically. Messianic Jews should not try to kid themselves that their list was the issue.

The list of 613 comes from Jewish tradition and a misnomer about pomegranates (supposedly they have 613 seeds, but they range from about 165 to over 1000). In Acts 15, we learn that the council of apostles and elders got together to decide whether or not Gentile Christians had to be physically circumcised. Many of the 613 'mitzvot' are not laws of the Torah, but are Jewish traditions.

The Messianics consider that the Protestants are real Christians and that they hold "the same core beliefs" (What is Messianic Judaism? Congregation Shema Yisrael. viewed 05/12/20). And that Emperors Constantine and Theodosius made actual "Christianity ... the state religion of the Roman Empire" (MESSIANIC JUDAISM. Messianic Jewish Alliance of America. https://mjaa.org/messianic-movement/ accessed 05/12/20).

We in the CCOG consider that Emperor Constantine was not a Christian and what became the state religion of the Roman Empire was not the biblical faith, but an apostate one.

Related to Protestant beliefs, Messianics tend to consider heaven the reward of the saved, that God is a trinity, Jesus was killed on a Friday, and that it is fine to celebrate Christmas and Easter. (https://www.shema.com accessed 12/20/19).

On the other hand, they advocate wearing things like tassels (specially knotted ritual fringes worn by observant Jews, also known as tzitzits) as well as "a Star of David, or a Star of David with a cross in it" (ibid). We in the CCOG do not. Some Messianic men wear head coverings known as kippah (also called a yarmulke) even at times they would be biblically prohibited by the New Testament (cf. 1 Corinthians 11:4,7).

The New Testament demonstrates the apostles did not appear to look like Jewish rabbis or Levitical priests, though many Messianic leaders seem to try to do so. When, for one example, the Apostle Paul was arrested, the authorities did not recognize him as a Jew, but thought he was an Egyptian (Acts 21:37-38). Paul had to tell the military commander he was a Jew (Acts 27:39). Thus, Paul did not look like a Jewish rabbi, nor was he apparently wearing distinguishing phylacteries or tzitzits as the Messianic Jews do. Christians have God's laws written on their hearts (Hebrews 10:16), hence do not need to wear visual reminders.

Some Messianics believe in the Black Israelite movement which, among other things, believe that Jesus and the Jews of His day were black African. Though, even coinage from that period disproves that theory.

Many Messianics use Hebrew names for deity. For some of them, it is based on the wrong idea that the New Testament was primarily written in Hebrew or Aramaic, which it was not (for more on that, see the free book, online at ccog.org, *Who Gave the World the Bible?*). Other than a very few Aramaic quotes, the New Testament was written in *koine* Greek. When one accepts that fact, one can see that God did not intend nor expect people to use Hebrew names for deity. Furthermore, because of the early lack of vowels in Hebrew, no one actually can be certain how those Hebrew names were originally pronounced.

Messianic Jews tend to consider themselves as at least similar to Protestants who accept Jesus, but believe that they should live somewhat like Orthodox Jews.

The Messianic Jewish movement is not part of the Church of God.

Nor are the Seventh-Day Baptists or the Seventh-day Adventists.

11. The Millennial Kingdom of God

The Sabbath helps picture the millennial reign.

Because of teachings and various scriptures, Jews (Psalm 90:4; Psalm 92) and early Christians (2 Peter 3:8; Hebrews 4:6-8; Revelation 20:4-6) believed that the Sabbath helped picture the millennium. Essentially, they taught that the six days of physical creation represented six one-thousand year days, followed by the Sabbath, representing the millennial rest. Jewish tradition also attributes supporting statements to that teaching, not recorded in the Bible, that were given by the prophet Elijah (Babylonian Talmud: Sanhedrin 97a).

Early Christians taught the millennium. Papias was a 1st century Church of God leader. Notice the following related to him:

> "These things are attested by Papias, an ancient man who was a hearer of John and a companion of Polycarp, in his fourth book. For five books have been written by him." ...

> Papias ... To these belong his statement that there will be a period of some thousand years after the resurrection of the dead, and that the kingdom of Christ will be set up in material form on this very earth. (Eusebius. The History of the Church, Book 3, Chapter XXXIX; Digireads, pp. 68-69)

So, Papias was a hearer of the Apostle John and friend of Polycarp and he clearly taught the millennium.

The Greco-Roman-Protestant saint Irenaeus also realized the millennial reality as he wrote:

> These are [to take place] in the times of the kingdom, that is, upon the seventh day, which has been sanctified, in which God rested from all the works which He created, which is the true Sabbath of the righteous, which they shall not be engaged in any earthly occupation; but shall have a table at hand prepared for them by God, supplying them with all sorts of dishes (Against Heresies. Book V, Chapter 33, Verse 2)

So did the 4th century Greco-Roman saint and bishop Methodius:

> For I also, taking my journey, and going forth from the Egypt of this life, came first to the resurrection, which is the true Feast of the Tabernacles, and there having set up my tabernacle, adorned with the fruits of virtue, on the first day of the resurrection, which is the day of judgment, celebrate with Christ the millennium of rest, which is called the seventh day, even the true Sabbath. (Methodius. Banquet of the Ten Virgins, Discourse 9, chapter 5)

Jerome observed that 5th century Sabbath-keeping Christians specifically believed that the seven-day Feast of Tabernacles pictured the millennium (Jerome, Commentariorum in Zachariam Lib. III. Patrologia Latina 25, 1529; 1536).

The Bible teaches that the millennial reign will be a fantastic time and that the law will be taught then (Isaiah 2:2-4; Micah 4:1-4) with reminders given by God's teachers to observe it (Isaiah 30:20-21). The Sabbath is a weekly reminder that God's millennial kingdom will come.

Followers of Martin Luther condemned the Anabaptists (called "they" below) for believing in the millennial Kingdom of God:

> **Article XVII: Of Christ's Return to Judgment.**
>
> 1] Also they teach that at the Consummation of the World Christ will appear for judgment, and 2] will raise up all the dead; He will give to the godly and elect eternal life and everlasting joys, 3] but ungodly men and the devils He will condemn to be tormented without end. 4] They condemn the Anabaptists, who think that there will be an end to the punishments of condemned men and devils. 5] They condemn also others who are now spreading certain Jewish opinions, that before the resurrection of the dead the godly shall take possession of the kingdom of the world, the ungodly being everywhere suppressed. (Melanchthon P. The Augsburg Confession. THE CONFESSION OF FAITH which was submitted to His Imperial Majesty Charles V at the Diet of Augsburg in the Year 1530. Loki's Publishing, 2018, pp. 13,20,21)

Some, but not most, of the Anabaptists held to *Continuing* Church of God doctrines.

Specifically like the Anabaptists, we do not believe that punishment is never ending. We also do believe that Christians will be part of the first resurrection and reign with Jesus on the earth for 1,000 years per Revelation 20:4-6.

Most modern Baptists disagree with the Anabaptist position that there will be an "end to the punishments of condemned men" (known as annihilation).

Protestant Reformers went along with the official position of the Roman and Eastern Orthodox Catholic churches and denounced the millennial view:

> Luther and Melanchthon, Zwingli and Bullinger, and Calvin and Beza repudiated the millenarian doctrine (Cogley, Richard W. The fall of the Ottoman Empire and the restoration of Israel in the 'Judeo-centric' strand of Puritan millenarianism. Church History. June 1, 2003)

That is a difference between them and the CCOG.

However, it should be pointed out that many Evangelical Protestants do accept that the Bible teaches a literal millennial reign on the earth.

Gospel of the Kingdom

Contrary to what some critics seem to feel, the message of the *Continuing* Church of God is one of hope for all humankind.

The message of the Bible includes the hope of the resurrection and the promises God made (Acts 26:6-8). It is the gospel, the GOOD NEWS, that God will intervene in world affairs and establish His kingdom on the earth (Mark 1:14; Acts 20:25; Revelation 11:15).

Those called and chosen in this age will be able to reign with Jesus during the millennium (Revelation 20:4-6) on this earth (Revelation 5:10) in what could be considered the first phase of the kingdom of God.

The first part of salvation for those called in this age. Part of why true Christians need to learn obedience and build character in this age is to teach others the way of Jesus during the millennium (cf. Isaiah 30:20) and the Last Great Day (cf. John 7:37). Resurrected Christians will be assisting others who will have an opportunity to be in the latter phase of the Kingdom of God.

Notice how the latter phase of God's kingdom will be:

> [3] And I heard a loud voice from heaven saying, "Behold, the tabernacle of God is with men, and He will dwell with them, and they shall be His people. God Himself will be with them and be their God. [4] And God will wipe away every tear from their eyes; there shall be no more death, nor sorrow, nor crying. There shall be no more pain, for the former things have passed away."
>
> [5] Then He who sat on the throne said, "Behold, I make all things new." And He said to me, "Write, for these words are true and faithful." (Revelation 21:3-5).

The Protestants (in general) and the *Continuing* Church of God accept this plain teaching from Revelation 21, but tend to understand many of the ramifications of the Gospel of the Kingdom differently.

Lutherans essentially teach that the Gospel is about personal salvation in this age:

> Lutherans showed how the Gospel of Jesus Christ is always the vibrant, beating heart of the biblical and historic Christian faith and life. (What Lutherans Teach about The Gospel. Concordia Publishing House, November 23, 2015)
>
> There is no Gospel but the Lutheran Gospel … It's Still All About Jesus (There is no Gospel but the Lutheran Gospel by Dr. Matthew C. Harrison, president of The Lutheran Church—Missouri Synod. YouTube, uploaded October 2, 2017)
> In the Greek New Testament, the noun *euangelion* ('gospel') appears just over seventy times. … The word *gospel* most simply means 'good news'. … In examining these texts, we discover that sometimes the word *gospel* refers broadly to all aspects of

the salvation and new life that Jesus gives His people, and sometimes it is used narrowly to refer to what Jesus does for us outside of us. In other words, sometimes the term *gospel* refers broadly to Jesus' work of justification and sanctification for and in His people, and sometimes it refers narrowly to Jesus' work of justification. (Godfrey WR. What Is the Gospel? Ligonier Ministries, April 12, 2019)

Yes, personal salvation for those called in this age is an important part of the gospel—but it is not the only part.

Lutherans repeatedly neglect that the focus of Jesus and His early disciples was on the good news of the Kingdom of God. That message was one that showed that human civilization would be replaced and God's government implemented—a government based on the laws of God (cf. Isaiah 2:3; Micah 4:2).

Laws that Martin Luther did not properly teach.

Here is the first public teaching from Jesus that Matthew records:

> [23] And Jesus went about all Galilee, teaching in their synagogues, preaching the gospel of the kingdom… (Matthew 4:23).

Matthew also records:

> [35] Then Jesus went about all the cities and villages, teaching in their synagogues, preaching the gospel of the kingdom… (Matthew 9:35).

The New Testament shows that Jesus will reign forever:

> [33] And He will reign over the house of Jacob forever, and of His kingdom there will be no end (Luke 1:33).

Luke records that the purpose that Jesus was sent was to preach the Kingdom of God. Notice what Jesus taught:

> ⁴³ but He said to them, "I must preach the kingdom of God to the other cities also, because for this purpose I have been sent" (Luke 4:43).

Have you ever heard that preached? Did you ever realize that Jesus' purpose for being sent was to preach the Kingdom of God?

Luke also records that Jesus *did* go and preach the Kingdom of God:

> ¹⁰ And the apostles, when they had returned, told Him all that they had done. Then He took them and went aside privately into a deserted place belonging to the city called Bethsaida. ¹¹ But when the multitudes knew it, they followed Him; and He received them and spoke to them about the kingdom of God… (Luke 9:10-11).

Notice something about a Roman Catholic and apparent COG leader in the 12th century:

> "Like St. Francis [of Assisi], Waldo adopted a life of poverty that he might be free to preach, **but with this difference that the Waldenses preached the doctrine of Christ while the Franciscans preached the person of Christ**" (*Encyclopaedia Britannica,* 11th ed.).

Protestants have continued that Roman Catholic practice of focusing more on the person of Christ than on His doctrines and messages. We in the CCOG teach about the person of Jesus, while we focus on His doctrines and messages --like the Gospel of the Kingdom of God.

Consider, Jesus taught that the Kingdom of God should be the top priority for those who would follow Him:

> ³³ But seek first the kingdom of God and His righteousness… (Matthew 6:33).

> ³¹ But seek the kingdom of God, and all these things shall be added to you. (Luke 12:31).

Christians are to SEEK FIRST the Kingdom of God. They make this their top priority by living as Christ would have them live and looking forward to His return and kingdom. Yet, most who profess Christ, not only do not seek first the Kingdom of God, they do not even know what it is. Many also falsely believe that being involved in worldly politics is what God expects from Christians. By not understanding God's kingdom, they do not live now as they should nor understand why humanity is so flawed.

Consider also that the kingdom will be given to a little flock (cf. Luke 12:32; Romans 11:5). It takes humility to be willing to be part of the true little flock. For more on the good news, check out the free book, online at ccog.org, titled: *The Gospel of the Kingdom of God.*

Worldly Politics

Early Christians looked to the Kingdom of God as the answer to the problems facing the world and did not place their hopes in worldly politics. However, Christians are to pray for those in authority (1 Timothy 2:1-3). And we in the CCOG do that.

The followers of Martin Luther, however, endorsed worldly politics and condemned people for opposing that:

> **Article XVI: Of Civil Affairs.**
>
> 1] Of Civil Affairs they teach that lawful civil ordinances are good works of God, and that 2] it is right for Christians to bear civil office, to sit as judges, to judge matters by the Imperial and other existing laws, to award just punishments, to engage in just wars, to serve as soldiers, to make legal contracts, to hold property, to make oath when required by the magistrates, to marry a wife, to be given in marriage. 3] They condemn the Anabaptists who forbid these civil offices to Christians.

In general, Protestants encourage military service, voting, jury duty, and other aspects of worldly politics. Modern Baptists generally agree with Protestants on these points (in the 20th century, Baptist Jimmy Carter also became President of the United States) and not with their claimed Anabaptist ancestors.

The following seems applicable to any Protestants who are militaristic, sexually immoral, and/or providing false teachings:

> [2] But your iniquities have separated you from your God; And your sins have hidden His face from you, So that He will not hear. [3] For your hands are defiled with blood, And your fingers with iniquity; Your lips have spoken lies, Your tongue has muttered perversity. (Isaiah 59:2-3)

The Apostle Paul wrote that Christians are to be ambassadors for Christ (2 Corinthians 5:20). Ambassadors do not take part in the direct affairs of the countries they are living in, and certainly not the wars of the nations they are in. Paul also wrote that Christians were to be separate (2 Corinthians 6:17), whereas the Apostle John warned against loving the world and its systems (1 John 2:15-17). CCOG members do not swear oaths per Jesus' statements against such in Matthew 5:33-37.

Unless legally required, CCOG members do not vote nor serve on secular juries. While one might think a Christian would render a better judgment than a non-Christian, because of rules of evidence, penalties, and other legalities, most governments would not want Christians to render decisions for a system that opposes God's justice.

Why unless "legally required"? Because scripture does not specifically prohibit these actions, but warns to be separate from the world (1 John 2:15-17) and to trust God for leaders (1 Samuel 8:6-9, Daniel 4:17). Hence, we believe our prayers for God's will to be done, and not some vote, is what matters. We do not 'swear' if legally required as that opposes Jesus' commands (Matthew 5:33-37), but can legally affirm to tell the truth. We in the CCOG believe that those who voluntarily choose to vote tend to put their hopes in human governments and not God's coming kingdom. But it is God's kingdom Jesus said Christians needed to seek first (Matthew 6:33). Perhaps it should be added that the only time the expression "cast my vote" was used in the New Testament, it had to do with condemning Christians (Acts 26:10, NKJV).

Proclaiming the Gospel of the Kingdom of God

Jesus taught:

> [14] And this gospel of the kingdom will be preached in all the world as a witness to all the nations, and then the end will come. (Matthew 24:14)

The *Continuing* Church of God does not believe that this preaching has been fulfilled, as the end has not yet come. Some Protestants also realize that it has not been fulfilled. Notice:

> Despite all the efforts of all the missionaries and evangelists and Christian workers for two thousand years past, the fact must be accepted that the majority of men pass into death without in any sense of the word coming into vital contact with Divine truth or knowing anything of the issues which are eventually to determine their destiny. (Hudson AO. Future Probation In Christian Belief, Chapters 1,2,3. Bible Fellowship Union, 1975)

> Jesus tells us when the end of the age will come in Matthew 24:14 where He says, "And this gospel of the kingdom will be proclaimed throughout the whole world as a testimony to all nations, and then the end will come." Has that happened? If not, it is so very, very close that you can almost taste it. (Wellman J. Has The Gospel Now Been Preached To All Nations? Faith-in-the-News, July 6, 2018)

Well, the age did not end in 70 A.D. nor has it yet ended. However, we are very close to the fulfilment of Matthew 24:14. Church of God leaders like Polycarp of Smyrna taught the Kingdom of God (Polycarp. Letter to the Philippians, Chapter V).

Now, there are some preterists (those who believe Matthew 24 was fulfilled by 70 A.D.) and other Protestants who teach that Matthew 24:14 has been fulfilled:

> **Great Commission Is Complete: As Jesus Predicted in Matthew 24:14**
>
> So what is the right number of unreached people groups? That's an impossible question to answer because the definitions are subjective. And it is the wrong question to even ask. Jesus' claim that "This gospel of the kingdom shall be preached in the whole

world as a testimony to all the nations, and then the end will come" is a general prediction of what happened between Pentecost and the destruction of Jerusalem in 70 AD. (Pentley PT. Great Commission Is Complete: As Jesus Predicted in Matthew 24:14. Re-enacting the Way. May 14, 2017)

Well, since the end will come after God determines that Matthew 24:14 is fulfilled, then it is not appropriate to say it is subjective. This prophecy by Jesus also could at least partially tie in with the full number of Gentiles to be converted (Romans 11:25).

2nd century Christians did not believe this had been fulfilled, otherwise missionaries would not have been sent out from places like Asia Minor and Palestine (Moore TV. The Culdee Church, chapters 3 and 4, and Wilkinson, Our Authorized Bible Vindicated, pp. 25, 26).

The *Continuing* Church of God believes that it needs to support the work of proclaiming the gospel of the Kingdom of God to the world as a witness. We have a booklet on the subject titled *The Gospel of the Kingdom of God*. It is also available in about 100 non-English languages.

We believe events will occur that will focus attention on the gospel message in the future and then God will determine that Matthew 24:14 has been fulfilled and the end of this age, and then the start of the Great Tribulation will begin consistent with Jesus' words in Matthew 24:15-21.

12. Saved to Do What?

One message that Protestantism tends to promote is that one has to accept Jesus as Lord to be saved (true) from its tradition that one would otherwise burn forever in Gehenna fire (which is not actually what the Bible teaches).

Overall, the Protestant message focuses on using fear of eternal condemnation to motivate people to "accept Jesus" so they can "go to heaven."

While the Bible shows that Christians are to repent and accept Jesus to be saved from their sins to be granted eternal life, is heaven the reward?

What are Christians saved for?

Why did God make people or anything else for that matter?

Within Protestantism, there seems to be some general agreements on why God made anything.

But do they have the right and biblical message?

Let's look at one Protestant view of why God made humans:

> **Why Did God Create Humans?**
>
> He did so to give himself glory. God created us to live and enjoy relationship as he did. Jesus said, "I have told you this so that my joy may be in you and that your joy may be complete" (John 15:11). ...
>
> To bring glory to God—that is, to exalt him, lift him up, give him praise, to reflect upon him honorable—is in fact our purpose in life. (Bell S. Josh McDowell Ministry. Posted April 11, 2016)

We in the CCOG would disagree. God did not create because He is some ego-driven spiritual entity that needed people to give Him glory. Nor is giving glory to God the purpose of human life. But it is true that God wanted to increase joy.

Here is another, somewhat similar Protestant response:

> **Why did God create in the first place? Was He bored? Was He lonely? Why did God go through the trouble of making humans?**
>
> The Bible tells us that God's ultimate purpose for the universe is to reveal His glory. The Bible tells us that God's ultimate purpose for mankind is to reveal His love. (Was God Bored? All About God Ministries, accessed 03/21/19)

This is slightly closer as love is part of it, but again the implication is that God made everything because of His need to have His ego stroked. God is not vain and does not need that.

Here are views from two others:

> **Why Did God Create the World?**
>
> *Why did God create the world*?
>
> The short answer that resounds through the whole Bible like rolling thunder is: *God created the world for his glory*. (Piper J. September 22, 2012 www.desiringgod.org/messages/why-did-god-create-the-world accessed 01/16/19)
>
> **Why Did God Create?**
>
> God did not create because of some limitation within Himself. Instead, He created everything out of nothing in order to put His glory on display for the delight of His created beings and that they might declare His greatness. (Lawson J. Ligonier Ministries, July 3, 2017)

Two more claiming God made things for His personal glory.

So, those Protestant (including Baptist) sources seem to agree. But that view is not scriptural. We in CCOG do not believe they really understand the mystery of God's plan.

The Beatific Vision

Some feel that eternity will be spent primarily gazing upon the face of God. This is known as the 'Beatific Vision.'

While the Bible teaches we can see God's face forever (Psalm 41:12), the Beatific Vision is taught by some as the Christian reward and purpose of the creation.

Here is how the *New World Encyclopedia* describes it:

> The **Beatific Vision** is a term in Catholic theology describing the direct perception of God enjoyed by those who are in Heaven, imparting supreme happiness or blessedness. In this view, humans' understanding of God while alive is necessarily indirect (mediated), while the Beatific Vision is direct (immediate). ...
>
> Thomas Aquinas explained the Beatific Vision as the ultimate goal of human existence after physical death. Aquinas' formulation of beholding God in Heaven parallels Plato's description of beholding the Good in the world of the Forms, which is not possible while still in the physical body. ...
>
> The philosophy of Plato hints at the concept of the Beatific Vision in the Allegory of the cave, which appears in the Republic Book 7 (514a-520a), speaking through the character of Socrates:
>
>> My opinion is that in the world of knowledge the idea of good (the Good) appears last of all, and is seen only with an effort; and, when seen, is also inferred to be the universal author of all things beautiful and right, parent of light and of the lord of light in this visible world, and the immediate source of reason and truth in the intellectual (517b,c).

> For Plato, the Good appears to correspond to God in Christian theology. ...
>
> St. Cyprian of Carthage (third century) wrote of the saved seeing God in the Kingdom of Heaven. How great will your glory and happiness be, to be allowed to see God, to be honored with sharing the joy of salvation and eternal light with Christ your Lord and God ... to delight in the joy of immortality in the Kingdom of Heaven with the righteous and God's friends. ...
>
> In the thirteenth century, philosopher-theologian Thomas Aquinas, following his teacher Albertus Magnus, described the ultimate goal of a human life as consisting in the intellectual Beatific Vision of God's essence after death. According to Aquinas, the Beatific Vision surpasses both faith and reason. ...
>
> George Fox and the other early Quakers believed that direct experience of God was available to all people, without mediation. (Beatific Vision. New World Encyclopedia, 2013. Accessed 04/16/19)

The editor of the *Lutheran Journal of Ethics* wrote:

> But the end goal of God's purpose for the human creature shines through an eschatological understanding of sanctification, where we are promised the beatific vision of holiness and full communion with God in eternity. (Santos C. Editor's Introduction: Lutherans and Sanctification. © September/October 2017. Journal of Lutheran Ethics, Volume 17, Issue 5)

Many, though not all, Protestants who believe in the Beatific Vision lean toward the view that this vision is a spiritual, not physical sight (e.g. Ortlund G. Why We Misunderstand the Beatific Vision. First Baptist Church of Ojai, September 26, 2018).

Those who accept versions of the Beatific Vision as the end goal, the real hope of salvation, tend to think that seeing God will fill them with His or their own happiness.

Here is an opposing view of that vision from a onetime Church of God writer:

> If eternity is to be spent gazing blissfully up into God's face, or having our every wish immediately fulfilled — as many religions teach — after a few months (or after a few octillion years, it doesn't really matter), life would get boring. And once life got boring, it would be sickeningly and fiendishly terrifying. Because there would remain nothing but an unending eternity of boredom to come — with death a wonderful but impossible way of escape (see Luke 20:35-38). This would indeed be the ultimate torture.
>
> But our Eternal Father has a better idea. He has designed a plan in which eternity will not grow progressively more boring. But, as unbelievable as it seems, eternity will grow progressively more exciting, more scintillating, and more enjoyable as each eon follows eon. (Kuhn RL. The God Family – Part Three: To Inhabit Eternity. Good News, July 1974)

Yes, God made what He did so that eternity could be better. Notice something from a deceased Church of God writer:

> The God who put this world together did so with a plan in mind. That plan was not the hopeless Nirvana of one major religion of the world which promises you will become an unconscious part of the great whole of nothing with no worries forever — because you have no individual consciousness forever. It is not the bliss of slumbering in a hammock slung between two date palms in an oasis, being fed by voluptuous maidens forever, the promise of which the followers of Allah are assured. It is not walking the golden streets with golden slippers, strumming on a harp with your only worry being how to keep your halo straight, as seems to be the promise of the majority of Protestant groups. It is most certainly not the promise of finally being able to look into the face of God and appreciate the beatific vision (whatever that is), as is the promise to those who follow the Catholic faith: What the God who created everything proposes is to bring you into His very family. To be God as God is God! Not just to be a God in the euphemistic sense of us all

being brothers and sisters with God as our figurehead Father, but to share His divine nature completely. ...

God's real plan is practical. He says of His family Kingdom that there will never be an end to its expansion. His plan is to continue adding sons and daughters who look, feel, act like Him and who are composed of the same self-regenerating eternal spirit life as He is, forever! That is why the goal God has set before Himself is a hope that not even He will ever fulfil. Endless, eternal, forever creating an ever-expanding family to enjoy and rule the great creation He has already made — and to have you and me share in future creations without end. A busy, practical, interesting, challenging, ongoing plan that gives an eternal reason to live.

There is no boredom in that plan. Never a time when your interest will run out. No mythical, religious-sounding folderol about some spiritual never-never land where you do nothing forever — but an eternal job of creating, governing! Problem-solving with visible benefit. ... He has the power to resurrect you ... (Hill DJ. What the World Needs Now Is...HOPE. Plain Truth, February 1979)

Notice something from a late Church of God leader:

"If a man die, shall he live again?" (Job 14:14). This should be a time of HOPE, because even if THIS WORLD dies — and it shall — there will follow **a RESURRECTION of a new and better world** — a world at PEACE — a world of contentment, happiness, abundance, JOY! God help us to comprehend! Not merely continuous existence — but the full, happy, interesting, ABUNDANT life! Yes — and that for ALL ETERNITY! (Armstrong HW. What Is the Purpose of the Resurrection? Good News, March 1982)

Because many do not fully understand scripture, they have promoted views, like the beatific vision, which are not fully consistent with God's plan.

Us looking at God does not, of itself, make eternity better. But He, in blessing us forever, certainly will result in that (cf. Psalm 72:17-19).

All Things Created for Jesus

The New Testament teaches this relating to Jesus and the creation:

> ^{15} He is the image of the invisible God, the firstborn over all creation. ^{16} For by Him all things were created that are in heaven and that are on earth, visible and invisible, whether thrones or dominions or principalities or powers. All things were created through Him and for Him. (Colossians 1:15-16)

> ^{2} ... His Son, whom He has appointed heir of all things, through whom also He made the worlds; ^{3} who being the brightness of His glory and the express image of His person, and upholding all things by the word of His power, (Hebrews 1:2-3)

Were we simply created to look at Jesus for eternity in heaven?

No, that is not the hope of salvation.

Notice why Jesus said He came:

> ^{10} ... I have come that they may have life, and that they may have it more abundantly. (John 10:10)

By have 'life' and having it 'more abundantly,' Jesus is teaching that He came so that we could have a better eternity and that we could help make eternity better.

God did not create humans for the purpose of humans staring at Him for all eternity.

Heaven

Are the deceased who are saved living their lives in heaven?

No.

Jesus said:

> [13] No one has ascended to heaven but He who came down from heaven, that is, the Son of Man who is in heaven. (John 3:13)

Hence, contrary to assertions by some Protestants, God's leaders such as Moses, Enoch, Elijah, Abraham had not done so according to Jesus' words.

Early writers spoke of death being like sleep, to be followed by the resurrection and Jesus' return. Notice that a late 1st century letter called *1 Clement* contains the following:

> The Lord shall suddenly come ... there shall be a future resurrection ... For [Scripture] says in a certain place, You shall raise me up, and I shall confess unto You; and again, I laid me down, and slept; I awoke, because You are with me; and again, Job says, You shall raise up this flesh of mine, which has suffered all these things. (1 Clement, Chapters 23, 24, 26)

Former Evangelical Protestant Bart Ehrman has written that Christians in the 1st century believed that the Kingdom of God was coming to earth within their own lifetimes and they looked forward to a divine future on earth. Bart Ehrman postulated that when the Kingdom of God did not arrive, the Greco-Romans who professed Christ gradually refined their hopes so that they came to look forward to an immediate reward in heaven after death, rather than to a future divine kingdom on earth—despite the churches' continuing to use the major creeds' statements of belief in a coming Resurrection Day and World to Come (Ehrman, Bart. Peter, Paul, and Mary Magdalene: The Followers of Jesus in History and Legend. Oxford University Press, USA. 2006).

Probably because of his endorsement of meeting on "the day said to be Helios" in his letter to the Mithra-honoring Roman Emperor Antoninus Pius (The First Apology. Chapter LXVII), which day we commonly call Sunday, Justin Martyr is considered an important Greco-Roman-Protestant saint.

Yet, Justin Martyr wrote something that most Protestants would be shocked to hear:

> For if you have fallen in with **some who are called Christians**, but ... **who say there is no resurrection of the dead, and that their souls, when they die, are taken to heaven; do not imagine that they are Christians** (Justin. Dialogue with Trypho. Chapter 80).

Early Christians did not teach that humans had an immortal soul or that they went to heaven upon death.

The apostle Paul was inspired to write Timothy that only Jesus was immortal (1 Timothy 6:16) – and this was about 30 years *after* Christ died, was resurrected, and ascended to heaven. This confirms that no dead human being, including Stephen who was martyred in Acts 7:54-60, had become immortal and gone to heaven.

Now, some have wondered about the following from Jesus:

> ^{2} In My Father's house are many mansions; if it were not so, I would have told you. I go to prepare a place for you. ^{3} And if I go and prepare a place for you, I will come again and receive you to Myself; that where I am, there you may be also. (John 14:2-3).

Jesus was saying that He would prepare a place for YOU if you were one of the Father's children. Notice that this does NOT say that you will go to heaven. When Jesus comes again, He will come to the earth.

The late COG evangelist, Dr. Herman Hoeh, explained:

> The Greek word "move" translated "mansion" means in more modern English, "a room, a place of staying, an abode, a chamber." So in the Father's house there are a number of ROOMS OR CHAMBERS.
>
> But what is the Father's house? What does the Bible declare the Father's house to be?
>
> When in the Temple, Jesus said to the Jews who were selling doves and cattle therein: "Make not my FATHER'S HOUSE an house of merchandise" (John 2:16).

Here is a simple Bible definition of the Father's house.

The TEMPLE at Jerusalem was an earthly type (Heb. 8:5) of the Father's house in heaven. Luke 19:46 and Isaiah 56:7, also quote the Lord as saying of the TEMPLE. "MY HOUSE is a house of prayer ...." So the Temple at Jerusalem in Christ's day was a type of the Father's house in heaven.

But did the Temple have many "mansions" or rooms and chambers in it?

Certainly!

In turning to Jeremiah 35:2, we read this: "Speak unto them, and bring them into the house of the Lord, INTO ONE OF THE CHAMBERS." In the fourth verse of the same chapter, we notice that different chambers were for persons of different rank. Hanan, a man of God, had his chamber or room "BY the chamber of the princes ... which was ABOVE the chamber of ... the keeper of the door."

The various chambers or "mansions" corresponded to the ranks of the persons residing in them. Each room of the Temple — a type of the Father's house — not only designated the RESIDENCE of each official, but also indicated his POSITION OR OFFICE, whether he was a doorkeeper or prince.

It Is NOT Heaven

Nowhere does the Bible call "heaven" the Father's house. The Father's house IS BEING BUILT IN heaven, but it is not heaven! Heaven is never said to have "mansions."

The ancient tabernacle built under Moses had two compartments, the inner, called the Holy of Holies, being an exact picture of the throne of God of heaven itself. IT HAD NO MANSIONS. Read Hebrews 8:5 and 9:1-7 to see exactly what the pattern of heaven is like.

> No, Jesus was not referring to heaven. He is referring to a place being prepared IN heaven. (Hoeh HL. What is the Place that Jesus is Preparing? Tomorrow's World magazine, February 1972)

What about the place that is now being prepared in heaven? It will come down to the earth. Let's look at something that the Apostle John was inspired to write:

> ² Then I, John, saw the holy city, New Jerusalem, coming down out of heaven from God, prepared as a bride adorned for her husband. ³ And I heard a loud voice from heaven saying, "Behold, the tabernacle of God is with men, and He will dwell with them, and they shall be His people. God Himself will be with them and be their God. (Revelation 21:2-3)

Notice that God will come down to the earth and dwell with His people. That dwelling is not in heaven according to those scriptures.

Getting back to Justin, he also specifically taught that souls were not immortal (Dialogue. Chapter 4-5). The Bible teaches that it is at a resurrection where the mortal put on immortality (1 Corinthians 15:50-54).

This is also consistent with the writings of the 3rd century theologian Hippolytus of Rome:

> The Father of immortality sent the immortal Son and Word into the world, who came to man in order to wash him with water and the Spirit; and He, begetting us again to incorruption of soul and body, breathed into us the breath (spirit) of life, and endued us with an incorruptible panoply. If, therefore, man has become immortal, he will also be God. And if he is made God by water and the Holy Spirit after the regeneration of the laver he is found to be also joint-heir with Christ after the resurrection from the dead (Hippolytus. The Discourse on the Holy Theophany, Chapter 8).

Notice the following related to some Protestant researchers:

One of the central stories of the Bible, many people believe, is that there is a heaven and an earth and that human souls have been exiled from heaven and are serving out time here on earth until they can return. Indeed, for most modern Christians, the idea of "going to heaven when you die" is not simply one belief among others, but the one that seems to give a point to it all.

But the people who believed in that kind of "heaven" when the New Testament was written were not the early Christians. ...

The followers of the Jesus ... believed that God would then raise his people from the dead, to share in — and, indeed, to share his stewardship over — this rescued and renewed creation. And they believed all this because of Jesus. ... Jesus taught his followers to pray: "Thy kingdom come on earth as in heaven." From as early as the third century, some ... **teachers tried to blend this with types of the Platonic belief, generating the idea of "leaving earth and going to heaven," which became mainstream by the Middle Ages. But Jesus' first followers never went that route**. (Wright NT. The New Testament Doesn't Say What Most People Think It Does About Heaven. Time, December 16, 2019)

(RNS) The oft-cliched Christian notion of heaven — a blissful realm of harp-strumming angels — has remained a fixture of the faith for centuries ... But scholars on the right and left increasingly say that comforting belief in an afterlife has no basis in the Bible and would have sounded bizarre to Jesus and his early followers ...

The most recent expert to add his voice to this chorus is the prolific Christian apologist N.T. Wright, a former Anglican bishop who now teaches about early Christianity and New Testament at Scotland's University of St. Andrews. Wright has explored Christian misconceptions about heaven ...

"This is a very current issue – that what the church, or what the majority conventional view of heaven is, is very different from what we find in these biblical testimonies," said Christopher Morse of Union Theological Seminary in New York. . .

> Wright and Morse work independently of each other and in very different ideological settings, but their work shows a remarkable convergence on key points. In classic Judaism and first-century Christianity, believers expected this world would be transformed into God's Kingdom — a restored Eden where redeemed human beings would be liberated from death, illness, sin and other corruptions.
>
> "This represents an instance of two top scholars who have apparently grown tired of talk of heaven on the part of Christians that is neither consistent with the New Testament nor theologically coherent," said Trevor Eppehimer of Hood Theological Seminary in North Carolina. "The majority of Christian theologians today would recognize that Wright and Morse's views on heaven represent, for the most part, the basic New Testament perspective on heaven."
>
> ..."And so it's not a Platonic, timeless eternity, which is what we were all taught," Wright said. "It is very definitely that there will come a time when God will utterly transform this world — that will be the age to come." (Have we gotten heaven all wrong? First Presbyterian Church of Newhall. January 16, 2014)

We in the *Continuing* Church of God teach the good news of the kingdom of God on earth and the age to come. For more details, see our free books, online at ccog.org titled *The Gospel of the Kingdom of God* and *Universal OFFER of Salvation, Apokatastasis: Can God save the lost in an age to come? Hundreds of scriptures reveal God's plan of salvation.*

While Greek philosophers (like Plato) and Mithraism taught going to heaven, the reality is that this was not a teaching of the New Testament nor of early professors of Christ.

A Roman Catholic priest wrote:

> The resemblances between Mithraism and Christianity may be quickly summed up,—belief in the immortality of the soul ... heaven ... (Aiken C.F., Mithraism and Christianity, p. 380).

The modern doctrine of going to heaven upon death simply was not part of early Christianity or taught in the New Testament. Christians taught the resurrection, that they would then reign with Jesus for 1,000 years on the earth (Revelation 20:4-6).

But after influence by people such as the sun-god worshipping Emperor Constantine in the 4th century, many ideas of his and his religion's became adopted by the Greco-Romans, out of whom, the Protestants later sprang.

The heaven as the reward of the saved doctrine has further been grabbed a hold of by Protestants. They tend to teach the physical earth is too flawed, but since heaven is spiritual people will not have problems like on earth.

They fail to realize some of the meaning of the statement that "we know that the law is spiritual" (Romans 7:14). The spiritual principles of the law apply now and will apply after Christians are made spirit beings. True Christians follow God's law now, which not only helps them build character, but will help them be able to teach others after the first resurrection (cf. Isaiah 30:20-21).

Jesus taught that in this age His followers are to "seek first the kingdom of God and His righteousness" (Matthew 6:33a). This focus motivates those who do so to have faith that God will provide (Matthew 6:33ab) and to strive to improve their lives and build character in this age.

When the millennial Kingdom of God comes, it will have a king (Jesus), laws, physical territory, and subjects. Christians are to pray for that kingdom to come (Matthew 6:10) and live their lives so that they will be able to reign with Jesus (cf. Revelation 20:4-6). Later, as Jesus taught (Revelation 3:12), New Jerusalem will come down from heaven to the earth (Revelation 21:2). Yet, many misunderstand that, and instead think heaven itself is the promise.

Eternity will not be better just because of being changed from mortal to immortal (1 Corinthians 15:54). Eternity will be better because God will only change those who willingly obeyed Him and built character in this life, so they will be better to reign with Him (Revelation 5:10).

Humans Were Created to Make Eternity Better

God has a job for each person individually (Romans 12:4-5; 1 Corinthians 12:11,27). Furthermore notice:

> [15] You shall call, and I will answer You; You shall desire the work of Your hands. (Job 14:15)

Each human being is the work of God's hands! You are not just "another brick in the wall," like the "beatific vision" seems to teach. God has a plan for everyone, individually, who will properly respond to Him and it involves doing a work to help make eternity better.

The CCOG teaches that God made humanity in order to reproduce Himself and be part of His family (Malachi 2:15). He made us to share in His glory (Romans 8:17) and to rule the universe (Hebrews 2:5-17).

Jesus taught that "It is more blessed to give than receive" (Acts 20:35). ("There is more happiness in giving than in receiving" Acts 20:35, Good News Translation).

God MADE humanity in order to give love (cf. 1 John 4:7-12), and so that there would be more love in the universe (cf. Matthew 22:37-39).

The CCOG teaches that God made humans so each one could give love in a unique way (cf. 1 Corinthians 12:20-13:10; 1 Thessalonians 3:12) to make eternity better for themselves and others. That, in essence, is the CCOG hope of salvation.

But how do we move towards that?

Essentially, by now living by faith and obedience to God in this life.

Christians, themselves, later will be changed and perfected at the first resurrection (1 Corinthians 15:50-54) in order to help give love and actually make eternity better.

The Apostle Paul referred to this change as "a mystery" (1 Corinthians 15:51).

Those who are currently non-Christian will have this opportunity after they are resurrected (see also the free book, available online at ccog.org, titled *Universal OFFER of Salvation, Apokatastasis: Can God save the lost in an age to come? Hundreds of scriptures reveal God's plan of salvation*). True Christians in this age will also be used by God to teach others (Isaiah 30:20) and reign during the millennium (Revelation 20:4-6).

The reason that God created humans is so that eternity would be better (cf. Hebrews 6:9,11:16; Philippians 1:23). God did not create humans so we would simply be in awe of Him for eternity.

More on God's plan can be found in the free book, available online at ccog.org titled, *The MYSTERY of GOD's PLAN Why Did God Create Anything? Why Did God Make You?*

Death

Are the Christian dead looking down on us now from heaven, as many Protestants teach?

No.

The Bible teaches that when people die, they basically are like being asleep.

So what are the dead now doing? The dead are dead. They are simply 'sleeping' in their graves, unconscious, waiting to be called to resurrection.

They are not strumming harps nor feeling the torment of pain and torture.

Here is a Protestant source that considers the biblical doctrine on death to be considered 'cultic':

> Soul sleep is the teaching that when a person dies that his soul "sleeps" until the time of the future resurrection. In this condition, the person is not aware or conscious. ...

The primary verses used to support soul sleep are found in Ecclesiastes:

- Eccl. 9:5, For the living know they will die; but the dead do not know anything, nor have they any longer a reward, for their memory is forgotten."
- Eccl. 12:7, "then the dust will return to the earth as it was, and the spirit will return to God who gave it."

Ecclesiastes must be understood in the context of its own commentary, which says at the opening of the book, "The words of the Preacher, the son of David, king in Jerusalem. 2 "Vanity of vanities," says the Preacher, "Vanity of vanities! All is vanity." 3 What advantage does man have in all his work which he does under the sun?" (Eccl. 1:1-3). The writer is telling us how things are from the human perspective from "under the sun." He is not telling us doctrinal statements about whether or not the soul continues after death. Besides, it's a mistake to use the Old Testament to interpret the New Testament. It is the New Testament that sheds light on the Old Testament.

In the New Testament, we see Paul say in 2 Cor. 5:8, "we are of good courage, I say, and prefer rather to be absent from the body and to be at home with the Lord." Paul is clearly telling us that when he dies that he will go and be with the Lord. Furthermore, at the Transfiguration of Jesus (Matt. 17:1-8), we see Moses and Elijah who were alive. There was no soul sleep with them.

Therefore, the doctrine of soul sleep is incorrect. (Slick M. President and Founder of the Christian Apologetics and Research Ministry. What is soul sleep? https://carm.org/soul-sleep accessed 01/13/16)

The above is wrong. It not only wants to discount the Book of Ecclesiastes, it misunderstands the Apostle Paul's writings, and misconstrues the Transfiguration. Plus, it ignores the direct teachings in both the Old and New Testaments on the state of the dead.

Notice some passages from the Old Testament Book of Psalms:

> ⁵ For in death there is no remembrance of You; In the grave who will give You thanks? (Psalm 6:5)
>
> ³ Consider and hear me, O Lord my God; Enlighten my eyes, Lest I sleep the sleep of death; (Psalm 13:3)
>
> ⁶ At Your rebuke, O God of Jacob, Both the chariot and horse were cast into a dead sleep. (Psalm 76:6)
>
> ¹⁰ Will You work wonders for the dead? Shall the dead arise and praise You? (Psalm 88:10)
>
> ¹⁷ The dead do not praise the Lord, Nor any who go down into silence. 18 But we will bless the Lord From this time forth and forevermore. Praise the Lord! (Psalm 115:17-18)

The Book of Psalms, and not just the Book of Ecclesiastes, teaches that the dead know nothing and that death is like sleep. The dead must be resurrected in order to praise God, and that will happen.

Consider also the following:

> ¹⁴ If a man dies, shall he live again? All the days of my hard service I will wait, Till my change comes. (Job 14:14)
>
> ²¹ Who knows the spirit of the sons of men, which goes upward, and the spirit of the animal, which goes down to the earth? (Ecclesiastes 3:21)

Upon death, the spirit of humans returns to God (cf. 2 Corinthians 5:8). The human spirit is there, sort of like a saved computer file of your memory and character—in a sleep-like state (Psalm 13:3; 76:6)—and is saved for the resurrection (Ecclesiastes 3:21; John 3:13; Ezekiel 37:11-14; 1 Corinthians 15:50-54). But, the spirit of animals seemingly comes to an end (Ecclesiastes 3:21), as they are not ever mentioned in any resurrection.

What about the New Testament?

The idea that death is like sleep is what Jesus Himself taught:

> ¹⁸ While He spoke these things to them, behold, a ruler came and worshiped Him, saying, "My daughter has just died, but come and lay Your hand on her and she will live." ...
>
> ²³ When Jesus came into the ruler's house, and saw the flute players and the noisy crowd wailing, ²⁴ He said to them, "Make room, for the girl is not dead, but sleeping." And they ridiculed Him.
>
> ²⁵ But when the crowd was put outside, He went in and took her by the hand, and the girl arose. ²⁶ And the report of this went out into all that land. (Matthew 9:18, 23-26)
>
> ¹¹ These things He said, and after that He said to them, "Our friend Lazarus sleeps, but I go that I may wake him up."
>
> ¹² Then His disciples said, "Lord, if he sleeps he will get well." ¹³ However, Jesus spoke of his death, but they thought that He was speaking about taking rest in sleep.
>
> 14 Then Jesus said to them plainly, "Lazarus is dead" (John 11:11-14).

In both of the above cases, the person was dead, but basically because this was normal physical death and NOT the permanent, second death, Jesus said the person was sleeping. All who sleep in the grave will be resurrected and hear His voice (John 5:28-29). Jesus showed a foretaste of this by resurrecting those He did.

As far as the Transfiguration supposedly disproving this goes, notice what the Bible actually teaches:

> ¹ Now after six days Jesus took Peter, James, and John his brother, led them up on a high mountain by themselves; 2 and He was transfigured before them. His face shone like the sun, and His clothes became as white as the light. ³ And behold, Moses and Elijah appeared to them, talking with Him. ...

> ⁹ Now as they came down from the mountain, Jesus commanded them, saying, "Tell the vision to no one until the Son of Man is risen from the dead." (Matthew 17:1-3,9)

Notice that Jesus said the Transfiguration was a VISION. A vision of something related to the future—not something that already happened.

Moses has not yet been resurrected nor has Elijah.

Consider that God called David "a man after His own heart" (1 Samuel 13:14). Yet, after Jesus was resurrected, notice what the Apostle Peter said:

> ²⁹ Fellow Israelites, I can tell you confidently that the patriarch David died and was buried, and his tomb is here to this day. ... ³⁴ For David did not ascend to heaven ... (Acts 2:29-34, NIV).

David has not yet been resurrected, nor is he in heaven. Nor is anyone other than Jesus, the Father, and the angels (cf. Matthew 18:10).

But what about 2 Corinthian 5:8 and desiring to be absent from the body? Does that not prove that 'soul sleep' was not taught?

No.

Notice what Pionius of Smyrna taught in the middle of the third century:

> When Pionius had been nailed down the public executioner said to him once again: "Change your mind and the nails will be taken out."
>
> But he answered: "I felt that they are in to stay."
>
> Then after a moment's reflection he said: "I am hurrying that I may awake all the more quickly, manifesting the resurrection from the dead." (The Martyrdom of Pionius and his Companions, Chapter 21. Text from H. Musurillo, The Acts of the Christian Martyrs (Oxford, 1972), 137-167)

Pionius desired to be with God quickly, but he understood that this would happen in the resurrection, which to him would seem to be the instant after he was killed.

Regarding 'soul sleep,' notice what some of what the Apostle Paul was inspired to write:

> [29] For he who eats and drinks in an unworthy manner eats and drinks judgment to himself, not discerning the Lord's body. [30] For this reason many are weak and sick among you, and many sleep. (1 Corinthians 11:29-30)

> [17] And if Christ is not risen, your faith is futile; you are still in your sins! [18] Then also those who have fallen asleep in Christ have perished. [19] If in this life only we have hope in Christ, we are of all men the most pitiable. [20] But now Christ is risen from the dead, and has become the firstfruits of those who have fallen asleep. (1 Corinthians 15:17-20)

> [51] Behold, I tell you a mystery: We shall not all sleep, but we shall all be changed — [52] in a moment, in the twinkling of an eye, at the last trumpet. For the trumpet will sound, and the dead will be raised incorruptible, and we shall be changed. [53] For this corruptible must put on incorruption, and this mortal must put on immortality. (1 Corinthians 15:51-53).

> [14] Therefore He says: "Awake, you who sleep, Arise from the dead, And Christ will give you light." (Ephesians 5:14)

> [14] For if we believe that Jesus died and rose again, even so God will bring with Him those who sleep in Jesus.

> [15] For this we say to you by the word of the Lord, that we who are alive and remain until the coming of the Lord will by no means precede those who are asleep. [16] For the Lord Himself will descend from heaven with a shout, with the voice of an archangel, and with the trumpet of God. And the dead in Christ will rise first. [17] Then we who are alive and remain shall be caught up together with them in the clouds to meet the Lord in the air. And thus we shall always be with the Lord. [18] **Therefore**

comfort one another with these words. (1 Thessalonians 4:14-18)

Luke also recorded that death was like sleep (Acts 7:60, 13:36), as did Peter (2 Peter 3:4).

It is proper for Christians to teach and believe that death is like sleep. Christians are to be comforted by God's plan, which includes the dead being asleep until they are resurrected.

Those who condemn 'soul sleep' are also condemning Jesus and the Apostle Paul, as well as Luke and Peter.

Did early Christians and others who professed Christ continue to teach this?

Yes.

The *Letter to the Corinthians*, also known as *1 Clement* teaches it in chapters 24 and 44. It is also consistent with chapter VII of Polycarp's *Letter to the Philippians*, as well the view his 'successor' Church of God bishop/pastor Polycrates of Ephesus held in the late second century:

> We observe the exact day; neither adding, nor taking away. For in Asia also great lights have fallen asleep, which shall rise again on the day of the Lord's coming, when he shall come with glory from heaven, and shall seek out all the saints. Among these are Philip, one of the twelve apostles, who fell asleep in Hierapolis; and his two aged virgin daughters, and another daughter, who lived in the Holy Spirit and now rests at Ephesus; and, moreover, John, who was both a witness and a teacher, who reclined upon the bosom of the Lord, and, being a priest, wore the sacerdotal plate. He fell asleep at Ephesus. And Polycarp in Smyrna, who was a bishop and martyr; and Thraseas, bishop and martyr from Eumenia, who fell asleep in Smyrna. Why need I mention the bishop and martyr Sagaris who fell asleep in Laodicea, or the blessed Papirius, or Melito, the Eunuch who lived altogether in the Holy Spirit, and who lies in Sardis, awaiting the episcopate from heaven, when he shall rise from the dead ? All these observed the fourteenth day of the passover according to the

> Gospel, deviating in no respect, but following the rule of faith. And I also, Polycrates, the least of you all, do according to the tradition of my relatives, some of whom I have closely followed. For seven of my relatives were bishops; and I am the eighth. And my relatives always observed the day when the people put away the leaven. I, therefore, brethren, who have lived sixty-five years in the Lord, and have met with the brethren throughout the world, and have gone through every Holy Scripture, am not affrighted by terrifying words. For those greater than I have said ' We ought to obey God rather than man'...I could mention the bishops who were present, whom I summoned at your desire; whose names, should I write them, would constitute a great multitude. And they, beholding my littleness, gave their consent to the letter, knowing that I did not bear my gray hairs in vain, but had always governed my life by the Lord Jesus (Polycrates as cited in Eusebius. The History of the Church, Book V, Chapter XXIV, Verses 2-7. Translated by A. Cushman McGiffert. Digireads.com Publishing, Stilwell (KS), 2005, p. 114).

Notice that five times, Polycrates, who claimed his teachings came from the Bible and the Apostles Philip and John referred to death as being like sleep. Various leaders of the Greco-Roman churches (including Roman Catholic and Eastern Orthodox saints) also taught this in the second and third centuries.

Protestants may wish to consider what Martin Luther wrote on 13 January 1522:

> It is probable, in my opinion, that, with very few exceptions indeed, the dead sleep in utter insensibility till the day of judgment ... On what authority can it be said that the souls of the dead may not sleep out the interval between earth and heaven ... (Luther M. Translated by W. Hazlitt. The life of Luther written by himself. M. Michelet, ed. Bohn's Standard Library. G. Bell, 1904, p. 133)

So, even Martin Luther somewhat understood that death is like sleep.

The Bible teaches "the dead know nothing" (Ecclesiastes 9:5).

According to A.N. Dugger, there were three unique doctrines that separated the COGs from Protestant sects: The observance of the seventh day Sabbath, nontrinitarianism, and teaching against the doctrine of the immortality of the soul.

Furthermore, according to A.N. Dugger, only the COGs held ALL three of those doctrines (Dugger AN, Dodd CO. A History of True Religion, 3rd ed. Jerusalem, 1972 (Church of God, 7th Day). 1990 reprint, p. 278). And he may have been correct in that.

Now, nearly all the Protestant faiths teach against what the Bible teaches regarding the state of the dead.

But some do know the truth.

The following is from an interview by *Time* with N.T. Wright, a high-ranking bishop in the Church of England:

> **Wright**: St. Paul is very clear that Jesus Christ has been raised from the dead already, but that nobody else has yet. Secondly, our physical state. The New Testament says that when Christ does return, the dead will experience a whole new life: not just our soul, but our bodies. And finally, the location. At no point do the resurrection narratives in the four Gospels say, "Jesus has been raised, therefore we are all going to heaven." It says that Christ is coming here, to join together the heavens and the Earth in an act of new creation.
>
> **TIME**: Is there anything more in the Bible about the period between death and the resurrection of the dead?
>
> **Wright**: ... Paul writes that ...it will be like being asleep. The Wisdom of Solomon, a Jewish text from about the same time as Jesus, says "the souls of the righteous are in the hand of God," and that seems like a poetic way to put the Christian understanding, as well (Van Biema D. Christians Wrong About Heaven, Says Bishop (N.T. Wright). Time, February 7, 2008).

Those who believe the Bible realize that it teaches that death is like sleep.

Annihilation or Eternal Punishing?

What is the fate of the incorrigibly wicked who will refuse God's offer of salvation?

What about the otherwise unconverted?

Protestants, in general, teach that any who have not accepted Jesus in this life will suffer eternal torment in the Gehenna fire that Jesus spoke of. People like Augustine of Hippo and Protestant Reformer John Calvin taught that included infants and the mentally-disabled.

Here is a historic Protestant view of punishment as expressed in the *Westminster Confession* (1646):

> "but the wicked, who know not God, and obey not the gospel of Jesus Christ, shall be cast into eternal torments, and punished with everlasting destruction from the presence of the Lord, and from the glory of his power." (Chapter XXXIII, Of the Last Judgment)

According to a year 2000 report from the *Alliance Commission on Unity & Truth* among Evangelicals the majority of Protestants have held that the unsaved will be in a place of unending conscious torment, both physical and spiritual. Because of influence from Dante Alighieri's 14th century poem known as *The Divine Comedy*, the area he called the Inferno/Infernus gave many people the wrong impression that God has a place of torturing that would last forever.

But that is not what the Bible teaches.

The Hebrew scriptures teach annihilation:

> [3] You shall trample the wicked, For they shall be ashes under the soles of your feet On the day that I do this," Says the Lord of hosts. (Malachi 4:3)

Here is what Jesus taught:

> [28] And you should not be afraid of those killing the body but not being able to kill the soul. Indeed rather you should fear the *One* being able to destroy both soul and body in Gehenna. (In Matthew 10:28, Berean Literal Bible)

Jesus taught annihilation.

Note: Gehenna IS a proper rendering above. Mistranslations of it and the words *hades* and *tartaroosas* have led to misunderstanding about annihilation among the Greco-Roman-Protestants. The word Gehenna represents "the Valley of HINNOM which lay just outside of Jerusalem and was the place where refuse was constantly being burned up" (The Ambassador College Bible Correspondence Course, Lesson 6, 1977). The word *hades* refers to the grave—it, of itself, is not a reference to "the lake of fire" (cf. Revelation 20:14).

It is first referred to in scripture in Joshua 15:8. It was also associated with pagan fire practices in 2 Kings 23:10; 2 Chronicles 28:3, 33:6; Jeremiah 7:31-32, 19:2-6, & 32:35. Trash, filth, the dead bodies of animals, and DESPISED CRIMINALS were thrown into Gehenna. Ordinarily, everything thrown into this valley was DESTROYED by fire. Christ used it to picture the terrible fate of UNREPENTANT SINNERS! Please understand that JESUS USED THE WORD GEHENNA 11 TIMES IN THE TEXTUS RECEPTUS (the text that the KJV was translated from). Jesus knew what it meant! But instead, various Protestant leaders do not want people to comprehend what Jesus was really teaching. For more details, check out *Lesson 15 of the STUDY THE BIBLE COURSE* of the *Continuing* Church of God, available online at www.ccog.org.

Despite Jesus' teaching on annihilation, as mentioned earlier, the early followers of Martin Luther condemned the annihilation view:

> XVII: ... They condemn the Anabaptists, who think that there will be an end to the punishments of condemned men and devils. (The Confession of Faith: Which Was Submitted to His Imperial Majesty Charles V. At the Diet of Augsburg in the Year 1530. By Philip Melanchthon, 1497-1560)

Notice more scriptures from the New Testament:

> [13] The sea gave up the dead who were in it, and Death and Hades delivered up the dead who were in them. And they were judged, each one according to his works. [14] Then Death and Hades were cast into the lake of fire. This is the second death. [15] And anyone not found written in the Book of Life was cast into the lake of fire. (Revelation 20:13-15)

> [8] But the cowardly, unbelieving, abominable, murderers, sexually immoral, sorcerers, idolaters, and all liars shall have their part in the lake which burns with fire and brimstone, which is the second death. (Revelation 21:8)

The second death is not like physical death—it is a permanent annihilation.

Ignatius of Antioch taught:

> Seeing, then, all things have an end, these two things are simultaneously set before us — death and life; and every one shall go unto his own place. (Letter to the Magnesians, Chapter 5).

> Let us not, therefore, be insensible to His kindness. For were He to reward us according to our works, we should cease to be. (Letter to the Magnesians, Chapter 10).

Annihilation, the second death, eliminates future suffering.

Annihilation is what Jesus taught and that is what we in the *Continuing Church of God* teach.

Furthermore, the purpose for all not annihilated is to give love in a unique way so that eternity will be better for all.

13. Plan of Salvation

Does God have a plan of salvation that makes sense?

Yes.

The Bible teaches that "God is love" (1 John 4:8), "God is the God of salvation" (Psalm 68:20), God is good (Mark 10:18), and God is all-powerful, all-knowing (Isaiah 46:9-11).

Would not such a God be wise enough to come up with a plan of salvation that works, and does not doom the overwhelming majority of humans who ever lived to punishing that never ends?

Could that be a major part of why He sent His Son (John 3:16-17; 10:10)?

Will God *offer* salvation to all human beings who ever lived?

The CCOG says yes. Protestants, in general, say no.

God's plan is a mystery to most. Notice something that the Bible teaches about that:

> [25] Now to Him who is able to establish you according to my gospel and the preaching of Jesus Christ, according to **the revelation of the mystery kept secret since the world began** [26] **but now made manifest, and by the prophetic Scriptures** made known to all nations, according to the commandment of the everlasting God, for obedience to the faith — [27] to God, alone wise, be glory through Jesus Christ forever. Amen. (Romans 16:25-27)

The Bible tells of the mystery which has been kept secret since the world began, but that it is revealed in prophetic scriptures—"the word of truth" (John 17:17, 2 Timothy 2:15; James 1:18). God's plan of salvation is a mystery to most Protestants, but not to the CCOG.

Protestants, in general, do not believe in keeping the biblical Holy Days nor understand how they tie in with God's plan of salvation.

Instead they tend to accept days like Christmas and Easter, which were not observed by early Christians.

The Protestant *Christianity Today* reported:

> The eventual choice of December 25, ... reflects a convergence of Origen's concern about pagan gods and the church's identification of God's son with the celestial sun. December 25 already hosted two other related festivals: *natalis solis invicti* (the Roman "birth of the unconquered sun"), and the birthday of Mithras, the Iranian "Sun of Righteousness" whose worship was popular with Roman soldiers. ... Seeing that pagans were already exalting deities with some parallels to the true deity, church leaders decided to commandeer the date and introduce a new festival. Western Christians first celebrated Christmas on December 25 in 336, after Emperor Constantine had declared Christianity the empire's favored religion. (Coffman E. Why December 25? For the church's first three centuries, Christmas wasn't in December—or on the calendar at all. Christianity Today, August 8, 2008)

The above is true. The name "Christmas" came later as *The Catholic Encyclopedia* reports:

> The word for Christmas in late Old English is *Cristes Maesse*, the Mass of Christ, first found in 1038, and *Cristes-messe*, in 1131. (Martindale C. Christmas, 1908).

Jesus never endorsed it. Even ignoring the pagan elements, Christmas focuses on elements that may be associated with the birth of Jesus as opposed to how He lived and what He will do with His kingdom.

Yet each December, it is common to hear what the 'multitude of heavenly hosts' said to the shepherds concerning Jesus' birth:

> [10] ... Do not be afraid, for behold, I bring you good tidings of great joy which will be to all people. [11] For there is born to you this day in the city of David a Savior, who is Christ the Lord. (Luke 2:10-11)

Yet, most Protestants not only do not realize that Jesus was born in the Fall (probably on one of the Holy Days), they do not seem to grasp that Jesus would be a joy to all people, as ALL will have an opportunity for salvation through Him: which is some of what the Fall Holy Days (particularly the Day of Atonement and the Last Great Day) help picture.

Although Jesus is a major part of God's plan (which is part of Protestant rationalization for promoting Christmas and Easter), by not keeping the Holy Days, Protestants tend to discount/deny aspects of the plan of salvation that the Holy Days help demonstrate. **All the biblical Holy Days have connections to Jesus and God's plan of salvation**.

Protestantism Dooms Most

Protestant salvation, in contrast to what the Bible teaches, tends to mainly rely on chance and circumstance. Some other Protestants (Calvinists come to mind) essentially teach that all humans are horrible sinners, but because God is a God of love, He predestined about 2% of people (mainly white ones) to be saved and that, essentially, God predestined all others to be lost.

Various Protestant leaders have clearly taught that most will be lost. Here are a few:

> ... most will be lost and not find salvation from sin (Price B. Romans Bible Commentary — Living By Faith Published by Brad Price, 2005, p. 96).

> ... most will not be saved (God's Plan of Salvation. Manassas Church of Christ, ©Manassas Church of Christ 1997-2003. http://manassaschurch.org/StudySer_Plan.htm viewed 06/11/09).

> The Bible says that most believe in God, but most will not be saved. (Andres GS. Do you have an Opposition to being saved? Up Dated Wednesday, March 18, 2009. G. Steven Andres Copyright — 1999 to 2009. http://andresusa.com/03-salvation/how-to-be-saved/do-you-have-an-objection.htm viewed 06/11/09).

> Even some two thousand years after the Great Commission, more people in the world have **not** heard the gospel than **have** heard it. The secret things do belong to God, but Christians and non-Christians alike cannot help wondering about the justice as well as the compassion of a God who assigns to eternal torment people who, for reasons beyond their control, never heard about fellowship with him through Jesus Christ....(Warren V. *What the Bible Says about Salvation* 1982, pp. 104-105, as cited in Estabrook J and Thompson B. Will Those Who Have Never Heard the Gospel Be Lost? Apologetics Press: Reason & Revelation, June 2001 — 21[6]:41-46. http://www.apologeticspress.org/articles/469 viewed 05/24/12).

The Bible, of course, does NOT teach that most will not be saved—there is NO scripture that states that.

The 'Protestant god' that condemns most, contrary to scripture (cf. John 3:17), does not have mercy (cf. Psalm 59:17, all of Psalm 136), does not offer salvation to all flesh (Luke 3:6), and is not the loving God of salvation (Psalm 68:20), and is not the God of the Bible that we in the CCOG serve.

Now consider some lyrics from the Protestant hymn *Untold Millions*:

> Untold millions are still untold
> Untold millions are still outside the fold
> Who will tell them of Jesus' love
> And the heavenly mansions awaiting above
> Jesus died on Calvary to save each one from sin
> Now he calls to you and to me
> To go and bring them in

Well, untold millions (actually, billions) have not been reached by

Protestantism. Partially because of that, there seems to be a basic acceptance within Protestantism that most people will not get a real chance to accept Jesus as Savior. Yet, unlike the Protestant trinity, the Godhead we in the CCOG worship will give every single person a real opportunity for salvation.

Protestants tend to hope that God will 'save sinners,' but tend to believe that most will not be reached and even more will never be saved.

Notice the following Protestant claim about the majority:

> ... the majority of those on earth will travel the wide road to destruction ... The average person in the world is lost in sin and does not know it ... **Why Will Most Be Lost?** ... Jesus said that if you die in your sins, you will be separated from Him forever, John 8:21 (Danklefsen B. If the Lord Returned Right Now Would you Be With Him for Eternity? *Eternal Life* series 1, 1977)

No, that explanation is in serious error. As often happens with improper exegesis (explanation of scriptures) verses cited often do not say what the author implies. John 8:21 has Jesus saying:

> "I am going away, and you will seek Me, and will die in your sin. Where I go you cannot come."

Notice that JESUS DID NOT say "separated from Him forever" or LOST IN YOUR SINS FOREVER! Consider that because there IS a resurrection, dying in ones' sins does not mean that there is no possible future hope (e.g. Ezekiel 37:11-14).

Since God is not a respecter of persons (Acts 10:34), while we in the CCOG accept that God predestined some to be called in this age, we do not believe the rest were predestined to be lost. We believe all will be granted an opportunity for salvation—the called in this age, and others in the ages to come.

John Calvin taught:

> That the vast majority of mankind will be lost (Farrar FW.
>
> MERCY AND JUDGMENT. LAST WORDS ON CHRISTIAN ESCHATOLOGY WITH REFERENCE TO DR. PUSEY'S "WHAT IS OF FAITH? 2nd edition, 1882. R. CLAY. SONS, AND TAYWR, BREAD STREET HILL, E.C., p. 58).

Thus, clearly Calvinistic Protestantism believes that a God of love wants to permanently punish and torment His creation. It makes no sense that an all-wise and loving God would do that. Do they not know that the Great Shepherd plans to look for those who are lost (Ezekiel 34:11-16)? How can He put an end to all crying, pain and suffering (Revelation 21:4) if He condemns most to eternal torment?

God Plans to Save People from All Over

Furthermore, if one takes those general views in Protestantism to their logical conclusion, the implication would be that God will mainly save people from the West, such as historical Europe and, later, North America (plus some parts of the Middle East). But notice what happened when Jesus was asked about salvation:

> [23] Then one said to Him, "Lord, are there few who are saved?" And He said to them, [24] Strive to enter through the narrow gate, for many, I say to you, will seek to enter and will not be able. ... [28] There will be weeping and gnashing of teeth, when you see Abraham and Isaac and Jacob and all the prophets in the kingdom of God, and yourselves thrust out. [29] **They will come from the east and the west, from the north and the south, and sit down in the kingdom of God.** [30] And **indeed there are last who will be first**, and there are first who will be last." (Luke 13:23-24,28-30)

There are several points concerning the above.

The first is that apparently people in this age who think that they are Christians (including being Protestant leaders) will not be saved unless they truly change and really know the Jesus of the Bible.

The second is it appears that Jesus is indicating that there will not be an overwhelming majority who are saved that are from the West. The West has no preeminence over those of the East (Asia), North (Russia, Scandinavia, and Inuit areas), or the South (Africa and islands). Yet, Protestantism really implies that people in those areas will have very few saved.

The third point is that many from non-Western lands, many whom now are not part of the so-called 'Christian' nations will be first, suggesting that many will have preeminence over Westerners in the Kingdom of God. Protestants need to understand that this truly is what the Bible is teaching.

Unlike Calvinistically-minded ones, we in the CCOG truly believe:

> [20] Our God is the God of salvation (Psalm 68:20).

Does it not make sense that "the God of salvation" actually has a plan of salvation that includes it being offered to all and accepted by most?

Yet, because Protestantism does not truly believe in *sola Scriptura* and is focused so much on this present age, it does not understand that or God's plan of salvation.

Perhaps, however, it should be mentioned that amongst 21st century Protestants, there are many among the Presbyterians and others that do realize that God must have a plan for all, and not just those who currently profess Christ (e.g. Some Presbyterians see salvation by other... Associated Press – Feb 10, 2010).

Consider the following about God:

> [3] For this is good and acceptable in the sight of God our Savior, [4] who desires all men to be saved and to come to the knowledge of the truth. (1 Timothy 2:3-4)

Since God wants all to be saved and is not biased, obviously God must have a plan so that all will have an opportunity to be saved.

Unlike most Protestants, we believe that the vast majority of people will ultimately truly accept Jesus and be saved. Protestants essentially believe that if because of circumstance one never hears about salvation through Jesus or for some reason, one did not accept it in this age, then one will be lost for eternity. Hundreds of scriptures support the CCOG's view (for details, check out the free book, available online at ccog.org, *Universal OFFER of Salvation, Apokatastasis: Can God save the lost in an age to come? Hundreds of scriptures reveal God's plan of salvation).*

The Real Jesus is Central to the Gospel

Like the Greco-Roman-Protestants, the CCOG teaches that Jesus is central to the gospel. The New Testament teaches:

> [16] For I am not ashamed of the gospel of Christ, for it is the power of God to salvation for everyone who believes, for the Jew first and also for the Greek (Romans 1:16).

> [4] Therefore those who were scattered went everywhere preaching the word. [5] Then Philip went down to the city of Samaria and preached Christ to them. ... [12] But when they believed Philip as he preached the things concerning the kingdom of God and the name of Jesus Christ, both men and women were baptized. ... [25] So when they had testified and preached the word of the Lord, they returned to Jerusalem, preaching the gospel in many villages of the Samaritans. [26] Now an angel of the Lord spoke to Philip ... [40] Philip was found at Azotus. And passing through, he preached in all the cities till he came to Caesarea. (Acts 8:4,5,12,25,26,40)

> [18] he preached to them Jesus and the resurrection. (Acts 17:18)

> [30] Then Paul dwelt two whole years in his own rented house, and received all who came to him, [31] **preaching the kingdom of God and teaching the things which concern the Lord Jesus Christ** with all confidence, no one forbidding him. (Acts 28:30-31)

Notice that the preaching included Jesus AND the kingdom. Sadly, a proper understanding of the gospel of the Kingdom of God tends to be missing from the teachings of the Greco-Roman-Protestant churches.

Salvation is ONLY available through Jesus (Acts 4:12). That is why He came and died to pay the penalty for the sins of humankind.

Notice also the following:

> [35] Then Philip opened his mouth, and beginning at this Scripture,

> preached Jesus to him. ³⁶ Now as they went down the road, they came to some water. And the eunuch said, "See, here is water. What hinders me from being baptized?"
>
> ³⁷ Then Philip said, "If you believe with all your heart, you may."
>
> And he answered and said, "I believe that Jesus Christ is the Son of God." (Acts 8:35-37)
>
> ⁹ Therefore God also has highly exalted Him and given Him the name which is above every name, ¹⁰ that at the name of Jesus every knee should bow, of those in heaven, and of those on earth, and of those under the earth, ¹¹ and that every tongue should confess that Jesus Christ is Lord, to the glory of God the Father. (Philippians 2:9-11)

The real Jesus kept the Sabbath, the Holy Days, kept the Ten Commandments, avoided unclean meats, and taught about the coming Kingdom of God, etc.

Protestants tend to have an issue with that as most of them will not "walk just as He walked" (1 John 2:6b).

Furthermore, although Christians like the Apostle Paul kept the Feast of Tabernacles after Jesus' resurrection, because many modern translations of the New Testament do not use the *Textus Receptus*, those who rely on those translations of Acts 18:21 would not realize that (for more on biblical manuscripts), see the free book, online at ccog.org, *Who Gave the World the Bible?*).

Keeping God's Holy Days Helps Christians to Understand

God's plan of salvation is actually laid out in the biblical Holy Days. Briefly, starting with the acceptance of the sacrifice of Jesus at Passover (cf. Luke 22:15) for the forgiveness of our sins, this is followed by the Days of Unleavened Bread which show that Christians are to strive to live without sin and hypocrisy (cf. Luke 12:2; 1 Corinthians 5:6-8).

The Feast of Pentecost, referred to as the Day of Firstfruits (Numbers 28:26) and Feast of Harvest (Exodus 23:16) in the Old Testament, pictures firstfruits of the small Spring harvest. This helps show the calling of the elect as the firstfruits in this age. These are those who will be raised in the first resurrection (Revelation 20:4-6). We see the start of the New Testament church and the outpouring of the Holy Spirit began on Pentecost in Acts 2. Christians now "have the firstfruits of the Spirit" (Romans 8:23).

The relatively long time gap between the Day of Pentecost (third month of the biblical calendar) and Feast of Trumpets (seventh month of the biblical calendar) helps picture the approximately 2,000 year-long church age that we are now in, which ends at the sounding of the seventh trumpet (Revelation 11:15).

The Feast of Trumpets, itself, points to the reality that God will pour out His wrath upon the world (Revelation 8:1-13, 9:1-19), Jesus will return to establish God's Kingdom (Revelation 11:15-19), and the first resurrection of the elect is coming (1 Corinthians 15:51-53).

The Day of Atonement helps show that Satan the devil and his role in our sins is real (cf. Leviticus 16:20-22,26), but also that his deceit will not exist in the millennial Kingdom (Revelation 20:1-3). Since it comes after the Feast of Trumpets (of which the final trumpet pictures the end of the church age), the ancient sin-offering sacrifice performed on it (Leviticus 16:9), helps picture that Jesus' sacrifice was not just for the called in this age, but for others who were to be later called. Yet, Protestants effectively "close the door" on that.

The Feast of Tabernacles helps picture the joys of the physical and spiritual abundance (cf. Deuteronomy 16:13-15) of the millennial kingdom of God on earth with Jesus as King.

The Last Great Day, also sometimes known as the eighth day of the Feast of Tabernacles points to the Great White Throne judgment (Revelation 20:11). It also points to the realization that God will offer salvation to all when parts of God's plan are revealed and made available to all as Jesus taught (cf. John 7:37-38). The dead will be raised (Revelation 20:5, 11-12) at this second resurrection, and live 100 years (Isaiah 65:20).

Notice the following from the old Worldwide Church of God:

The Eighth Day

Numbers in Scripture often carry special significance. The number 7, for instance, symbolizes completion or perfection, while the number 40 indicates trial or testing. The same is true in the case of the Last Great Day, which is referred to as the eighth day of the Feast (Lev. 23:36).

The word for the number 8 is related to a Hebrew word meaning 'fatness', and can imply abundance, fertility, resurrection or regeneration. This last and great day of the annual festival days foreshadows the greatest time of salvation for the greatest number of people at one time.

Listen now to God's words of warning and encouragement concerning these latter days: "Give a serving to seven, and also to eight, for you do not know what evil will be on the earth" (Eccl. 11:2).

We are told, "Cast your bread upon the waters, for you will find it after many days" (verse 1).

This exhortation should ring loud and clear to us in the context of the Last Great Day, for God sets the example, follows His own instructions and inspires us to do the same. God Himself will cast His spiritual bread upon the waters or nations of this earth both during the 1,000-year period, portrayed by the seven-day Feast of Tabernacles, and during the Great White Throne Judgment, symbolized by the Last Great Day Festival or the eighth day of the Feast. (Aust J. What the Last Great Day Means for You. Good News, October-November, 1983)

Together, the Feast of Tabernacles and the "Last Great Day," are also referred to as the Feast of Ingathering in the Old Testament (Exodus 23:17; 34:22). The Last Great Day pictures the great Fall harvest when others will be called (cf. John 7:37-38).

As did early Christians, Jews place great spiritual significance on the Holy Days. Notice the words of a prayer that Jews cite on the Last Great Day (which they call Shemini 'Atzeret):

> You are eternally mighty, my Lord, the Resuscitator of the dead are You; abundantly able to save" ("Mashiv HaRuach U'Morid HaGeshem" The Jewish Prayer for Wind and Rain).

Yes, God is abundantly able to save and His Holy Days help outline the plan.

Jews refer to the Last Great Day as Shemini 'Azeret or "the day of rain." And their sages placed great importance on it. In the Talmud, Jewish sage Rabbi Abahu said this was the best holy day because it "benefits both the righteous and the unrighteous" (Babylonian Talmud, Ta'anit 7a). And yes, it will benefit all.

> R. Shilah said: "The day of rain is as hard [to bear] as the day of judgment" (Babylonian Talmud, Baba Mezi'a 85a). Well, since it represents the day of judgement, that is in a sense so.

> "Rabbi Ḥama, son of Rabbi Ḥanina, said: The day of the rains is as great as the day on which the heavens and earth were created" (Babylonian Talmud, Ta'anit 7b). Traditionally, Jews believe the creation was on Rosh Hoshana (otherwise known as the Feast of Trumpets).

Rabbi Tanchum Bar Chiyah said it was greater than the day the Torah was given (traditionally believed to have been on Pentecost) because it will provide "joy to all nations and to the entire world" (Midrash Shocher Tov on Tehillim 117). And that great day will bring joy to all nations.

While some Protestants call God's plan to call others on the Last Great Day as "unorthodox" or even "cultic," the Eastern Orthodox teach:

> It is heretical to say that all must be saved, for this is to deny free will; **but it is a legitimate hope that all may be saved. Until the Last Day come, we must not despair of anyone's salvation**, (Ware T. The Orthodox Church. Penguin Books, London, 1997, p. 262).

2nd century COG writers like Ignatius (Letter to Polycarp, Chapter 1) and Theophilus (To Autolycus, Book 2, Chapter 17) taught about a future salvation past this age. So did Eastern Orthodox saints like Irenaeus of Lyon, Origen of Alexandria, Gregory of Nyssa, and Ambrose of Milan.

In the New Testament, the Apostle John referred to the eighth day as "the last day, that great day of the feast" (John 7:37a). On that day, Jesus confirmed that was when those who are spiritually thirsty can drink (John 7:37b).

God long ago laid out aspects of His plan:

> [11] The counsel of the Lord stands forever, The plans of His heart to all generations. (Psalm 33:11)

Did you know that the Bible talked about the existence of religious festivals in its very first book? One reason that God actually made the moon was to mark His holy day seasons:

> [14] Then God said, "Let there be lights in the sky to separate the day from the night. They will be signs and will mark religious festivals, days, and years. (Genesis 1:14, GWT)

The Hebrew word '*mowed*' (or *moad*) is properly translated as "religious festivals."

The Book of Psalms also confirms His festivals is basically why God made the moon:

> [19] He made the moon to mark the festivals (Psalm 104:19, Holman Christian Standard Bible)

Is this something you have heard before?

What are the religious festivals that the 'lights in the sky' God placed there were to mark? They are those listed in Leviticus 23 where the Hebrew word '*mowed*' is used seven times.

Now, notice the following scriptures:

> [11] The counsel of the Lord stands forever, The plans of His heart to all generations. (Psalm 33:11)

> [8] The end of a thing is better than its beginning; (Ecclesiastes 7:8)

Yes, God's plan will end well. It will not end with most of His children eternally being tormented. And the biblical Holy Days help picture this.

Now, Protestants are correct to point out that "all have sinned" (Romans 3:23), the "wages of sin is death" (Romans 6:23) and that it is appointed to humans "to die" (Hebrews 9:27). Yet, they sometimes overlook the fact that this is a physical death as people will be resurrected and judged (Hebrews 9:27; Romans 14:10; Revelation 20:11-12).

Someone with a Protestant background who realized that the Protestant concepts of salvation had problems and wondered about the Hebrew roots movement, sent this author an email that asked:

> If "it is appointed unto man once to die and then the judgment" (Hebrews 9:27), how does a person who isn't already saved make it to that 8th day after they have died? I have wondered a long time how it is not "fair" for babies to get a free pass into heaven without making a deliberate choice to serve God, so I do believe that they, as well as certain others, will get that chance, but how to get around Hebrews 9:27?

This author's response was:

> What happens to babies when they die was one of the first items that interested me in the Church of God. And is a doctrine that I have not seen explained in the Hebrew roots movements. Anyway, being appointed once to die does not limit death to only once. The Bible is clear that there is a "second death" that non-believers risk (Revelation 2:11; 20:6,14; 21:8). So, there really is no need to "get around" Hebrews 9:27—just consider it in the context of other scriptures. People "make it" to that "8th day" time by being part of the second resurrection (cf. Revelation 20:4-14) (email 8/21/12).

Protestants also seem to overlook/misunderstand biblical statements such as the following:

> ⁴ Who are you to judge another's servant? To his own master he stands or falls. Indeed, he will be made to stand, for God is able to make him stand. (Romans 14:4)
> ¹³ Mercy triumphs over judgment. (James 2:13)

So, yes, people can be judged and found guilty, but still receive mercy. God can make them stand.

How else could mercy triumph over judgment?

Joel pointed out that God relents of punishment for those who will turn to Him:

> ¹² "Now, therefore," says the Lord, "Turn to Me with all your heart, With fasting, with weeping, and with mourning."
>
> ¹³ So rend your heart, and not your garments; Return to the Lord your God, For He is gracious and merciful, Slow to anger, and of great kindness; And He relents from doing harm. (Joel 2:12-13)

God's mercy and judgments are unsearchable for most:

> ³³ Oh, the depth of the riches both of the wisdom and knowledge of God! How unsearchable are His judgments and His ways past finding out!
>
> ³⁴ "For who has known the mind of the Lord? Or who has become His counselor?" (Romans 11:33-34)

God's mercy is beyond what most Protestants seem to think it is. Many do not understand how the mind of the Lord loves.

The Bible then tells of a time called the great white throne judgment, which happens after the second resurrection:

> ¹¹ Then I saw a great white throne and Him who sat on it, from whose face the earth and the heaven fled away. And there was found no place for them. ¹² And I saw the dead, small and great, standing before God, and books were opened. And another book was opened, which is the Book of Life. And the dead were judged according to their works, by the things which were written in the books. (Revelation 20:11-12)

Thus, the Bible foretells judgment for those not judged by God in this life. And that books would be opened. Yes, people will be found guilty of sin (cf. Romans 3:23), but remember, that eternal life will be granted to repentant sinners who accept Jesus (Romans 6:23). The future time for this is also known as the age to come (cf. Matthew 12:31-32).

However, according to Dr. David Jeremiah (a well-known tele-evangelical Protestant minister), all who come before the white throne judgment are essentially doomed. Here are some things he wrote:

> Revelation 20. The Great White Throne Judgment is an event where those that did not know Jesus as their Savior during their life will come before the Lord and be judged by Christ. ...
>
> We see Buddhists and Muslims and Hindus and Protestants and Catholics and Baptists and Presbyterians. ... What will happen to these religious people when they stand before God? ... Let the Lord Jesus answer that question. "Many will say to Me in that day, 'Lord, Lord, have we not prophesied in Your name, cast out demons in Your name, and done many wonders in Your name?' And then I will declare to them, 'I never knew you; depart from Me, you who practice lawlessness!' (Matthew 7:21-23) ...
>
> (Revelation 3:5) ... If we come to the end of our life and we haven't accepted Him, the Bible says our name is blotted out of the Book of Life ... (Jeremiah D. What is the Great White Throne Judgment in Revelation? https://davidjeremiah.blog/what-is-the-great-white-throne-judgment-in-revelation/ accessed 06/26/19)

Despite David Jeremiah's last claim, the Bible (including Revelation 3:5) does NOT say those who were not called in this age are automatically "blotted out" of the Book of Life. No scripture states that.

Furthermore, notice something from evangelical Protestant Don Stewart:

> The Great White Throne is the final judgment. Those who are judged are assigned to their final state. The Bible does not indicate any chance for belief after this final judgment. (Steward D. What Is the Last Judgment? (The Great White Throne)

> https://www.blueletterbible.org/faq/don_stewart/don_stewart_146.cfm accessed 04/28/20)

But Jesus did teach a legitimate opportunity at the time of judgment (cf. Matthew 11:22-24). The Bible shows that God will plead with people (Isaiah 3:13; Jeremiah 25:31; Ezekiel 20:33-44). God will plead for true repentance! This pleading will be for people considered to be "lost sinners"! He will give them an opportunity to live His way. God's plan is to maximize those who could be saved. His word teaches that the time will come that, "whoever calls on the name of the Lord shall be saved" (Romans 10:13).

After the hundred year white throne judgment, the righteous and the wicked die (Isaiah 65:20). All then dead will hear Jesus' voice (cf. John 5:28-29) as this is the third resurrection (Revelation 20:13; Acts 24:15).

Eric Meyers published the following about Christians In the 2nd to 4th centuries:

> These Jewish Christian groups, referred to by Epiphanius (Williams, 1987) as Nazarenes or Elkasaites, professed the following beliefs: They proclaimed Jesus as Messiah; insisted upon the validity of the Torah & laws of ritual purity; spoke of three resurrections; professed a millennarian eschatology; ... & preferred the designation "Nazarene" over "Christian." (Meyer E. Early Judaism and Christianity in the Light of Archaeology. Biblical Archaeologist, Vol. 51, No. 2, June 1988: 69-79).

Early Christians taught three resurrections (and the millennium).

Though most Protestants do not teach three resurrections, some realize that the Bible does teach that:

Here are two items from the 19th century related to that:

> Rev xx. ... In this chapter there are THREE resurrections mentioned. The first takes place *before* or *at* the Millennium, the second *immediately after* it, and the third not until the *end* of the season that *succeeds* the Millennium. It is evident, from the language that these are *distinct* and *separate* resurrections.

> (The Original Secession Magazine. A Short and Easy Method with the Ultra-Millenarians. September 1865, later published by J. Maclaren, 1866, pp. 274-275)

> The theorists of the literal school lose all the righteous except martyrs and confessors; else they must have three resurrections ... (Campbell A. The Christian Messenger and Reformer. Churches of Christ, May 1843, p. 79)

In the 20th century, the late COG evangelist Raymond McNair wrote:

> When the time for the third resurrection arrives, everyone will have had his chance. (McNair R. The Third Resurrection: Part V. Good News, May 1974)

In the late 20th century, the late COG evangelist Dr. Herman Hoeh wrote:

> How, then, does one understand the expression that "the child shall die"? Because the righteous will not continue to live in the flesh. They shall be given immortality by becoming spirit beings, the eternal sons of God, just as the righteous who are alive when Christ returns at His Second Coming: "Behold, I tell you a mystery: we shall not all sleep, but we shall all be changed-in a moment, in the twinkling of an eye" (I Corinthians 15:51-52). ... The change from mortal to immortal is a death of the cells of the natural body, but it will happen "in a moment," as Paul said, so one will not even be aware of a loss of consciousness!

> Isaiah 65:20 is describing this kind of momentary death, when one is changed to immortality; not the lake of fire, which is the second death, which the sinner who is accursed suffers. So the great purpose of the second resurrection will be finished in 100 years! (Hoeh H. The. Resurrection at the LAST DAY. Good News. Sept-Oct 1988, p. 22)

For believers at the end of this period, the change at the 'third resurrection' will be like what happens to living Christians at the time of the first resurrection (1 Corinthians 15:51-53).

We in the *Continuing* Church of God teach the three resurrections (see also the free online book: *Universal OFFER of Salvation, Apokatastasis: Can God save the lost in an age to come? Hundreds of scriptures reveal God's plan of salvation*). We believe that God's plan of salvation makes sense, is fair, and is not as illogical and happenstance as the bulk of Protestantism teaches.

Some Protestants have improperly claimed that the biblical Holy Days only can be kept in Jerusalem. However, the Bible shows that the Apostle Paul and his companions kept the Days of Unleavened Bread in Philippi of Macedonia (Acts 20:6), Jewish records show the festivals kept outside of Jerusalem (Schausse H. The Jewish Festivals: A Guide to Their History and Observance, 1938. Schocken (September 9, 1996), p. 184), and history shows that early Christians like Polycarp of Smyrna observed them outside of Jerusalem (Danielou, Cardinal Jean-Guenole-Marie. The Theology of Jewish Christianity. Translated by John A. Baker. The Westminster Press, 1964, pp. 345-346).

If the world's churches would have continued to keep the biblical Holy Days like the original Christians did, and not rely on unbiblical traditions (Matthew 15:3-9), they would have understood much more about God's wonderful plan of salvation. They would have been better able to understand that God is not desperately trying to save everyone now, but that His plan includes offering salvation to all!

For more information on the Holy Days and how they tie in with God's plan of salvation, check out the free online booklet, *Should You Keep God's Holy Days or Demonic Holidays?*

Only Few Find the Way Now

Currently in this age, most in the world are cut off from God. There are those selected individuals with whom God chose to work with now that He reserved to Himself. Those are called the elect (more on God's calling is available in the free online booklet, *Is God Calling You?*).

Jesus and Paul made it clear only a relative few in this age are called:

> [32] Do not fear, little flock, for it is your Father's good pleasure to give you the kingdom. (Luke 12:32)

> ²⁷ Though the number of the children of Israel be as the sand of the sea, The remnant will be saved. ²⁸ For He will finish the work and cut it short in righteousness, Because the Lord will make a short work upon the earth. (Romans 9:27-28)

We in the CCOG are among the remnant (see also Romans 11:5) called in this age to be part of that "little flock" and we also are working on preparations to support the "short work."

During this 6,000-year stage of His plan, the flock is called to carry out special assignments in this age (Matthew 24:14; 28:19-20; 1 Corinthians 12:20-28), as well as to be prepared to assist after the first AND second resurrections. The elect of this age will be able to relate to, and assist, those who are to be called in the age to come.

In this age, only a few will truly find Christ as Jesus teaches in Matthew 7:13-14:

> ¹³ Enter by the narrow gate; for wide is the gate and broad is the way that leads to destruction, and there are many who go in by it. ¹⁴ Because narrow is the gate and difficult is the way which leads to life, and there are few who find it.

Remember that this is the same Jesus who came to save more than a few. And He will in the age to come, since only a few were prophesied to remain faithful in this age. Furthermore, Jude made it clear that only "ten thousands of His saints" would return with Jesus (Jude 14). Since the Apostle Paul wrote "all His saints" (1 Thessalonians 3:13) return with Him at His second coming, that number is not tens of millions or billions.

Would a loving God make the way so difficult that only a relative few would ever be able to be saved?

No, of course not!

God made the way to find it difficult in this age as He realized that would be the best way to make it so the vast majority of people who ever lived could be saved. That is the plan.

We in the Philadelphia remnant of the Church of God, specifically in the *Continuing* Church of God, understand that God will offer salvation to everyone either in this age or the ages to come (millennium and 100 year period), and even those in nations without many Bibles will respond.

Notice also Zephaniah 2:11:

> [11] The Lord will be awesome to them, For He will reduce to nothing all the gods of the earth; People shall worship Him, Each one from his place, Indeed all the shores of the nations.

God has a plan for those who worshiped pagan gods.

Now, partially because of improper teachings from major faiths that claim Christianity, an Islamic website claimed:

> Unlike Jews and Christians, Muslims believe that Heaven (Paradise) is accessible to believers from all nations (Islam for Christians. The Last Day according to Judaism, Christianity and Islam (2/2), December 28, 2016).

But Christians faithful to scripture do teach that what Muslims may consider to be 'paradise' is accessible to all nations. Notice what the New Testament shows:

> [9] After these things I looked, and behold, a great multitude which no one could number, of all nations, tribes, peoples, and tongues, standing before the throne and before the Lamb, clothed with white robes, with palm branches in their hands, [10] and crying out with a loud voice, saying, "Salvation belongs to our God who sits on the throne, and to the Lamb!" (Revelation 7:9-10)

Notice that this is telling about all nations, tribes, peoples, and tongues.

Not All Called Now

In 2 Thessalonians 2:13-14, Paul teaches that God planned to call the elect now from the beginning:

> [13] But we are bound to give thanks to God always for you, brethren beloved by the Lord, because God from the beginning chose you for salvation through sanctification by the Spirit and belief in the truth, [14] to which He called you by our gospel, for the obtaining of the glory of our Lord Jesus Christ.

The Feast of Pentecost helps show that only some are called now, for a small, initial harvest. But many Protestants seem to overlook that aspect of Pentecost since they do not keep the other biblical Holy Days.

In Romans 11:1-5, Paul shows that while God has not cast away His people forever, He only has called a remnant now:

> [1] I say then, has God cast away His people? Certainly not! For I also am an Israelite, of the seed of Abraham, of the tribe of Benjamin. [2] God has not cast away His people whom He foreknew. Or do you not know what the Scripture says of Elijah, how he pleads with God against Israel, saying, [3] "LORD, they have killed Your prophets and torn down Your altars, and I alone am left, and they seek my life"? [4] But what does the divine response say to him? "I have reserved for Myself seven thousand men who have not bowed the knee to Baal." [5] Even so then, at this present time there is a remnant according to the election of grace.

A remnant, at this present time, according to the election of grace, is not a relatively large amount.

Yet, Zechariah 10:6 shows:

> [6] "I will strengthen the house of Judah, And I will save the house of Joseph. I will bring them back, Because I have mercy on them. They shall be as though I had not cast them aside;

How can people be as though they were not cast aside if they will not have an opportunity for salvation? These also would include those who were cast off in Hosea 9:16-17. And this ties in with the Last Great Day, which Protestants generally do not observe.

Mark 4:33-34 shows that Jesus only explained what He meant to a few who heard Him:

> [33] And with many such parables He spoke the word to them as they were able to hear it. [34] But without a parable He did not speak to them. And when they were alone, He explained all things to His disciples.

Why?

Many could not believe, even though they saw Jesus' miracles, because they had been blinded:

> [37] But although He had done so many signs before them, they did not believe in Him, [38] that the word of Isaiah the prophet might be fulfilled, which he spoke:
>
> "Lord, who has believed our report? And to whom has the arm of the LORD been revealed?"
>
> [39] Therefore **they could not believe, because** Isaiah said again: [40] **"He has blinded their eyes and hardened their hearts, Lest they should see with their eyes, Lest they should understand with their hearts and turn**, So that I should heal them." (John 12:37-40, NKJV)

> [40] He hath blinded their eyes, and hardened their heart; that they should not see with their eyes, nor understand with their heart, and be converted, and I should heal them. (John 12:40, KJV)

Therefore, the Bible is clear that people were blinded so that even when they saw the signs from Jesus they could not be converted in this age. This is because this was not the age for most to be saved as God's plan, which involves the age to come, will result in the highest possible percentage of people being saved.

Also notice Job 17:4a and Luke 13:24:

> [4] For You have hidden their heart from understanding ...

> [24] Strive to enter through the narrow gate, for many, I say to you, will seek to enter and will not be able.

Some, including some who wanted to know, have been prevented from understanding!

There is No Partiality with God

Is God partial?
No, there is no partiality with God as Romans 2:11, Ephesians 6:9, and Acts 10:34 show:

> [11] For there is no partiality with God.

> [9] ... there is no partiality with Him.

> [34] In truth I perceive that God shows no partiality.

Hence, ***there must be a plan for the rest!***

A plan for those NOT called and chosen in this age as God is NOT partial, nor does He love them any less.

In a Day of Salvation

Contrary to the view that some interfaith leaders promote, the Bible makes it clear that there is only one name that can save as Acts 4:10-12 plainly teaches:

> [10] let it be known to you all ... that by the name of Jesus Christ of Nazareth, ...[11] This is the 'stone which was rejected by you builders, which has become the chief cornerstone.' [12] Nor is there salvation in any other, for there is no other name under heaven given among men by which we must be saved.

It should be clear that God has hidden parts of His plan, since the name of Jesus as the true Christ is not known by many today. Nor has the name of Jesus been known for thousands of years by many. Yet, since God plans to offer salvation to the ends of the earth, and since no one can be saved without Jesus, it should be obvious to any who will believe their Bibles that God must have planned to offer salvation to everyone at a later time.

Furthermore, please study, pray, and meditate about what Ephesians 2:11-12 says:

> [11] Therefore remember that you, once Gentiles in the flesh—who are called Uncircumcision by what is called the Circumcision made in the flesh by hands— [12] that at that time you were without Christ, being aliens from the commonwealth of Israel and strangers from the covenants of promise, having no hope and without God in the world.

Notice that those Gentiles HAD NO HOPE! Up until Christ came, almost no Gentile that ever lived had any HOPE! And since most Gentiles (and most Israelites) have STILL never heard the truth about Christ (the only name by which men can be saved—Acts 4:12), will your God condemn those who never had hope? People who are still blinded by Satan so that they, in this age (2 Corinthians 4:4), cannot see?

But most Protestants say, doesn't the Bible teach NOW IS THE DAY OF SALVATION?

Well, let's look at the scriptures cited relating to that.

This view comes, initially, from Isaiah 49:8a. Since some versions have not translated it from the Hebrew literally, people can get confused. Here are some translations that get it right:

> [8] Thus saith the Lord, In an acceptable time have I heard thee, and in a day of salvation have I helped thee: (KJV)

> [8] Thus saith the LORD: In an acceptable time have I answered thee, And in a day of salvation have I helped thee; (Jewish Publication Society Tanakh 1917)

> [8] Thus said Jehovah: 'In a time of good pleasure I answered thee, And in a day of salvation I helped thee, (Youngs Literal Translation)

Notice that the above does not say the only day of salvation, but only "a day of salvation" (note: the complete passage as well as the next several verses that follow it do refer to the age to come).

Now, the New Testament was written in Greek, and Greek has different grammar rules than English. Some who read translations in English have concluded that the word of God says something it does not quite say.

Some have been confused by many Protestant translations of 2 Corinthians 6:2 which seems to say that now is the only day of salvation.

Yet, this verse has often been improperly translated. Notice one example of that:

> [2] For He says: "In an acceptable time I have heard you, And in the day of salvation I have helped you." Behold, now is the accepted time; behold, now is the day of salvation. (NKJV)

It is mistranslated because the word "the" in the New King James version is actually absent in the Greek, as a review of the original language makes clear. Not one of the three times "the" is included in the NKJV is it in the Greek.

Let's look at two actually more literal Protestant translations:

> [2] For He says, "In *the* acceptable time I listened to you, and in *the* day of salvation I helped you." Behold, now is *the* time of favor; behold, now is *the* day of salvation. (2 Corinthians 6:2, Berean Literal Bible)

> [2] for He saith, 'In an acceptable time I did hear thee, and in a day of salvation I did help thee, lo, now is a well-accepted time; lo, now, a day of salvation,' – (2 Corinthians 6:2, Young's Literal Translation)

The use of italics in the Berean Literal Bible shows that the word "the" was not in the original, but inserted several times.

When you consider that the definite article "the" is used in *koine* Greek much more than English, this further drives home the point (since 'the' is absent from the New Testament text) that the Bible is NOT teaching that this is the only day of salvation, but only *a* day of salvation).

That being said, for those who have truly been called and accepted the call, yes, it is the/their day of salvation.

For others, their opportunity comes later, at a time when they will be more able to accept it.

There is no second chance. ALL HUMAN BEINGS WILL HAVE ONE REAL OPPORTUNITY FOR SALVATION.

Who Will Totally Lose Their Opportunity for Salvation?

The Bible clearly shows that everyone will have a one real opportunity for salvation. Those who truly already had their opportunity will be destroyed without this later opportunity (Hebrews 2:3; 6:4-5). Only the ones who truly had their opportunity in this life and discarded it, have blasphemed the Holy Spirit.

That is the one, and only, thing Jesus said would not be forgiven:

> [31] Therefore I say to you, every sin and blasphemy will be forgiven men, but the blasphemy against the Spirit will not be forgiven men. [32] Anyone who speaks a word against the Son of Man, it will be forgiven him; but whoever speaks against the Holy Spirit, it will not be forgiven him, either in this age or in the age to come (Matthew 12:31-32, see also Hebrews 6:4-6).

Notice that Jesus said that speaking against Him would be forgiven in the age to come—hence hearing the name of Christ and not responding to it IS NOT AN UNPARDONABLE SIN. But blasphemy against the Holy Spirit will not be forgiven.

What would constitute blasphemy against the Holy Spirit?

Hebrew 10:26-27 teaches:

> [26] For if we sin willfully after we have received the knowledge of the truth, there no longer remains a sacrifice for sins, [27] but a

certain fearful expectation of judgment, and fiery indignation which will devour the adversaries.

So, one way would be to become a true Christian and reject that way. Peter noted:

> [21] For it would have been better for them not to have known the way of righteousness, than having known it, to turn from the holy commandment delivered to them (2 Peter 2:21).

Another way would be truly knowing better, but not acting on it as Jesus noted:

> [41] Jesus said to them, "If you were blind, you would have no sin; but now you say, 'We see.' Therefore your sin remains" (John 9:41).

Note that any sin that remains is NOT sin that is forgiven. And the only sin that is not forgiven is "blasphemy against the Holy Spirit."

Only those who have truly blasphemed the Holy Spirit have lost their opportunity—they do not get 'a second chance'—they had their opportunity.

And that helps explain why there are very few real Christians on the earth. Since God is love and wants none to permanently remain lost, He is only calling a relatively few now, so that even fewer would blaspheme the Holy Spirit and not receive eternal salvation. This is a biblical concept that greatly sets apart the bulk of the Protestant world from the genuine Church of God.

The Bible is clear that some are called now, and others to be called later—in the age to come (for more scriptures that specifically use that term, please see our free online booklet *Universal OFFER of Salvation, Apokatastasis: Can God save the lost in an age to come? Hundreds of scriptures reveal God's plan of salvation*). This is the hope of not just physical Israel, but also those who will be called later and to be part of spiritual Israel (Romans 9:6-8). While there may be more than one way to interpret various scriptures, what the *Continuing* Church of God teaches on this subject is consistent with the Bible.

Since God is love and intentionally has not called or chosen everyone in this age, then it is clear that He does have a plan for all. The Apostle Paul asked King Agrippa:

> [8] Why should it be thought incredible by you that God raises the dead? (Acts 26:8).

So, why should it be incredible that God truly has a plan for salvation? There are reportedly around 800,000,000 nominal Protestants currently alive with some fraction of those being devout. If one takes the primary Protestant view to its logical conclusion, then 7,000,000,000 (or more) people currently alive are doomed to burn forever, as well as countless billions throughout history. This Protestant view seems to lead to the conclusion that God will show His love by saving a relatively few Protestants while tormenting the greatest majority of humankind forever. Surely, any thinking Protestant can see the gross error in the traditional Protestant view.

What about any lovingly logical explanation from Protestant scholars on what Jesus meant on these matters, especially related to the expression "in the age to come" (Matthew 12:32)?

The *Wycliffe Bible Commentary*, for example, ignores the expression (see The Wycliffe Bible Commentary, Electronic Database, Matthew 12:31-32. Copyright I 1962 by Moody Press), while *Matthew Henry's Commentary* states:

> [2.] What the sentence is that is passed upon it; It shall not be forgiven, neither in this world, nor in the world to come. As in the then present state of the Jewish church, there was no sacrifice of expiation for the soul that sinned presumptuously; so neither under the dispensation of gospel grace, which is often in scripture called the world to come, shall there be any pardon to such as tread underfoot the blood of the covenant, and do despite to the Spirit of grace: there is no cure for a sin so directly against the remedy. It was a rule in our old law, No sanctuary for sacrilege. Or, It shall be forgiven neither now, in the sinner's own conscience, nor in the great day, when the pardon shall be published. Or, this is a sin that exposes the sinner both to temporal and eternal punishment, both to

present wrath and the wrath to come (Matthew Henry's Commentary on the Whole Bible: New Modern Edition, Electronic Database, Matthew 12:22-37. Copyright 1991 by Hendrickson Publishers, Inc.).

The above commentary seems to basically ignore what Jesus was saying—somewhat like it would rather discuss other portions of the verse. But there is an age to come that IS part of God's plan.

The Indescribable Gift

Consider that this impartial One is "one God and Father of all" (Ephesians 4:6).

> [17] Every good gift and every perfect gift is from above, and comes down from the Father of lights, with whom there is no variation or shadow of turning. (James 1:17)

Jesus taught that fathers are to give their children good gifts (Matthew 7:9-11).

Will not God the Father of all human beings at least offer the gift of salvation to all of His children?

While referencing those called now who have the "grace of God" (2 Corinthians 9:14), the Apostle Paul wrote:

> [15] Thanks be to God for His indescribable gift! (2 Corinthians 9:15)

Is it only those called now who can have that gift?

No.

> [15] But *should* not the free gift be even as the offense *was*? For if by the transgression of the one man many died, how much more did the grace of God, and the gift of grace, which *is* by the One Man, Jesus Christ, abound unto many?

> ¹⁶ And *should* not the free gift *be* like that which came by *the* one who had sinned? For on the one hand, judgment *was* by one unto condemnation; but on the other hand, the free gift *is by one* to *the* justification of many offenses.
>
> ¹⁷ For if by the offense of the one man death reigned by the one, how much more shall those who receive the abundance of grace and the gift of righteousness reign in life by the One, Jesus Christ.)
>
> ¹⁸ So then, even as by the one transgression condemnation *came* unto all men, in the same way also, by the one act of righteousness *shall* justification of life *come* unto all men. (Romans 5:15-18, AFV)

Notice also the last verse above as shown in the Berean Literal Bible:

> ¹⁸ So then, just as through one trespass, *it is* unto condemnation to all men, so also through one act of righteousness *it is* unto justification of life to all men. (Romans 5:18, BLB)

Justification of life cannot come to all humans unless they are given an opportunity.

But how?

Consider that Isaiah 9:2 is clear that those who walked in darkness will see the light:

> ² The people who walked in darkness Have seen a great light; Those who dwelt in the land of the shadow of death, Upon them a light has shined.

Notice that Isaiah 42:16-18 teaches that and shows this includes those who had followed idols:

> ¹⁶ I will bring the blind by a way they did not know; I will lead them in paths they have not known. I will make darkness light before them, And crooked places straight. These things I will do for them, And not forsake them. ¹⁷ They shall be turned back,

> They shall be greatly ashamed, Who trust in carved images, Who say to the molded images, 'You are our gods.' ¹⁸ "Hear, you deaf; And look, you blind, that you may see.

Jeremiah 6:10 further shows that many simply cannot hear God's message:

> ¹⁰ To whom shall I speak and give warning, That they may hear? Indeed their ear is uncircumcised, And they cannot give heed.

Thus, not only can some NOT SEE, some apparently CANNOT GIVE HEED.

Isaiah was inspired to write:

> ¹⁵ Whereas you have been forsaken and hated, So that no one went through you, I will make you an eternal excellence, A joy of many generations. (Isaiah 60:15)

The masses of humanity throughout history in places like Asia, Africa, remote islands, and the old Western Hemisphere will get an opportunity. Yes, including peoples of China, Siberia, India, and the Americas (Incas, Mayans, Inuits, etc.). Plus "many who are first will be last, and the last first" (Mark 10:31).

Consider the following from the Book of Acts:

> ⁴⁸ ... And as many as had been appointed to eternal life believed. (Acts 13:48)

But since God wants ALL saved (cf. 1 Timothy 2:4), truly there will be an opportunity for those not 'appointed to eternal life' in this age.

The biblical Holy Days help lay out how God is calling some now and will call others later. This is not something that general Protestantism understands.

Instead, Protestantism clings to the views of people like Marcion and John Calvin that most people who ever lived will not be saved.

14. Crosses, Trees, Valentine's, and Collars

Early Christians did not have crosses or icons.

Notice an accusation against those who professed Christ in the second/third century (date uncertain) in a supposed argument between the heathen Caecilius and the claimed Christian Octavius:

> Why have they no altars, no temples, no acknowledged images? (Minucius. Octavius. Excerpted from Ante-Nicene Fathers, Volume 4, Chapter 10).

If the cross was an oft used symbol or sacred image for early Christians, the above accusation would not have been made against them.

The use of images like crosses started to change by practices of some of the Greek heretics in the late 2nd and early 3rd centuries. Later, this was adopted by many of the rest of the Greco-Romans in the 4th century after being influenced by Emperor Constantine.

History records that crosses were used by pagans centuries before Jesus was born. There is an Assyrian statue of King Samsi-Vul (prior to 1000 B.C.) wearing a cross around his neck, the Greek goddess Diana was often portrayed with a cross above her head looking very much like later medieval portrayals of the 'Virgin Mary,' and in India Buddha was depicted as a cross centuries before Jesus was executed (Brock M. The Cross, Heathen and Christian: A Fragmentary Notice of Its Early Pagan Existence and Subsequent Christian Adoption, 3rd edition. Seeley Jackson, and Halliday, 1879, pp. 1-4). But the original usage seems to be even older. In the Old Testament, worship of Astarte/Ashtoreth (1 Kings 11) is condemned and that goddess has been featured on coins with crosses (Brock, p. 11).

Now, what does the Bible, specifically the New Testament, say about crosses?

Not as much as most believe as it is not certain that the word is ever used.

Why?

Amongst other reasons, the Greek word commonly translated as "cross" in the New Testament is *stauros*, which literally means pole or stake.

> NT:4716 *stauros* (stow-ros'); from the base of NT:2476; a stake or post (as set upright), i.e. (specifically) a pole ... (Biblesoft's New Exhaustive Strong's Numbers and Concordance with Expanded Greek-Hebrew Dictionary. Copyright 1994, Biblesoft and International Bible Translators, Inc.)

> σταυρός...'upright, pointed stake' or 'pale'; ... **a pole to be placed in the ground and used for capital punishment** (Bauer W, Danker FW. *A Greek-English Lexicon of the New Testament*, 3rd edition. University of Chicago, 2000, p. 941)

It should be noted that according to *Strong's Exhaustive Concordance*, every time in the NT (KJV) the word cross appears, it comes from word #4716.

But, some may ask, what about the word "crucify" or "crucified"? Does this mean being killed on a cross? While that is how people interpret that in English, the two Greek words translated as crucify in the NT (KJV) come from *stauros* and mean impale:

> NT:4717 *stauroo* (stow-ro'-o); from NT:4716; to impale (Biblesoft's New Exhaustive Strong's Numbers and Concordance with Expanded Greek-Hebrew Dictionary. Copyright © 1994, 2003, 2006 Biblesoft, Inc. and International Bible Translators, Inc.)

> NT:4957 *sustauroo* (soos-tow-ro'-o); from NT:4862 and NT:4717; to impale in company with (literally or figuratively) (Biblesoft's New Exhaustive Strong's Numbers and Concordance with Expanded Greek-Hebrew Dictionary. Copyright © 1994, 2003, 2006 Biblesoft, Inc. and International Bible Translators, Inc.)

There is a third word once incorrectly translated as "crucify" in the KJV NT, but it means to "kill again," and thus has nothing to do with an actual cross.

Neither the apostles nor their immediate followers (who would know first century *koine* Greek better than any currently alive) ever were recorded using or wearing or honoring any cross. The fact is that modern scholars know that *stauros* meant a stake, but many have chosen, because of tradition, to translate it as "cross." In Greece now, because of 'tradition', the word *stauros* is now considered to mean "cross" even though it clearly did not originally.

Furthermore, consider that in the second half of the second century, a Greek satirist and anti-Christian named Lucian wrote in his *The Death of Peregrinus* about Christians:

> that one whom they still worship who was impaled because he brought this new form of initiation into the world.

Lucian used the Greek word *anaskolopizien*, which means "to impale" (McDowell J, McDowell S. Evidence that Demands a Verdict. Thomas Nelson, 2017, p. 148). Impalement had been understood by many after Jesus' death.

Notice what Polycarp, Bishop of Smyrna, wrote in the second century:

> Let us then continually persevere in our hope, and the earnest of our righteousness, which is Jesus Christ, "who bore our sins in His own body on the tree" ... If a man does not keep himself from covetousness, he shall be defiled by idolatry, and shall be judged as one of the heathen (*Polycarp's Letter to the Philippians*, Chapter VIII).

He, like others, referred to Jesus being killed on a tree and warned against professors of Christ being involved with idolatry. Notice some passages from the New Testament related to Jesus on a tree:

> [30] The God of our fathers raised up Jesus whom you murdered by hanging on a tree. (Acts 5:30)

> [39] And we are witnesses of all things which He did both in the land of the Jews and in Jerusalem, whom they killed by hanging on a tree. (Acts 10:39)
>
> [29] Now when they had fulfilled all that was written concerning Him, they took Him down from the tree and laid Him in a tomb. [30] But God raised Him from the dead. (Acts 13:29-30)
>
> [24] who Himself bore our sins in His own body on the tree, that we, having died to sins, might live for righteousness — by whose stripes you were healed. (1 Peter 2:24)
>
> [13] Christ has redeemed us from the curse of the law, having become a curse for us (for it is written, "Cursed is everyone who hangs on a tree"), (Galatians 3:13)

The Greek word *xulon* (ξύλον) translated as 'tree' above, basically means tree, stick or piece of timber. As far as Galatian 3:13 goes, that contains a reference to Deuteronomy 21:23–and the Hebrews were NOT crucifying people on crosses then.

Even though Greco-Romans titled his writing *The Discourse on the Cross*, Melito of Sardis (late 2nd century) actually wrote Jesus was killed on a tree:

> God who is from God; the Son who is from the Father; Jesus Christ the King for evermore...He that bore up the earth was borne up on a tree. The Lord was subjected to ignominy with naked body–God put to death, the King of Israel slain!

Melito also wrote in his *Discourse on Faith* and elsewhere:

> **He who was hanged on the tree**; ... He that bore up the earth was borne up on a tree.

Early Christians reported Jesus was killed on a tree.

In what appears to be circa 135 in Jerusalem, there was a group of compromised, Roman supporting 'Christians' that wrote down what they thought were (or perhaps could have been) the gospel accounts.

Yet, according to a later source, "In all this there was no mention of the cross or crucifix" (Pines S. The Jewish Christians of the Early Centuries of Christianity according to a New Source. Proceedings of the Israel Academy of Sciences and Humanities, Volume II, No.13; 1966. Jerusalem, p. 16).

Furthermore, according to the historical records, no real Christian prior to the late second or early third century is ever described as carrying an idol, having images in any worship services, or even wearing a cross (though some apostates started to advocate crosses in the second and third centuries).

Some have suggested that catacombs and funeral-related items for Christians proves an early acceptance of the cross. But this is not the case. Let it be added that this author has visited various catacombs (including in the vicinity of Rome) to verify this.

While some have pointed to the letter "X" (the Greek letter 'chi') or other symbols on certain Christian documents and/or artifacts as a sign for the cross and/or proof of the early widespread acceptance of crosses, notice what Roman Catholic priest and scholar B. Bagatti discovered:

> The doctrine of millenarianism, being widespread, left many iconographical traces. As a sign of millenarianism, also called chiliasm, we find the Greek letter X, initial for the word *chilioi* (thousand) ... Studying funeral monuments we find ourselves face to face with very many signs which lead us to millenarian iconographic repertoire. (Bagatti, The Church from the Circumcision, pp. 297, 298)

Ancient artifacts showing versions of "+," (Bagatti, From the Church of the Circumcision, pp. 298-299) or "YO (=Ω), YT, YX," (Saller SJ, Testa E. The archaeological setting of the shrine of Bethphage; Issue 1 of Smaller series. Franciscan Press, 1961. Franciscan Press, 1961, p. 108) and "Σ" (Saller, p. 113) also were sometimes used as a symbol of the pre-millennial resurrection of the saints (1 Corinthians 15:51-53; Revelation 20:4-6)—this resurrection coinciding with Jesus' return was, and still should be, a blessed hope of Christians (Titus 2:13; Acts 23:6; 1 Corinthians 15:12-23).

Icons and crosses were generally discouraged by Greco-Roman leaders until the fourth century.

> Scholars believe that the first surviving public image of Jesus's crucifixion was on the fifth-century wooden doors of the Basilica of Santa Sabina, which is located on the Aventine Hill in Rome. Since it took approximately 400 years for Jesus's crucifixion to become an acceptable public image, scholars have traditionally believed that this means the cross did not originally function as a symbol for Christians. ...
>
> Perhaps the earliest portrayal of the cross by Christians occurred in the iconography of their papyrus manuscripts, specifically the Staurogram, or shape of the cross made by the overlapping of the Greek letters "Rho" and "Tau" (⳨). A more obvious depiction of the cross is seen in a third-century gem in the British Museum, which depicts a crucified Jesus with an inscription that lists various Egyptian magical words. ...
>
> Undoubtedly, though, Constantine's adoption of the cross was the most important development that resulted in its becoming the preeminent symbol of Christianity. (Shisley S. Jesus and the Cross. Biblical Archaeology Society, February 23, 2020)

Should anyone think that **real** Christians were using "magic words" with crosses? Obviously not!

As far as a staurogram goes:

> The *tau-rho* staurogram, like other christograms, was originally a pre-Christian symbol. A Herodian coin featuring the Staurogram predates the crucifixion. (The Staurogram. Biblical Archaeology Society, April 14, 2019)

So, no, a staurogram was not originally a Christian symbol, but a pagan one that was later adopted by the Greco-Romans. While a "tau" (τ) resembles the letter T (which some claim is the symbol of the cross), the fact that the staurogram contains a "rho" (ρ) should show the discerning that it had nothing to do with Jesus, but was a pagan symbol that also resembled ancient Egyptian ankh crosses. The first known staurograms associated with Christian literature were from Alexandrian Egypt.

Some Protestants have pointed to the passages in Revelation 7:2-4 about God placing a seal on the 144,000 as that seal being the cross. Yet, the word for seal is the Greek word transliterated as *sphragída*, and that word is not related to any word for cross. Nor was it the view of early Christians that this seal was a cross—if so, the cross would likely have been a first century symbol and would not resemble pagan ones.

The cross was an important symbol for Mithraism:

> Mithras signed his soldiers on the forehead with a Cross. (Pike A. Morals and dogma of the Ancient and Accepted Scottish Rite of Freemasonry. First published 1871. Forgotten Books, 1962, p. 246)

> A curious bas-relief recently published shows us ... a tripod bearing four tiny loaves of bread, each marked with a cross. ... these love feasts are evidently the ritual commemoration of the banquet which Mithra celebrated before his ascension. (Cumont F. The Mysteries of Mithra. Open Court, 1903, p. 160)

> Mithratic ... initiates ... would henceforth have the Sun Cross on their foreheads. The similarity to the cross of ashes made on the forehead on the Christian Ash Wednesday is striking. (Nabarz P. The mysteries of Mithras: the pagan belief that shaped the Christian world. Inner Traditions / Bear & Company, 2005, p. 36).

Emperor Constantine practiced a version of the idolatrous religion of Mithraism. Now, in 310 he had a vision of the sun god Sol in a grove of Apollo in Gaul (Rodgers BS. "Constantine's Pagan Vision," Byzantion, vol. 50, 1980, pp. 259–78). Then in 312, Constantine claimed he had a vision of a spear that had a bar overlaid on it to look like a cross. He interpreted this to mean he would win the Battle of Milvian Bridge. So he had his forces paint crosses on their shields to fight, and later had a golden spear cross with glittering jewels made to commemorate his vision (Eusebius. The Life of Constantine, Book I, Chapters 28,30,31).

Notice something that happened a year or so after the Council of Nicea:

> Constantine appointed his mother Helena as Augusta Imperatrix, he gave her access to the imperial treasury in order to locate the relics of the Judeo-Christian tradition. (Morgan R. History of the Coptic Orthodox People and the Church of Egypt. FriesenPress, 2016, p. 67)

So his mother Helena came back with various idolatrous icons. Helena claimed to have located Jesus' 'true cross' in the Jerusalem area on September 14, 326. She then brought a piece back along with other 'relics.' The veneration of her cross relic quickly led to broader acceptance and veneration of crosses by those of the Greco-Roman faiths outside of Egypt.

Now, it should be pointed out that some, but not most, Protestants recognize that Emperor Constantine was not a real Christian, but a pagan as the following from one shows (**bolding** in source):

> Constantine was a **pagan** just like most of the Romans were. He worshipped the sun god SOL INVICTUS, which means the "**unconquered sun**." If you were the devil and wanted this guy to obey you, what would you do? Use his devotion to the **sun god** of course! ...
>
> So in 312 AD ... he saw an **ankh** in the sky and the words ***EN HOC SIGNO VINCES*** ("**in this sign conquer**"). And Satan's forces made sure he won. ... Constantine was the Pontifex Maximus ...
>
> - **He set the holidays**
> - **He set the sacrifices for the gods**
>
> **That way Constantine could hold tight control over the pagan religions**. But he *also* made himself the head of the "church." ... FALSE CONVERSIONS WERE EVERYWHERE. ... Now he wanted to **UNITE these so-called "Christians."** So in 325 AD, Constantine as Bishop of Bishops presided over the Council of Nicea. It was to decide whose doctrine of the Godhead would be followed. The emperor's plan **worked**. ... In 321 AD this last great Caesar had made the "venerable day of the sun" (Sunday) into a

"Christian" holy day. (Daniels DW. Did the Catholic Church Give Us the Bible? Chick Publications, 2013, pp. 43-49).

Egyptian angk

Most Protestants follow several Constantinian doctrines to this day. Since he had been a follower of the militaristic Mithras/Sol Invictus cult, Constantine had no problem with crosses of various types (an ankh was originally a pagan symbol from Egypt). It should be pointed out that even after his alleged conversion related to his claimed version cross vision, Emperor Constantine continued to put the sun god Sol on his coins, and he chose to be buried in a grave in 337 dedicated to the sun god.

Constantine's acceptance of crosses and other Icons proved highly popular with the Greeks, though some in Rome had problems with them for a time. Centuries later, the Eastern Orthodox considered their getting the Roman Church to formally accept icons at the end of the "Seventh Ecumenical Council" was "the triumph of Orthodoxy" in 843 (Ware T. The Orthodox Church. Penguin Books, London, 1997, pp. 31-33).

Now, since the time of Emperor Constantine, cross-bearers who claim Christ have been involved in military and persecutory actions. The term "Crusader" meant cross-bearer, to cite just one example.

In Italy, and elsewhere, others who professed Christ objected to crosses:

> About the year 1040, the Paterines had become very numerous at Milan, which was their principal residence, and here they flourished at least two hundred years. They ... they rejected not only Jerome of Syria, Augustine of Africa, and Gregory of Rome, but Ambrose of Milan; considering them, and other pretended fathers, as corrupters of Christianity ... **They called [the adoration of] the cross the mark of the beast.** (Jones W. The history of the Christian church from the birth of Christ to the xviii. Century, Volumes 1-2, 3rd edition. R.W. Pomeroy, 1832, p. 289)

> ... the **Cathari also renounced priestly vestments, altars, and crosses as idolatrous. They called the cross the mark of the beast**, and declared it had no more virtue than a ribbon for binding the hair. (Schaff, Philip, History of the Christian Church, Chapter X. 1923, p. 480)

It is of historical interest to note the following doctrinal admissions in the article on the Paulicians in *The Catholic Encyclopedia* (bolding mine):

> **They honoured not the Cross, but only the book of the Gospel** ... Since Gibbon **the Paulicians have often been described as a survival of early and pure Christianity**, godly folk who clung to the Gospel, rejecting later superstitions, who were grossly calumniated by their opponents ...

The cross remained a concern in the Middle Ages to some opposed to the Church of Rome.

The famous Roman Catholic inquisitor, Bernard Gui, claimed the following about the Albigenses, a small minority of whom were COG:

> In the first place, they usually say of themselves that ... they are good men and good Christians, and that they are persecuted just as Christ and his apostles were by the Pharisees. ...

> They assert, moreover, that the cross of Christ should not be adored or venerated, because, as they urge, no one would venerate or adore the gallows upon which a father, relative, or friend had been hung. They urge, further, that they who adore

the cross ought, for similar reasons, to worship all thorns and lances, because as Christ's body was on the cross during the passion, so was the crown of thorns on his head and the soldier's lance in his side, (From the Inquisitor's Manual of Bernard Gui [d.1331], early 14th century, translated in J. H. Robinson, Readings in European History, Boston: Ginn, 1905, pp. 381-383)

Perhaps it should be mentioned that the cross, along with a sword, was on the 'coat of arms' for the Spanish Inquisition:

Both Sir Isaac Newton and a Roman Catholic priest named Huchedé pointed to a cross as a possible symbol for the final Antichrist:

> His mark is ✠✠✠ and his name ΛΑΤΕΙΝΟΣ {Lateinos}, and the number of his name 666. (Sir Isaac Newton's Daniel and the Apocalypse with an introductory study of the nature and the cause of unbelief, of miracles and prophecy, by Sir William Whitla; 1922; Murray, London, p. 327)

> *Priest P. Huchedé* (19th century): Antichrist will further make all men, great and small, rich and poor, freemen and bondmen, bear a sign on their right arm or their forehead. (*Apoc.* 13:16). What this sign shall be time alone will reveal. Yet there are some {Catholic} commentators of the Holt Writ, who, according to a special revelation pretend to say that it shall be formed out of the Greek letters X and P, interlaced ... which resembles the

number of Christ. (Cornelius a Lapide in Epis. 2 to Thes.). No one can either buy or sell without this mark, as specified in the Apocalypse (13:17). (Huchedé P. Translated by JBD. History of Antichrist. Imprimatur: Edward Charles Fabre, Bishop of Montreal. English edition 1884, Reprint 1976. TAN Books, Rockford (IL), p. 24)

Since these reports about the cross being an Antichrist symbol are traditions (not in conflict with scripture, but not directly taught in scripture) it is not CCOG doctrine that a cross must be a mark of the Beast or Antichrist. But a cross could be a "mark of" or associated with the "image of the Beast" (Revelation 13:15-17).

Perhaps it should be pointed out that there are Roman Catholic writings which indicate that some in the future who wear crosses will be persecutors:

St. Francis de Paul (1470): the Great Monarch ... shall be a great captain and prince of holy men, who shall be called 'the holy Cross-bearers of Jesus Christ,' with whom he will destroy the Mahometan sect and the rest of the infidels. ... God Almighty will exalt a very poor man of the blood of Emperor Constantine ... who shall on his breast wear a sign which you have seen at the beginning of this letter (a red Cross) ... He will gather a grand army, ... An infinite number of wicked men shall perish through the hands of the Cross-bearers ... most faithful Crossbearers elected by the Most High, who, not succeeding in converting heretics with science, shall make vigorous use of their arms ... **These holy Cross-bearers shall reign and dominate holily over the whole world until the end of time** ... (Culleton G. The Prophets and Our Times. Nihil Obstat: L. Arvin. Imprimatur: Philip G. Scher, Bishop of Monterey-Fresno, November 15, 1941. Reprint 1974, TAN Books, Rockford (IL), p. 157-161).

Latin Tiburtine Sibyl (c. 4th-11th century): The king of the Romans will claim the whole Christian empire for himself. ... in every temple the Cross of Christ will be erected. Whoever does not adore the Cross of Jesus Christ will be punished by the sword. ... At that time the Prince of Iniquity who will be called Antichrist will arise ... (McGinn B. Visions of the End: Apocalyptic

Traditions in the Middle Ages. Columbia University Press, 1998, pp. 49-50).

St. Bridget of Sweden (died 1373): war shall ... be victorious

through the sign of the Cross. He shall destroy the Jewish and Mahometan sects ... (Culleton, p. 154).

Anne Catherine Emmerich (October, 1820): warriors, led by a rider on a white horse; and ... citizens and peasants, many of whom were marked on the forehead with a red cross. As this army drew near, the captives and oppressed were delivered and swelled the ranks whilst the demolishers and conspirators were put to flight on all sides (Emmerich AC. The Life of Lord Jesus Christ and Biblical Revelations. Schmöger edition, Vol. II. Nihil Obstat: D. Jaegher, 14 Februari 1914. Imprimatur: A.C. De Schrevel, Brugis, 14 Februari 1914. Reprint TAN Books, Rockford (IL), 2004, pp. 290-291).

The Bible warns about the rider of the white horse (Revelation 6:1-2), who represents the final Antichrist. The Bible also warns that those who refuse the Beast's "mark" (Revelation 13:16-17) are subject to be being killed by those with a mark on their forehead (Revelation 14:9) through the direction of the Antichrist (Revelation 13:11-15). The fact that Roman Catholic prophecy points to people who are doing the persecuting wearing a cross and going against "Jewish" sects (which Greco-Roman Catholics tend to consider the COG to be) and "heretics" is consistent with the view that a cross may well be a mark or image of the Beast and Antichrist.

Protestants, while opposing certain icons, generally have accepted cross-related icons.

Though we in the CCOG have not accepted them as true Christian symbols, we do not believe that use of crosses by civic organizations (like the Red Cross) or their use on government documents (including identification cards) means such should be avoided by Christians.

But yes, there is a real threat that persecutors will use a cross and that a version of it could be a or the mark of the Beast.

Christmas Trees

Although Jesus was killed on a tree, lighted trees are not proper religious symbols for Christians.

In his book *Two Babylons*, Alexander Hislop reported:

> The wassailing {punch} bowl of Christmas had its precise counterpart in the "Drunken festival" of Babylon; and many of the other observances still kept up among ourselves at Christmas came from the very same quarter. The candles, in some parts of England, lighted on Christmas-eve, and used so long as the festive season lasts, were equally lighted by the Pagans on the eve of the festival of the Babylonian god, to do honour to him: for it was one of the distinguishing peculiarities of his worship to have lighted wax-candles on his altars. The Christmas tree, now so common among us, was equally common in Pagan Rome and Pagan Egypt. In Egypt that tree was the palm-tree; in Rome it was the fir; the palm-tree denoting the Pagan Messiah, as Baal-Tamar, the fir referring to him as Baal-Berith. The mother of Adonis, the Sun-God and great mediatorial divinity, was mystically said to have been changed into a tree, and when in that state to have brought forth her divine son. If the mother was a tree, the son must have been recognised as the "Man the branch." And this entirely accounts for the putting of the Yule Log into the fire on Christmas-eve, and the appearance of the Christmas-tree the next morning. As Zero-Ashta, "The seed of the woman," which name also signified Ignigena, or "born of the fire," he has to enter the fire on "Mother-night," that he may be born the next day out of it, as the "Branch of God," or the Tree that brings all divine gifts to men. But why, it may be asked, does he enter the fire under the symbol of a Log? To understand this, it must be remembered that the divine child born at the winter solstice was born as a new incarnation of the great god (after that god had been cut in pieces), on purpose to revenge his death upon his murderers. Now the great god, cut off in the midst of his power and glory, was symbolised as a huge tree, stripped of all its branches, and cut down almost to the ground. But the great serpent, the symbol of the life restoring Aesculapius, twists itself around the

dead stock, and lo, at its side up sprouts a young tree—a tree of an entirely different kind, that is destined never to be cut down by hostile power—even the palm-tree, the well-known symbol of victory. The Christmas-tree, as has been stated, was generally at Rome a different tree, even the fir; but the very same idea as was implied in the palm-tree was implied in the Christmas-fir; for that covertly symbolised the new-born God as Baal-berith, * "Lord of the Covenant," and thus shadowed forth the perpetuity and everlasting nature of his power, not that after having fallen before his enemies, he had risen triumphant over them all.

Therefore, the 25th of December, the day that was observed at Rome as the day when the victorious god reappeared on earth, was held at the Natalis invicti solis, "The birth-day of the unconquered Sun." Now the Yule Log is the dead stock of Nimrod, deified as the sun-god, but cut down by his enemies; the Christmas-tree is Nimrod redivivus—the slain god come to life again. In the light reflected by the above statement on customs that still linger among us, the origin of which has been lost in the midst of hoar antiquity, let the reader look at the singular practice still kept up in the South on Christmas-eve, of kissing under the mistletoe bough. That mistletoe bough in the Druidic superstition, which, as we have seen, was derived from Babylon, was a representation of the Messiah, "The man the branch." The mistletoe was regarded as a divine branch *—a branch that came from heaven, and grew upon a tree that sprung out of the earth.

While certain Protestants and Greco-Roman Catholics have criticized Alexander Hislop for having a few errors among the hundreds of references his book cites, the reality is that lighted trees for religious purposes do not come from the Bible.

Most who have looked into the subject of Christmas trees are familiar with the passages in Jeremiah 10 that clearly condemn pagan tree practices:

> [2] "Do not learn the ways of the nations or be terrified by signs in the sky, though the nations are terrified by them. [3] For the

customs of the peoples are worthless; they cut a tree out of the forest, and a craftsman shapes it with his chisel. ⁴ They adorn it with silver and gold; they fasten it with hammer and nails so it will not totter. ⁵ Like a scarecrow in a melon patch, their idols cannot speak; they must be carried because they cannot walk. Do not fear them; they can do no harm nor can they do any good." (Jeremiah 10:2-5, NIV).

The Bible is clear that God's people are not to incorporate pagan practices into true worship (1 Corinthians 10:20-22; 1 Timothy 4:1-2, Deuteronomy 12:19-31). While the trees themselves cannot harm us (cf. 1 Corinthians 10:19-22), God says that they cannot do any good. Protestants are NOT honouring the God of the Bible with Christmas trees.

Even though there is nothing in the Bible to encourage putting a tree in one's house to honor Jesus or the Father, many Protestants believe that they have legitimate reasons to.

According to the Historic Trinity Lutheran Church of Detroit, "Dr. Martin Luther is credited with originating the use of lighted pine trees in the home for Christmas."

Although they changed, Roman Catholics condemned the use of fir trees at Christmas calling Protestantism the 'Tannenbaum religion' (meaning "fir tree religion" in German) centuries ago because of Martin Luther's advocacy of Christmas trees. And the truth is that the evergreen tree had long been a pagan religious symbol in northern Europe.

Protestants who claim *sola Scriptura* should ponder the following scriptures:

> ² **You shall utterly destroy all the places where the nations which you shall dispossess served their gods, on the high mountains and on the hills and under every green tree**. ³ And you shall destroy their altars, break their sacred pillars, and burn their wooden images with fire; you shall cut down the carved images of their gods and destroy their names from that place. ⁴ **You shall not worship the Lord your God with such things**. (Deuteronomy 12:2-4)

> ⁹When you come into the land which the Lord your God is giving you, you shall not learn to follow the abominations of those nations. … ¹² For all who do these things are an abomination to the Lord, and because of these abominations the Lord your God drives them out from before you. (Deuteronomy 18:9,12)

Is not having Christmas trees like the heathen consistent with what God warned His people not to do?

We in the CCOG do not have Christmas trees.

Gregory Thaumaturgus' and Constantine's Influence

The use of green branches, new holidays, use of lights, and various other things came to Protestants through the influence of a demon-influenced man named Gregory and the pagan Emperor Constantine.

Notice something written by former Anglican bishop, then Roman Catholic Cardinal, John Henry Newman in the late 19th century:

> Confiding then in the power of Christianity to resist the infection of evil, and to transmute the very instruments and appendages of demon-worship to evangelical use, … the rulers of the Church from early times were prepared, should the occasion arise, to adopt, to imitate, or to sanctify the existing rites and customs of the population, as well as the philosophy of the educated class.
>
> St. Gregory Thaumaturgus supplies the first instance on record of this economy. He was the Apostle of Pontus, and one of his methods for governing an untoward population is thus related by St. Gregory of Nyssa. "On returning," he says, "to the city, after revisiting the country round about, he increased the devotion of the people everywhere by instituting festive meetings in honour of those who had fought for the faith. The bodies of the Martyrs were distributed in different places, and the people assembled and made merry, as the year came round, holding festival in their honour. This indeed was a proof of his great wisdom …

> We are told in various ways by Eusebius, that Constantine, in order to recommend the new religion to the heathen, transferred into it the outward ornaments to which they had been accustomed in their own. It is not necessary to go into a subject which the diligence of Protestant writers has made familiar to most of us. The use of temples, and these dedicated to particular saints, and ornamented on occasions with branches of trees; incense, lamps, and candles; votive offerings on recovery from illness; holy water; asylums; holydays and seasons, use of calendars, processions, blessings on the fields; sacerdotal vestments, … are all of pagan origin, and sanctified by their adoption into the Church. (Newman JH. An Essay on the Development of Christian Doctrine. J. Toovey, 1845, pp. 358-360.)

Notice that pagan items were considered to be an evangelical tool. Please understand that the appeal to "the philosophy of the educated class" means that pagan philosophy (as taught by the Greeks and Romans) was to be accepted. Are Protestant supposed to accept the Church of Rome sanctified (made holy) pagan practices, special water, garments, and holidays? Yet, that is, in essence, the case for many of those.

The 3rd century bishop Gregory of Neocaesarea (also known as Gregory the Wonder Worker or Gregory Thaumaturgus) was a major doctrinal influencer. Gregory was from a pagan family, which likely influenced some of his views and doctrines. He claimed to see an apparition of Mary (and seems to be the first we have a clear record of to make this claim)—which obviously was not Jesus' mother as she is awaiting the resurrection. He was essentially influenced by demons in multiple ways. Notice the following:

> "Gregory … the demons were subject to him … he could cast his cloak over a man, and cause his death … he could bring the presiding demons back to their shrine. (Roberts A, Donaldson J. Ante-Nicene Christian Library. Translations of the Writings of the Fathers down to A.D. 325, Volume 20: The Works of Gregory Thaumaturgus, Dionysius of Alexandria, and Archelaus. Syriac documents attribute. Originally 1871, modern printing by Elibron.com, 2006, p. 3).

No Christian would cast their cloak on someone to cause someone's death. Therefore, it should be clear that, Gregory was a demonically-connected leader. Yet, Because Gregory's power over demons and other "wonders" were apparently accepted by many, he had influence. It seems that Gregory's enchantments and/or sorceries: (cf. Isaiah 47:5-12; Nahum 3:4), along with Imperial persecutions, may have greatly assisted the compromised Greco-Roman faction, essentially eliminating the dominance of the organized faithful in Asia Minor in the 3rd century.

Gregory was also a factor in the Marian cults that began to rise up around that time. His writings teach praise and excessive devotion to the "Holy Virgin," including the blasphemous teaching that Mary "blotted out" Eve's "transgressions" (Gregory Thaumaturgus, Homily concerning the Holy Mother of God. The Expositor 5th series vol.3, 1896, pp.161-173), He was also among the first to push the biblically false idea that Mary never sinned (cf. Romans 3:23), as well as to tell people it was better to hold a festival for her than to keep biblical Holy Days (Gregory Thaumaturgus. The Second Homily on the Annunciation to the Holy Virgin Mary).

Gregory pushed also the pagan concept of the immortality of the soul (Gregory Thaumaturgus. On the Soul, Chapters 5, 6. Translated by S.D.F. Salmond. From Ante-Nicene Fathers, Vol. 6. Edited by Alexander Roberts, James Donaldson, and A. Cleveland Coxe. Buffalo, NY: Christian Literature Publishing Co., 1886).

He is credited by many for expanding Greco-Roman influence by incorporating profane pagan practices in worship and festivals to make their churches more desirable among the heathen (Gregory of Neocaesarea, Saint. The Catholic Encyclopedia, 1910). He is among the first to have used the term "Holy Trinity" (Gregory Thaumaturgus, Homily concerning the Holy Mother of God, Section 35. Translated from the Armenian by F. C. CONYBEARE. The Expositor, 1896, 5th series vol.3, p. 173).

Many biblical deviations that entered the Greco-Roman churches essentially were promoted by him. Sadly, today, many Protestants hold onto many of his views (including his view on the Godhead) without realizing that they basically came from demonic influence.

Notice also the basic admission that Constantine pushed branches of trees, new "holydays," and sacerdotal vestments (meaning special distinctive, and generally pagan, clothing for the clergy) which Protestantism adopted (though some Protestant clergy have not adopted the special dress). He also likely would have pushed the immortality of the soul doctrine, as that was a tenet of the sun god he worshipped.

These vestiges of paganism were not part of the original Christian faith. Additionally, prior to Emperor Constantine, Greco-Romans were not militaristic, but he pushed that change as well.

The Apostle Paul wrote, "the things that the nations sacrifice — they sacrifice to demons and not to God; and I do not wish you to come into the fellowship of the demons" (1 Corinthians 10:20, YLT).

Hence, we in the CCOG cannot accept modified holidays and other clearly pagan items that were endorsed by Emperor Constantine, Gregory, or others. Yet, many Protestants (often unknowingly) do. They certainly did not get them from early Christians or from the Bible!

Valentine's Day

Although not all Protestants celebrate Valentine's Day, many do.

This is despite the fact that it is well recognized that what became known as Valentine's Day was essentially a holiday for illicit sex to honor the pagan god Lupercus and goddess Juno (Valentine's Day. World Book Encyclopedia, Volume 19. 1966, pp. 205-206). Notice also:

> Valentine's Day had originated as a pagan festival honoring the birth of Nimrod under the name of Lupercus, meaning hunter of wolves. On this day in ancient Babylon, the evening of February 14th on the Christian calendar, the Babylonian Queen Semiramis proclaimed a celebration in honor of her son Nimrod who she had married (Dan Strickenberger, Jim Pitts. The Signs of the Sun Matrix. AuthorHouse, 2008, p. 13)

Presuming that is correct, Nimrod may have been the original "Valentine." Nimrod was the founder of Babel:

> ⁸ Cush fathered Nimrod, who began to be powerful in the land. ⁹ He was a **powerful hunter** in the sight of the Lord. That is why it is said, "Like Nimrod, a **powerful hunter** in the sight of the Lord." ¹⁰ His kingdom started with Babylon ... (Genesis 10:8-10 CSB)

The Latin word *valens* from hence came the name Valentine, means strong, healthy, or powerful. The term Valentine seems to have a connection, thus to the hunter Nimrod.

Consider that God confused languages at Babel/Babylon (Genesis 11:9), because the people had rebelled against God there. In the Old Testament, God tells of a coming "daughter of Babylon" who will be punished (Isaiah 47; Jeremiah 50,51). And in the New Testament, God condemns *Mystery Babylon* as "the mother of harlots and of the abominations of the earth" (Revelation 17:5). Nimrod, thus, is not one to celebrate. Presuming Nimrod is distantly connected to modern Valentine's Day, and that pagan worship absolutely was, those who claim to believe the Bible obviously should not want anything to do with it.

Reverend and Collars

Protestants often refer to their ministers with the title "The Reverend" or simply "Reverend."

We in the CCOG do not.

God's name is reverend, "holy and reverend is his name" (Psalm 111:9, KJV).

The practice of calling Greco-Roman clergy "Reverend" seems to have begun in English-speaking lands in the 15th century, and was in habitual use by Protestants in the 17th century (Reverend. Encyclopaedia Britannica. Updated by Britannica editors January, 04, 2007). It is certainly not a biblical nor original Christian practice.

Furthermore, the white collar that many Protestant ministers wear did not come from the Bible. Though the modern reverse white collar was reported to have been invented in the 19th century, something similar was worn by Roman and Eastern Orthodox priests much earlier. Egyptian pagan priests wore some version of collars thousands of years ago (e.g. Jarus O. 2,300-Year-Old Cemetery with Mummy Priests Found in Egypt. LiveScience, February 26, 2018).

A collar was also associated with the sun-god Mithras:

> Mithra wears the Phrygian cap ... Rays of light emerge from Mithra's head much like a halo. His choke collar is a serpent. (Cooper JD. Mithras: Mysteries and initiation rediscovered. Samuel Weiser, Inc., 1996).

The ministry in the CCOG does not wear the priestly collar like many of the Protestant ministers do. Distinctive clothing for the ministry was not employed by early Christians—they dressed the same as their congregants.

However, after influence from Emperor Constantine, the Greco-Roman clergy adopted versions of many of the clothing styles that sun-god priests and other members of his court had worn (including versions of the collar and Phrygian cap). Scholars admit that special clerical clothing came from pagans and was adopted because of Emperor Constantine (e.g. Newman, pp. 358-360)

While not all Protestant minister adopted symbols of pagan dress, many (like the Anglicans) have.

We in the CCOG do not believe that the Christian ministry should wear distinctively religious clothing.

Nor do we believe we should incorporate pagan icons, including crosses, as part of our worship.

15. Godhead

There is one God (Deuteronomy 6:4). In the New Testament, the term Godhead is sometimes used (Romans 1:20; Colossians 2:9).

What does the Godhead consist of?

A small percentage of Protestants are unitarian. Unitarians claim that the Godhead is one and that God is exclusively the one known as the Father and they deny the deity of Jesus.

The vast bulk of Protestants are trinitarian. Trinitarians claim that there are, and always will be, three co-equal parts of the one God.

Like the first Christians, the CCOG holds a binitarian view. Binitarians claim that God is one family, currently consisting of two beings, with humans having the potential to enter into that family after a resurrection into the Kingdom of God.

One of the reasons that self-proclaimed 'cult-watchers' tend to call groups like the *Continuing* Church of God a "cult" is because we do not accept the trinitarian conclusion of the Council of Constantinople called by the warring Emperor Theodosius in 381 A.D.

Although unitarians reject more than one being in the Godhead, Genesis 1 uses the Hebrew term transliterated as "Elohiym" for God, Elohim is a uniplural noun, like church, which means it is normally referring to more than one being (Biblesoft says Elohiym literally is the plural of the word God).

Furthermore, Jesus did not define "one" the same way unitarians do. Jesus clearly taught that two distinct beings of a family can be one as can members of God's family:

> [5] 'For this reason a man shall leave his father and mother and be joined to his wife, and the two shall become one flesh'? [6] So then, they are no longer two but one flesh. Therefore what God has joined together, let not man separate." (Matthew 19:5-6)

> [11] ... Holy Father, keep through Your name those whom You have given Me, that they may be one as We are. (John 17:11b)

Therefore, a family consisting of a husband and wife as well as one consisting of the Father and Son are considered one by our Savior. The divine family is how the currently binitarian deity is one. Furthermore, notice something else Jesus stated:

> [20] "I do not pray for these alone, but also for those who will believe in Me through their word; [21] that they all may be one, as You, Father, are in Me, and I in You; that they also may be one in Us, (John 17:20-21)

Jesus is saying His true followers, the children of God, will also become one as part of the divine family. The binitarian view does not limit the oneness of the Godhead like the trinitarian view does.

Now see a binitarian statement from the Apostle Peter:

> [1] Simon Peter, a bondservant and apostle of Jesus Christ, To those who have obtained like precious faith with us by the righteousness of our God and Savior Jesus Christ: [2] Grace and peace be multiplied to you in the knowledge of God and of Jesus our Lord, (2 Peter 1:1-2)

In what should be considered as a binitarian statement, the Apostle Paul taught Christians were to know:

> [2] ... the knowledge of the mystery of God, both of the Father and of Christ (Colossians 2:2)

The nature of the Godhead, however, remains a mystery to Protestants as most do not understand it.

Notice, for example, what one Protestant scholar wrote:

> How did the Word, which was "in the beginning" (John 1:1) come to be "made flesh" (John 1:14) as the "one mediator between God and men, the man Christ Jesus" (1 Tim. 2:5)? No full answer can be given, because the incarnation, like the

Trinity, is a mystery, and will remain so (Brown HOJ. Heresies: Heresy and Orthodoxy in the History of the Church. Hendrickson Publishers, Peabody (MA), 1988, pp. 158-159).

The Word clearly was made flesh when Jesus emptied Himself of His divinity (Philippians 2:7). But most Protestants do not fully grasp that or enough of the truth about the Godhead, yet true Christians do (cf. Colossians 2:2).

In the 2nd century, like the apostles had also done earlier, Church of God leaders taught that the Father and Son were God. Ignatius of Antioch taught this (Ignatius. Letter the Ephesians, 0.0; 19,3). Polycarp taught this (Polycarp. The Epistle to the Philippians, 12:6,7). Melito taught this (Melito. A Discourse Which Was in the Presence of Antoninus Caesar). Theophilus of Antioch taught this (Theophilus. To Autolycus, Book II, Chapter XV).

Even 21st century scholars like the Roman Catholic Mauricio Saavedra Monroy recognize that Polycarp and Ignatius made binitarian statements:

> As for the binitarian confessional formula, which confesses the Father and the Son, we likewise find examples in Polycarp and Ignatius. (Monroy MS. The Church of Smyrna: History and Theology of a Primitive Christian Community. Peter Lang edition, 2015, p. 292)

Notice also even a 2nd century Greco-Roman-Protestant saint, Irenaeus, made a clear binitarian pronouncement:

> ... **there is none other called God by the Scriptures except the Father of all, and the Son**, and those who possess the adoption (Irenaeus. Adversus haereses, Book IV, Preface, Verse 4).

Notice that Irenaeus states that only the Father, the Son, and those who possess the adoption (Christians who will be born into God's family) are God. This is a binitarian, not a trinitarian view.

Some, who have chosen to misinterpret scriptures and history, have claimed that the idea of God consisting of two beings is a relatively recent invention. However, even Protestant scholars have noted:

> Earliest Christian worship specifies two figures, God and Jesus, as recipients (Hurtado Larry. Abstract: "The Binitarian Shape of Early Christian Worship." International Conference on the Historical Origins of the Worship of Jesus. 13-17 June 1998).

> The argument that Christianity is not binitarian but trinitarian, hence could not be perceived as a two-powers heresy, ignores the fact that it is not so much what Christianity thought of itself that counts but how it appeared to its rabbinic critics. And there we see clearly that it was often described as binitarian or dualistic rather than trinitarian (Summary of response by Alan F. Segal. International Conference on the Historical Origins of the Worship of Jesus. 13-17 June 1998).

And in the New Testament and among second century Christians historians it is recognized:

> ... there are a fairly consistent linkage and subordination of Jesus to God "the Father" in these circles, evident even in the Christian texts from the latter decades of the first century that are commonly regarded as a very 'high' Christology, such as the Gospel of John and Revelation. This is why I referred to this Jesus-devotion as a "binitarian" form of monotheism: there are two distinguishable figures (God and Jesus), but they are posited in a relation to each other that seems intended to avoid the ditheism of two gods, and the devotional practices show a similar concern ... In my judgment this Jesus-devotion amounts to a treatment of him as a recipient of worship at a surprisingly early point in the first century, and is certainly a programmatic inclusion of a second figure unparalleled in the monotheistic tradition of the time (Hurtado LW. Lord Jesus Christ, Devotion to Jesus in Earliest Christianity. William B. Eerdmans Publishing, Grand Rapids, 2003, pp. 52-53).

Notice also something from a 2nd century Greco-Roman second apologist named Athenagoras:

> And, the Son being in the Father and the Father in the Son, in oneness and power of spirit, the understanding and reason (*nous kai logos*) of the Father is the Son of God ... The Holy Spirit ... which operates in the prophets, we assert to be an effluence of God, flowing from Him, and returning back again like a beam of the sun...Who, then, would not be astonished to hear men who speak of God the Father, and of God the Son, and of the Holy Spirit (Athenagoras. A Plea for the Christians, Chapter X. Translated by B.P. Pratten. Excerpted from Ante-Nicene Fathers, Volume 2. Edited by Alexander Roberts & James Donaldson. American Edition, 1885).

Thus, Athenagoras explained that the Father and the Son are God, have a oneness of power and spirit, and that the Holy Spirit is the effluence of God (an "effluence" is something that flows out from something). Athenagoras never called the Holy Spirit God. And he stated that both, the Father and the Son (the term in English refers to two), are both God and distinct—this is a binitarian view.

Into the 4th century, the majority of people who professed Christ held to a binitarian view of the Godhead (e.g. Seminarians and Semiarianism. The Catholic Encyclopedia, Volume XIII. Published 1912.). But, in time, a trinitarian change emerged, which most Protestants now accept.

Introduced by Apostates

The trinity is a doctrine that was not originally taught by the Christian Church. It was originally introduced by a famous Gnostic heretic named Valentinus in the mid-2nd century. Gnostics combined Greek philosophy and tradition with scripture.

Valentinus wrote this in the heretical *Gospel of Truth*:

> The Father uncovers his bosom, which is the Holy Spirit, revealing his secret. His secret is his Son! (Valentinus. Gospel of Truth. Verse 17. English translation by Patterson Brown).

Valentinus is the earliest known professing Christian writer to make clear trinitarian claims.

Then, also in the 2nd century, an apostate named Montanus did as well (though he, himself, did not come up with the term *trinity*; Tertullian, who eventually followed him, seemingly did).

It also should be noted that Valentinus was denounced as a heretic by Polycarp of Asia Minor, when Polycarp visited Rome— (Irenaeus. Adversus Haereses. Book III, Chapter 3, Verse 4).

Eusebius records (Eusebius. Church History, Book V, Chapters 18-19) that church leaders in Asia Minor and Antioch, (such as Apollonius of Ephesus, Serapion of Antioch, Apollinaris of Hierapolis, and Thraseas of Eumenia) opposed the Montanist heresies.

Both Valentinus and Montanus are considered to have been heretics/apostates by Roman Catholics, Orthodox, most Protestants, and those in the Churches of God. Despite this, Valentinus and Montanus were tolerated by the Greco-Romans for decades. Hence, they had some influence.

But not a huge amount.

Later came a major trinitarian and pagan influencer, the 3rd century bishop Gregory Thaumaturgus. He may have been the first to use the expression "the mystery of the Holy Trinity" in writing when he was promoting aspects of Marian devotion after being influenced from demonic sources (Gregory Thaumaturgus, Homily concerning the Holy Mother of God, p. 173).

Partially because of him, up to 10 to 15% of the Greco-Roman bishops ended up accepting a trinitarian view of the Godhead by the early 4th century.

Yes, it was from false teachers that the trinity began to be accepted by the Greco-Roman churches—it was NOT an original Christian doctrine.

Furthermore, notice the following from the prophet Nahum:

> 3 Horsemen charge with bright sword and glittering spear. There is a multitude of slain, A great number of bodies, Countless corpses — They stumble over the corpses — 4 Because of the

multitude of harlotries of the seductive harlot, The mistress of sorceries, Who sells nations through her harlotries, And families through her sorceries. (Nahum 3:3-4)

This harlot with sorceries is called Mystery Babylon the Great in Revelation 17. In 312, Emperor Constantine claimed to see a glittering/golden spear in a vision. It does not seem to be a coincidence that Emperor Constantine also promoted a compromised church that supported the use of the sword. And that church ultimately accepted a trinitarian deity.

Trinity is Not a Given

The position of most Roman Catholic scholars is that the term 'trinity' (from the Latin *trinitas*) was developed 85 years after the last book of the Bible was written as *The Catholic Encyclopedia* states:

> **In Scripture there is as yet no single term by which the Three Divine Persons are denoted together** ... The word trias (of which the Latin *trinitas* is a translation) is first found in Theophilus of Antioch about A.D. 180 ... Afterwards it appears in its Latin form of trinitas in Tertullian ("De pud." C. xxi) (The Blessed Trinity. The Catholic Encyclopedia, Volume XV Copyright © 1912 by Robert Appleton Company Online Edition Copyright © 2003 by K. Knight).

It should be understood that claims of certain Greco-Roman scholars to the contrary, Theophilus of Antioch did not teach the trinity or that the Holy Spirit was a person. But it is true that Tertullian did somewhat, about 150 years after the start of the New Testament church in Acts 2.

Protestants have claimed that the trinity is a central doctrine of the New Testament. Yet, here is what Dr. Bart Ehrman has written about it:

> Like other doctrines that became central to the faith, however, belief in the Trinity was a historical development, not a "given" from the early years of the faith.
>
> **A.** The basic notion of the Trinity is that there are three persons in the Godhead: Father, Son, and Holy Spirit. These are all

equally God and of the same substance, but despite the fact there are three persons, together, they compromise only one God, indivisible in nature.

B. This doctrine does not appear to be a doctrine pronounced by the historical Jesus, Paul, or any other Christian writer during the first hundred years or so of Christianity.

C. It cannot be found explicitly stated in the earliest Christian writings. The only passage of the New Testament that declares the doctrine (1 John 5:7-8) was not originally part of the text but was added by doctrinally astute scribes at a later date (it is not found in any Greek manuscripts until the 11th century) (Ehrman B. From Jesus to Constantine: A History of Early Christianity, Part 2. The Teaching Company, Chantilly (VA), 2004, p. 43).

It was, at least partially, because of findings like this that former "fundamentalist Protestant" Dr. Ehrman basically became agnostic. Those who understand the truth of early church history cannot remain Protestant if they want to act on that truth.

Before going further, consider what Jesus Himself taught:

> [27] All things have been delivered to Me by My Father, and no one knows the Son except the Father. Nor does anyone know the Father except the Son, and the one to whom the Son wills to reveal Him. (Matthew 11:27)

Notice that ONLY the Father and Son know each other (other than those Jesus reveals). This shows, for example, that the Holy Spirit (which is not mentioned) is not part of that 'only.' It should be clear, according to Jesus' words, that the Holy Spirit is NOT a co-equal member of a Greco-Roman trinity. But Jesus' words are consistent with the binitarian view of the Godhead.

The terms *trinity*, *threeness*, or *trinitarian* are not found in the Bible.

Martin Luther, himself, admitted:

> **It is indeed true that the name "Trinity" is nowhere to be found in the Holy Scriptures, but has been conceived and invented by man.** (Luther Martin. The Sermons of Martin Luther, Church Postil, 1522; III:406-421)

Thus, even Martin Luther admitted that the trinity doctrine was not from *sola Scriptura*. Here is something from a renowned Protestant scholar:

> For Luther, as for the German mystics, God is Deus absconditus, the "hidden God," inaccessible to human reason" ... By emphasizing the sole authority of Scripture and downgrading the work of the church fathers and the decisions of the ecumenical councils, Luther created a problem for his followers. One the one hand, Luther wanted to affirm traditional theology with respect to the doctrine of the Trinity and Christ, but on the other those doctrines are not explicit in Scripture. They are the product of church fathers and the councils (Brown HOJ. Heresies: Heresy and Orthodoxy in the History of the Church. Hendrickson Publishers, Peabody (MA), 1988, p. 314).

So, like mystics and other pagans, Martin Luther did not understand the Godhead and pushed a non-biblical explanation of it.

1 John 5:7-8

Protestants often point to 1 John 5:7-8 as "proof" of the trinity.

The truth is that the KJV, NKJV, and Douay Rheims for 1 John 5:7-8 include words not in the original text:

> [7] For there are three that bear record in heaven, the Father, the Word, and the Holy Ghost: and these three are one. [8] And there are three that bear witness in earth, the spirit, and the water, and the blood: and these three agree in one. (1 John 5:7-8, KJV)

> [7] For there are three that bear witness in heaven: the Father, the Word, and the Holy Spirit; and these three are one. [8] And there are three that bear witness on earth: the Spirit, the water,

and the blood; and these three agree as one. (1 John 5:7-8, NKJV)

> [7] And there are three who give testimony in heaven, the Father, the Word, and the Holy Ghost. And these three are one. [8] And there are three that give testimony on earth: the spirit, and the water, and the blood: and these three are one. (1 John 5:7-8, Douay-Rheims)

On page 1918, *The Ryrie Study Bible* reminds everyone, while referring to the NKJV:

> "Verse 7 should end with the word *witness*. The remainder of v. 7 and part of v. 8 are not in any ancient Greek manuscript...".

In other words the words "*in heaven: the Father, the Word, and the Holy Spirit; and these three are one. And there are three that bear witness on earth*" are not inspired and are not supposed to be in the Bible.

Notice how the *Interlinear Bible* translates the Greek:

> [7] For three there are that ......bear record in heaven,
> 3754 5140 1526 3588 3140 <9999> <9999>
> the Father, the Word, ...and the
> <9999> <9999> <9999> <9999> <9999>
>
> Holy Ghost: ....and ...these ....three are one.
> <9999> <9999> <9999> <9999> <9999> <9999> <9999>
>
> [8] And there are three that bear witness in earth, ...
> <9999> <9999> <9999> <9999> <9999> <9999> <9999>
>   the spirit, and ...the water, and...the
>   3588 4151 2532 3588 5204 2532 3588
>
>   blood: and these ..three... in.... ....one. agree
>   129 2532 <3588> 5140 1519 3588 1520 1526

> (Interlinear Transliterated Bible. Copyright © 1994, 2003, 2006 by Biblesoft, Inc.)

<9999> means that the word does not exist. Thus, the Father, the Word, and Holy Ghost were NOT part of what John was inspired to write in verse 7.

The NIV gets 1 John 5:7-8 right:

> [7] For there are three that testify: [8] the Spirit, the water and the blood; and the three are in agreement.

Some other translations, like the Berean Literal Bible and the A Faithful Version, get it right as well.

Now lest any Roman Catholics have a different view about this, consider that the *Codex Amiatinus* (Codex Amiatinus. Novum Testamentum Latine interpreter Hieronymo. Epistula Iohannis I V:6-8. Constantinus Tischendorf, Lipsiae. 1854), which is believed to be the closest to the original document that Jerome originally translated, also does not have this as *The Catholic Encyclopedia* states:

> **Codex Amiatinus** The most celebrated manuscript of the Latin Vulgate Bible, remarkable as the best witness to the true text of St. Jerome ... (Fenlon, John Francis. "Codex Amiatinus." The Catholic Encyclopedia. Vol. 4. New York: Robert Appleton Company, 1908)

Note: Yes, I personally read the Latin in the *Codex Amiatinus* and compared it to the changed version and more modern version of the Latin Vulgate which differs from the early version in that the modern version adds *"in caelo, Pater, Verbum, et Spiritus Sanctus. Et hi tres unum sunt. Et tres sunt qui testimonium dant in terra:"* (Latin Vulgate.com is provided by Mental Systems, Inc. http://www.latinvulgate.com/verse.aspx?t=1&b=23&c=5 viewed 04/21/12).

Well, *"in caelo, Pater, Verbum, et Spiritus Sanctus. Et hi tres unum sunt. Et tres sunt qui testimonium dant in terra:"* translates into English as:

> "in heaven, the Father, the Son, and Holy Spirit. And these three are. And there are three that bear witness in earth"

In other words, the text that Jerome originally translated DID NOT include the above. What we see in the Douay-Rheims is from a CHANGED version of the *Latin Vulgate*. It is NOT a translation of what Jerome originally wrote.

Notice also a copy of the relevant section of a Greek document called the *Codex Sinaiticus* c. 350 (the *Codex Sinaiticus* is considered as the oldest complete copy of the New Testament):

```
ΚΑΙΤΩΑΙΜΑΠΚΝ
ΤΟΙΙΝΑΕΟΤΙΝΤΟ
ΜΑΡΤΥΡΟΥΝΟΤΙΤ·
ΠΝΑΕΟΤΙΝΗΑΝΙ
ΟΟΙΛΟΤΙΟΙΤΡΕΙ··)
ΟΙΝΟΙΜΑΡΤΥΡΟΙ
ΤΟΟΤΟΙΙΝΑΚΑΙΤΟΤ
ΛΩΡΚΑΙΤΟΑΙΜΑ
ΚΑΙΟΙΤΡΕΙΟΕΙΟΤ·
ΕΝΟΙΟΙΝΕΙΙΙΝΜΗ
ΤΥΡΙΑΝΤΟΥΘΥΛΜ
ΡΑΝΟΜΕΝΗΜΑΡ
```

Here is a translation of 1 John 5:7-8 as shown in the *Codex Sinaiticus* from a scholastic source:

> [7] For they that testify are three, [8] the Spirit, and the water, and the blood, and the three are one. (CodexSinaiticus.org accessed 07/02/20)

The added statements, found in some translations, was not in the *Codex Sinaiticus*.

Furthermore, *"Verse 7 is nonexistent in the Eastern Peschitta"* (Roth AG, Daniel BB. Aramaic English New Testament, 5th edition. Netazari Press, 2012, p. 658)—in other words, it is not in the primary Aramaic version of the New Testament. Here is what that has for verse 8:

> [8] And there are three witnesses, the Spirit and the water, and the blood: and these three are in union. (First Yochanan 5:8, AENT).

So, when did the extra statement get put in?

Notice what seems probably to be the most accepted view from Dr. Daniel Wallace:

> the earliest manuscript, codex 221 (10th century), includes the reading in a marginal note which was added sometime after the original composition. Thus, there is no sure evidence of this reading in any Greek manuscript until the 1500s; each such reading was apparently composed after Erasmus' Greek NT was published in 1516. Indeed, the reading appears in no Greek witness of any kind (either manuscript, patristic, or Greek translation of some other version) until AD 1215 (in a Greek translation of the Acts of the Lateran Council, a work originally written in Latin)...
>
> The Trinitarian formula (known as the *Comma Johanneum*) made its way into the third edition of Erasmus' Greek NT (1522) because of pressure from the Catholic Church ...
>
> In reality, the issue is history, not heresy: How can one argue that the *Comma Johanneum* must go back to the original text when it did not appear until the 16th century in any Greek manuscripts? (Wallace DB, professor of New Testament Studies at Dallas Theological Seminary. The Textual Problem in 1 John 5:7-8. http://bible.org/article/textual-problem-1-john-57-8 viewed 07/03/20)

Basically, what seems to have happened is that a monk put a personal note related to his interpretation of the 'three' mentioned in the first part of 1 John 5:7. One or more scribal monks after him, inserted his note actually in the text. It was NOT inspired by God.

Notice more of what the trinitarian Dr. Wallace has said about it:

> In 1516, Desiderius Erasmus, a Dutch humanist scholar, published the first printed Greek New Testament—on March 1, 1516. When it came out, he did not have this verse, 1 John 5:7 in there, affirming the Trinity. There were Catholic scholars who got very upset with him for not putting it in there. And in his

second edition of 1519, he didn't have it. What he mentioned in his notes in that second edition is "I did not put it in because I did not see it in any Greek manuscripts." ... his third edition of 1522 now has 1 John 5:7-8 in it with that Trinitarian formula.

That is something that has plagued English readers of the Bible, but not German readers. Because Martin Luther based his New Testament on the 1519 edition that didn't have that. So, in 1519 Luther was using that edition and it didn't have that Trinitarian formula. German Christianity has never had a problem the Bible, never had the Trinitarian formula in 1 John 5:7-8. As stated, it made it into Erasmus' 1522 text and then in the King James Version Bible after that. Erasmus basically puts it in under protest. ... It seems that this particular reading was never part of the Greek New Testament until after there was a protest. ... It never affected Christians through any of the church councils. They never pointed out that verse, because it did not exist in the Bible. So, they came up to the doctrine of the Trinity on some other basis. (Wallace D. What are Some Passages You Interpret Differently than Dr. Ehrman?, 1 John 5:7-8. YouTube video. Jan 15, 2011)

Yes, "the Trinitarian formula in 1 John 5:7-8" was not part of the true *Textus Receptus*. Notice that the church councils did not mention it, as it did not exist. Understand that it is from the councils of men (influenced by Imperial authorities and others) that the trinitarian doctrine came from.

Some wish to believe the expanded passage of 1 John 5:7-8 was real because early heretics seem to have possibly referred to it. At least one popular online source falsely claims that Tertullian, who followed the trinitarian heretic Montanus, quoted the omitted words in *Against Praxeas. However,* this is not true as I have read that writing and it is not a full quote of 1 John 5:7-8. Yet, even if it were, Tertullian was a heretic who did not seem to have the proper canon.

The so-called "trinitarian formula" was never part of the biblical text. Notice also the following from Dr. Bruce Metzger:

(1) The text is missing from all Greek manuscripts except eight and these contain the passage of in what appears to be a translation of the Latin Vulgate ...

(2) The passage is quoted in none of the Greek Fathers, who, had they known it, would most certainly have employed it in the Trinitarian controversies (Sabellian and Arian). Its first appearance in Greek is in a Greek version of the (Latin) Acts of the Lateran Council in 1215.

(3) The passage is absent from the manuscripts of all ancient versions (Syriac, Coptic, Armenian, Ethiopic, Arabic, Slavonic), except the Latin; and it is not found (*a*) in the Old Latin in its early form (Tertullian Cyprian Augustine), or in the Vulgate (*b*) as issued by Jerome ... or (*c*) as revised by Alcuin...

The earliest instance of the passage being *quoted as a part of the actual text of the Epistle* [italics added] is in a fourth century Latin treatise entitled *Liber Apologeticus* (chap. 4), attributed either to the Spanish heretic Priscillian (died about 385) or to his follower Bishop Instantius. (Metzger B. A Textual Commentary on the Greek New Testament, 2nd ed. Hendrickson Publishers, 2005, pp. 647-648)

Despite the facts of history, what some seem to want to do is claim that because some writers wrote statements similar to the extra words added to 1 John 5:7-8 that this proves that they were originally in the inspired manuscripts of scripture (e.g. Rogers J. Why Creeds and Confessions? Lulu.com, pp. 98-99).

Instead, if such trinitarian writings prove anything, they point to a monk of some type who read non-biblical texts (probably the late 4th century document known as the *Latin Liber Apologeticus* by the gnostic Priscillian) and then decided to insert a comment he read elsewhere.

The truth is that the current Protestant and Greco-Roman Bibles which have the added words are relying on very late documents that were not considered to be original or faithful to the original text of the Bible. Some, of course, have ignored the truth about the origin of 1 John 5:7-8. The reality is that scholars realize that 1 John 5:7-8 additions were added centuries after the New Testament was originally written and finalized.

It is partially because of intentional errors like including words that should not be in 1 John 5 that Muslims claim that the New Testament cannot be trusted because 'Christians' (so-called) changed it. The Apostle Peter warned, "there will be false teachers among you, who will secretly bring in destructive heresies ... And many will follow their destructive ways, because of whom the way of truth will be blasphemed" (2 Peter 2:1-2). Certainly, that warning applies to any who intentionally changed the Bible on their own.

According to Protestant Dr. Wallace, here is what the original Greek supports for 1 John 5:7-8:

> "**5:7** For there are three that testify, **5:8** the Spirit and the water and the blood, and these three are in agreement." —NET Bible

Furthermore, other Protestant trinitarian scholars have concluded that what should be in 1 John 5:6-8 essentially has to do with baptism and Jesus—not the "trinity":

> **5:6 Water and blood** have been interpreted ... (1) as Jesus' baptism and death, (2) as His incarnation ... Most scholars favor the first interpretation ...
>
> **5;7, 8 The Holy Spirit** testifies in accord with **the water** and **the blood** (v. 6) that Jesus is the Son of God (Radmacher ED, general editor. Nelson Study Bible. New King James Version, 1997, p. 2147).

Properly understood, 1 John 5 simply is not teaching the modern Greco-Roman trinity that most who profess Christ claim to believe in.

Matthew 28:19 and Isaiah 6:3

Another passage that is often cited by trinitarians is Matthew 28:19. But it does not teach the trinity.

It should be explained here that perhaps the reason the Bible teaches, "baptizing them in the name of the Father and of the Son and of the Holy Spirit" (Matthew 28:19) is that through being begotten by the Holy Spirit through baptism (Luke 3:16), we will ultimately be born in the family of God (this is discussed further below)—and that is part of the relationship between us, the Holy Spirit, the Son, and the Father (this is also consistent with what Theophilus, a second century leader, wrote).

Even the Greco-Roman-Protestant saint and bishop Irenaeus did not teach that Matthew 28:19 endorsed the trinity as he felt:

> And for this reason the baptism of our regeneration proceeds through these three points: God the Father bestowing on us regeneration through His Son by the Holy Spirit. For as many as carry (in them) the Spirit of God are led to the Word, that is to the Son; and the Son brings them to the Father; and the Father causes them to possess incorruption. Without the Spirit it is not possible to behold the Word of God, nor without the Son can any draw near to the Father: for the knowledge of the Father is the Son, and the knowledge of the Son of God is through the Holy Spirit; and, according to the good pleasure of the Father, the Son ministers and dispenses the Spirit to whomsoever the Father wills and as He wills (Irenaeus, St., Bishop of Lyon. Translated from the Armenian by Armitage Robinson. The Demonstration of the Apostolic Preaching, Chapter 7. Wells, Somerset, Oct. 1879. As published in SOCIETY FOR PROMOTING CHRISTIAN KNOWLEDGE. NEW YORK: THE MACMILLAN CO, 1920).

Notice that Irenaeus clearly is teaching that the Father and Son have separate wills and that they dispense the Holy Spirit—one does not dispense a person.

In addition, in another attempt to find scriptural justification for the trinity, some trinitarians have declared that the "Holy, holy, holy" expression used twice in the Bible is proof of a trinitarian God.

The first time that expression occurs is Isaiah 6:3, so let us notice what it actually states:

> ¹ I saw the Lord sitting on a throne, high and lifted up, and the train of His robe filled the temple. ² Above it stood seraphim; each one had six wings: with two he covered his face, with two he covered his feet, and with two he flew. ³ And one cried to another and said: "Holy, holy, holy is the LORD of hosts; The whole earth is full of His glory!" (Isaiah 6:1-3)

Now in the vision in Daniel of God's throne, there were two divine beings (Daniel 7:13-14).

The expression "Holy, holy, holy" is repeated in Revelation 4:8-9 and it also clearly shows that this is a discussion of one being, not three. Notice:

> ⁸ ... And they do not rest day or night, saying: "Holy, holy, holy, Lord God Almighty, Who was and is and is to come!"
>
> ⁹ Whenever the living creatures give glory and honor and thanks to Him who sits on the throne, who lives forever and ever ...

The expression 'Who was and is and is to come' is also three, but not a reference to three divine beings—this is clearly a reference to Jesus. Notice that the four living creatures are giving glory to the Him who sits on the throne. This does not seem to be a discussion of a plurality of Him. If trinitarians are trying to convince non-trinitarians of their point they would be wise to be more careful about their supposed proofs.

"Jesus, the author and finisher of our faith" (Hebrews 12:2) taught:

> ²⁴ God is Spirit, and those who worship Him must worship in spirit and truth. (John 4:24)

The truth is that God is NOT a trinity and Christians should not vainly worship God based on improper traditions from men (cf. Matthew 15:3-9).

Yet, most who claim Christianity ignore the Bible and teach the trinitarian tradition that was formally adopted centuries later by a council of men who did not properly understand the Bible.

The Ancient of Days

In the Old Testament, Daniel saw a vision of two divine beings:

> [13] "I was watching in the night visions, And behold, One like the Son of Man, Coming with the clouds of heaven! He came to the Ancient of Days, And they brought Him near before Him. [14] Then to Him was given dominion and glory and a kingdom, That all peoples, nations, and languages should serve Him. His dominion is an everlasting dominion, Which shall not pass away, And His kingdom the one Which shall not be destroyed. (Daniel 7:13-14)

The Ancient of Days is the one called the Father in the New Testament, who gives the Kingdom to Jesus (Luke 22:29). The Father and Son are NOT the same. And the New Testament shows Jesus will ultimately turn the Kingdom over to the Father (1 Corinthians 15:24)—which He could not do if they were the same being.

Regarding the New Testament, even a Protestant trinitarian scholar has admitted that the Bible has a binitarian emphasis, and does not teach what is now considered to be the trinity:

> The binitarian formulas are found in Rom. 8:11, 2 Cor. 4:14, Gal. 1:1, Eph. 1:20, 1 Tim 1:2, 1 Pet. 1:21, and 2 John 1:13 ... **No doctrine of the Trinity in the Nicene sense is present in the New Testament** ... There is no doctrine of the Trinity in the strict sense in the Apostolic Fathers ... (Rusch W.G. The Trinitarian Controversy. Fortress Press, Phil., 1980, pp. 2-3).

The above book endorses the trinity, yet admits that it was NOT part of the original faith (Jude 3).

Now consider the following scripture:

> [16] For God so loved the world that He gave His only begotten Son, that whoever believes in Him should not perish but have everlasting life. (John 3:16)

This was supreme love of the Father to give the Son, His eternal companion. For if the Son sinned, their relationship would have been destroyed. This is something that the Ancient of Days risked, so that people could have everlasting life (John 3:16-17).

Yet, in the trinitarian view, the Ancient of Days risked nothing as it teaches that Jesus was 'fully divine' when He was 'fully human'.

Scripture teaches that the Father is greater than the Son (John 14:28). The Father, not wanting glory just for Himself, sent His Son as a focus for humanity's salvation, which gives great glory to Jesus (cf. Hebrews 13:20-21; 1 Peter 4:11).

Biblical or Protestant Jesus?

Jesus is divine.

In the New Testament, John begins by making binitarian statements which demonstrate the divinity of Jesus:

> [1] In the beginning was the Word, and the Word was with God, and the Word was God. [2] He was in the beginning with God. [3] All things were made through Him, and without Him nothing was made that was made (John 1:1-3).

Thus, the Word was God and was with God. And the Word, Jesus, is a lot like the Father, notice that Jesus became flesh:

> [14] And the Word became flesh and dwelt among us, and we beheld His glory, the glory as of the only begotten of the Father, full of grace and truth (John 1:14).

An important point to notice is this shows that Jesus was God and He actually became flesh—scripture does not state that He remained fully God on the earth. Jesus was aware of His divine existence before coming to the earth as a human and did point that out (John 6:62-8:58). Note: In an attempt to denounce binitarianism, some Protestants have claimed that Melito wrote that Jesus was 'fully God' on the earth, but he did not. Melito basically wrote that Jesus had the natures of deity and humanity after His resurrection (Hall S. ed., Melito of Sardis on Pascha and fragments. Oxford, 1979, Peri Pascha, verse 8, pp. 6-7), which Jesus certainly did when appearing in bodily form (John 20:24).

Since Protestant scholars do not insist that the post-resurrected Jesus was fully man, none should suggest that Melito said so.

The Bible teaches that Jesus gave up various divine attributes to come to the earth.

Notice what the Apostle Paul was inspired to write:

> ^{7} ... Christ Jesus, who subsisting in (the) form of God thought (it) not robbery to be equal to God, but emptied Himself, taking (the) form of a slave, becoming in (the) likeness of men" (Philippians 2:7. Literal translation. Green J.P. ed. Interlinear Greek-English New Testament, 3rd ed. Baker Books, Grand Rapids (MI), 1996, p. 607).

Note that "emptied Himself" is the literal translation in the Greek. We in the CCOG teach that Jesus made the supreme sacrifice. He had everything as a member of the Godhead. Yet, He emptied Himself of His divinity in order to become human.

This took massive love towards humanity and massive faith towards the one known as the Father. This, for example, would have been the opportunity for the Father to, so to speak, eliminate the competition. Jesus would have known that prior to His incarnation. Yet, He fully trusted the Father and went through it.

One of the many problems with Protestantism's embracing of the trinity is that it leads people away from worshipping the Jesus of the Bible.

The trinitarian Jesus did not empty Himself of His divinity, nor did He truly die.

Canadian Protestant theologian J. I. Packer wrote:

> The really staggering Christian claim is that Jesus of Nazareth was God made man—that the second person of the Godhead became the "second man" (1 Cor. 15:47), determining human destiny, the second representative head of the race, and that He took humanity without loss of deity, so that Jesus of Nazareth was as truly and fully divine as He was human. Here

are two mysteries for the price of one—the plurality of persons within the unity of God, and the union of Godhead and manhood in the person of Jesus. (Packer Jl. Knowing God. InterVarsity Press, 2011, p. 53).

While, yes, Jesus was "made man," Jesus was not fully God and fully human at the same time. Jesus did voluntarily give up His divinity to become human.

There are other scriptures that help prove that.

Notice the following:

> [5] and he was not able there any mighty work to do, (Mark 6:5a, YLT)
>
> [5] Now He could do no mighty work there (Mark 6:5, NKJV)

If Jesus was FULLY DIVINE, He would have been able to do mighty works then (whether He actually would have is another question). But notice that He could not, which proves He was NOT fully divine at that time. Jesus did not regain His full divinity until after His resurrection (cf. Matthew 28:18; John 20:28).

Jesus declared:

> [30] I can of Myself do nothing. (John 5:30)

If Jesus was fully God at that time, He could have done basically anything. But, since He was truly human, He could only do what the Father allowed Him to do.

Jesus had faith. His saints keep the commandments and have the "faith of Jesus" (Revelation 14:12).

By claiming that Jesus was "fully God" on the earth, that limits what Protestants think about faith. But Jesus said of His followers that God would work great signs through them (Mark 16:17; cf. Acts 2:4, 17-18, 5:12). And, since Jesus is now divine, we can do all things through Him (Philippians 4:13).

As far as Jesus' humanity goes, consider also the New Testament makes it clear that Jesus was tempted:

> [18] For in that He Himself has suffered, being tempted, He is able to aid those who are tempted. (Hebrews 2:18)

Since the New Testament also teaches that God cannot be tempted by evil according to James 1:13 (which uses the same Greek word for "tempted"), this shows that Jesus was not fully God after His incarnation and prior to His resurrection.

Furthermore, notice:

> [14] Seeing then that we have a great High Priest who has passed through the heavens, Jesus the Son of God, let us hold fast our confession. [15] For we do not have a High Priest who cannot sympathize with our weaknesses, but was in all points tempted as we are, yet without sin. (Hebrews 4:14-15)

Humans, of course, can sin.

Consider that the Bible teaches God cannot lie (Hebrews 6:18, Titus 1:2). For Jesus to have been "in all points tempted as we are" to position Him to fully "sympathize with our weaknesses," He had to be capable of actually sinning, otherwise He was NOT tempted as we are. Therefore, since God cannot sin, and scripture cannot be broken (John 10:35), we must conclude Jesus could not have been fully God while on earth. For, if Jesus was fully God on earth, He was not tempted as we are.

The false Jesus that Protestant trinitarians actually claim to worship did NOT give up all so that humans could be saved, was not subject to transgression like humans, did not have to the faith to rely on the Father for miracles or to be resurrected, did not really die, and, hence, did not really come in the flesh.

Although Protestants do not word it that way, their view of Jesus is warned against by the Apostle John:

> ⁷ For many deceivers have gone out into the world who do not confess Jesus Christ as coming in the flesh. This is a deceiver and an antichrist (2 John 7).

This scripture says that antichrist is a deceiver who does "not confess Jesus Christ as coming in the flesh."

Jesus is to live His life in us (as taught in Galatians 2:20), and did come in the flesh.

What doctrine is popular amongst Protestants yet teaches that:

> 1) Jesus is only the physical representation of the Father, thus denying the actual Lord?
> 2) the Godhead is a closed triangle, hence we cannot truly become one with Jesus and His Father?
> 3) Jesus did not truly empty Himself of his divinity as He was supposedly "fully God" while on the earth?
> 4) God never really died since He was in heaven (allegedly only His physical representation appeared to have died, and even then it went to preach to demons for those three days and three nights)?
> 5) the Father and Son could not have different wills, thus it denies the Father and the Son?

Is it not a version of the Greco-Roman trinity as adopted by the Council of Constantinople called for by the Emperor Theodosius in 381 A.D.?

If Jesus was not truly human while on earth, does not standard trinitarianism actually deny Jesus' humanity?

Protestantism essentially teaches a Jesus who appeared as a human and appeared to die (but supposedly did not really die for our sins), and that if someone is lucky enough to be persuaded about Him, they can be saved through Him.

That is not the biblical Jesus.

The Apostle Paul warned about people who would preach another Jesus:

> [3] But I fear, lest somehow, as the serpent deceived Eve by his craftiness, so your minds may be corrupted from the simplicity that is in Christ. [4] For if he who comes preaches another Jesus whom we have not preached, or if you receive a different spirit which you have not received, or a different gospel which you have not accepted — you may well put up with it! (2 Corinthians 11:3-4)

The simple truth is that Jesus became flesh as the Son of God. Since the resurrection, He is divine and is the Son of God in the Family of God. He gave all that He possibly could for us. He taught repentance (Mark 1:15). And, He came to be the Savior for all (1 Timothy 4:10), not just those who received instructions and/or social pressures that persuaded them to consider themselves Christians in this life.

Do not put up with the Protestant 'Jesus.' The unbiblical Protestant one is "another Jesus" with a "different gospel."

Holy Spirit

There is a "spirit in man" (Job 32:8; cf. 1 Corinthians 2:11).

Is that spirit human?

Essentially, since it is part of a human, it is a human spirit.

The same is essentially true of the Holy Spirit.

Since it proceeds from God, it is God's spirit. But just like the spirit in man is not a separate person, neither is the Spirit of God a separate person.

This is why the following verses (which are the ones most frequently cited by trinitarians to supposedly prove that the Holy Spirit is God, thus a third person of their trinity) only show that sin against the Holy Spirit is a sin against God, as opposed to teaching that the Holy Spirit, itself, is a separate God being:

> [1] But a certain man named Ananias, with Sapphira his wife, sold a possession. [2] And he kept back part of the proceeds, his wife

also being aware of it, and brought a certain part and laid it at the apostles' feet.

³ But Peter said, "Ananias, why has Satan filled your heart to lie to the Holy Spirit and keep back part of the price of the land for yourself? ⁴ While it remained, was it not your own? And after it was sold, was it not in your own control? Why have you conceived this thing in your heart? You have not lied to men but to God." (Acts 5:1-4).

There are two main points about the above. The first is that Ananias did lie to men and the Holy Spirit. The second is that Peter and others in the Bible (Moses, Aaron, Joshua, Micah, etc.) ultimately equate all sin to being sin against God.

Perhaps it may be of interest to note that after David sinned against Uriah the Hittite, he claimed he had only sinned against God (2 Samuel 12:13). Notice the following:

> ³ For I acknowledge my transgressions, And my sin is always before me. ⁴ Against You, You only, have I sinned, And done this evil in Your sight (Psalm 51:3-4).

Similarly, all sin is against God.

Is the Holy Spirit in Acts 5 the Spirit of the Father, the Spirit of the Lord, or a separate person only called the Holy Spirit? Continuing on in Acts 5 we find the answer:

> ⁷ Now it was about three hours later when his wife came in, not knowing what had happened. ⁸ And Peter answered her, "Tell me whether you sold the land for so much?"
>
> She said, "Yes, for so much."
>
> ⁹ Then Peter said to her, "How is it that you have agreed together to test the Spirit of the Lord? Look, the feet of those who have buried your husband are at the door, and they will carry you out." (Acts 5:7-9).

Notice that Peter makes it clear both Ananias and his wife Sapphira tested "the Spirit of the Lord." This is not some separate being.

Therefore, contrary to the assertion by many trinitarian scholars, Acts 5 is not definitive proof that the Holy Spirit is a separate God or person in any trinity.

What about Acts 13:2? It states:

> ² As they ministered to the Lord and fasted, the Holy Spirit said, "Now separate to Me Barnabas and Saul for the work to which I have called them." (Acts 13:2)

While some conclude that the above must mean an audible voice, this is not necessarily the case. The Bible is clear that in the past the Holy Spirit spoke through the prophets (cf. 1 Kings 14:18; Hebrews 1:1; 2 Peter 1:20). Also, the word translated as "said" (εἶπε) can include concepts other than direct personal speech.

Some Protestant commentators seem to also realize this:

> *The Holy Ghost said*; either with an articulate voice, or by an internal impulse, upon the minds of three of the prophets: (Gills Exposition of the Entire Bible.)

> 13. *As they ministered to the Lord*-The word denotes the performance of official duties of any kind, and was used to express the priestly functions under the Old Testament. Here it signifies the corresponding ministrations of the Christian Church.
>
> *And fasted*-As this was done in other cases on special occasions (Ac 13:3, 14, 23), it is not improbable that they had been led to expect some such prophetic announcement at this time.
>
> *The Holy Ghost said*-through some of the prophets mentioned in Ac 13:1. (Jamieson-Faucett-Brown)

> *The Holy Ghost said.* By an inspiration given to some one of these prophets. God has spoken at sundry times and in divers

manners unto the fathers by the one of these prophets (Heb 1:1). Compare Ac 20:23. (Peoples New Testament)

Precisely how this information was conveyed is not completely clear and it is possible that this information came from a prophet who told the apostles. Hence, to declare Acts 13:2 as proof of personhood for the Holy Spirit is shaky ground at best.

The Apostle Paul mentions the Father and Jesus in every introduction of every book he wrote (Romans 1:7; 1 Corinthians 1:3; 2 Corinthians 1:2; Galatians 1:3; Ephesians 1:2; Philippians 1:2; Colossians 1:2; 1 Thessalonians 1:1; 2 Thessalonians 1:2; 1 Timothy 1:2; 2 Timothy 1:2; Titus 1:1; Philemon 1:3; Hebrews 1:1-2), but he never mentions the Holy Spirit. This is known as a binitarian position.

If the Holy Spirit was a coequal member of the trinity, could this possibly be blasphemy against the Holy Spirit (Luke 12:10)? Jesus Himself made that clear when He said that blasphemy against Him would be forgiven, but not blasphemy against the Holy Spirit (Mark 3:28-29). If they were coequal entities, there would be no such distinction.

Certainly no one thinks that the Apostle Paul was guilty of that.

Like Paul, the Apostle Peter also made the duality of God clear in the introduction of his two books (1 Peter 1:3; 2 Peter 1:2), where he, too, left out the Holy Spirit.

Peter confirmed that he knew that Jesus was part of the God Family when he said to Jesus, "You are the Christ, the Son of the living God" (Matthew 16:16). Peter also helped to confirm that the Holy Spirit is not a person when in Acts 2:17-18, he quotes Joel about God pouring out His Spirit.

Early Christians did not teach the Holy Spirit was a third member of a trinity.

Perhaps it should be mentioned here that the reason that the Bible teaches, "baptizing them in the name of the Father and of the Son and of the Holy Spirit" (Matthew 28:19) is that through being begotten by the Holy Spirit through baptism (Luke 3:16), we will ultimately be born in the family of God.

At least one Protestant trinitarian scholar has admitted:

> The language of the New Testament permits the Holy Spirit to be understood as an impersonal force or influence more readily than it does the Son ... The attempt to develop an understanding of the Holy Spirit consistent with the trinitarian passages ... came to fruition at Constantinople in 381. There were a number of reasons why the personhood of the Holy Spirit took longer to acknowledge than the Son: (1) the term *pneuma*, breath, is neuter in general and impersonal in ordinary meaning; (2) the distinctive work of the Holy Spirit, influencing the believer, does not necessarily seem as personal as that of the Father ... in addition, those who saw the Holy Spirit as a Person, were often heretical, for example, the Montanists; (3) many of the early theologians attributed to the Logos or Word, the revelatory activity later theologians saw as the special, personal work of the Holy Spirit (Brown HOJ. Heresies: Heresy and Orthodoxy in the History of the Church. Hendrickson Publishers, Peabody (MA), 1988, p. 140).

Hence, trinitarian scholars understand that:

1) a concept close to what trinitarians teach about the Holy Spirit was not widely accepted until the fourth century,
2) **normal understanding of *koine* Greek reveals that the Holy Spirit would be impersonal**, not a person,
3) the work of the Holy Spirit can be attributed to an impersonal force from God,
4) **second-century heretics were associated with treating the Holy Spirit as a person**,
5) early church writers made statements contradicting the current trinitarian view of the Holy Spirit,
6) after the trinity was accepted, later writers decided biblical statements that were not considered trinitarian must support the trinity, hence essentially PROVING that the Holy Spirit as part of a divine trinity WAS NOT an original Christian teaching, and

7) the primary portion of scripture that many have pointed to as proof of the trinity—1 John 5:7-8—is a fraud.

What were the views of 2nd century Christian writers?

Around 108 A.D., Ignatius of Antioch referred to the Father as *God* and Jesus as *God*, but not the Holy Spirit. Here is what he actually taught about the Holy Spirit:

> ... using as a rope the Holy Spirit (Ignatius. Letter to the Ephesians, 9:1. In Holmes, p.143).
>
> For our God, Jesus Christ, was conceived by Mary according to God's plan, both from the seed of David and of the Holy Spirit (Ignatius. Letter to the Ephesians, 18:2, p.149).
>
> appointed by the mind of Jesus Christ, whom he, in accordance with his own will securely established by his Holy Spirit ... the Spirit is not deceived as it is from God (Ignatius. Letter to the Philadelphians. 0:1,7:1, pp.177,181).

Referring to the Holy Spirit as *it* and a *rope* points to it as a manifestation of the power of God and not a person.

Also, Polycarp specifically called the Father *God* and Jesus *God* (Polycarp's Letter to the Philippians, chapter XII), he never referred to the Holy Spirit that way. Here is the only extant direct quote from Polycarp that clearly mentions the Holy Spirit:

> I bless you because you have considered me worthy of this day and hour, that I might receive a place among the number of martyrs in the cup of your Christ, to the resurrection of eternal life, both of soul and of body, in the incorruptibility of the Holy Spirit. May I be received among them in your presence today, as a rich and acceptable sacrifice, as you have prepared and revealed beforehand, and have now accomplished, you who are the faithful and true God. For this reason, indeed for all things, I praise you, I bless you, I glorify you, through the eternal and heavenly High-priest, Jesus Christ, your beloved Son, through whom to you with him and the Holy Spirit be glory both now

and for the ages to come. Amen (The Martyrdom of Polycarp, 14:2-3. In Holmes M.W. The Apostolic Fathers, Greek Texts and English Translations. Baker Books, Grand Rapids (MI), 2004, p.143).

Contrary to claims from some who are misinformed, Polycarp was not a trinitarian, but a binitarian.

Furthermore, Melito of Sardis was a leader who Polycrates claimed to be faithful to the teachings he learned from the Apostle John and Polycarp. And here is what Melito (whom the Greco-Roman Catholics and others consider to be a saint) wrote:

> No eye can see Him, nor thought apprehend Him, nor language describe Him; and those who love Him speak of Him thus: 'Father, and God of Truth" (Melito. A Discourse Which Was in the Presence of Antoninus Caesar).

Melito also wrote:

> For the deeds done by Christ after His baptism, and especially His miracles, gave indication and assurance to the world of the Deity hidden in His flesh. For, being at once both God and perfect man likewise ... He concealed the signs of His Deity, although He was the true God existing before all ages (Melito. On the Nature of Christ. From Roberts and Donaldson).

This clearly shows that Melito considered Christ to be God, as well as the Father. There is no indication in any of the known surviving writings of Melito that he considered that the Holy Spirit was also God. His writings, like those of Ignatius and Polycarp, suggest that the Holy Spirit was simply a manifestation of the power of God as he wrote:

> *The tongue of the Lord*-His Holy Spirit. In the Psalm: "My tongue is a pen." (Melito. From the Oration on Our Lord's Passion, IX).

> *The finger of the Lord*-the Holy Spirit, by whose operation the tables of the law in Exodus are said to have been written (Melito. From the Oration on Our Lord's Passion, XVI).

Since God had written the Ten Commandments Himself (Exodus 31:18), this shows that Melito only considered the Holy Spirit to be the power of God, not a separate person.

While the Hebrew word for spirit is feminine and the Greek word for spirit is neuter, those designations, of themselves, either do not tell us gender or at least show us not to use "He" like most Protestant translators improperly have done. Because the English language does not have masculine or feminine nouns, "it" is a more linguistically proper pronoun.

Plus, realize that early Christians simply did NOT believe that the Holy Spirit was a person and was not referred to as "He." Nor precisely something that was male or female based upon the early writings that are available.

Many have been misled by improper translations of Greek personal pronouns into English.

Evangelical Baptist scholar Dr. Daniel Wallace explained some of this as follows:

> About half a dozen texts in the NT are used in support of the Spirit's personality on the grounds of gender shift due to *construction ad sensum* ("construction according to sense" or, in this case, according to natural as opposed to grammatical gender). That is to say, these passages seem to refer to the Spirit with the masculine gender in spite of the fact that πνεῦμα is neuter, and grammatical concord would normally require that any reference to the Spirit also be in the neuter gender. ...
>
> Many theologians treat these passages as a primary proof of the Spirit's personality. ...
>
> John 16:7 can be dismissed ... Whatever the reason for the masculine participle in v. 7, it is evident that the grammaticization of the Spirit's personality is not the only, nor even the most plausible, explanation. Since this text also involves serious exegetical problems (i.e., a variety of reasons as to why the masculine participle is used), it cannot be

marshaled as unambiguous syntactical proof of the Spirit's personality. In sum, none of the gender shift passages clearly helps establish the personality of the Holy Spirit.

There is no text in the NT that clearly or even probably affirms the personality of the Holy Spirit through the route of Greek grammar. ...

Evangelical defenses of various doctrines occasionally are poorly founded. We sometimes claim things to be true because we want them to be true, without doing the exhaustive spadework needed to support our conclusions. ...

In sum, I have sought to demonstrate in this paper that **the *grammatical* basis for the Holy Spirit's personality is lacking in the NT**, yet this is frequently, if not usually, the first line of defense of that doctrine by many evangelical writers. But if **grammar cannot legitimately be used to support the Spirit's personality, then perhaps we need to reexamine the rest of our basis for this theological commitment.** (Wallace D. Greek Grammar and the Personality of the Holy Spirit. Bulletin for Biblical Research 13.1 (2003) 97-125)

John 15:26 ... The use of ἐκεῖνος {*that one*} here is frequently regarded by students of the NT to be an affirmation of the personality of the Holy Spirit. ... 42 ...

But this is erroneous. In all these Johannine passages, πνεῦμα {*spirit*} is appositional to a masculine noun. The gender of ἐκεῖνος has nothing to do with the natural gender ending of πνεῦμα. ...

42 The view is especially popular among theologians, not infrequently becoming their mainstay for their argument for the personality of the Holy Spirit ... (Wallace D. Greek Grammar. Pp. 331-332).

For those who wish to read many of the technical reasons above, Dr. Wallace put up entire papers at the following link: https://www.ibr-bbr.org/files/bbr/BBR_2003a_05_Wallace_HolySpirit.pdf

The grammatical reality is that the Greek noun *pneuma* (πνεῦμα), in all its various forms, is always and only neuter in gender. Likewise, all pronouns that refer to *pneuma* are always and only can be neuter in gender. If the Holy Spirit were a masculine person, the nouns and pronouns in the Greek text would have to have been written in the masculine gender, as are all the nouns and pronouns that refer to God the Father and Jesus Christ.

Yet, as Dr. Wallace and others have concluded, nowhere in the Greek text of the New Testament is the Holy Spirit ever designated by a noun or pronoun in the masculine gender.

If Protestants truly accept *sola Scriptura*, they would not insist that the Holy Spirit is a masculine third person of a trinity. The original Greek text of the New Testament absolutely does not teach it.

Imperial Councils in the 4th Century

How did the Protestants get trinitarianism?

Well, it started as a corrupting heresy.

Here is an explanation from the 4th century Orthodox Catholic and binitarian bishop Marcellus of Ancyra:

> Now with the heresy of the Ariomaniacs, which has corrupted the Church of God ... These then teach three hypostases, just as Valentinus the heresiarch first invented in the book entitled by him 'On the Three Natures'. For he was the first to invent three hypostases and three persons of the Father, Son and Holy Spirit, and he is discovered to have filched this from Hermes and Plato (Source: Logan A. Marcellus of Ancyra (Pseudo-Anthimus), 'On the Holy Church': Text, Translation and Commentary. Verses 8-9. Journal of Theological Studies, NS, Volume 51, Pt. 1, April 2000, p.95).

So, yes, the trinity was pushed by apostates, such as Valentinus who was denounced in the 2nd century by Polycarp of Smyrna (Irenaeus. Adversus Haereses. Book III, Chapter 4, Verse 3). In the 4th century, the apostasy became widespread and official.

But the vast majority of the Greco-Romans, even in the 4th century, had not started out that way.

Emperor Constantine, himself, was heavily involved pushing the change to trinitarianism:

> Although **Constantine** is usually remembered for the steps he took toward making Christianity the established religion of the Roman Empire, it would not be wrong to consider him the one who **inaugurated the centuries of trinitarian orthodoxy**. It was he who proposed and perhaps even imposed the expression *homoousis* at the Council of Nicea in 325, and it was he who provided government aid to the orthodox and exerted government pressure against nonconformists. (Brown HOJ. Heresies: Heresy and Orthodoxy in the History of the Church. Hendrickson Publishers, Peabody (MA), 1988, pp. 332-333).

Thus, a pagan emperor, pushed and imperially imposed a doctrine on his own. And this did not come from the Bible into the world's largest churches, but from a pagan. Constantine still honored the pagan sun deities after his supposed conversion to Christianity. He was not even baptized into the Greco-Roman world's church when he convened the Council of Nicea in 325 A.D. In 337 A.D., he allegedly converted on his death bed—and even then he insisted upon being buried in a grave dedicated to a pagan deity.

The 4th century Roman Emperor Constantine followed Mithraism, a religion that had a trinitarian component (Paine LL. The Ethnic Trinities and Their Relations to the Christian Trinity: A Chapter in the Comparative History of Religions. Kessinger Publishing, 1901, p. 84).

Constantine called for, and essentially forced via legal summons, the Council of Nicea in 325 A.D. Protestant Philip Schaff wrote the following about the Emperor and that Council:

> How great the contrast between this position of the church and the time of her persecution but scarcely passed! What a revolution of opinion in **bishops who had once feared the Roman emperor as the worst enemy of the church, and who now greeted the same emperor in his half barbarous attire as**

> an angel of God from heaven, and gave him, though not yet even baptized, the honorary presidency of the highest assembly of the church! (Schaff P. History of the Christian Church, Volume 3. C. Scribner's sons, 1923, p. 625)

Emperor Constantine remained an enemy of the true church as he took persecuting steps against COG Christians shortly after the Council of Nicea.

The vast majority of the Greco-Roman bishops who attended the Council of Nicea were not trinitarian (ibid). The Holy Spirit was simply not considered to be the third member of the Godhead by the vast majority of Greco-Romans then.

The biggest group (75-80%) at the Council of Nicea were Semi-Arians (Feldmeth N. Early Christianity. CD Lecture. Fuller Theological Seminary, c. 2003). The rest were unitarians (10%) and trinitarians (10-15%).

Notice what a Roman Catholic priest wrote about the trinitarian Athanasius at the Nicene Council:

> Remember the example of St. Athanasius, the great champion for the true Faith in the 4th-Century crisis concerning the Person and nature of Jesus Christ. St. Athanasius stood up against 90% of all the bishops in the Church, and even endured the appearance of being excommunicated by Pope Liberius . . . (Gruner N., Priest. Part II FATIMA: Roadblocks and Breakthroughs. The Fatima Crusader 110, Fall 2014, p. 48)

Notice that the above account claims that 90% of Greco-Roman bishops did NOT support the trinity. The idea that the trinity was a fundamental part of even the Greco-Roman faith simply does not agree with the historical facts.

Emperor Constantine was familiar with a trinitarian viewpoint since Mithraism had a type of triad/trinity leading it. After an impassioned speech by trinitarian Athanasius, Emperor Constantine arose. And since he was the Emperor, plus he was dressed as a golden "angel," his standing was noticed (Feldmeth N. Early Christianity. CD Lecture. Fuller Theological Seminary, c. 2003).

The attendees then correctly interpreted the Emperor as now supporting Athanasius. Because of Athanasius' speech and the Emperor's approval, the bulk of the attendees decided to come up with a statement on the Godhead that the unitarians could not support.

Furthermore, to this day, trinitarian theologians tend to use Constantine's *homoousis* term to describe aspects of the trinity.

Yet not everyone at the Nicene Council agreed with Emperor Constantine.

Into the middle of the fourth century, even many major leaders of the Greco-Roman churches endorsed Semi-Arian, non-trinitarian positions (we in the CCOG continue to do so today).

But through Imperial and other pressures, the Greco-Romans changed.

In 380, Theodosius issued an Imperial decree that said any who would not embrace the trinity would be labelled differently (they could legally no longer use the term "catholic," though some in places like Armenia, like the Paulicians, still did) **and he called them "heretics" and "foolish madmen"** (Theodosian Code XVI.1.2. Cited in Bettenson H, ed., Documents of the Christian Church, London: Oxford University Press, 1943, p. 31). In other words, Theodosius was the one who set the stage to declare that any who were not trinitarian were part of a cult. From the Book of Acts to present, the true faith has often been "spoken against everywhere" (Acts 28:22). It is reported that:

> On February 27, 380, in Thessaloniki, the Eastern Roman Emperor Theodosius I (347 - 395) signed a decree in the presence of the Western Roman Emperor Valentinian II (371 - 392) that made {Nicene} Christianity the religion of the state. (von Hellfeld M. Christianity becomes the religion of the Roman Empire - February 27, 380. Deutsche Welle, November 16, 2009)

What kind of man was the name-calling Theodosius?

Let's see something written about his actions in 390 A.D. by a contemporary witness and Greco-Roman theologian named Theodoret who reported:

> The emperor was fired with anger when he heard the news, and unable to endure the rush of his passion, did not even check its onset by the curb of reason, but allowed his rage to be the minister of his vengeance. When the imperial passion had received its authority, as though itself an independent prince, it broke the bonds and yoke of reason, unsheathed swords of injustice right and left without distinction, and slew innocent and guilty together. No trial preceded the sentence. No condemnation was passed on the perpetrators of the crimes. Multitudes were mowed down like ears of grain in harvest-tide. It is said that seven thousand perished. (Theodoret. Ecclesiastical History of Theodoret. Dalcassian Publishing Company, 2019, p. 200).

Theodosius also had people killed (called Quartodecimans) who retained the biblical date of Passover (Gibbon E. Decline and Fall of the Roman Empire, Volume III, Chapter XXVII. Ca. 1776-1788). "To the reign of Theodosius belonged the glory or the infamy of establishing Inquisitors of Faith, who seem to have been specially enjoined to look after the crime of the Quartodecimans" (Smith W. A Dictionary of Greek and Roman Biography and Mythology: Oarses-Zygia. J. Murray, 1890 Item notes: v.3, p. 1064).

The change to trinitarianism was finalized by the Council of Constantinople, which was convened by Theodosius, in 381 A.D. The *Catechism of the Catholic Church* states:

> **245** The apostolic faith concerning the Spirit was announced by the second ecumenical council at Constantinople (381) (Catechism of the Catholic Church. Imprimatur Potest +Joseph Cardinal Ratzinger. Doubleday, NY 1995, p. 72).

Remember that the apostles had all been dead for hundreds of years before the trinitarian position with the Holy Spirit was agreed upon.

Most Protestants have accepted the trinitarian change and many follow Theodosius' general example of considering non-trinitarians as part of a cult.

Deification

Consistent with numerous scriptures (e.g. Malachi 2:14-15; Acts 17:29; Ephesians 3:14-19; Romans 8:29; 1 Peter 1:15-16; 2 Peter 1:3-4), early Christians taught deification and that humans were not immortal.

Protestant Dr. Malcolm Jeeves admitted pagan views affected the Greco-Roman-Protestants:

> Malcolm Jeeves ... is one of many believing scientists who think the Christian concept of the soul should be relieved of its Cartesian and Platonic overlays. 'The immortality of the soul is so often talked about that it is easy to miss that the Jewish view did not support it,' Jeeves says. 'Furthermore, the original Christian view was not the immortality of the soul but the resurrection of the body.' But Platonism did creep in, Jeeves acknowledges, winning over such influential Christian theologians as Augustine and John Calvin. (Tolson J. Is There Room for the Soul? New challenges to our most cherished beliefs about self and the human spirit. US NEWS AND WORLD REPORT, October 23, 2006)

As far as Platonism being a factor, notice what the Greco-Roman supporting Tertullian (155-220 A.D.) wrote:

> I may use, therefore, the opinion of a Plato, when he declares: 'Every soul is immortal'" (Tertullian. On the Resurrection of the Flesh. Ante-Nicene Fathers, vol. III, VI, 3, p. 547)

Notice that Tertullian did not write that the Bible taught the immortality of the soul, but referenced a Greek philosopher. The Greeks, themselves, allegedly got this teaching from the ancient Egyptians (see Euterpés statements in the second book of Herodotus' History).

Like early real Christians (we do not consider Tertullian to have been one), we in the CCOG still teach humans do not have immortal souls (1

Corinthians 15:51-54; Romans 2:6-7). We do not consider that John Calvin or Augustine or Gregory Thaumaturgus (who preceded Augustine) were true Christians and do not believe that pagan sources should have changed biblical beliefs.

We also teach that deification is to be granted to resurrected Christians (2 Timothy 1:10; 1 John 3:2), like early Christians did.

For example, in the early 2nd century, Ignatius of Antioch wrote:

> For neither shall I ever have such [another] opportunity of attaining to God ... It is good to set from the world unto God, that I may rise again to Him ... it will be granted me to attain to God (Ignatius. Letter to the Romans, Chapters 2,4).

> He is the door of the Father, by which enter in Abraham, and Isaac, and Jacob, and the prophets, and the apostles, and the Church. All these have for their object the attaining to the unity of God (Ignatius. Letter to the Romans, Chapter 9).

The false idea that humans could not really die as they already possessed immortality was, according to Justin Martyr (considered a saint by Protestants), believed by false Christians who descended from Simon Magus:

> "To Simon the holy God." And almost all the Samaritans, and a few even of other nations, worship him, and acknowledge him as the first god; and a woman, Helena, who went about with him at that time, and had formerly been a prostitute, they say is the first idea generated by him. And a man, Meander, also a Samaritan, of the town Capparetaea, a disciple of Simon, and inspired by devils, we know to have deceived many while he was in Antioch by his magical art. He persuaded those who adhered to him that they should never die, and even now there are some living who hold this opinion of his ... All who take their opinions from these men, are, as we before said, called Christians; just as also those who do not agree with the philosophers in their doctrines, have yet in common with them the name of philosophers given to them...But I have a treatise against all the heresies that have existed already composed, which, if you wish

> to read it, I will give you (Justin. First Apology, Chapter XXVI. Excerpted from Ante-Nicene Fathers, Volume 1. Edited by Alexander Roberts & James Donaldson. American Edition, 1885).

Also in the 2nd century, Theophilus of Antioch taught deification and that humans were not immortal.

Although some claim Theophilus was the first to write about the trinity, what he actually wrote had to do with a non-trinitarian threeness with God. Theophilus' writings refer to the Father, Son, but not also the Holy Spirit as part of the threeness. The third part he wrote about had to do with human deification.

Though the following has often been mistranslated, here is a more proper translation from the Greek of something that Theophilus wrote:

> In like manner also the three days which were before the luminaries, are types of the three of God, and His Word, and His wisdom. And the fourth is the type of man, who needs light, that so there may be God, the Word, wisdom, man. (Theophilus of Antioch. To Autolycus, Book 2, Chapter XV)

Now trinitarian Protestants may argue that this is just a semantics issue and that Theophilus was actually teaching about the trinity. Well, he was not as the third part has to do with teaching that humans become God. And that is what Theophilus was teaching—that now man is a fourth part, but will become part of God, a third part, when humans become God's resurrected offspring! And that clearly is a binitarian view.

Furthermore, Theophilus did not teach that the Holy Spirit was one of three persons in any trinity. He verified that when he taught the following about the Spirit of God:

> ... if I say He is Spirit, I speak of His breath ... For as the pomegranate, with the rind containing it, has within it many cells and compartments which are separated by tissues, and has also many seeds dwelling in it, so the whole creation is contained by the spirit of God, and the containing spirit is along

with the creation contained by the hand of God (Theophilus of Antioch. To Autolycus, Book 1, Chapters III,V).

The threeness, if you will, of God is that those begotten of the Holy Spirit who do not commit the unpardonable sin will be born again in the Family of God (Ephesians 3:15). The converted, through the Holy Spirit, will become the third part after the resurrection.

Now, notice that Jesus Himself prayed that His followers would be in the same oneness with Him and the Father as He had with the Father:

> [20] "I do not pray for these alone, but also for those who will believe in Me through their word; [21] that they all may be one, as You, Father, are in Me, and I in You; that they also may be one in Us, that the world may believe that You sent Me. [22] And the glory which You gave Me I have given them, that they may be one just as We are one: (John 17:20-22)

Christians are to be one with the Father and Son as they are one as "they also may be one in Us"!

This is a oneness that the trinitarian concept really does not allow for.

True Christians, after we are resurrected and deified, become the 'third' part of the Godhead that Theophilus was referring to! This is something that most trinitarians either deny or do not realize. In essence, trinitarianism denies this important part of the plan of God!

Lest anyone suggest that we are reading something into Theophilus' writings that he does not mean, he verifies that conclusion when he wrote:

> ... if I call Him Wisdom, I speak of His offspring (Theophilus of Antioch. To Autolycus, Book 1, Chapter III).

So, the 'third type of God' Theophilus refers to as Wisdom is NOT the Holy Spirit, but a reference to Christians. Christians are to be God's offspring! We are to be God in the family of God.

Notice what Paul wrote along those lines:

> [29] For whom He foreknew, He also predestined to be conformed to the image of His Son, that He might be the firstborn among many brethren (Romans 8:29).

> [29] Therefore, since we are the offspring of God, we ought not to think that the Divine Nature is like gold or silver or stone, something shaped by art and man's devising. (Acts 17:29)

God wants godly offspring, and that is why God made humans male and female and created marriage, as the prophet Malachi was inspired to write:

> [14] ... she is your companion And your wife by covenant. [15] But did He not make them one, Having a remnant of the Spirit? And why one? He seeks godly offspring. (Malachi 2:14-15)

Now, notice something that the Apostle John wrote:

> [12] But as many as received Him, to them He gave the right to become children of God, to those who believe in His name (John 1:12).

We all understand that the offspring of cows are cows and the offspring/children of humans are humans. The offspring of God who accept His way, become children of God, and will become God. Although, unlike the Father and Son, deified humans will have always had a beginning and will never be equal in authority to the Son (who is under the Father's authority; cf. John 14:28) or the Father.

If anyone questions the view that Theophilus of Antioch's writings mean deification, he verifies that conclusion when he wrote:

> For if He had made him immortal from the beginning, He would have made him God ... so that if **he should incline to the things of immortality, keeping the commandment of God, he should receive as reward from Him immortality, and should become God** ... For God has given us a law and holy commandments; and every one who keeps these can be saved, and, obtaining the resurrection, can inherit incorruption (Theophilus of Antioch. To

Autolycus, Book 2, Chapter XXVII. Translated by Marcus Dods, A.M. Excerpted from Ante-Nicene Fathers, Volume 2).

Theophilus was explaining that people were not created immortal and that Christians are to be God's offspring and become God when we are resurrected. We are to be God in the family of God:

> [14] For this reason I bow my knees to **the Father of our Lord Jesus Christ, [15] from whom the whole family in heaven and earth is named**, [16] that He would grant you, according to the riches of His glory, to be strengthened with might through His Spirit in the inner man, [17] that Christ may dwell in your hearts through faith; that you, being rooted and grounded in love, [18] may be able to comprehend with all the saints what is the width and length and depth and height — [19] to know the love of Christ which passes knowledge; that you may **be filled with all the fullness of God**. (Ephesians 3:14-19).

Those who accept God's way will become literal parts of the family of God and literally, after the appropriate resurrection, be filled with the fullness of God.

The Protestant trinity is supposedly composed of three co-equal parts, yet the Bible clearly teaches that Jesus is subservient to the Father (cf. John 14:28; Matthew 26:39), that He and the Father have different wills (Luke 22:42) and words (John 14:10; 17:8). Furthermore, nor does it teach 'equality' of the Holy Spirit to the Father (John 14:26) or Jesus (cf. John 15:26).

So how do trinitarians reconcile these and other problems? They do not. Instead they say that the trinity cannot be understood. Notice these admissions from Protestant and Roman Catholic trinitarian scholars:

> ...the Trinity...it has proven impossible for Christians actually to understand the doctrine or to explain it in any comprehensive way (Brown HOJ. Heresies: Heresy and Orthodoxy in the History of the Church. Hendrickson Publishers, Peabody (MA), 1988, p. 128).

The Vatican Council further defined that the Christian Faith contains mysteries strictly so called (can. 4). All theologians admit that the doctrine of the Trinity is of the number of these. Indeed, of all revealed truths this is the most impenetrable to reason...The Fathers supply many passages in which the incomprehensibility of the Divine Nature is affirmed. St. Jerome says, in a well-known phrase: "The true profession of the mystery of the Trinity is to own that we do not comprehend it" (De mysterio Trinitatus recta confessio est ignoratio scientiae — "Proem ad 1. xviii in Isai."). (The Blessed Trinity, The Catholic Encyclopedia, 1912).

Actually, it is so impenetrable to reason, that one must deny both logic, biblical revelation, and early church history to accept it.

One of the many problems with the ramifications of trinitarianism is that it pushes the concept of a closed Godhead. Early Christians, like Theophilus, did not hold to that view.

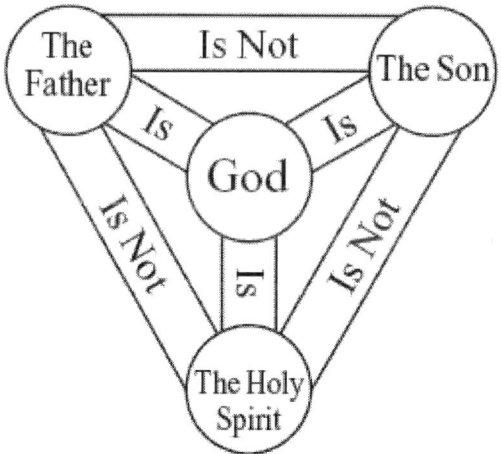

Shield of the Trinity (Wikipedia)

While the trinity is shown as a closed system, it distorts the nature of God and His plan.

God is one family, currently consisting of the Father and the Son—which is clearly a family relationship. As Jesus was the "firstborn among many brethren" (Romans 8:29), Christians are to be His brothers. Upon conversion, the new Christian is "begotten" by the Holy Spirit (1 Peter 1:23 Young's Literal Translation). The Christian's remaining physical life can be considered analogous to human gestation.

Christians will be reborn (John 3:5-8) and transformed into divine spirit beings in the first resurrection (1 Corinthians 15:50-53). This is not a new teaching, but one that early Christians held.

Getting back to Theophilus, he taught about being born again at the resurrection:

> But the moon wanes monthly, and in a manner dies, being a type of man; then it is born again, and is crescent, for a pattern of the future resurrection" (Theophilus of Antioch. To Autolycus, Book 2, Chapter XV)

Anciently, King David knew that he would be as God when he was resurrected into God's Kingdom:

> 15 As for me, I will see Your face in righteousness; I shall be satisfied when I awake in Your likeness. (Psalm 17:15)

In the 16th century, notice that Martin Luther taught:

> God becomes man in order that man might become God (On the Word Became Flesh Martin Luther, 1483-1546 From: Sermo Lutheri in natali Christi, [December 25, 1514]) _D. Martin Luthers Werke. Kritische Gesammtausgabe_ (Weimar: Hermann Boehlau, 1883) Vol. 1, p. 28).

However, many Evangelical Protestants no longer teach or believe this as they tend to falsely view deification as a strange and cultic doctrine.

Like (but not exactly the same way as) the Roman and Eastern Orthodox Catholic churches, we in the CCOG still teach deification.

But unlike them, we teach the original Christian view of the Godhead.

16. Tithing

Tithing is discussed, with many specifics, in the Old Testament. The terms "tithe," "tithing," or giving a "tenth" occur ten times in the New Testament (NKJV), thus it is also a New Testament subject.

Jesus stated:

> [23] "Woe to you, scribes and Pharisees, hypocrites! For you pay tithe of mint and anise and cumin, and have neglected the weightier matters of the law: justice and mercy and faith. These you ought to have done, without leaving the others undone. (Matthew 23:23)

While justice and mercy and faith are weightier matters of the law, tithing was endorsed by Jesus as something to be done. The Church of God in Jerusalem would have taught tithes until the rise of Marcus around 135 A.D.

Early Christians tithed. And it takes faith to do so.

Collier's Encyclopedia stated:

> "TITHE [taith] {O.E. teotha, a tenth}, generally defined as the tenth part of fruits and profits justly acquired, owed to God in recognition of his supreme dominion, and paid to the ministers of region. ... Adopted in principle by the Christian Church from apostolic times ... (Collier's Encyclopedia: With Bibliography and Index, Bernard Johnston (M.A.). 1993, ISBN 0029425484, p.336)

An Antiochian (likely Eastern Orthodox related), but spurious, source from the 3rd century states:

> Set by part-offerings and tithes and first fruits to Christ, the true High Priest, and to His ministers ... the priests and Levites now are the presbyters and deacons ... (Didascalia Apostolorum, Chapter IX. Translated by Hugh Connelly. Oxford: Clarendon Press, 1929)

The above suggests that at least some affiliated with the Greco-Romans tithed in the 3rd century.

The Greco-Roman saint Jerome recorded that there were people in the late 4th/early 5th century who claimed descent from the Church of God who had fled to Pella from Jerusalem. Jerome reported that these "Nazarenes" kept the 'old law' and had the 'Judeao-Christian' practices of the Sabbath, Holy Days (including the Feast of Tabernacles), millenarianism, etc. (Pritz R. Nazarene Jewish Christianity. Magnas, Jerusalem, 1988, pp. 58,62,63. Bagatti, The Church from the Circumcision, p. 202). Such a group would have tithed. Jerome's report, thus, indicates tithing was still in place towards the end of the Smyrna era of the Church of God.

Even Augustine of Hippo [Append. Serm. Cclxxcii] [qu. I Can. Decimae], said: "It is a duty to pay tithes, and whoever refuses to pay them takes what belongs to another."

Anciently, the Jews understood that the Bible told of multiple tithes as confirmed by Jewish historian Josephus:

> "Besides those two tithes, which I have already said you are to pay every year, the one for the Levites, the other for the festivals, you are to bring every third year, a third tithe to be distributed to those that want" (Antiquities of the Jews. Book IV, Chapter VIII, Paragraph 22).

The tithe for the festivals was not donated to the synagogue. Instead it was saved by to be used to finance the biblical Holy Days, such as the Feast of Tabernacles.

The Thyatira era of the Church paid multiple tithes:

> "The three-part division of tithes paid the Waldensian Church is significant. Even in the 1500's the same division continued. "The money given us by the people is carried to the aforesaid general council, and is delivered in the presence of all, and there it is received by the most ancients (the elders), and part thereof is given to those that are wayfaring men, according to their necessities, and part unto the poor" (George Morel, Waldensian

> elder, quoted by Lennard, "History of the Waldenses"). 1. Compare this practice with Num. 18:21 and Deut. 14:22-25, 28-29. Isn't it exactly what the Bible commands? ... Most authors have ASSUMED the "wayfaring men" were the traveling "barbel." But THEIR expenses would have been paid from the money given the elders, at EVERY time of year, for the direct conduct of the Work – "first" tithe and offerings. Notice that in Numbers 18:21. What Morel then mentions is a "second" tithe, for those traveling to and from the festivals – wayfaring men; and following it, the "third" to the poor. See the explanation in Deut. 14. Feast goers who had more "second tithe" than they needed shared their excess with those who had need, even as they do today! (LESSON 51 (1968) AMBASSADOR COLLEGE BIBLE CORRESPONDENCE COURSE "And the woman fled into the wilderness, where she hath a place ..." Rev. 12:6).

Those in the *Continuing* Church of God continue this practice to this day. The general COG position has been that since the third tithe is for the poor, they do not necessarily have to pay it (and it is only paid every third and sixth year in a seven-year cycle). However, it is my personal view that those who do not pay third tithe because they are poor are very likely to remain poor unless they really try to change that way.

As far as Protestants go, notice the following:

> During the 16th-century Protestant Reformation, Martin Luther approved in general of paying tithes to the temporal sovereign, and the imposition of tithes continued for the benefit of Protestant as well as Roman Catholic churches. Gradually, however, opposition grew. (Tithing. Encyclopaedia Britannica, viewed 09/20/19)

Currently, Protestants are divided on tithing.

But other than some of those known as Messianic Jews, Protestants generally do not teach multiple tithes.

One of the reasons for that is that Protestants generally do not observe the biblical Holy Days, like the Feast of Tabernacles. As a pilgrimage feast (cf. Psalm 42:4), it normally involves travel and is 'financed' by individuals for themselves and their families to attend through what is called second or festival tithe (cf. Deuteronomy 14:23-27; 16:13-15).

The New Testament teaches that an aspect of tithing changed from the Levitical priesthood because of Jesus (Hebrews 7:4-16). Early Christians understood that they were to tithe.

Of course, there were people not willing to give up physical possessions to follow Jesus (Mark 10:17-22). Jesus also taught:

> [27] And whoever does not bear his cross {Gr. *stauros*} and come after Me cannot be My disciple. [28] For which of you, intending to build a tower, does not sit down first and count the cost, whether he has enough to finish it — [29] lest, after he has laid the foundation, and is not able to finish, all who see it begin to mock him, [30] saying, 'This man began to build and was not able to finish.' [31] Or what king, going to make war against another king, does not sit down first and consider whether he is able with ten thousand to meet him who comes against him with twenty thousand? [32] Or else, while the other is still a great way off, he sends a delegation and asks conditions of peace. [33] So likewise, whoever of you does not forsake all that he has cannot be My disciple. (Luke 14:27-33)

As tithing is something that the Bible enjoins, we in the CCOG tithe. We do not consider that cost is too great though it can be a struggle in this world (cf. John 16:33).

Jesus taught, "where your treasure is, there your heart will be also" (Matthew 6:21; Luke 12:34).

Tithing supports the work of God, the poor, and festival travel.

It also helps build faith.

Those who truly trust God are willing to tithe (cf. Malachi 3:8-12; Galatians 6:6-10; James 2:14-18).

In the Hebrew scriptures God states:

[8] "Will a man rob God? Yet you have robbed Me! But you say, 'In what way have we robbed You?'

In tithes and offerings. ...

[10] Bring all the tithes into the storehouse, That there may be food in My house, And try Me now in this," Says the Lord of hosts,

"If I will not open for you the windows of heaven And pour out for you such blessing That there will not be room enough to receive it." (Malachi 3:8,10)

Many Protestants do not seem to have the faith to tithe and believe that with God's help and blessings multiple tithing can be done.

The Bible shows that Jesus denounced those who wanted to accept the "doctrines of men" so they would not feel the need to give as God commands (Matthew 15:3-9).

17. Clean and Unclean Meats

Most Protestants believe that it is appropriate to eat biblically unclean meat.

One claimed 'proof' that some have referred to is the vision the Apostle Peter had at Joppa in Acts 10:9-16, where Peter said (after Jesus had been resurrected), "I have never eaten anything common or unclean" (Acts 10:14).

Related to that vision most Protestants have concluded something very different than the Apostle Peter did:

> ² And when Peter came up to Jerusalem, those of the circumcision contended with him, ³ saying, "You went in to uncircumcised men and ate with them!"
>
> ⁴ But Peter explained it to them in order from the beginning, saying: ⁵ "I was in the city of Joppa praying; and in a trance I saw a vision, an object descending like a great sheet, let down from heaven by four corners; and it came to me. ⁶ When I observed it intently and considered, I saw four-footed animals of the earth, wild beasts, creeping things, and birds of the air. ⁷ And I heard a voice saying to me, 'Rise, Peter; kill and eat.' ⁸ But I said, 'Not so, Lord! For nothing common or unclean has at any time entered my mouth.' ⁹ But the voice answered me again from heaven, 'What God has cleansed you must not call common.' (Acts 11:2-9)

The above is a Protestant translation of the Bible and it clearly shows that Peter understood that the vision was for him not to call any human common, not that he and others were to eat biblically unclean meat (see also Acts 10:17,28).

Even Origen of Alexandria taught that after the resurrection Peter did not believe he could eat unclean meats:

> Peter himself seems to have observed for a considerable time the Jewish observances enjoined by the law of Moses, not

> having yet learned from Jesus to ascend from the law... Peter "went up into the upper room to pray about the sixth hour. And he became very hungry, and would have eaten" ... Peter is represented as still observing the Jewish customs respecting clean and unclean animals. (Origen. Contra Celsum, Book II, Chapter 1)

Peter was still believed to have observed 'Jewish practices' and, also, never ate unclean meat (Acts 10:14).

Furthermore, much later than the time of the Joppa vision, the Apostle Peter wrote:

> [14] ... not conforming yourselves to the former lusts, as in your ignorance; [15] but as He who called you is holy, you also be holy in all your conduct, [16]because it is written, *"Be holy, for I am holy."* (1 Peter 1:14-16).

Now where is that *first written* in the Bible: to *"be holy because God is holy"*?

It is Leviticus 11:44 & 45 where God is talking about avoiding unclean meat! The statement Peter quoted about being Holy as God is holy is repeated only three more times in the Hebrew Bible. The first is in Leviticus 19:2-3 where it then discusses the Sabbath and the second in Leviticus 20:7-8 where it teaches about not being involved with witchcraft and then keeping God's statutes. Does your church teach that you are to be holy as God is?

Protestant churches, however, generally do not teach that a sign of being unholy would be eating biblically unclean meats or violating the Sabbath.

The final time *"be holy because God is holy"* occurs is in Leviticus 20:25-26 where God explains about avoiding unclean animals and being holy.

So what could Peter have been talking about? The only subjects from the Old Testament could have been unclean meat, the seventh-day Sabbath, or the statutes in the Law, including witchcraft. However, the context says to avoid lusts. Lust is unlawful desire. Apparently, Peter is including desires such as eating that which is unlawful.

Paul emphasized that Christians were not to be unclean nor be misled by those who did not teach that:

> [7] For God did not call us to uncleanness, but in holiness. [8] Therefore he who rejects this does not reject man, but God, who has also given us His Holy Spirit. (1 Thessalonians 4:7-8)

Notice that God says that eating unclean animals makes one abominable and that God's people are to be separate:

> [25] You shall therefore distinguish between clean animals and unclean, between unclean birds and clean, and you shall not make yourselves abominable by beast or by bird, or by any kind of living thing that creeps on the ground, which I have separated from you as unclean. [26] And you shall be holy to Me, for I the LORD am holy, and have separated you from the peoples, that you should be Mine (Leviticus 20:25-26).

Notice what the Apostle Paul wrote:

> [17] Come out from among them and be separate, says the Lord. Do not touch what is unclean, and I will receive you (2 Corinthians 6:17).

Now, see something the Apostle John was inspired to write:

> [11] He who is unjust, let him be unjust still; he who is filthy, let him be filthy still; he who is righteous, let him be righteous still; he who is holy, let him be holy still (Revelation 22:11).

Notice that the holy are distinguished from the filthy (the unclean). Notice also that the Bible warns about those who love and believe a lie:

> [15] But outside are dogs and sorcerers and sexually immoral and murderers and idolaters, and whoever loves and practices a lie. (Revelation 22:15)

And, in my view, those who believe that God's people are to eat biblically unclean animals are accepting a lie. Consider also that dogs are biblically unclean animals.

All should realize that Paul did not want Gentile Christians to participate in uncleanness and that is something that they should repent of. Paul also wrote:

> [5] For this you know, that **no** fornicator, **unclean person, nor covetous man**, who is an idolater, **has any inheritance in the kingdom of Christ and God.** [6] **Let no one deceive you with empty words**, for because of these things the wrath of God comes upon the sons of disobedience. [7] Therefore do not be partakers with them (Ephesians 5:5-7).

Is eating biblically prohibited foods or not eating them a sign of disobedience? Is not consuming what the Bible prohibits covetous?

Peter added:

> [9] ... the Lord knows how ... to reserve the unjust under punishment for the day of judgment, [10] and especially those who walk according to the flesh in the lust of uncleanness and despise authority (2 Peter 2:9-10).

Some, sadly, despise biblical authority in order to eat whatsoever they lust after.

The inability of non-Sabbath-keeping religious leaders to properly distinguish between things such as clean and unclean was prophesied long ago (Ezekiel 22:26).

Pronouncements of Men

Although Articles XV and XXVI of the Lutheran Augsburg Confessions of 1530 take exception to bishops being able to tell what meats people should eat, the reality is that it has been asserted by the Church of Rome that one of its bishops made a determination that people did not need to obey the dietary restrictions in the Old Testament, despite Jesus pointing to their validity in the New Testament (cf. Matthew 7:10; Luke 11:11).

History shows that in order to be allowed back into the city of Jerusalem after the Jewish Bar Kochba revolt in 135 A.D., Roman soldiers said that the professors of Christ needed to eat unclean animals like they did (Pines S. The Jewish Christians of the Early Centuries of Christianity according to a New Source. Proceedings of the Israel Academy of Sciences and Humanities, Volume II, No.13; 1966. Jerusalem, pp. 14-15). The compromisers who followed the lead of 'Bishop Marcus' of Jerusalem did so in order to be able to live in Jerusalem.

Also, in Alexandria, the falsely named *Epistle of Barnabas* (the biblical Barnabas did not write it) came out around 135 A.D. and advocated an allegorical interpretation of scripture and said since the Bible was allegorical unclean animals could be eaten. Around the same time, it appears that the apostate Justin (who was uncomfortable with the Ten Commandment keeping Christians in Asia Minor and went to Rome) also ate unclean meat. Probably because he grew up eating it.

The Protestant saint Irenaeus endorsed not eating unclean meats in the late 2nd century (Irenaeus. Adversus haereses, Book V, Chapter 8, Verse 4). However, shortly thereafter, according to the Church of Rome, its Bishop Eleutherus made a pronouncement that all animal flesh could be eaten (Kirsch J.P. Pope St. Eleutherius/Eleutheros. The Catholic Encyclopedia, Volume V). This is interesting as it shows that even in Rome about 150 years after Jesus' resurrection, many professors of Christ did NOT believe that Jesus cleansed unclean animals to make them food. Should Protestants accept a Roman bishop's pronouncement contrary to scripture on this? Well, the vast majority of Protestants do.

Church of God Christians, however, continued to avoid consuming unclean animals as the 3rd century testimony from Pionius (a successor to Polycarp) supports (The Martyrdom of Pionius and his Companions, Chapters 3,6, & 9. Text from H. Musurillo, The Acts of the Christian Martyrs (Oxford, 1972), 137-167).

Furthermore, after Church of God Christians moved back to Jerusalem, they refused to eat unclean animals. To try to change that in the 4th century, Emperor Constantine ordered the death penalty for those who would not eat pork (Bagatti, The Church from the Circumcision, pp. 13-14). The Bible tells that "those who had been slain for the word of God" (Revelation 6:9) and the truly faithful (as well as some not faithful) have been subject to that throughout history.

Those called Nazarenes by 4th and 5th century Greco-Roman writers would have avoided unclean meat.

Various Sabbath-keeping Celts in the early Middle Ages did not eat unclean meat (Hardinge, p. 196).

Sabbath keepers in the 12th century also reportedly avoided eating unclean animals (Mosheim, p. 333).

In 1402, Sabbatarian John Seygno said that swine were unclean to eat (Ball, p.33).

In the 15th and 16th centuries, the Sabbatarians in the area now known as Hungary did not eat biblically unclean animals and also kept the Holy Days (Bacher W. The Sabbatarians of Hungary. The Jewish Quarterly Review, Volume 2. Macmillan, 1890, Original from the University of Michigan, Digitized Nov 10, 2008, p. 473).

Church of God Sabbatarians in England taught against eating biblically unclean meats in the 17th and 18th centuries and kept Passover on the 14th (Ball, pp. 9-10,15,49,153).

Throughout history, faithful Christians would not intentionally eat things like pigs, shrimp, bats, dogs, shellfish, snakes, snails, or other creatures prohibited in Leviticus 11, Deuteronomy 14, or Matthew 7:9-10.

Even the last book of the Bible, in Revelation 16:13 and Revelation 18:2, confirms that frogs and certain birds are still unclean.

We in the *Continuing* Church of God do not eat biblically unclean animals.

18. Rapture or Fleeing?

It should be pointed out that there are many, many, prophetic differences that the *Continuing* Church of God has with Protestantism. Detailed articles, on many prophetic topics, can be found at cogwriter.com and ccog.org.

But let's cover a few of the differences related to the time of the Great Tribulation and the Day of the Lord.

Many Evangelical Protestants believe that they will be raptured prior to the start of the Great Tribulation.

But notice that Jesus taught that Christians would have to flee before He returned:

> 23 When they persecute you in this city, flee to another. For assuredly, I say to you, you will not have gone through the cities of Israel before the Son of Man comes. (Matthew 10:23)

Notice that the fleeing is to happen until Jesus returns.

Jesus also taught:

> 15 "Therefore when you see the 'abomination of desolation,' spoken of by Daniel the prophet, standing in the holy place" (whoever reads, let him understand), 16 "then let those who are in Judea flee to the mountains. 17 Let him who is on the housetop not go down to take anything out of his house. 18 And let him who is in the field not go back to get his clothes. 19 But woe to those who are pregnant and to those who are nursing babies in those days! 20 And pray that your flight may not be in winter or on the Sabbath. (Matthew 24:15-20)

Is it only those in Judea who will flee?

No.

Jesus taught:

> [36] Watch therefore, and pray always that you may be counted worthy to escape all these things that will come to pass, and to stand before the Son of Man. (Luke 21:36)

So, only a part of the church that prays to escape all these things (and takes steps to be accounted worthy) will be able to do so (cf. Revelation 3:10).

In the latter portion of the twelfth chapter of the Book of Revelation, we see two parts of the Christian church:

> [13] Now when the dragon saw that he had been cast to the earth, he persecuted the woman who gave birth to the male Child. [14] But the woman was given two wings of a great eagle, that she might fly into the wilderness to her place, where she is nourished for a time and times and half a time, from the presence of the serpent. [15] So the serpent spewed water out of his mouth like a flood after the woman, that he might cause her to be carried away by the flood. [16] But the earth helped the woman, and the earth opened its mouth and swallowed up the flood which the dragon had spewed out of his mouth. [17] And the dragon was enraged with the woman, and he went to make war with the rest of her offspring, who keep the commandments of God and have the testimony of Jesus Christ. (Revelation 12:13-17)

Revelation 12:13 shows that persecution will come. Jesus said to flee when that happened (Matthew 10:23), and we see that happening in verses 14-16.

But notice that not all Christians will flee to the place of safety in the wilderness. The wilderness is obviously not heaven, as even Protestant commentators admit (e.g. *Jamieson, Fausset, and Brown*).

Notice also that Revelation 12:6 speaks of this same woman (the church) fleeing into the wilderness for 1260 days (prophetic years) *after* "her Child {Christ} was caught up to God and His throne." While this had not yet happened when John was inspired to write this, it has since happened (c. 380-1640). Nobody believes that there was a rapture of the church during that time, so why should the end-time described fleeing into the wilderness be interpreted any differently?

Why bring any of this up?

Because some Evangelicals teach that the entire Christian church is raptured to heaven and does not flee prior to the start of the tribulation.

Scripture is in conflict with that.

Furthermore, even early Greco-Roman writers such as Irenaeus, Hippolytus, and Victorinus taught that the church would flee. No early writer understood the New Testament to be teaching a rapture of saints to heaven prior to the tribulation.

Although the pre-tribulation rapture theory has been claimed by some to have originated earlier, it was not until the 19th and 20th centuries that it started appearing much in Protestant literature.

Not only was that not an original Christian belief, notice what Jesus taught about His return and the tribulation:

> 29 "Immediately after the tribulation of those days the sun will be darkened, and the moon will not give its light; the stars will fall from heaven, and the powers of the heavens will be shaken. 30 Then the sign of the Son of Man will appear in heaven, and then all the tribes of the earth will mourn, and they will see the Son of Man coming on the clouds of heaven with power and great glory. 31 And He will send His angels with a great sound of a trumpet, and they will gather together His elect from the four winds, from one end of heaven to the other. (Matthew 24:29-31)

Early Christians did not teach a pre (or mid) tribulation rapture. Jesus taught He would return after the tribulation (more scriptures explaining this can be found at www.cogwriter.com/rapture.htm).

Gather Together

Some Protestants teach that all Christians will be raptured together, generally before a seven-year tribulation or the worst 3-½ years (the second half of that).

But let's consider, not only does the Book of Revelation NOT teach that all Christians will be protected, but the Hebrew scriptures also give information about who may be protected.

Around 630 B.C., God inspired the Prophet Zephaniah to write the following:

> [1] Gather yourselves together, yes, gather together, O undesirable nation, (Zephaniah 2:1)

This is a command for end of the age Christians.

Although it has certain misunderstandings, the Protestant *Jamieson, Fausset, and Brown Commentary* realized that the gathering together was intended for a religious group or assembly:

> **Zephaniah 2:1**
>
> Gather yourselves together – to a religious assembly, to avert the judgment by prayers, (Joel 2:16, "Gather the people, sanctify the congregation, assemble the elders," etc.) (Jamieson, Fausset, and Brown Commentary, Electronic Database. Copyright © 1997, 2003, 2005, 2006 by Biblesoft, Inc.)

When are they to gather together?

> [2] Before the decree is issued, Or the day passes like chaff, Before the Lord's fierce anger comes upon you, Before the day of the Lord's anger comes upon you! (Zephaniah 2:2)

The gathering is to take place well before the day of the Lord (which happens about 2 ½ years after the Great Tribulation of Matthew 24:21 begins) and before some type of decree is issued.

Who does God want to gather together?

The most faithful end of the age Christians. Notice what Jesus stated and something the Apostle Peter wrote:

> [19] If you were of the world, the world would love its own. Yet because you are not of the world, but I chose you out of the world, therefore the world hates you. (John 15:19, NKJV)

> [9] But ye are a chosen generation, a royal priesthood, an holy nation, a peculiar people; that ye should shew forth the praises of him who hath called you out of darkness into his marvellous light: [10] Which in time past were not a people, but are now the people of God: which had not obtained mercy, but now have obtained mercy. (1 Peter 2:9-10, KJV)

This is a peculiar people. These are people whom the world does not desire. These are Philadelphian Christians. They are to "continue" (Hebrews 13:1, NKJV) "remain" (Hebrews 13:1, YLT) until the time of needed protection is passed (cf. Revelation 3:7-10).

How do we know that Zephaniah 2:1-3 is related to Christians? Because the decree is for the end time and because of what else God inspired Zephaniah to write:

> [3] Seek the Lord, all you meek of the earth, Who have upheld His justice. Seek righteousness, seek humility. (Zephaniah 2:3a)

The above is a reference to Christians as they are to be the "meek of the earth" (Matthew 5:5) and to Philadelphians who "have upheld His justice. Seek righteousness, seek humility."

These are Philadelphian Christians who are supporting the end time work, accept biblical church governance, accept the last days manifestations of God's Holy Spirit (cf. Acts 2:17-18), and are humble enough to not think that they should remain 'independent.'

Why does God tell them they may wish to be gathered together? So:

> [3] ... It may be that you will be hidden In the day of the Lord's anger. (Zephaniah 2:3b)

Interestingly, the Hebrew words translated as Zephaniah means "Yahweh Hides" or "Yahweh Has Hidden" (Holy Bible: Vine's Expository Reference Edition, p. 826).

Philadelphian Christians are the only ones who will actually 'gather together' as they should.

Why?

Because it is they who will lead the final phase of the work and it is only to the Philadelphians that Jesus promises to protect from the coming hour of trial, also referred to as the Great Tribulation and the Day of the Lord:

> [7] "And to the angel of the church in Philadelphia write, 'These things says He who is holy, He who is true, "He who has the key of David, He who opens and no one shuts, and shuts and no one opens": [8] **"I know your works. See, I have set before you an open door**, and no one can shut it; for you have a little strength, have kept My word, and have not denied My name. [9] Indeed I will make those of the synagogue of Satan, who say they are Jews and are not, but lie — indeed I will make them come and worship before your feet, and to know that I have loved you. [10] Because you have kept My command to persevere, **I also will keep you from the hour of trial which shall come upon the whole world, to test those who dwell on the earth**. [11] Behold, I am coming quickly! Hold fast what you have, that no one may take your crown. [12] He who overcomes, I will make him a pillar in the temple of My God, and he shall go out no more. I will write on him the name of My God and the name of the city of My God, the New Jerusalem, which comes down out of heaven from My God. And I will write on him My new name.
>
> [13] "He who has an ear, let him hear what the Spirit says to the churches."' (Revelation 3:7-13)

Notice that the Philadelphians are doing the work of God, going through the open doors (to reach others), have kept God's word, have not denied Christ's name/authority, and are persevering in the truth.

Yet, other actual Christian churches existing at the end, such as the remnants of Thyatira (Revelation 2:18-29) and Sardis (Revelation 3:1-6) are not promised that protection. Nor are the many Laodiceans (Revelation 3:14-22), whether in churches or independent.

Notice something Jesus taught:

> 34 "But take heed to yourselves, lest your hearts be weighed down with carousing, drunkenness, and cares of this life, and that Day come on you unexpectedly. 35 For it will come as a snare on all those who dwell on the face of the whole earth. 36 **Watch therefore, and pray always that you may be counted worthy to escape all these things that will come to pass, and to stand before the Son of Man.**" (Luke 21:34-36)

Notice that Jesus said to watch and pray ALWAYS for Christians to be counted worthy to escape. And the watching refers not just to our lives, but He was also referring to prophetic matters. It is ONLY the Philadelphian Christians that are promised a way of escape from the coming Great Tribulation. If all Christians were to be granted protection and raptured to heaven, there would be no reason to give Christians instructions as Jesus did. Although THIS CAME FROM JESUS, MANY SCOFF AT PROPHECY for differing reasons (cf. 2 Peter 3:1-7)–yet being a prophetic scoffer is a mistake (cf. 2 Peter 3:8-9).

The Book of Daniel prophesies some of what the faithful Philadelphians will do before (and probably also while) they flee:

> [33] Those with insight will instruct many, though for a time they will fall by sword or flame, or be captured or plundered. (Daniel 11:33, BSB)

Hopefully, you now have insight, are faithful, and have the willingness to instruct many. Along with the Bible, this book, our other literature, and truly being with God's Spirit will help the truly faithful be able to do that.

Jesus realized that if real Christians did not pay attention to prophecy and pray always, they would not properly take the steps to "be counted worthy to escape all these things." Yes, God uses prophecy as a motivator for people. Remember that God used Jonah to warn Nineveh (Jonah 3:1-4) and they repented (Jonah 3:5-9), and they did not receive the punishment they were going to get then (Jonah 3:10).

As Revelation 12:17 shows, not all real Christians are going to be protected. The Book of Revelation is clear that after the Philadelphians are persecuted (cf. Daniel 7:25a; 11:29-36; Revelation 12:13), they will flee to a place of protection, while the rest of the true Christians will not flee and then be subject to severe persecution (Daniel 7:25b, 8:24, 12:1; Revelation 12:17, 13:5-10, 14:12-13, 20:4).

Protestants tend to not properly understand that. That being said, people who truly will be willing to believe the Bible and resist the "mark of the beast" (Revelation 14:11-12) during the Great Tribulation and the preaching of the two witnesses (Revelation 11:3), will be part of the "great multitude" that comes out of the tribulation (Revelation 7:9-14). This would be expected to include many who were Evangelical/Protestant/Baptist who truly will believe in and properly act on the word of God. Yet, those who survive long enough to do that would be better off to change now rather than later.

Believe the prophetic word.

As hopefully this book has helped you see, we in the CCOG "have also a more sure word of prophecy; whereunto ye do well that ye take heed, as unto a light that shineth in a dark place, until the day dawn, and the day star arise in your hearts" (2 Peter 1:19, KJV).

19. Polycarp or Martin Luther?

Who were faithful Christian leaders?

Not knowing that can result in accepting false teachings.

Were 1st and 2nd century leaders like Polycarp, Papias, Ignatius, and Theophilus faithful as the *Continuing* Church of God claims?

Or instead were people who contradicted them like Justin, Augustine, John Chrysostom, John Calvin, and Martin Luther faithful?

Most Protestant scholars improperly claim both those sets were faithful (and some Baptists also add Novatian). But that does not make sense as both sets held very different beliefs and practices.

Protestant scholars sometimes call Polycarp a "proto-orthodox" Christian. This essentially means that they believe Polycarp was a faithful Christian, but that various doctrines people like him held were changed to be what is now considered to be acceptable (or "orthodox").

The following chart has religious details about Polycarp and Martin Luther (which includes understandings of their early successors) which is intended to highlight many of their differences:

Polycarp	Martin Luther
Baptized at age 18 by a Church of God leader.	Baptized as an infant by Roman Catholic priest.
Trained by the original apostles.	Trained by the Church of Rome.
Ordained by the original apostles.	Ordained by the Church of Rome.
Related all things in accordance with scripture.	Relied on tradition if he did not care for the scriptural position.
Taught the word of God.	Felt he could change parts of the word of God.
Taught the importance of all the scriptures.	Diminished the importance of many books of the Bible.
Had a binitarian view of the Godhead.	Taught a trinitarian view of the Godhead.

Only baptized adults.	Promoted infant baptism and condemned those who did not accept it.
Did not eat unclean meat.	Ate biblically unclean meat.
Taught the Ten Commandments.	Taught a version of the Ten Commandments.
Kept the Sabbath.	Promoted Sunday.
Observed biblical Holy Days.	Observed non-biblical holidays.
Kept Passover on the 14th.	Kept Easter Sunday.
Had no idols or icons.	Had crosses and Christmas trees.
Warned that a Latin man would be 666.	Taught that the Pope was the Antichrist.
Believed in "soul sleep."	Taught "soul sleep."
Understood that God would offer salvation to all and that most would be saved.	Taught that most would be lost and that most would not get a real offer of salvation.
Taught the Kingdom of God was the reward.	Taught that heaven was the reward.
Endorsed the millennial doctrine.	Condemned the millennial doctrine.
Walked in the ways taught by the Apostle John, who was considered to be a Jew.	Ordered followers to burn Jewish synagogues, take Jewish wealth, and hunt Jews down.
Taught against Christian military involvement.	Condemned those who did not endorse Protestant military involvement.
Warned about the "vanity of many."	Warned against select Roman Catholic positions.
Died as a martyr.	Had ill health for many years and died shortly after having a stroke.

Polycarp stood for and taught the original apostolic Christian faith (additional details on Polycarp's specific teachings can be found at https://www.cogwriter.com/polycarp.htm), while Martin Luther often did not.

Although Martin Luther had some positive positions, he compromised too much and did not truly accept his own *sola Scriptura* rallying cry. You do not have to dig very deep into history to prove that.

We in the *Continuing* Church of God do not believe that Martin Luther was a true and faithful leader. We believe that he accepted the "vanity of many," which is also happening in the 21st century with the ecumenical movement.

20. Ecumenism

Currently, the Protestant world is split on ecumenism.

Notice something in favour of it from the Lutherans:

> The Lutheran World Federation (LWF) General Secretary, Rev. Dr Martin Junge has sent greetings to the president of the Pontifical Council for Promoting Christian Unity (PCPCU), Cardinal Kurt Koch, to mark the 60th anniversary of the founding of the Vatican's ecumenical office. In the congratulatory letter, the Lutheran leader says that, for the past sixty years, this office has "forged a way forward on the path of ecumenism". (LWF's General Secretary sends greetings to PCPCU President recalling longstanding ecumenical relationship LWF, June 8, 2020)

Although the Lutherans and many Protestants in places like Europe seem to favour it, many American Protestants (particularly among the Evangelicals and certain Baptists) are currently opposed to it.

Early Protestant leaders were bitterly opposed to ecumenical unity with the Church of Rome:

> (1) Martin Luther: ... We here are of the conviction that the Papacy is the seat of the true and real antichrist ...

> (2) John Calvin: I deny him to be the vicar of Christ. ... He is an antichrist — I deny him to be the head of the Church (*John Calvin Tracts*, Volume 1, pages 219, 220). (Standish CD, Standish RR. The Evangelical Dilemma. Hartland Publications, 1996, p. 162)

> Samuel Lee (a seventeenth century Rhode Island minister): It is agreed among all main lines of the English Church that the Roman pontiff is the Antichrist (Samuel Lee, *The Cutting off of Antichrist*, p. 1). (Standish CD, Standish RR. The Antichrist is Here. Hartland Publications, 1988, p. 16)

As far as the final Antichrist goes, the position of the CCOG is that the false prophet of Revelation 16:13, 19:20, and 20:10 will likely be some type of antipope who will initially claim the Roman Catholic religion, but will betray the church of the "great city" of Rome (cf. Revelation 17:15-18). Consistent with a teaching sometimes ascribed to Polycarp, we teach that the King of the North Beast is 666. It is not likely that Polycarp would have taught that the Church of Rome was the Antichrist as it did not have a massive amount influence in Polycarp's day. That being said, in the 2nd century both Polycarp and Polycrates denounced Rome for its change of the date of Passover, not holding to scripture, and essentially seeking ecumenical unity.

Yet now, even many American Protestant leaders like Kenneth Copeland, Joel Osteen, and Rick Warren have endorsed aspects of ecumenical unity with Rome. Furthermore, the late Billy Graham was quite ecumenical with the Church of Rome (Bynum EL. Why We Cannot Support The Billy Graham Crusade. Tract # G-603. TABERNACLE BAPTIST CHURCH, Lubbock, Texas).

In 2020 it was reported:

> Almost two-thirds of Protestant pastors view Pope Francis as a genuine Christian and their "brother in Christ." ... Five hundred years ago, Protestants were calling the Pope, "AntiChrist" as they were tortured and killed for their unwillingness to compromise ... (Gendron M. Is Roman Catholicism Still a Mission Field? Proclaiming the Gospel newsletter, March 2020)

Martin Luther, himself, specifically taught that the Roman Catholic Church was the "great harlot of the Apocalypse" (O'Hare PF. The Facts About Luther, originally 1916, 1987 ed., p.9).

Let's notice some of the "great harlot" chapter in scripture that Martin Luther said pictured the Church of Rome:

> [5] And on her forehead a name was written: MYSTERY, BABYLON THE GREAT, THE MOTHER OF HARLOTS AND OF THE ABOMINATIONS OF THE EARTH. (Revelation 17:5)

> [9] "Here is the mind which has wisdom: The seven heads are seven mountains on which the woman sits. ... [18] And the

woman whom you saw is that great city which reigns over the kings of the earth." (Revelation 17:9,18)

Rome is the famous city of seven hills/mountains and even Roman Catholic scholars admit that Revelation 17:9 is a reference to Rome—though they say it is to the old Roman Empire and not their church (e.g. Kurz, W. What Does the Bible Say About the End Times? A Catholic View. Servant Books, Cincinnati, pp. 165-166).

Notice what the Church of Rome has taught:

> The MOTHER CHURCH of Christendom lovingly invites the descendants of all the CHILDREN torn from her bosom by irrelevant issues to return to the practice of their forebears [meaning the Roman Catholic Church] (90 Common Questions about the Catholic Faith, by John O'Brien, p. 11 as cited in McNair R. Why Church Unity Eludes Theologians. Plain Truth, September 1968)

> The Church recognizes that in many ways she is linked with those who, being baptized, are honored with the name of Christian, though they do not profess the faith in its entirety or do not preserve unity of communion with the successor of Peter. ... the desire to be peacefully united, in the manner determined by Christ, as one flock under one shepherd, and He prompts them to pursue this end. Mother Church never ceases to pray, hope and work that this may come about. She exhorts her children to purification and renewal so that the sign of Christ may shine more brightly over the face of the earth. (Pope Paul VI. Dogmatic Constitution of the Church, Lumen Gentium. Promulgated on November 21, 1964)

In at least two places in the *Catechism of the Catholic Church* (#1163 & 1667) the Church of Rome calls itself the "Holy Mother Church." And it wants unity with the Protestants it considers its daughters.

The idea that Rome claims to be the mother of the Protestants and other churches of this world is clear from the following which is on the outside of St. John Lateran Church, which is within the seven hills of Rome:

Inscription in the Basilica of St. John Lateran
(photo by Joyce Thiel)

Translated from the Latin it states:

Sacred Lateran Church Mother and Head of All Churches of the City and the World

The Basilica of St. John Lateran is the cathedral of the Bishop of Rome, that contains its papal throne (*Cathedra Romana*), This is the official ecclesiastical seat of the Pope (it ranks above all other churches in the Roman Catholic Church, even above St. Peter's Basilica in the Vatican).

So, it is clear to all who will see that the Vatican claims to be the Mother of the World's Churches. And the Bible warns that Mystery Babylon is the Mother of the WORLD's churches. However, the Vatican is NOT the mother of the Church of God which preceded the formation of the Church of Rome and did not come from the Church of Rome. Yet, the Protestants did come from the Church of Rome (and even many Protestants who claim otherwise still hold Roman Catholic doctrines which are in conflict with scripture).

17th and 18th century Church of God writers considered that the Protestant (including Puritans who claimed to be "proper Protestants") movement was a failure as it did not reform enough (Ball, p. 14) and because it retained papal pronouncements (Saller W. An Examination of a late book published by Doctor Owen ... A Sacred Day of Rest. 1671, London, pp. 32,35; Ball, pp. 12,319; Philotheos, p. 67). A Sabbatarian of that period said he "abandoned Babylon's customs and traditions" that Protestants had (Ball, p. 273).

The position of the late WCG evangelist Dean Blackwell was that the Protestant Reformation, itself, was prophesied to arise (Revelation 2:24-25) during the Thyatira church era (it did), to be unfaithful to scripture (it has been), and was essentially a Satanic plot to try to swallow up the faithful who believed in a version of *sola Scriptura* (Blackwell DC. A Handbook of Church History. Chapter V - Series: 1: Waldenses and Anabaptists. Ambassador College Thesis, 1973, pp. 20-21).

The essentially official position of the old Worldwide Church of God, itself, was that the Protestants were the harlot daughters of Mystery Babylon (Revelation 17:4-5) and daughters of Jezebel (Revelation 2:22-23) that arose in the 1500s (and subsequent centuries). And that many of those remaining Protestants who would not repent, would be destroyed after the start of the Great Tribulation consistent with Revelation 2:23 (LESSON 51, AMBASSADOR COLLEGE BIBLE CORRESPONDENCE COURSE "And the woman fled into the wilderness, where she hath a place ..." Rev. 12:6. Ambassador College, 1968). The CCOG prayer is that Protestants who do not respond now, but survive into the Great Tribulation, will be part of the "great multitude" that comes out of that tribulation (Revelation 7:9-14).

Lutherans, Anglicans, Rome, and WCC

Despite biblical warnings, many Protestants are pushing for more unity with Rome.

Without citing Rome, part of the claimed Lutheran doctrinal continuity is its adherence to Greco-Roman documents. Notice the following Lutheran teaching from 1577:

> The Apostles Creed, the Nicene Creed, and the Athanasian Creed, we pledge ourselves to them, and hereby reject all heresies and dogmas which, contrary to them, have been introduced into the Church of God. (Bente F, Dau WHT, editors. Concordia Triglotta: Die Symbolischen Bücher Der Evangèlisch-lutherischen Kirche, Deutsch-lateinisch-englisch. Northwestern 1931, p. 777)

But the actual *Church of God* could never have accepted the Athanasian Creed, such as it contains unscriptural parts such as:

> *And in this Trinity none is before after another; none is greater or less than another;*
>
> *But the whole three persons are coeternal with each other and coequal, so that in all things, as has been stated above, the Trinity in Unity and Unity in Trinity is to be worshiped.*
>
> *Therefore, whoever desires to be saved must think thus about the Trinity.*

Jesus taught the Father was greater than He (John 14:28) and there is nothing in scripture stating that having a particular belief in the 'trinity' is necessary for salvation (cf. Acts 2:38). The acceptance of this creed shows another fallacy of the Lutheran view of salvation.

A Lutheran source asserts that the Athanasian Creed has been in use since the 6th century (The Athanasian Creed. Redeemer Lutheran Church. https://redeemer-fortwayne.org/what-we-believe/the-athanasian-creed/ accessed 06/22/20). Hence, it obviously does not reflect original Christian doctrine in many ways—but it was accepted by the Greek Orthodox, Roman Catholic, Lutherans, and other churches. It should perhaps be pointed out that the oldest known form of the "creed" (called the "old Roman form") was NOT trinitarian.

As far as trinitarian ecumenism goes, the Vatican's 2020 handbook, *The Bishop and Christian Unity: An Ecumenical Vademecum*, basically divides professing Christians into two groups. One that accepts the godhead definition adopted by the 381 Council of Constantinople and the other that does not accept it. The Vatican's handbook only calls for ecumenical unity with the first group. Furthermore, that is consistent with the trinitarian position adopted last century by the World Council of Churches (WCC Approves a Trinitarian Basis, Christianity Today, December 22, 1961), that has remained in effect in the 21st century (Thomas TK. "WCC, Basis of," in Dictionary of the Ecumenical Movement, 2nd ed., ed. Nicholas Lossky et al. Geneva: WCC Publications and Grand Rapids: Eerdmans, 2002: 1238–1239). Thus, since the CCOG does not accept the 381 trinitarian adoption, it would not even be a target of the ecumenical efforts of the Vatican or the WCC.

Meetings and Declarations

Over the past several decades, the Roman Catholics have held a lot of ecumenical meetings to point out similarities. In terms of the Lutherans, two groundbreaking events of their ecumenical dialogue was a joint statement on the doctrine of *Justification by Faith* in 1983 and the *Joint Declaration on the Doctrine of Justification* (JDDJ) on October 31, 1999.

In February 2014, Anglican Episcopal Bishop Tony Palmer pointed to that last document and stated:

> The protests have been over for 15 years ... If there is no more protests, how can there be a Protestant church ... We now teach the same gospel, we now teach the same faith ... The protest is over, the protest is over. Brothers and sisters, Luther's protest is over. Is yours?

In October 2017, the archbishop of Canterbury, Justin Welby, presented a text by the Anglican community affirming a joint declaration by the Roman Catholic church and global Protestant bodies which was described as "a sign of healing after 500 years of division."

Additionally, notice some from 2020:

> A historical "Ecumenical Charter" was signed by Seventh-day Adventists, Roman Catholics, Orthodox, Anglicans, Evangelicals and Methodists on January 25th, in Bologna, Italy. The charter says that "the most important task of the Churches is to proclaim the Gospel together through word and action, for the salvation of all human beings. (Gendron M. Catholics Seek Unity with SDA's and Evangelicals. Proclaiming the Gospel newsletter, March 2020)

Yes, many within the Protestant world believe that they are basically unattached versions of the same church based in Rome. The ecumenical movement is pushing ahead.

The SDA signer of the "Ecumenical Charter" was SDA Pastor Giovanni Caccamo, who was the former Secretary of the Italian Union of Seventh-day Adventist Churches.

However, it should be noted that the Inter-European Division of the SDA church denounced that signing, essentially stating that it went too far towards unity (Statement on the position of the Inter-European Division on the involvement of an Italian Seventh-day Adventist Pastor in the signing of the Ecumenical Charter of the Council of the Christian Churches of Bologna. Press release EUD: "Charta Ecumenica di Bologna". February 24, 2020). So, some SDAs have opposition. Yet officially, "Seventh-day Adventists ... stress the conviction that many Roman Catholics are brothers and sisters in Christ" (How Seventh-day Adventists View Roman Catholicism. This statement was recorded on April 15, 1997, by the General Conference of Seventh-day Adventists Administrative Committee (ADCOM) and released by the Office of the President, Robert S. Folkenberg).

Notice, now, something written from a Protestant against those who dare to resist the ecumenical movement (**bolding** added):

> The Latter Rain is God's great end-time ministry. This concept, as revealed in the Bible, comprises the restitution of the church to it's rightful place, the enormous last day revival soon to come, and the harvest of souls before the great and terrible Day of the Lord. It is the outpouring of the Holy Spirit upon all flesh promised to us in the last days and the restoration of apostolic and prophetic gifts. It has been explained like this, the latter rain, the latter reign and the latter rein; first the spiritual outpouring, then the spirit and Bride says come in power and authority and then the ingathering. (Atkinson J. The Latter Rain. The Latter Rain Page. http://latter-rain.com/eschae/latter.htm retrieved 03/29/19)
>
> **The worst churches in Christendom are not those that need to repent but those in pride that are unwilling to repent, especially those that are opposed to ecumenicism**. They are easy to identify, they think that they are the chosen saints of God, they have an illiberal nature and are intolerant of others, self-righteous, they oppose dialogue, independent, a sinful

spirit of division and particularistic exclusivism. ... The Lord has given Christians the grace to reconcile the children to their Fathers As One Body We prepare for the Marriage Supper of the Lamb Harvest the Fruit of the Latter Rain Follow Him as the Army of the Lord into His Glory (Atkinson J. Ecumenical. The Latter Rain Page. http://latter-rain.com/kingdom/ecu.htm retrieved 03/28/19)

The assertion that Jesus came so that the world would be united in this age is false (cf. Matthew 10:34-38; information concerning the biblical truth about the "latter rain" can be found in the free online book: *Universal OFFER of Salvation, Apokatastasis: Can God save the lost in an age to come? Hundreds of scriptures reveal God's plan of salvation*).

Notice what Jesus actually taught:

> [34] "Do not think that I came to bring peace on earth. I did not come to bring peace but a sword. [35] For I have come to 'set a man against his father, a daughter against her mother, and a daughter-in-law against her mother-in-law'; [36] and 'a man's enemies will be those of his own household.' [37] He who loves father or mother more than Me is not worthy of Me. And he who loves son or daughter more than Me is not worthy of Me. [38] And he who does not take his cross and follow after Me is not worthy of Me. [39] He who finds his life will lose it, and he who loses his life for My sake will find it. (Matthew 10:34-39)

> [51] Do you suppose that I came to give peace on earth? I tell you, not at all, but rather division. (Luke 12:51)

Protestant and other religious leaders who profess Christ and the interfaith and ecumenical agendas clearly are overlooking what Jesus taught. Jesus taught His people should be willing to stand alone, even among family members. Let it be pointed out that in the first half of the 21st century a 'revival' will come to Europe and other lands. Many Protestants will applaud this and some have long hoped for this and some have called it "the blessed reflex" (Martin S. 'The Blessed Reflex' is Re-Evangelizing Europe. Love for His People, March 10, 2020). Yet, the Bible warns against the type of improper religious unity that will occur before the second coming of Jesus.

The Apostle Paul taught that true unity of faith would not happen until after Jesus returns:

> [13] till we all come to the unity of the faith and of the knowledge of the Son of God, to a perfect man, to the measure of the stature of the fullness of Christ; (Ephesians 4:13)

While getting along peaceably with one another is biblically promoted (cf. Romans 12:18), those who believe that true unity of faith comes prior to Jesus' return are in error. We are not 'perfect' until after He comes (cf. 1 John 1:8). The prophesied unity of faith does not happen prior to Jesus' return.

Understand that Pope Francis considers "all believers" daughters of the Church of Rome:

> "In drawing close to Mary," the Pope elaborated, "the Church discovers herself, She finds her center and her unity."
>
> "The enemy of our human nature," the devil, the Jesuit Pope warned, "seeks instead to divide, highlight differences, ideologies, partisan thinking and parties. But we do not understand the Church if we regard her by starting with structures, programs and trends, ideologies and functions. We may grasp something, but not the heart of the Church. Because the Church has a mother's heart."
>
> The Holy Father encouraged all believers, as her sons and daughters, "invoke today the Mother of God, who gathers us together as a people of believers." (Lubov DC. Pope on New Year's Day: 'Let's Stand & Acclaim the Lady, the Holy Mother of God' ... 'All Together Now, Three Times'. Zenit, January 1, 2020)

Pope Francis is referring to, at least, the Protestants as its daughters (cf. Revelation 17:5). Francis does not want people to look at true doctrinal differences, nor apparently warnings from the word of God. Francis wants unity—his way.

Lutherans tend to believe that the Church of Rome was the true church, but since it would not correct the errors it had, it had to form. Now that

Rome has adopted nearly all the changes that Martin Luther objected to, Lutherans and many others seem to want to embrace unity with Rome.

Perhaps it should also be pointed out that the Muslims tend to revere Mary. Pope Francis has often used his version of 'Mary' to promote both ecumenical and interfaith unity.

Although some Protestants have warned that the Roman Catholic "Mary" may be the "image of the beast" (e.g. Hull. England's Fall is Babylon's Triumph: An Original Interpretation of the Apocalypse, with a Special Reference to the Greek Church. J. Pulleyn, 1855, p. 94), many Protestants have accepted unbiblical aspects of Marianism. A female involved with sorcery, signs, and lying wonders is warned against in scripture (cf. Isaiah 47:8-9; Nahum 3:4; 2 Thessalonians 2:9-12; Revelation 18:7-8,23).

Do Not Be Unequally Yoked

We in the *Continuing* Church of God do not consider we should be yoked together with Protestants, as we do not see Protestantism as a reflection of the original and true faith.

While many of those who do not wish to accept the biblical and original Christian faith want unity with Rome, the Apostle Paul warned about believers being yoked together with unbelievers, including idolaters:

> [14] Do not be unequally yoked together with unbelievers. For what fellowship has righteousness with lawlessness? And what communion has light with darkness? [15] And what accord has Christ with Belial? Or what part has a believer with an unbeliever? [16] And what agreement has the temple of God with idols? For you are the temple of the living God. As God has said:
>
> "I will dwell in them And walk among them. I will be their God, And they shall be My people."
>
> [17] Therefore

> "Come out from among them And be separate, says the Lord. Do not touch what is unclean, And I will receive you."
>
> [18] 'I will be a Father to you, And you shall be My sons and daughters, Says the Lord Almighty." (2 Corinthians 6:14-18)

Christians are to be separate from paganism. Those who accept the true God as their Father must realize that. Isaiah wrote:

> [11] Depart! Depart! Go out from there, Touch no unclean thing; Go out from the midst of her, Be clean, You who bear the vessels of the Lord. (Isaiah 52:11)

To depart means to separate. Notice that Isaiah's sentiments here are captured in the New Testament in Paul's writing (2 Corinthians 6:17) and the Book of Revelation (18:2-4).

Notice also the following end time warning to not be part of the Babylonian religious system:

> [4] And I heard another voice from heaven saying, "Come out of her, my people, lest you share in her sins, and lest you receive of her plagues." (Revelation 18:4).

Sadly, even Christians have to be warned.

James berated those who wanted to be close to the world:

> [4] Adulterers and adulteresses! Do you not know that friendship with the world is enmity with God? Whoever therefore wants to be a friend of the world makes himself an enemy of God. (James 4:4)

Throughout history, the truly faithful have resisted unifying with the Greco-Roman churches.

> In the late 19th century, an important manuscript was discovered at the Etchmiadzin library by F. C. Conybeare, bearing the title *The Key of Truth*. Many scholars, having carefully studied this text, concluded that this was a very

ancient religious manual belonging to the Paulicians of the 8th century. (Kasparian V., Archpriest. Defending the Faith. Publication financed by St. Leon Armenian Cathedral LADIES GUILD. Western Diocese of the Armenian Church of North America, 2015, Burbank (CA), p. 113)

In *The Key of Truth*, the Paulicians of Armenia made these statements against the Greco-Romans:

> Behold, O ye blind, how our Lord deems your procedure false and vain, and pronounces you to be deniers of him, and calls you children of Satan, as was written above. Lo, now do ye recognize right well your lying father; recognize of a truth your spirit; recognize even your false God. Nay, recognize also your teacher; yea, and furthermore do ye recognize the Pope, the Catholicos, and your president; and recognize your sham Messiah, and the rest. Of whom our mediator and intercessor, our life and refuge, doth manifestly speak, saying: 'And that which he speaketh false, he speaketh out of his own, and his father is Satan.' Thus our Lord Jesus and the holy universal and apostolic church saw and spoke as we wrote above. (Conybeare FC. The Key of Truth: A Manual of the Paulician Church of Armenia. Clarendon Press, Oxford, 1898, pp. 85-86).

Sadly, today, most who profess Jesus fail to truly recognize important aspects of the truth. And many want to make further compromises away from the truth for the sake of an unbiblical unity.

This unbiblical unity will result, not only in destruction of the final compromised church or the end-time religio-political alliance(cf. Revelation 17:14-18; 18:1-23), but also in persecution against true believers (Daniel 7:25; Revelation 13:7-10; 18:24). Such persecution will include beheading (cf. Revelation 20:4) and burning (Daniel 11:33).

Perhaps related to that, it should be noted that there is an Eastern Orthodox prophecy that looks forward to the time of the "public executioner of the Sabbatians {Sabbath keepers}" (Tzima Otto H. The Great Monarch and WWIII in Orthodox, Roman Catholic, and Scriptural Prophecies. The Verenika Press, Rock Hill (SC), 2000, pp. 127, 132-135, with a partial translation from page 240).

Also, there is a Roman Catholic prophecy that looks forward to the time the "sect" that does not go along with this unity will have its supporters executed and burned (Schmöger Carl E. The Life and Revelations of Anne Catherine Emmerich, Volume 2. Approbation: Bishop of Limbourgh Peter Joseph. TAN Books, reprint 1976, p.292). Quite, unchristian of them.

Will you be on God's side or the side of the Greco-Romans? The side of the word of God or the side of traditions and doctrines of men? The Father seeks those who worship Him according to true doctrines (John 4:23), as the truth sets us free from error (John 8:31).

Signs and Lying Wonders

Sadly, not all who claim to believe the Bible, truly live by every word of it.

Kenneth Copeland is a Charismatic Protestant and has embraced ecumenical unity with the Vatican. The author of this book saw him do that as he praised Pope Francis in a video. He then uttered gibberish, which he indicated was 'being moved by the Spirit.' Some of what the Pentecostals do seems to be faked or delusionally influenced by emotions that are whipped up or demonic. The Bible does not endorse the emotional whipping up of 'the Spirit' that various Pentecostals are involved in.

Many Pentecostalists believe they speak in tongues from God and give prophetic utterances.

Some of their 'prophecies' even seem to come to pass.

Are those proof of God's approval?

No, not according to the word of God which teaches:

> [1] If there arises among you a prophet or a dreamer of dreams, and he gives you a sign or a wonder, [2] and the sign or the wonder comes to pass, of which he spoke to you, saying, 'Let us go after other gods' — which you have not known — 'and let us serve them,' [3] you shall not listen to the words of that prophet

or that dreamer of dreams, for the Lord your God is testing you to know whether you love the Lord your God with all your heart and with all your soul. ⁴ You shall walk after the Lord your God and fear Him, and keep His commandments and obey His voice; you shall serve Him and hold fast to Him. (Deuteronomy 13:1-4)

So, the word of God shows if the prophet does not keep and advocate keeping God's commandments, he/she is false. The 'prophecy' from such, if not from their own imagination (cf. Ezekiel 13:17), is demonic.

Because God answers prayers, even sometimes for those not necessarily converted (c.f. Genesis 24:12-27), some consider answered prayer or other blessings as proof that their religion is right. But they should be cautious about that.

Consider also that many Roman Catholics are convinced that theirs is the right church because of various mystics, Marian apparitions, Eucharistic 'miracles,' stigmatics (stigmatics are people who display what they claim to be wounds of Jesus from a supernatural source), and incorruptibles (incorruptibles are dead people whose bodies do not decay like normal deceased humans). Of course, the Eastern Orthodox also have claims of Marian apparitions and miracles of various types. In addition, the Muslims have their version of stigmatics and some other religions have "incorruptibles."

Throughout the church age, there have been those with signs and wonders.

Should we 'believe our eyes' without question?

No. The Apostle Paul warned about signs and lying wonders:

> ⁹ The coming of the lawless one is according to the working of Satan, with all power, signs, and lying wonders, ¹⁰ and with all unrighteous deception among those who perish, because they did not receive the love of the truth, that they might be saved. ¹¹ And for this reason God will send them strong delusion, that they should believe the lie, ¹² that they all may be condemned

> who did not believe the truth but had pleasure in unrighteousness. (2 Thessalonians 2:9-12)

This does not mean that the CCOG does not believe that God cannot perform various miracles. We believe that He does, and has done so in relation to various healings, for example. Plus, we believe that God has shown the CCOG supernatural favor in regards to last days signs such as are listed in Acts 2:17-18.

But we do NOT accept things such as Pentecostal tongues/prophecies, Marian apparitions, stigmatics, incorruptibles, and 'Eucharistic miracles', as from God for primarily four reasons.

The first is that many of these signs are not scriptural (or are contrary to scripture).

The second, and perhaps most important, is that none of those we are aware of involved true Christians (though God can use false prophets, e.g. Balaam in Numbers 23-24).

The third is that they teach a gospel different than the Bible:

> 6 I marvel that you are turning away so soon from Him who called you in the grace of Christ, to a different gospel, 7 which is not another; but there are some who trouble you and want to pervert the gospel of Christ. 8 But even if we, or an angel from heaven, preach any other gospel to you than what we have preached to you, let him be accursed. (Galatians 1:6-8)

Christians are to walk by faith, not by sight (2 Corinthians 5:7). Therefore, the message is considered more important than the messenger or something appearing to be supernatural.

Before getting to the last reason, it should be pointed out that whether or not someone is in the Church of God, God has a plan for all. God fashions all of us individually (Psalm 33:11-15) and all that you went through matters (see our free book, online at ccog.org, *The MYSTERY of GOD's PLAN: Why Did God Create Anything? Why Did God Make You?*), whether you are truly being called in this age (see our free book, online at ccog.org, *Is God Calling You?*) or the age to come (see the free book, online at ccog.org, *Universal Offer of Salvation*). Hence, we accept that God will sometimes answer prayers from those He has not called in this age, as well as, of course, from those He has.

The fourth, and last, of the primary reasons for Divine rejection is that the Greco-Roman-Protestant purveyors of signs and wonders do not have the biblical "fruits."

Notice Jesus' words:

> [15] "Beware of false prophets, who come to you in sheep's clothing, but inwardly they are ravenous wolves. [16] You will know them by their fruits. Do men gather grapes from thornbushes or figs from thistles? [17] Even so, every good tree bears good fruit, but a bad tree bears bad fruit. [18] A good tree cannot bear bad fruit, nor can a bad tree bear good fruit. [19] Every tree that does not bear good fruit is cut down and thrown into the fire. [20] Therefore by their fruits you will know them.
>
> [21] "Not everyone who says to Me, 'Lord, Lord,' shall enter the kingdom of heaven, but he who does the will of My Father in heaven. [22] Many will say to Me in that day, 'Lord, Lord, have we not prophesied in Your name, cast out demons in Your name, and done many wonders in Your name?' [23] And then I will declare to them, 'I never knew you; depart from Me, you who practice lawlessness!' (Matthew 7:15-23).

So, even those who believe that they cast out demons in God's name, prophesy, do-wonders, etc. are not accepted by Jesus if they were practicing lawlessness or preaching a false gospel (more on lawlessness can be found in the free online book: *The Ten Commandments: The Decalogue, Christianity, and the Beast*).

Yes, Jesus will tell the vast majority of those who consider themselves Protestant (some in the non-Philadelphian COGs have considered themselves as a type of Protestant) that He never knew them (see also Luke 13:24-28).

Jesus also said:

> [24] "Make every effort to enter through the narrow door, because I tell you, many will try to enter and won't be able [25] once the homeowner gets up and shuts the door. Then you will stand outside and knock on the door, saying, 'Lord, open up for us!' He will answer you, 'I don't know you or where you're from.' ... [27] But He will say, '**I tell you, I don't know you or where you're from. Get away from Me, all you workers of unrighteousness!**'" (Luke 13:24-25,27 HCSB)

Since "all God's commandments are righteousness" (Psalm 119:172), Jesus's words here look to be directed towards those who claim Christianity and even called Him "Lord," but would not live as He taught.

A Protestant minister named Tommy Waller indicated on in a television interview (Focus on Israel, TBN, January 2020) that Jesus' warning was to many exposed to Protestantism. Tommy Waller said Jesus twice was asking "Where are you from?," and basically taught that many who thought they were Christian would be FROM some place that Jesus would not recognize as His church. Protestantism does not represent His church.

Are you one who will respond to the truth or is your faith based on feelings, on a foundation of sand?

Notice some statements from John Stuart Mill in 1869:

> So long as an opinion is strongly rooted in the feelings, it gains rather than loses in stability by having a preponderating weight of argument against it. For if it were accepted as a result of argument, the refutation of the argument might shake the solidity of the conviction; but when it rests solely on feeling, the worse it fares in argumentative contest, the more persuaded its adherents are that their feeling must have some deeper ground, which the arguments do not reach; and while the feeling remains, it is always throwing up fresh intrenchments of argument to repair any breach made in the old. (Mill JS. The Collected Works of John Stuart Mill: Utilitarianism, The Subjection of Women, On Liberty, Principles of Political Economy, A System of Logic, Ratiocinative and Inductive, Memoirs. Google ebook, 2017)

Notice that John Stuart Mill highlighted the frequent reality that many opinions aren't based on facts at all, but feelings. Sadly, this is the case of inaccurate theological opinions that many hold.

This author has a shared well and liked drinking from the water from the well. This author THOUGHT it was good and pure and making him healthy. Later, the author learned that it had unhealthy levels of arsenic. No matter how good the author felt about the water, the water still had always been contaminated.

That is often also the case with contaminated religion.

Even if you think God answered some of your prayers (He may have), even if you confessed Jesus as Lord, and even if you had special spiritual gifts—according to Jesus that is not real proof of your Christianity (Matthew 7:21-23). And according to the Apostle Paul, even if one or more ministers make you feel that they are "ministers of righteousness" (2 Corinthians 11:15), that is not proof they are not Satan's ministers (2 Corinthians 11:14).

Feelings are not a proper biblical foundation. Eve made a disobeying decision based on feelings (cf. Genesis 3:6). Is it possible that your religion is based more on feelings than the word of God?

The Book of Proverbs warns:

> [16] The lazy man is wiser in his own eyes Than seven men who can answer sensibly. (Proverbs 26:16)

> [11] A fool vents all his feelings, But a wise man holds them back. (Proverbs 29:11)

So, we see a warning against one who relies on feelings and is unwillingly to deal with sensible answers. And a warning about venting all feelings. Of course, this Satanically-influenced world (1 John 5:21) tells people to trust their feelings above the word of God.

The Bible essentially teaches that many are too lazy to accept the challenge to "prove all things" (1 Thessalonians 5:21, KJV), but instead they are comfortable with leaders they think look good. They also think their feelings are more important than making wise (which means biblically appropriate for this purpose) decisions. But Christians are not to walk in the futility of mind or non-biblical feelings (Ephesians 4:17-19).

The Apostle Paul warned:

> [12] But what I do, I will also continue to do, that I may cut off the opportunity from those who desire an opportunity to be regarded just as we are in the things of which they boast. [13] For such are false apostles, deceitful workers, transforming themselves into apostles of Christ. [14] And no wonder! For Satan himself transforms himself into an angel of light. [15] Therefore it is no great thing if his ministers also transform themselves into ministers of righteousness, whose end will be according to their works. (2 Corinthians 11:12-15)

Some unfaithful ministers look real good.

Yet, God's ministers are to "guard the deposit" (1 Timothy 6:20, BLB, ESV) or "guard the doctrine" (1 Timothy 6:20, AFV) of faith (or "truths" per the WNT) to which they have been entrusted and not fall for "opposing arguments falsely called knowledge" (1 Timothy 6:20, BLB).

True Christians, ministers or otherwise, have the Spirit of Christ (Romans 8:9). While God knows who they are (2 Timothy 2:19), His word helps us identify those who are not real Christians.

Hence, we consider that the warnings in Deuteronomy 13:1-4, Matthew 7:15-23, and 2 Thessalonians 2:9-12 apply to signs and wonders. Those warnings are also consistent with what the Apostle John wrote:

> [1] Beloved, do not believe every spirit, but test the spirits, whether they are of God; because many false prophets have gone out into the world. (1 John 4:1)

> [19] ... the whole world lies under the sway of the wicked one. (1 John 5:19).

The Bible gives the proper criteria to "test the spirits" to avoid being under Satan's sway.

The New Testament also repeatedly warns about false prophets (Matthew 7:15, 24:11, 24; Mark 13:22; 2 Peter 2:1; Revelation 20:10), including at least one with Satan's support in the end time who performs 'miraculous' signs (Revelation 16:13-14; 19:20). In other scriptures, such as Revelation 13:11-15 and 2 Thessalonians 2:9-12, it is clear there will be supernatural signs that are false, but overwhelmingly accepted by nearly all of humanity.

The final Antichrist will be a false prophet (cf. 1 John 4:1-3). Contrary to scripture, he will promote an improper unity (Revelation 13:11-18).

The position of the CCOG is that proper discourse among religions can be helpful. But scripture does not endorse the type of coming ecumenical unity that Pope Francis, many of the Eastern Orthodox, and various Protestant leaders seemingly endorse now. We believe the coming ecumenical-interfaith unity that many are promoting is not only contrary to scripture, but warned against by the word of God.

21. Summary

Protestantism has two basic problems. As this book has pointed out, one is that it really does not believe in its *sola Scriptura* rallying cry.

The other is that there is no record of a faithful early church that resembles modern Protestantism.

Greco-Roman Catholic apologists have written about Protestantism:

> "Where was your church before the Reformation? Show us a people who before Calvin and Luther had the same beliefs as you. ... Let us see the uninterrupted link which binds you to the Church of the first centuries and through her to the apostles and to Jesus Christ. This conjunction should exist. But it is impossible for you to point to such a link. You are introducing a new movement; you have a beginning. It is possible to assign to your movement a precise date; and this simple fact condemns you." (Dumoulin, op. cit., I, 28, 29; Rébelliau, op. cit., p. 345; Jean-Baptiste Dantecourt, Remarques sur le livre d'un potestant, intitulé Considerations sur les lettres circulaires de l'assemblke du clergk de France, de l'annke 1682 ... Paris, 1683: as cited in Walther D. WERE THE ALBIGENSES AND WALDENSES FORERUNNERS OF THE REFORMATION? Andrews University Seminary Studies. 1986 (2), 5, p. 199)

It is true that the Protestant movement had a post-New Testament date. It is also true that many views held by John Calvin and Martin Luther were not held by the original church. More modern Protestants also cannot find their beliefs in the first couple of centuries of the Christian church era.

Furthermore, Protestant scholars tend to push a false and unbiblical view as the following admits:

> The "Parting of the Ways" is typically depicted as an inexorable development ... the inevitable separation of Christianity (in all its varieties) from its theological, social, and cultural ties to Judaism ... the narratives told in modern research echo proto-

orthodox/orthodox Christian historiography in asserting that "Jewish-Christian" forms of belief and worship should have never survived - let alone thrived - long beyond the apostolic age. Accordingly, scholars largely follow the lead of the heresiologists, by minimizing, marginalizing, and explaining away the evidence to the contrary. (Reed AY. 'Jewish Christianity' after the 'Parting of the Ways': Approaches to Historiography and Self-Definition in the Pseudo-Clementine Literature. In: The Ways that Never Parted: Jews and Christians in Late Antiquity and the Early Middle Ages, Tübingen: Mohr Siebeck, 2003, 189-231).

As this book points out, "Jewish-Christian" forms of belief and worship did survive and thrive after the apostles. The so-called "inevitable separation" from scriptural practices considered 'Jewish' by many Protestant scholars and nearly all Protestants is not what the Bible calls for. Those who believe the true faith was to change are clinging to a lie (cf. Revelation 22:15)—and sadly, that lie is what Greco-Roman-Protestants tend to accept.

Furthermore, it is not just a "Parting of the Ways" that is a problem for the Greco-Roman-Protestants, it is a departing from what the Book of Acts often refers to as THE WAY (Acts 9:2,19:9,19:23,24:22).

The departure from THE WAY is what Protestantism has accepted.

The original faith was not to change, and in reality, the true one never did (though some parts were not always embraced throughout history as they should have been per Revelation 2:1-5; 3:1-6).

But what about the *Continuing* Church of God?

Not only do we hold to a proper *sola Scriptura* view, we can document our beliefs in early churches as well as later churches throughout history. Yet, some point to a declaration date in the 21st century to try to callously dismiss our continuity. However, consistent with New Testament teachings that the true church would not remain headquartered in any one place during the church age (Hebrews 13:14), that it would change locations because of persecutions (Matthew 10:23) and be called by different names (e.g. Matthew 5:11; Acts 24:5), we have documented that we are a continuation of the original Christian church established in the 2nd chapter of the Book of Acts (see also the free book, online at ccog.org, titled: *Continuing History of the Church of God*).

So, is Protestantism or the CCOG truly faithful?

When we look at the New Testament, as well as into early church history, we do not see a religion that looks like most of what is called Protestantism.

That does not mean that some Protestant researchers and translators have not made positive contributions in document preservation, archaeology, translations, etc.

Yet, while many Protestant scholars and theologians have helped convey the concept of *sola Scriptura*, they have also misled people through mistranslations and non-biblical teachings.

The Apostle Paul taught:

> [16] All Scripture is given by inspiration of God, and is profitable for doctrine, for reproof, for correction, for instruction in righteousness, [17] that the man of God may be complete, thoroughly equipped for every good work. (2 Timothy 3:16-17)

The word of God rebukes much of Protestantism.

If Protestantism would have truly believed in *sola Scriptura*, many of its current doctrines would be pushed aside.

Yet, mainly because of the acceptance of later traditions from the Greco-Roman churches (including many from the influence of Emperor Constantine), Protestants do not hold to many of the beliefs of early Christians as the following shows:

Doctrine	Original Christian Belief and/or Change
Baptism	Early Christians taught that baptism was by immersion for those who repented and accepted Jesus. In time, Greco-Romans implemented

	sprinkling, even for those without repentance. Some Protestants accepted this change.
Beatific Vision	Early Christians did not teach what is called the Beatific Vision. In time, the Greco-Romans adopted it and many Protestants hold to that teaching. Early Christians believed that they would, instead, be part of God's kingdom making eternity better.
Biblical Holy Days	Early Christians kept biblical Holy Days, sometimes now called Jewish Holy Days. Greco-Romans formally condemned them in the 4th century, and Protestants generally do not keep them.
Church Services	Church services in the *Continuing* Church of God are consistent with the scripture and Psalm focus of the early Christians. Protestant services vary, but generally are not consistent with those of early Christians.
Christmas	Early Christians did not celebrate Christmas or use lighted trees. In the 4th century, Greco-Romans adopted the 25th of December as Christ's birthday, as it was long celebrated as the birthday of the sun god Mithras, who was worshiped by Emperor Constantine.
Crosses and Icons	Early Christians did not have crosses or icons. This started to change by some of the Greeks in the 3rd century and was adopted by the Greco-Romans in the 4th century after being influenced by Emperor Constantine and his mother Helena.
Death	Early Christians, and even Martin Luther, taught that death is like sleep. Most Protestants do not teach that.
Deification	Early Christians taught deification of the saved. While the Eastern Orthodox and Roman Catholic churches officially teach this, most Evangelical Protestants do not. Instead, many consider the original belief a cultic idea.
Ecumenism	Early Christians were not ecumenical. In the 21st century, many Protestants are.

Eternal torment	Jesus taught that the incorrigible would be destroyed, whereas the Protestant position is eternal torturing.
History	We do not see evidence of modern Protestantism in the first centuries of the Christian era, and the closest claimed original Protestant was the apostate Marcion. Protestant groups who claim apostolic succession through Antioch, Smyrna, and/or Jerusalem do not have the teachings that early leaders in those areas held to.
Godhead	The trinitarian view of the Godhead, that was formally adopted in 381 A.D., was not the original Christian teaching, but it is accepted by most Protestants.
Gospel of the Kingdom of God	Early Christians believed that Jesus' message of the Kingdom of God was a major theme, which included salvation through Him. Many Protestants do not understand the importance of the literal kingdom teachings or how it should affect their lives, but instead focus on their views of certain aspects of the person of Jesus more than the kingdom message or how the real Jesus lived.
Heaven	Early Christians did not teach that heaven was the reward of the saved. They taught that the reward of the saved was to be part of the Kingdom of God on earth.
Holy Spirit	Early Christians believed that the Holy Spirit was the power of God given to baptized Christians who obeyed God. The personhood of the Holy Spirit was declared by Greco-Roman councils in the mid-late 4th century and this change was accepted by the Protestants.
Infant Baptism	Early Christians did not baptize infants, though they probably blessed little children like Jesus did. In time, Greco-Romans did baptize infants. Protestant Reformers like Martin Luther and John Calvin endorsed that change.
Immortality	Early Christians did not teach that souls were immortal. Most Protestants teach souls are immortal.

Jesus	Early Christians accepted Jesus as the divine Savior and strove to imitate Him. Many Protestants believe that He lived a perfect life in their stead, hence they do not really believe that they need to imitate Him.
Jews	Initially, most Christians were Jews. Protestant reformers including Martin Luther held anti-Semitic views and took horrible actions against Jews. Antisemitism still exists within Protestantism and is at least a latent factor for those not keeping the Sabbath or biblical Holy Days.
Lost Tribes?	While early Christians realized that not all the tribes of Israel lived in the area of the Roman province of Judea, most Protestants do not understand what nations best represent the "lost tribes" of Israel.
Marcion	Marcion was an apostate denounced by Polycarp of Smyrna, Melito of Sardis, Theophilus of Antioch, and Serapion of Antioch, but was tolerated by the Church of Rome for decades. He denied Jesus. Some scholars have referred to Marcion as the first Protestant.
Matthew 24:14	Some Protestants believe that the gospel of the kingdom has been sufficiently preached to the world as a witness. 2nd century Christians did not believe this had been fulfilled. Since the end (meaning the Great Tribulation per Matthew 24:21) has not come, Matthew 24:14 has not yet been fulfilled—and we in the CCOG are working towards its fulfilment.
Military Service	Early Christians did not voluntarily participate in military service nor watch intentionally violent sports. The Greco-Romans changed in the 4th century after being highly influenced by Emperor Constantine. Most Protestants accept the change.
Millennium	Early Christians taught a literal millennial reign. During the 381 Council of Constantinople, the Greco-Romans condemned this biblical doctrine. Though some Protestants accept the millennium,

	Martin Luther and his followers did not as they officially condemned it in 1531.
Ministers	Early Christians ministers were all biological males and were not called "Reverend." Nor did they wear special collars or other clothing distinctive from their congregants. Protestants have often changed/compromised on those matters.
New Testament Canon	Early Christians believed that the Apostle John did, in essence, canonize the New Testament—the CCOG holds that view. Many modern Protestant scholars do not believe the New Testament was canonized until centuries later.
Passover	Early Christians kept Passover after sunset on the 14th of Nisan. Greco-Romans began to change that to Sunday in the 2nd century and also implement a more frequent 'eucharist' ceremony. The Sunday Passover change was formally accepted at the Council of Nicea. In time, the Greco-Romans, also, basically dropped the vestiges of Passover from their observance and changed it to a resurrection holiday, called Easter in English. Most Protestants accepted those changes.
Persecution	Early Christians were often persecuted, but were never the persecutors. Starting in the 4th century, Greco-Romans began official persecutions. Protestants adopted aspects of this in the 16th century.
Rapture	Early Christians understood that they were to flee in the end times. Certain Protestants promoted the rapture theory in the 19th and later centuries.
Sabbath	Early Christians kept the Sabbath on Saturday. The Greco-Roman churches formally accepted Sunday at the Council of Nicea, 325 A.D. Most Protestants accept the change.
Salvation	Early Christians believed that God had a plan to offer salvation to all and most would ultimately accept that offer. Apostates, like Marcion, taught most people would be lost. Most Protestants share Marcion's view of this.

Signs and Wonders	While the Bible tells of proper last days' signs of God's Spirit (e.g. Acts 2:17-18), it also warns that people with insufficient love of the truth would be deceived by signs and lying wonders. 'Pentecostal' Protestants accept leaders and signs that the CCOG consider to be either faked, delusional, or demonic.
Swearing Oaths	Consistent with Jesus' command (Matthew 5:33-37), early Christians did not swear oaths. Martin Luther and most Protestant faiths have not followed that command.
Ten Commandments	Early Christians taught that the Ten Commandments were enjoined on Christians. It was originally only apostates like Simon Magus, Marcion, and their followers that taught against them. Many modern Protestants have followed the example of Simon Magus and Marcion.
Three Days and Three Nights	Early Christians believe that Jesus was in the grave for a full three days and three nights. In the early 5th century, Augustine of Hippo tried to claim a lesser time to justify a Good Friday to Easter Sunday tradition. Protestants have generally accepted that change, plus believe Jesus was resurrected on a Sunday. The CCOG did not accept that change and teaches that Jesus was resurrected on a Saturday.
Three Resurrections	Early Christians taught three resurrections. Protestants tend to believe that the Bible teaches two, but that they are of little importance as they claim immortality of the soul.
Tithing	Early Christians gave tithes and offerings. Some Protestants believe in tithing, but few believe in multiple tithes.
Tradition	While tradition that is not in conflict with the word of God can have a place, Protestants have accepted traditions derived from Mithraism and other sources that are in conflict with scripture that the CCOG has not.

Unclean Meat Consumption	Early Christians avoided biblically unclean meats. Greco-Romans, however, changed in the 2nd century. Most Protestants accept the change.
Valentine's Day	Early Christians did not celebrate the pagan Lupercalia, which later was renamed Valentine's Day. Many Protestants endorse it.
White Throne Judgment	Early Christian believed God would provide an opportunity to the uncalled during an age to come with the white throne judgment, whereas Protestants consider the white throne judgment essentially a time of condemnation and doom.
Worldly Politics	Early Christians generally stayed separate from worldly politics unless legally required to do so. Followers of Martin Luther condemned those who chose not to be voluntarily involved in worldly politics. Most Protestants endorse being involved in worldly politics.

That there was no early church that had a substantial amount of modern 'traditional' Protestant beliefs is truly a fact of history. A fact that Roman and Eastern Orthodox Catholic scholars are well aware of.

Many beliefs and practices associated with modern Protestantism were either:

1) not views of the original Christians,
2) not the views of the Reformation Protestants, and/or
3) were adopted from non-biblical sources (such as demonic "traditions" from places like Mithraism).

Can you handle the truth?

False religion and false worship is not what Jesus wants:

> 23 But the hour is coming, and now is, when the true worshipers will worship the Father in spirit and truth; for the Father is seeking such to worship Him. 24 God is Spirit, and those who worship Him must worship in spirit and truth. (John 4:23-24)

Protestantism is not the biblically true faith. The Apostle Paul admonished Christians to:

> [21] Prove all things; hold fast that which is good. (1 Thessalonians 5:21, KJV)

This book has provided scriptures as well as historical references to assist you in doing so.

All people have done wrong (Roman 3:23). And God knew that would happen before the foundation of the world (1 Peter 1:20; Revelation 13:8).

Is the true Christian church too 'Jewish' for you? Notice the following:

> [2] ... Tertullus presented the charges against **Paul** in the following address to the governor: "Your Excellency ... [5] We have found this man to be a troublemaker who is constantly stirring up riots among the Jews all over the world. **He is a ringleader of the cult known as the Nazarenes** ...
>
> [10] ...Paul said, [14] "... **I admit that I follow the Way, which they call a cult. I worship the God of our ancestors, and I firmly believe the Jewish law and everything written in the prophets.** (Acts 24:2,5,10,14, NLT)

The Bible shows that not only did Paul hold to practices considered Jewish, he praised Gentile Christians for imitating such practices (1 Thessalonians 2:14). History shows that Christians with "Nazarene" practices have long been accused of being part of a cult (or "sect," Acts 24:14, NKJV/NJB) by persecutors of various types.

Jesus warned that the faithful would be persecuted and insulted:

> [10] Blessed are those who are persecuted for righteousness' sake, For theirs is the kingdom of heaven. [11] "Blessed are you when they revile and persecute you, and say all kinds of evil against you falsely for My sake. [12] Rejoice and be exceedingly glad, for great is your reward in heaven, for so they persecuted the prophets who were before you. (Matthew 5:10-12)

Paul also stated that "all who desire to live godly in Christ Jesus will suffer persecutions" (2 Timothy 3:21). So, of course, keeping the same practices that Jesus of Nazareth, the Nazarene ringleader called the Apostle Paul and others throughout history does not make one part of an inappropriate "cult."

Can you stand for the truth (cf. Ephesians 6:14), despite name calling? If you are a true Christian, you must (cf. Matthew 10:33).

Do not be one who claims Jesus, yet will be thrust out of His Kingdom:

> [25] When once the Master of the house has risen up and shut the door, and you begin to stand outside and knock at the door, saying, 'Lord, Lord, open for us,' and **He will answer and say to you, 'I do not know you, where you are from,'** [26] then you will begin to say, 'We ate and drank in Your presence, and You taught in our streets.' [27] But He will say, 'I tell you I do not know you, where you are from. Depart from Me, all you workers of iniquity.' [28] **There will be weeping and gnashing of teeth, when you see Abraham and Isaac and Jacob and all the prophets in the kingdom of God, and yourselves thrust out.** (Luke 13:25-28)

Protestantism is not truly from the Bible nor part of the original church. The Apostle Paul warned people who thought they were Christians:

> [33] Do not be deceived: "Evil company corrupts good habits." [34] Awake to righteousness, and do not sin; for some do not have the knowledge of God. I speak this to your shame. (1 Corinthians 15:33-34)

Although many hope that they are in God's church, consider the following:

> Yet none is truly the Church OF GOD, unless it is GOD'S CHURCH, continuing doctrine, practice, organization, in all ways on the original biblical pattern, headed by Jesus Christ, yet belonging to God the Father, empowered by the Holy Spirit, having GOD'S TRUTH, fulfilling Christ's commission of proclaiming his GOOD NEWS of the KINGDOM OF GOD to the world as a whole.

(Armstrong HW. Mystery of the Ages. Dodd, Meade, 1985)

We in the *Continuing* Church of God have been continuing in the original doctrines and practices while we proclaim the gospel of the kingdom to the world as a witness (Matthew 24:14).

While many focus on outward differences such as the Sabbath, Holy Days, and unclean meats, a major difference between Protestants and the *Continuing* Church of God is the hope of salvation and *why* we live differently.

Regarding salvation, if you are Protestant (or Baptist) and cannot yet accept the view of the *Continuing* Church of God that the God of love's plan will result in most people being saved, we certainly can understand your reluctance to accept what you may at first consider to be such a radical view.

But it is both a biblical and historical view. It is also a very logical view.

Whether or not you are Protestant, God has a plan for you involving Jesus.

Jesus taught for those who would be faithful:

> [32] And you shall know the truth, and the truth shall make you free. (John 8:31)

This book contains scriptural truths and verifiable facts about doctrine and church history. Can you properly handle and act on the truth?

The full truth is not found in Protestantism.

All should properly do what the Apostle James wrote:

> [21] Therefore lay aside all filthiness and overflow of wickedness, and receive with meekness the implanted word, which is able to save your souls.
>
> [22] But be doers of the word, and not hearers only, deceiving yourselves. [23] For if anyone is a hearer of the word and not a

> doer, he is like a man observing his natural face in a mirror; [24] for he observes himself, goes away, and immediately forgets what kind of man he was. [25] But he who looks into the perfect law of liberty and continues in it, and is not a forgetful hearer but a doer of the work, this one will be blessed in what he does.
>
> [26] If anyone among you thinks he is religious, and does not bridle his tongue but deceives his own heart, this one's religion is useless. (James 1:21-26)

Many Protestants tend to be hearers more than doers. That is part of why they do not truly understand the hope of salvation we really have in Jesus.

Do you feel that God has a plan that is intended to save nearly all who ever lived or condemn most that ever lived?

Protestants, like the apostate Marcion, doom most human beings to eternal torment.

We in the CCOG realize that God is wise, all knowing, loving, and all powerful. We have faith that He has a plan of salvation that will result in the salvation of the vast majority of people who ever lived.

Consider that since the CCOG believes that Christians will be rewarded for their works (Matthew 16:7; Revelation 22:12), deified after being resurrected (1 Corinthians 15:53), and will have dominion over the universe (Hebrews 2:5-10), we live our lives with all of that in mind (cf. Hebrews 11:13-16).

Do you really believe the Bible? Do you have enough of "the love of the truth" (2 Thessalonians 2:10) to change from teachings of men to accept the true and original Christian faith?

Can you be like the Bereans of old, who when they heard teachings that they had not expected, they "received the word with all readiness, and searched the Scriptures daily to find out whether these things were so" (Acts 17:11)?

Hopefully, you are willing to believe the word of God and facts of history over unbiblical traditions.

(To learn more about living as a Christian, check out the free book, available online at ccog.org, titled *Christians: Ambassadors for the Kingdom of God, Biblical instructions on living as a Christian*.)

Notice the instructions in the Book of Proverbs:

> [5] Trust in the Lord with all your heart, And lean not on your own understanding; [6] In all your ways acknowledge Him, And He shall direct your paths. [7] **Do not be wise in your own eyes; Fear the Lord and depart from evil.** [8] It will be health to your flesh, And strength to your bones.
>
> [9] Honor the Lord with your possessions, And with the firstfruits of all your increase; [10] So your barns will be filled with plenty, And your vats will overflow with new wine.
>
> [11] My son, do not despise the chastening of the Lord, Nor detest His correction; [12] For whom the Lord loves He corrects, Just as a father the son in whom he delights. (Proverbs 3:5-12)

Shouldn't we all want to be those in whom God delights?

In this life, we are to develop the love of God by living our lives HIS way. Any other way is evil.

Trust God and do not be wise in the eyes of unbiblical traditions of men.

The Christian purpose for this life is to build character so you can maximize your potential and increase how much better you can give love in your own unique way to make the millennium better after the first resurrection and later to make eternity better for everyone, including yourself, in Jesus' service.

That is what real Christianity is all about.

The true Christian faith once delivered to the saints is taught by and contended for in the 21st century by the *Continuing* Church of God. The same cannot be said of Protestantism.

Continuing Church of God

The USA office of the *Continuing* Church of God is located at: 1036 W. Grand Avenue, Grover Beach, California, 93433 USA. We have supporters all around the world, and in all inhabited continents (all continents, except Antarctica).

Continuing Church of God Website Information

CCOG.ORG The main website for the *Continuing* Church of God.
CCOG.ASIA Asian-focused website, with multiple Asian languages.
CCOG.IN India-focused website, with some Indian languages.
CCOG.EU European-focused website, with multiple European languages.
CCOG.NZ Website targeted towards New Zealand.
CCOGAFRICA.ORG Website targeted towards Africa.
CCOGCANADA.CA Website targeted towards Canada.
CDLIDD.ES This is a totally Spanish language website.
CG7.ORG Explains which is the most faithful of the 7th day observant groups.
PNIND.PH Philippines-focused website, with some Tagalog.
STUDY THE BIBLE COURSE Free online course to help you better understand the Bible.

Radio & Video Channels

BIBLENEWSPROPHECY.NET Bible News Prophecy online radio.
Bible News Prophecy channel. Sermonettes on YouTube, Brighteon, BitChute, & Vimeo.
CCOGAfrica channel. Video messages from Africa on YouTube & BitChute.
CCOG Animations Animated messages on YouTube & BitChute.
CDLIDDsermones channel. YouTube messages in Spanish.
ContinuingCOG channel. Video sermons on YouTube & BitChute.

News and History Websites

CHURCHHISTORYBOOK.COM Church history website.

COGWRITER.COM News, history, and prophecy website

Made in the USA
Columbia, SC
06 September 2021